Published with the assistance of the
Louis and Minna Epstein Fund
of the American Academy for Jewish Research

ISBN 965-226-032-0

Printed in Israel 1982

Phototypesetting & printing – Yeda Sela Ltd.,
P.O.B. 25051, Tel Aviv 61250, Tel. 03-331061

LEON NEMOY

STUDIES IN JUDAICA, KARAITICA AND ISLAMICA

Presented to LEON NEMOY on his Eightieth Birthday

edited by
SHELDON R. BRUNSWICK

BAR-IL

CONTENTS

LIBRARY SCIENCE AND BIBLIOGRAPHY

HEBREW AND YIDDISH

PREFACE

Leon Nemoy is best known as a scholar in the field of Judaeo-Arabic and Karaite studies, having edited and translated important texts and treatises. He is also the devoted and indefatigable editor of the Yale Judaica Series and many of the contributors are indebted to him for sharpening their insights, suggesting the proper word, and providing patient guidance and advice. His achievement is hailed by the participation in this volume of scholars in a variety of fields, and the broad nature of their contributions bespeaks the breadth of his own interest. When Sheldon Brunswick, of the General Library of the University of California, Berkeley, first approached Nemoy's friends and associates for articles for this volume they responded warmly to the idea of publishing a volume of essays in his honor. Typical was the letter from the late Edward Kiev, the librarian of the New York School of the Hebrew Union College – Jewish Institute of Religion, who passed away before submitting his article:

> I am pleased to reply to your recent invitation to contribute an article to the Festschrift you are planning to publish in honor of Prof. Leon Nemoy.
>
> Doctor Nemoy holds a special place among us for his contributions to Jewish learning and Jewish librarianship. It has been a wonderful experience to have shared with him many important undertakings. He deserves our admiration and it is proper to celebrate his achievement by publishing a volume on the occasion.
>
> I gladly accept your invitation and hope to be able to send you an article which you will want to include in the volume.

The articles were assembled by Sheldon Brunswick, who also did the initial editorial work. It was hoped that the volume would appear in time for Leon Nemoy's seventy-fifth birthday, but the usual delays that afflict Jubilee volumes have affected this one too. After Bar-Ilan University agreed to undertake the publication of the volume, Dr. William Braude of Providence, Rhode Island, helped raise part of the funds needed for this. We appreciate the efforts that he has expended in true friendship for Leon Nemoy. Without his encouragement and prodding the volume might not have appeared. We are also grateful to the American Academy for Jewish Research for its support of this volume. The editors would like to thank Mr. David Louvish who copy-edited the articles and prepared the volume for publication with skill and judgment.

Daniel Sperber, Jonas C. Greenfield

LEON NEMOY – A BIOGRAPHICAL SKETCH

S. R. Brunswick

Leon Nemoy was born in Balta, Russia on December 29, 1901, into a middle class family. He grew up in Odessa and studied Classical and Slavic languages at the local university. During the Russian civil war he served as an artillery officer.

When he and his father realized that there was no future for them under the Soviet regime, they stole across the border into neighboring Poland in 1921. Their newly found freedom was to be of little help to his father, who passed away three days later of acute pneumonia. His mother, who was unwell and had refused to accompany them on their perilous attempt to escape from Russia, for fear of endangering them, died in 1923 before he could obtain the necessary documents and means to bring her out. From Poland he emigrated to the United States in 1923.

He had always worked in libraries, both in czarist Russia and in Poland. In New York City he sought the advice of Abraham Freidus, who told him of an opening for a Judaica cataloguer in the Yale University Library, where he proceeded to serve as curator of Hebrew and Arabic Literature and principal rare-book cataloguer until his retirement in 1966. (More detailed autobiographical reminiscences can be found in the February 1965 issue of *Yale University Library Staff News*.) It was at Yale University that he also completed his sought-for education, under such famous mentors as Albert Clay and Charles Torrey, with a dissertation concerning an Arab poet of the fourteenth century. Subsequent years would see him centering his attention on Karaite history and literature, including his edition of al-Qirqisani's monumental Code of Karaite Law, a *Karaite Anthology* in English translation and other studies. And it was at Yale University in 1930 that he married the former Elizabeth McGinley.

While at Yale he endeared himself to his many colleagues by the many anecdotes and humorous comments that he included in his service memoranda, sent to them in the departmental mail. He similarly endeared himself to the scholarly world at large by his prompt and generous response to inquiries, requests for help, and so on.

A recent letter describing academic life at Yale during Nemoy's first period of service is both illustrative and informative. It reads, in part: "Your tale of the young lady starting at the HUC Library at $9800 per annum brings back the memory of my starting wage (1923) at Yale – $85 per month. Of course, my furnished cubbyhole of a room cost me $3 a week, and a dinner at Silverberg's kosher restaurant in New Haven (no longer in existence, alas) cost 55 cents (plate of soup, main course, pie or fruit compote, coffee). The Yale Commons charged a whopping 75 cents for a Sunday dinner (half a roast chicken, or a 3/4 pound slab of roast ham, plus fruit cup, soup, a huge sector of pie or cake). When I happen to tell all this to a student at Dropsie, I could swear I can see by his eyes that he's saying to himself, 'This old fellow is a regular Fibber McGee,' and I can't really blame him. I felt the same way when my room landlord (a tree surgeon, native of Tennessee, whose accent was a delight to my ear) used to reminisce how, around 1900, he used to buy a good woollen suit for $3, and how his regular lunch cost 5 cents (schooner of beer, plus a plateful of cold cuts and salads from the free lunch counter). Oh well, where are the snows of yesteryear?"

Upon retirement from Yale he left his correspondence files to the Yale University Library. At that time, some said it would take three or four people to accomplish what he had managed to do within the same amount of time. An indication of the esteem in which he is held is the D.H.L. degree *honoris-causa* which he was awarded by the Hebrew Union College – Jewish Institute of Religion in 1976.

After retirement from Yale he settled with his wife in Philadelphia, where Dropsie University gave him an office as well as an appointment as Research Professor in Karaitic Literature. He continued his work (begun in 1956) as editor of the Yale Judaica Series from his office in Philadelphia, except for an occasional trip back to Yale to attend editorial meetings and to check over a newly acquired group of Near Eastern manuscripts. He once wrote and told me: "My editorial salary comes from an annual grant from the National Endowment for the Humanities. This year they are way behind schedule, and I haven't received a cent this year so far. I'm not worrying about it, and even if the series should go broke, I'd go on editing it (it's after all *le-shem shamayim*) – I wouldn't dream of saying no-pay-no-work."

Perhaps the finest tribute that can be paid to him is to quote a recent letter to me describing his work as editor of the Yale Judaica Series: "Heaven knows, thousands of hours of my labor are sunk in them. Not only did I have to put the manuscripts into decent English, but in the case of deceased translators I had to rewrite the introductions, compile the indices, check the bibliographies, etc., etc., *'avodat perekh'* withal."

Sheldon R. Brunswick

BIBLIOGRAPHY OF LEON NEMOY

S. R. BRUNSWICK

A. Monographs

'Umar ibn Ibrâhîm, Abû 'Alî al-Anṣârî, *Selected Poems from the Kitâb Zahr al-Kimâm fî Qiṣṣat Yûsuf,* edited from manuscripts preserved at the Cambridge University Library and the Yale University Library; New Haven 1930. 17 ll.

Yale University Library, Check-list of an exhibition of Judaica and Hebraica held at the Sterling Memorial Library, April-June 1933; New Haven 1933. 23 pp.

al-Qirqisânî, Ya'qûb, *Kitâb al-Anwâr wal-Marâqib,* Code of Karaite Law, edited from manuscripts in the State Public Library, Leningrad, and the British Museum, London; New York, Alexander Kohut Foundation, 1939–1943. 5 vols.

Ibn Kammûnah, Sa'd ibn Manṣûr, *The Arabic Treatise on the Immortality of the Soul,* Facsimile reproduction of the only known manuscript (Cod. Landberg 510, fol. 58–70) in the Yale University Library, with bibliographical note, New Haven, Yale University Library, 1944. 26 pp.

Yale University Library, Catalogue of Hebrew and Yiddish manuscripts and books from the library of Scholem Asch, New Haven, Yale University Library, 1945. 20, 69 pp. (Yale University Library Miscellanies, 5).

Karaite Anthology, Excerpts from the early literature, translated from Arabic, Aramaic and Hebrew sources, with notes, New Haven, Yale University Press, 1952. 26, 412 pp. (Yale Judaica Series, vol. 7).

The Scroll of Antiochus (original Aramaic version), Facsimile of Codex Hebrew 51 in the Yale University Library, copied in 1558 at Voltaggio, Italy, by Joseph ben Joshua ha-Kohen (author of *'Emek ha-Baḵa*), with bibliographical note, New Haven, Yale University Library, 1952. 8 ll.

Yale University Library, Arabic manuscripts in the Yale University Library; New Haven 1956. 273 p. (*Transactions of the Connecticut Academy of Arts and Sciences,* 40 [1956], 1–273).

*B. Articles and Book Reviews**

As this is a bibliography of scholarly articles and book reviews, popularistic items published in the *B'nai B'rith Magazine, Jewish Spectator* and *Synagogue Light* have not been included. Encyclopedia articles, such as those in the *Universal Jewish Encyclopedia, Ha-Entsiklopediyah ha-ʿivrit,* the *Encyclopaedia of Islam,* 2d ed., and the *Encyclopaedia Judaica,* 1971 ed., have also been excluded.

1930

"The Yiddish Yosippon of 1564," *Yale University Library Gazette,* 4 (1930), 36–39.

"al-Qirqisānī's Account of the Jewish Sects and Christianity," *HUCA*, 7 (1930), 317–397.

1933

"A Hitherto Undescribed Edition of Leon de Modena's 'Sod Yesharim'," *JQR*, new ser., 24 (1933), 49–50.

1934

"Pirke Shabat me-al-Kirkisānī," *Ḥorev*, 1 (1934), 200–206.

1936

"Maʿaseh-bukh hotsa'at Homburg, 5487," *ʿAlim,* 2 (1936), 53.

"Contributions to the Textual Criticism of Judah Ha-Levi's Kitāb al-Khazarī," *JQR*, new ser., 26 (1936), 221–226. Reprinted in: Judah ha-Levi, *Sefer ha-Kuzari,* Jerusalem 1970.

* Key to Abbreviations:

HUCA	*Hebrew Union College Annual*
JAOS	*Journal of the American Oriental Society*
JBL	*Journal of Biblical Literature*
JQR	*Jewish Quarterly Review*
JSS	*Jewish Social Studies*
PAAJR	*Publications of the American Academy for Jewish Research*
PAJHS	*Publications of the American Jewish Historical Society*
REJ	*Révue des Études Juives*

1937

Review of: Salmon ben Yeruhim, *Sefer Milḥamot Adonai,* New York 1934; in *JQR*, new ser., 28 (1937), 91–94.

1938

Review of: Zvi Cahn, *The Rise of the Karaite Sect,* New York 1937; in *JQR*, new ser., 28 (1938), 355–356.

"Hasagat Ya'akov al-Kirkisani 'al isur melechet ha-refu'ah le-'Anan rosh ha-Kara'im," *ha-Rofe ha-'Ivri* (1938), 2: 73-83.

"al-Qirqisani's Criticism of Anan's Prohibition of the Practice of Medicine," *ha-Rofe ha-'Ivri* (1938), 2: 207–198.

"Notes on some Arabic Manuscripts on Curious Subjects in the Yale University Library," in *Yale University Library, Papers in honor of Andrew Keogh,* New Haven 1938, pp. 45–66.

"A Tenth Century Disquisition on Suicide According to Old Testament Law," *JBL*, 57 (1938), 411–420.

1939

"William Gottlieb Schauffler," *PAJHS*, 35 (1939), 304–306.

"The Treatise on the Egyptian Pyramids, by Jalāl al-Dīn al-Suyūṭī (Tuḥfat al-kirām fī khabar al-ahrām)," edited with introduction, translation and notes, *Isis*, 30 (1939),17–37.

"Hebrew and Kindred Manuscripts in the Yale University Library," *Journal of Jewish Bibliography,* 1 (1939), 107–111.

"Terumat Ya'akov al-Kirkisani le-torat maḥalot ha-nashim veha-'ubar be-sifro 'Kitāb al-anwār'," *ha-Rofe ha-'Ivri* (1939), 2: 35–41. Reprinted: *Ibid.* (1961), 1: 159–165.

"Contributions to Gynaecology and Embryology from the Kitāb al-Anwār of al-Qirqisani," *ha-Rofe ha-'Ivri* (1939), 2: 173–167. Reprinted: *Ibid.* (1961), 1: 210–205.

1940

"Biblical Quasi-Evidence for the Transmigration of Souls," *JBL*, 59 (1940), 159–168.

Review of: Moses ben Maimon, *Sefer ha-katseret*, Jerusalem 1939/40; in *ha-Rofe ha-'Ivri* (1940), 2: 133–134.

"ha-Reshimot 'al ha-Rambam u-veno Avraham be-milono shel Ibn Avi Atsivah (Uṣaybi'ah) le-rof'im 'arvim," *ha-Rofe ha-'Ivri* (1940), 2: 78–81.

"The Sketches of Maimonides and his Son, Abraham, in Ibn Abi Usaybia's Dictionary of Arab Physicians," *ha-Rofe ha-'Ivri* (1940), 2: 173—171.

1941

"Al-Qirqisānī on Leviticus 18.18," in Sándor Scheiber, ed., *Jubilee Volume in Honour of Professor Bernhard Heller,* Budapest 1941, pp. 258-264.

"The Arabic Pharmacopoeia of Abū al-Minā al-Kūhīn al-'Attar, 13th Century," *ha-Rofe ha-'Ivri* (1941), 2: 166—156; (1942), 2: 148—144; (1943), 2: 150—144.

"Sefer ha-rakaḥut ha-'arvi shel Abū al-Minā al-Kūhīn al-'Attar," *ha-Rofe ha-'Ivri* (1941), 2: 68—76; (1942), 2: 88—93; (1943), 2: 77—85.

Review of: Walter C. Klein, al-Ash'ari's al-'Ibanah 'an uṣūl al-diyānah, New Haven 1940; in *JQR*, new ser., 32 (1941), 215—217.

1942

"Hebrew and Kindred Manuscripts in the Yale University Library, 2d series," *Journal of Jewish Bibliography,* 3 (1942), 44—47.

"From the Kitāb al-anwār of Ya'qūb al-Qirqisānī (Discourse XII, Chapter 30: On Vapors and Odors)," *Medical Leaves,* 4 (1942), 96—102.

1943

Review of: Japheth ben Eli, the Karaite, *The Arabic Commentary on the Book of Hosea,* Philadelphia 1942; in *JQR* new ser., 33 (1943), 501—506.

"'U-mi-zar'akha lo titen le-ha'avir la-Molekh,' perush al-Kirkisani 'al ha-pasuk," in David Fränkel, ed., *Sefer ha-yovel li-khevod Professor Aleksandr Marks*, New York 1943, pp. 131—134.

1944

ha-Kara'im, *Riv'on Katan,* no. 2 (summer 1944), 264—277.

1945

"A Yidishe iberzetsung fun Yirmiyahu, Prag, 1602," *Yivo Bleter,* 26 (1945), 236—240.

"A Tenth Century Criticism of the Doctrine of the Logos (John 1,1)," *JBL*, 64 (1945), 515—529.

1946

Review of David ben Abraham, Karaite, *The Hebrew-Arabic Dictionary of the*

Bible, New Haven 1936–45, 2 vols. (Yale Oriental Series, Researches, vols. 20–21); in *JBL*, 65 (1946), 221–223.

"A Yidishe iberzetsung fun Oylen-shpigl, Prag, 1735," *Yivo Bleter,* 27 (1946), 198.

Review of: Eli Ashtor, *Toldot ha-Yehudim be-Mitsrayim ve-Suryah*, Jerusalem 1944–50, 2 vols.; in *Historia Judaica*, 8 (1946), 200–204; 13 (1951), 163–166.

1947

"Anan ben David; a Re-appraisal of the Historical Data," in Sándor Scheiber, ed., *Semitic Studies in Memory of Immanuel Löw*, Budapest 1947, pp. 239–248. Reprinted in: Philip Birnbaum, ed., *Karaite Studies*, New York 1971, pp. 309–318.

"Ibn-Kammunah rofe yehudi," *ha-Rofe ha-'Ivri* (1947), 2: 123–125.

"A Forgotten 13th Century Jewish Physician – Ibn Kammuna," *ha-Rofe ha-'Ivri* (1947), 2: 159–157.

1948

"Did Salmon ben Jerohām Compose a Commentary on Ruth?" *JQR*, new ser., 39 (1948), 215–216.

"Ibn Kammūna's Treatise on the Immortality of the Soul," in David S. Löwinger, ed., *Ignace Goldziher Memorial Volume*, Budapest, etc. 1948–58, vol. 2, pp. 83–99.

"Ketsat segulot u-refu'ot min ha-folklor ha-yehudi ha-'arvi," *ha-Rofe ha-'Ivri* (1948), 1: 70–73.

"Some Bits of Judeo-Arabic Medical Folklore," *ha-Rofe ha-'Ivri* (1948), 1: 151–148.

1949

"Henry Obookiah; the First Hawaiian Student of Hebrew," *PAJHS*, 39 (1949), 190–192.

"ha-Ma'amar shel al-Kirkisani 'al ha-psikho-fisiyologiyah shel ha-shenah veha-ḥalomot," *ha-Rofe ha-'Ivri* (1949), 2: 88–95.

"al-Qirqisani's Essay on the Psycho-Physiology of Sleep and Dreams," *ha-Rofe ha-'Ivri* (1949), 2: 165–158.

"Sotsiale un ekonomishe faktorn in fri'ikn kara'imizm," *Yivo Bleter,* 33 (1949), 95–112.

1950

"Early Karaism (the Need for a New Approach)," *JQR*, new ser., 40 (1950), 307–315.

Review of: Judah Rosenthal, *Hiwi al-Balkhi,* Philadelphia 1949; in *Historia Judaica,* 12 (1950), 80–82.

1951

"Ḥomer refu'i be-sefer ha-ḥukim ha-kara'i shel Eliyahu Bashyatsi," *ha-Rofe ha-ʻIvri* (1951), 1: 108–117.

"Medical Material in the Code of Karaite Law by Elijah Bashyatchi," *ha-Rofe ha-ʻIvri* (1951), 1: 167–156.

1952

"From 'The Mantle of Elijah' (by) Elijah Bashyatchi (*Excerpt from Karaite Anthology*)," *Commentary,* 14 (1952), 65–69.

Review of: William Popper, *The Cairo Nilometer,* Berkeley 1951; in *JAOS*, 72 (1952), 130–131.

"Shemu'el ben Mosheh al-Magribi," *ha-Rofe ha-ʻIvri* (1952), 1: 121–124.

"Samuel ben Moses al-Maghribi," *ha-Rofe ha-ʻIvri* (1952), 1: 153–150.

1953

Review of: Moses ben Maimon, *Epistle to Yemen,* New York 1952; in *JQR*, new ser., 44 (1953), 170–175.

"Heʻarot le-ḥibur shel Ibn Kammunah ʻal ha-hevdelim ben ha-Rabanim veha-Kara'im," *Tarbits*, 24 (1953/54), 343–353.

1955

"ha-Rambam ve-hitnagduto li-kheshafim le-or ketavav shel Yaʻakov al-Kirkisani," *ha-Rofe ha-ʻIvri* (1954), 2: 102–109; (1955), 1: 139–147.

"Maimonides' Opposition to Occultism; the Influence of the Writings of Jacob al-Qirqisani, a Karaite Scholar of the Tenth Century, on Maimonides," *ha-Rofe ha-ʻIvri* (1954), 2: 167–164; (1955), 1: 147–139.

Review of: D. M. Dunlop, *The History of the Jewish Khazars,* Princeton, N.J., 1954 (Princeton Oriental Series, vol. 16); in *JQR*, new ser., 46 (1955), 78–81.

Review of: Abraham I. Katsh, *Judaism in Islam*, New York 1954; in *JQR*, new ser., 45 (1955), 262–265.

"A kristlekhe imitatsiye fun Reb Yedayeh ha-Peninis Bakoshes ha-memi"n,"

Yivo Bleter, 39 (1955), 283–284.

Review of: Mubashshir ha-Levi, *Kitāb istidrākh al-sahu,* New York 1955; in *JQR*, new ser., 46 (1955), 198–202.

"An unbakante oysgabe fun Megilas Vints," *Yivo Bleter,* 39 (1955), 284–286.

1956

Review of: Shlomo D. F. Goitein, *Jews and Arabs*, New York 1955; in *JQR*, new ser., 46 (1956), 384–389.

1957

Review of: Nahman Avigad and Yigael Yadin, *A Genesis Apocryphon,* Jerusalem 1956; in *Studies in Bibliography and Booklore*, 3 (1957), 69–71.

Review of: Salmon ben Yeruhim, *The Arabic Commentary on the Book of Psalms, Chapters 42–72*, Philadelphia 1956; in *JQR*, new ser., 48 (1957), 58–66.

1958

"Matrūn Once More," *JQR*, new ser., 49 (1958), 155–157.

1959

Review of: Leo Baeck, *Aus drei Jahrtausenden*, Tübingen 1958; in *JBL*, 78 (1959), 269–271.

Review of: Abraham I. Katsh, *ha-Yahadut be-Islam*, Jerusalem 1957, in *JBL*, 78 (1959), 185–186.

1960

"Arabic, Persian, Hebrew, Syriac, and Ethiopic Manuscripts," in *Exhibitions in the Yale University Library on the occasion of the 170th meeting of the American Oriental Society, Yale University, March 29–31, 1960*, New Haven 1960, pp. 7–11.

"Corrections and Emendations to al-Qirqisānī's Kitāb al-Anwār," *JQR*, new ser., 50 (1960), 371–383.

Review of: P. S. Goldberg, *Karaite Liturgy and its Relation to Synagogue Worship*, Manchester (England) 1957; in *JQR*, new ser., 50 (1960), 277–278.

1961

Review of: Zvi Ankori, *Karaites in Byzantium*, New York 1959; in *JQR*, new ser., 51 (1961), 332–354.

Review of: Peshitta Institute, Leiden, *List of Old Testament Peshitta Manuscripts*, Leiden 1961; in *JBL*, 81 (1962), 201–202.

1962

Review of: Edward Robertson, *Catalogue of the Samaritan Manuscripts in the John Rylands Library, Manchester, Vol. II: The Gaster Manuscripts*, Manchester (England) 1962; in *JBL*, 81 (1962), 430–431.

"Ibn Kammunah u-masato ʿal hishaʾarut ha-nefesh," *ha-Rofe ha-ʿIvri* (1962), 2: 131–136.

"Ibn Kammunah's Treatise on the Immortality of the Soul," *ha-Rofe ha-ʿIvri* (1962), 2: 239–213.

"Ibn Kammunah ve-ḥiburo ʿal ha-ḥilufim she-ben ha-Rabanim veha-Karaʾim," in Yehudah L. Maimon, ed., *Sefer yovel mugash li-khevod Yisrael Elfenbeyn*, Jerusalem 1962, pp. 201–208.

1963

Review of: Naphtali Wieder, *The Judean Scrolls and Karaism*, London 1962; in *JBL*, 82 (1963), 22–24.

1964

Review of: British Museum, Department of Oriental Printed Books and Manuscripts, *Catalogue of the Hebrew books in the Library of the British Museum*, London 1867 [i. e. c1964]; in *JBL*, 83 (1964), 438–439.

"New Data for the Biography of Saʿd ibn Kammūnah," *REJ*, 4. sér., 123 (1964), 507–510.

1965

Review of: Pinchas Wechter, *Ibn Barun's Arabic Works on Hebrew Grammar and Lexicography*, Philadelphia 1964; in *JBL*, 84 (1965), 200–201.

1966

Review of: Haim Z. Hirschberg, *Toldot ha-yehudim be-Afrikah ha-tsefonit*, Jerusalem 1965, 2 vols.; in *JBL*, 85 (1966), 122–123.

1968

Review of: Shlomo D. F. Goitein, *A Mediterranean Society*, vol. 1, Berkeley 1967; in *JQR*, new ser., 58 (1968), 338–343.

"Ibn Kammunah's Treatise on the Differences between the Rabbanites and the Karaites," *PAAJR*, 36 (1968), 107–165.

Review of: *Jewish Book Annual*, vol. 25, 5728; in *JSS*, 30 (1968), 275.

Review of: Seyyed H. Nasr, *Ideals and Realities of Islam*, Boston 1966; in *JSS*, 30 (1968), 179–181.

1969

Review of: Gerson D. Cohen, *A Critical Edition... of the Book of Tradition by Abraham ibn Daud*, Philadelphia 1967; in *JSS*, 31 (1969), 48–51.

Review of: Toshihiko Izutsu, *Ethico-religious Concepts in the Qur'an*, Montreal 1966; in *JQR*, new ser., 60 (1969), 69–71.

Review of: Ibn Kammūnah Sa'd ibn Manṣūr, *Tanqīh al-abhāth lil-milal al thalāth*, Berkeley 1967 (University of California Publications, Near Eastern Studies vol. 6); in *JSS*, 31 (1969), 333–335.

Review of: Obshtestvena kulturno-prosvetna organizatsi͡ia na evreite v narodna Republika Bulgari͡ia, *Tsentralno rukovodstvo Annual*, Sofia, vol. 2:1, 1967; in *JSS*, 31 (1969), 61–62.

1970

Review of: Paul André, *Écrits de Qumran et sectes juives aux premiers siècles de l'Islam*, Paris 1969; in *JBL*, 89 (1970), 489–491.

"The Epistle of Sahl ben Maṣlīah," *PAAJR*, 38/39 (1970/71), 145–177.

1971

Review of: Francesco Gabrieli, *Arab Historians of the Crusades*, London 1969; in *JQR*, new ser., 62 (1971), 133–137.

"A Modern Egyptian Manual of the Karaite Faith," *JQR*, new ser., 62 (1971), 1–11.

"Studies in the History of the Early Karaite Liturgy: the Liturgy of al-Qirqisānī," in *Studies in Jewish Bibliography, History, and Literature in Honor of I. Edward Kiev*, New York 1971, pp. 305–332.

1972

"The Rescher Collection of Arabic, Persian and Turkish Manuscripts," *Yale University Library Gazette*, 47 (1972), 57–99.

"Ibn Kammūnah's Treatise on the Differences between the Rabbanites and the Karaites," *JQR*, new ser., 63 (1972), 97–135.

Review of: *Islam and its Cultural Divergence; Studies in Honor of Gustave E. von Grunebaum*, Urbana 1971; in *JQR*, new ser., 63 (1972), 178–179.

Review of: Jacob Mann, *The Jews in Egypt and Palestine under the Fatimid Caliphs*, New York 1970; in *JQR*, new ser., 62 (1972), 222–224.

Review of: Erwin I. J. Rosenthal, *Studia Semitica*, Cambridge 1971, 2 vols. (University of Cambridge, Oriental Publications, no. 16–17); in *JQR*, new ser., 62 (1972), 320–321.

"A Scurrilous Anecdote concerning Maimonides," *JQR*, new ser., 62 (1972), 188–192.

Review of: M. A. Shaban, *The Abbāsid Revolution*, Cambridge 1970; in *JQR*, new ser., 63 (1972) 86–89.

1973

Review of: Philip Birnbaum, ed., *Karaite Studies*, New York 1971; in *JQR*, new ser., 64 (1973), 92–93.

"Ibn Kammūnah's Treatise on the Differences between the Rabbinites [*sic*] and the Karaites," *JQR*, new ser., 63 (1973), 222–246.

Review of: Reynold A. Nicholson, *Studies in Islamic Poetry*, London 1969; in *JQR*, new ser., 63 (1973), 361–362.

Review of: Andrew Sharf, *Byzantine Jewry*, London 1971; in *JQR*, new ser., 63 (1973), 363–364.

1974

"The Attitude of the Early Karaites towards Christianity," in *Salo Wittmayer Baron Jubilee Volume on the Occasion of his Eightieth Birthday*, English Section, Jerusalem 1974, vol. 2, pp. 697–715.

Review of: *Bar-Ilan, sefer ha-shanah le-mada'e ha-yahadut veha-ruaḥ*, vol. 9–10, 1972 (*Sefer Ḥ. M. Shapira)*; in *JQR*, new ser., 64 (1974), 331–334.

Review of: Shlomo D. F. Goitein, *A Mediterranean Society*, vol. 2, Berkeley 1971; in *JQR*, new ser., 65 (1974), 56–62.

Review of: A. M. Habermann, *Tave sefer yehudiyim*, Safed [1972?]; in *JQR*, new ser., 65 (1974), 136–137.

Review of: Stephan and Nandy Ronart, *Lexikon der arabischen Welt*, Zürich 1972; in *JQR*, new ser., 65 (1974), 138–139.

1975

Review of: Abū Iṣhāq Ibrāhīm al-Sāmirī, *Kitāb al-mīrāth*, ed. Heinz Pohl, Berlin 1974 (*Studia Samaritana*, II); in *JQR*, new set., 66 (1975), 62–65.

"Anan ben David, Karaite. English Translation of the Eupatoria Fragment of

Anan's Sefer ha-mitsvot," *JQR*, new ser., 66 (1975), 115–119.

Review of: Bahya ben Joseph ibn Pakuda, *The Book of Direction to the Duties of the Heart*, tr. by M. Mansoor, London 1973; in *JQR*, new ser., 65 (1975), 258–259.

Review of: Majid Khadduri, *Political Trends in the Arab World*, Baltimore 1972; in *JQR*, new ser., 65 (1975), 260–261.

Review of: Jean Le Moyne, *Les Sadducéens*, Paris 1972; in *JQR*, new ser., 66 (1975), 121–123.

Review of: Levi ben Gershom, *Les Guerres du Seigneur*, Livres III et IV, tr. Charles Touati, Paris 1968; in *JQR*, new ser., 66 (1975), 124–125.

Review of: Jacob Mann, *Texts and Studies*, New York 1972, 2 vols.; in *JQR*, new ser., 65 (1975), 190–191.

1976

Review of: Jamil N. Abun-Nasr, *A History of the Maghrib*, Cambridge (England) 1971; in *JQR*, new ser., 66 (1976), 251.

Review of: Henry Corbin, *Creative Imagination in the Sufism of Ibn ʿArabī*, Princeton 1969; in *JQR*, new ser., 67 (1976), 160–162.

"The Factor of Script in the Textual Criticism of Judeo-Arabic Manuscripts," *JQR*, new ser., 66 (1976), 148–159.

Review of: David M. Goodblatt, *Rabbinic Instruction in Sasanian Babylonia*, Leiden 1975; in *JBL*, 95 (1976), 517–518.

Review of: Fritz Homeyer, *Deutsche Juden als Bibliophilen und Antiquare* (2. Aufl.), Tübingen 1966; in *JQR*, new ser., 66 (1976), 172.

Review of: Moses ben Maimon, *On the Causes of Symptoms*, edited by J. O. Leibowitz, Berkeley 1974; in *JQR*, new ser., 67 (1976), 175–176.

"The Pseudo-Qūmisian Sermon to the Karaites," *PAAJR*, 43 (1976), 49–105.

"Mourad Farag and His Work *The Karaites and the Rabbanites*," *REJ*, 4. ser., 135 (1976), 87–112.

1977

Review of: L. Khayyāt, *Majmūʿat al-amthāl al-ʿāmmīyah*, vols. 1–2, Jerusalem – New York 1968–76; in *JQR*, new ser., 67 (1977), 242–243.

Review of: Menahem Stern, *Greek and Latin Authors on Jews and Judaism*, vol. I, Jerusalem 1974; in *JQR*, new ser., 67 (1977), 246.

1978

"Two Controversial Points in the Karaite Law of Incest," *HUCA*, 49 (1978), 247–265.

Review of: David Corcos, *Studies in the History of the Jews of Morocco*, Jerusalem 1976; in *JQR*, new ser., 68 (1978), 61–62.

Review of: Ben Siegel, *The Controversial Sholem Asch*, Bowling Green, Ohio, 1976; in *JQR*, new ser., 68 (1978), 121–122.

Review of: Patricia Crone and Michael Cook, *Hagarism, the Making of the Islamic World*, Cambridge (England) 1977; in *JQR*, new ser., 68 (1978), 179–181.

Review of John Wansbrough, *Quranic Studies*, Oxford 1977; in *JQR*, new ser., 68 (1978), 182–184.

Review of: *Humaniora Islamica*, vols. I–II, The Hague – Paris 1973–74; in *JQR*, new ser., 69 (1978), 62–63.

1979

"The Ascension of Enoch and Elijah, a Tenth Century Karaite Interpretation," in *Essays on the Occasion of the Seventieth Anniversary of the Dropsie University*, Philadelphia 1979, pp. 361–364.

Review of: Abraham Elijah Harkavy, *Ḥadashim Gam Yeshanim*, Jerusalem 5630; in *JQR*, new ser., 69 (1979), 243–244.

Review of: S. D. Goitein, *A Mediterranean Society*, vol. III, Berkeley – Los Angeles – London 1978; in *JQR*, new ser., 70 (1979), 50–56.

1980

Review of: Harry A. Wolfson, *Repercussions of the Kalām in Jewish Philosophy*, Cambridge, Mass.. 1979; in *JQR*, new ser., 70 (1980), 117–118.

Review of: Hayyim Liebermann, *Natsruto shel Sholem Asch*, Tel Aviv [1977?]; in *JQR*, new ser., 70 (1980), 183–184.

"A Modern Karaite Arabic Poet: Mourad Farag," *JQR*, new ser., 70 (1980), 195–209.

Review of: Moshe Seltzer, *Ideologies in the Near East, 1946–1972*, New York [1975]; in *JQR*, new ser., 71 (1980), 58–60.

Review of: Norman Stillman, *The Jews of Arab Lands*, Philadelphia 1979; in *JQR*, new ser., 71 (1980), 123–125.

"Elijah ben Abraham and His Tract Against the Rabbanites," *HUCA*, 51 (1980), 63–87.

"Al-Qirqisānī on the Value/Weight of the Shekel," *PAAJR*, 46/47 (1980), 389–395.

1981

Review of: Alexander Marx, *Bibliographical Studies*, New York 1977; in *JQR*, new ser., 71 (1981), 191–192.

Review of: *The Arabs, People and Power, Prepared by the Editors of Encyclopaedia Britannica*, New York 1978; in *JQR*, new ser., 71 (1981), 259–260.

Review of: *Readings in Arab Middle Eastern Societies and Cultures*, edited by Abdulla M. Lutfiyya and Charles W. Churchill, The Hague – Paris 1970; in *JQR*, new ser., 71 (1981), 261–262.

Review of: Jacob Lassner, *The Shaping of 'Abbasid Rule*, Princeton 1980; in *JQR*, new ser., 71 (1981), 263–265.

ON SOME AUXILIARY VERBS IN JUDAEO-ARABIC

J. Blau

1. L. Nemoy is one of the pioneers of Judaeo-Arabic studies in general and Karaite scholarship in particular. In the following, I shall endeavor to deal with some auxiliary verbs in Judaeo-Arabic which have not been sufficiently treated in my book *A Grammar of Mediaeval Judaeo-Arabic*.[1] I shall cite Karaite authors as well, including Kirkisânî's *Kitâb al-anwâr wal-marâqib* in Nemoy's excellent edition.[2] In most cases, however, it can be demonstrated that the linguistic usage of Rabbanite and Karaite authors was alike, and it stands to reason that no difference obtained even where, by chance it seems, so far a certain construction is attested in Karaite writings only.

2. *kân 'an* is used to denote what should have been: Tanḥûm,[3] *s.v. tzz: fa-kân 'aṣl hittîz 'alâ hâdhâ 'an yakûn bi-ṣêrê* "therefore, *hittîz* should have been originally with *ṣêrê*"; *fa-sh-shadda 'iwaḍa-s-sâkin 'alladhî kân ba'd 'al-mem 'alâ aṣlih(î) 'an yakûn mithl mêqîm* "and the doubling is instead of the long vowel, which originally should have been after the *mem* like *mêqîm*."

3. *Grammar,* p. 188, note 30 *tamm* "to remain," used as the main verb, is cited. Dozy,[4] *s.v.,* adduces it from Bocthor as an auxiliary verb in the sense of "continuing." In the Arabian Nights and in modern dialects, *tamm* (sometimes also *tann/dann*) with pronominal suffixes is used in the same sense; v. Brockelmann,[5] II, p. 39 and especially Barthélemy,[6] p. 93. I have noted it in Ms. Paris Heb. 583 (from Egypt, 1840) in a passage parallel to *Pereq*,[7] p. 7b, 5

1 Jerusalem 1961 (in Hebrew; henceforth: *Grammar*). [Since this paper went to press, a second edition of this grammar has been published (1980).]

2 New York 1939–43 (Henceforth: Nemoy).

3 Tanḥûm Yerûshalmî, *Al-murshid al-kâfî*, according to Weimar m.a. 252a.

4 R. Dozy, *Supplément aux dictionnaires arabes* (2nd ed.), Leiden–Paris 1927.

5 C. Brockelmann, *Grundriss der vergleichenden Grammatik der semitischen Sprachen,* Berlin 1908–13.

6 A. Barthélemy, *Dictionnaire arabe-français, Dialectes de Syrie: Alep...,* Paris 1935 ff.

7 R. David ben Abraham ben Rambam, *Sefer Pirqê 'Âbhôth 'im pêrûsh be-lâshôn 'arâbhî...,* ed. B. H. Ḥânân, Alexandria 1900–01.

tannô ʿalayh(i) "he always (causes) him (inconvenience)."

4. *ḥaṣal* is used in the sense of "to become": Maimonides,[8] p. 441, –6 *ḥaṣalat hatrâ'â* "it has become a warning"; Friedlaender,[9] p. 19, 8 *lâ taḥṣul bâqiya* "it does not become enduring," p. 25, 11 *wa-'idhâ ḥaṣal 'insân kâmil* (read so, according to the autograph!) "and if he becomes a perfect man."

5. Dozy, *s.v. rajaʿa*, adduces *rajaʿa* in the sense of "to become." I have noted it, preceding another verb in the imperfect, denoting "to begin": Friedlaender, p. 5, 12 *wa-rajaʿ yu'thir* "and he started preferring"; Abraham Maimuni, *Kifâyat al-ʿAbidîn,* Bodl. Neubauer 1274, p. 73, 1 *yarjiʿû mustaqbilîn* "they start turning."

6. Ingressive verbs are, in all stages of Arabic, often "stretched" into duratives; for particulars v. *Leshonenu,* 32 (1967–68), pp. 53–58. This applies as well to *ṣâr* which, preceding another verb in the imperfect, denotes "to begin" and, by stretching, has come to mark continuation and habit. This is the case, e.g., in the modern dialect of Damascus (v. Grotzfeld,[10] p. 90) and the phenomenon is already attested in Judaeo-Arabic: Nemoy, p. 138, 1–2 *wa-lima ṣâr man ṭaraʾ 'ila-sh-Sha'm min 'ahl al-ʿIrâq yattaxidh bi-sh-Sha'm yawmayn* "why were Babylonians who came to Palestine accustomed to celebrate two days?" It often occurs in Tanḥûm, e.g., s.v. *lʿs: fa-bi-hâdhâ ṣarû yaghsilû aṭ-ṭibʿa* "and by dint of it they were used to wash the stain."

7. *Grammar,* p. 189, §298, invariable *kâd* "almost" with pronominal suffixes is cited. Yet, as I learn from Y. Raṣabi, *kâd* with pronominal suffixes is also attested in conjugated form: Saadya's Commentary to Job 13:14 (ed. Derenbourg) *takâdnî 'an 'anhash laḥmî* "I almost bite my flesh."

8. *Grammar,* p. 214, note 32, the use of *'arâd* "to want" denoting the imminent future was mentioned in passing. In the following, we shall deal with this phenomenon in detail, also mentioning its linguistic background.

It is a very widespread phenomenon that verbs of volition lose their volitive sense and come to be used as markers of simple future. For the speaker of English, *will* denoting future is an outstanding instance. For this phenomenon in other Indo-European languages v., e. g., O. Jespersen, *The Philosophy of Grammar,* London 1925, pp. 260–61; H. Paul, *Deutsche Grammatik* iv, Halle 1920, pp. 147–48, §368; M. Grevisse, *Le bon usage*[8], Gembloux 1964, p. 587,

8 R. Moses ben Maimon, *Responsa*, ed. J. Blau, I-II, Jerusalem 1957–60.

9 I. Friedlaender, *Selections from the Arabic Writings of Maimonides*, Semitic Study Series XII, Leiden 1909.

10 H. Grotzfeld, *Syrisch-Arabische Grammatik*, Wiesbaden 1965.

§655.15; C. Bally, *Linguistique générale et linguistique française*[3], Berne 1950, p. 218, §343. It is also attested in Semitic languages; Biblical Aramaic: Daniel 2:13 *u-bhəʻô dânîʼēl wə-ḥabhrôhî lə-hitqəṭâlâ* "and Daniel and his fellows were on the point of being slain." Targum Jonathan to Jonah 1:4 uses *bəʻâ* in the same sense (as translation of Hebrew *ḥishshəbhâ*), and it is utilized in Neo-Syriac as marker of the future as well (v. Koehler-Baumgartner,[11] *s.v. bəʻâ*, where, however, read Nöd NsG 250 instead of 259). Cf. also *infra*.[12]

In Biblical Hebrew, cf. Genesis 43:30 *wa-ybhaqqesh li-ḇhkôt* "and he was about to weep," translated by Targum Onkelos as *u-bəʻâ lə-mibhkê* and by Saadya Gaon as *fa-ṭalab ʼan yabkî*. Cf. also the Aramaic translation of Palestinian origin (Paul Kahle, *Masoreten des Westens*, II, Stuttgart 1930, p. 20) *u-tbhaʻ lə-mebhkê*, and further, Biblical Hebrew: Jonah 1:4 (cf. *supra*) *wə-hâ-ʼŏniyyâ ḥishshəbhâ lə-hishshâbher* "and the ship was about to be broken."

biqqesh in this usage is attested in Middle Hebrew as well (v. Koehler-Baumgartner[3],[13] *s.v. bqsh*): Mishnah Yoma 1, 7 *biqqesh lə-hitnamnem* "he was about to fall asleep." One may also compare *nìtyâʼesh* "to despair," which may lose its mental shade (just as verbs of volition lose their volitive sense) and be used in Middle Hebrew and *piyyût* in the meaning of "to be negligent, to refrain"; for details v. M. Zulay, *ʻInyənê lâshôn*, ed. H. Yalon, Jerusalem 1941, pp. 5–6; S. Lieberman, *Tosefta Ki-fshuṭah, Order Zeraʻim*, New York 1955, pp. 3, 623.

Similarly, Arabic *ʼarâda* "to want" loses its volitive sense in the various layers of Arabic and may mark simple future. It occurs already in the Qurʼân: 18:77 *wajadâ jidâran yurîdu ʼan yanqaḍḍa* "they found a wall about to tumble down." As far as I know, the first who called attention to this passage was Landberg,[14] p. 1552 (who, however, quoted it with a slight change from Buxârî; v. also M. Gaudefroy-Demombynes — R. Blachère, *Grammaire de l'arabe classique*, Paris 1952, p. 272, §200b); cf. Zamaxhsharî's *al-Kashshâf ad locum*: *ʼustuʻîrati- l-ʼirâdatu li-l-mudânati wa-l-mushârafati* "will is metaphorically used for being imminent and impending," and he adduces, alongside passages in which personification, rather than imminence, is the central issue, sentences like *ʻazama -s-sirâju ʼan yaṭfaʼa, ṭalaba ʼan yaṭfaʼa* "the lamp was about to be extinguished." ⌈*ʼarâd*⌉ is attested in this usage in modern dialects as well (v. Landberg, *loc. cit.*, and further, e.g., the passage adduced by Brockelmann, II,

11 L. Koehler—W. Baumgartner, *Lexicon in Veteris Testamenti libros*, Leiden 1953.

12 Accordingly, one will not accept the other interpretations proposed for Daniel 2:13; v. Koehler—Baumgartner (1st ed.), *loc. cit.*, and also F. R. Blake, *JAOS*, 35 (1915), 384.

13 L. Koehler—W. Baumgartner, *Hebräisches und aramäisches Lexikon zum Alten Testament*, Leiden 1967 ff.

14 Le comte de Landberg, *Glossaire Daṯînois*, I-III, Leiden 1920—42.

p. 620, 1). It is well attested in Ancient South-Palestinian Christian Arabic (v. J. Blau, *A Grammar of Christian Arabic,* Louvain 1966–67, p. 445, §338.4): Ms. Sinai ar. 516, p. 13b, –7 f. *wa-huwadhâ qiddîs 'allâh yurîd yuḥraq* "and behold, the saint of God is about to be burnt"; p. 69b, 2 *qawm-h(û) yurîdûn yaddûn* (cf. Blau, *op. cit.,* p. 171, §74.1) *'al-jizya* "his nation will pay the poll tax"; Ms. Sinai ar. 431, p. 190b, 11–12 = Ms. Sinai ar. 428, p. 44b, 5 *yurîd yamût* "he was going to die"; Ms. Sinai ar. 460, p. 70b, –7 *kânat turîd 'an tuqtal* "she was about to be killed"; Ms. British Museum ar. 8605 Act xvi 27 *'arâd yaqtul nafs-hû* (the Greek original has ἔμελλεν) "he was about to kill himself," xxvi 22 *mimmâ yurîd 'an yakûn* (translating μελλόντων γίνεσθαι) "of what will happen."

In Judaeo-Arabic (v. *Grammar*, p. 214, note 32) I have noted Obermann,[15] p. 12, 6 *turîd tamût* "she was about to die."[16]

It is impossible to say whether Middle Arabic *'arâd* marking imminence exhibits a genuine Middle Arabic feature or replaces a dialectal word denoting will, used in dialects also as marker of the future. Very frequent is *bidd-* with pronominal suffixes in various dialects, originally, it seems, *bi-wudd-*, denoting will and non-volitive future as well (v. e.g. *Bîr Zêt,*[17] pp. 147 ff., especially §88b1′ and 3′, Grotzfeld, p. 89). Other verbs of volition used as markers of the future attested in dialects are *ḥbb, bghy, 'by* (v. e.g. Marçais-Guîga,[18] pp. 710–11, §9, Landberg, pp. 16; 1552).[19]

The use of *'arâda* as marker of the future in Modern Standard Arabic (as Maḥfûẓ, *Shahru -l-'asali,* Cairo 1971, p. 166, 9–10 *wa-naḥnu numanni -n-nafsa bi-tarqiyatin lâ turîdu 'an tataḥaqqaqa 'abadan* "and we harbor the hope that we will rise, which, however, will never be carried out into effect")

15 J. Obermann, *The Arabic Original of Ibn Shâhîn's Book of Comfort...,* New Haven 1933.

16 Obermann, p. 6, 5 (quoted *Grammar, ibid.*) *râd 'an yaḍill* "he was about to err," the original reading being *kâd 'an yaḍill* "he almost erred" (v. the parallel manuscripts in S. Abramson, *R. Nissim Gaon libelli quinque,* Jerusalem 1956, p. 428, –5, and especially p. 429 note 14). Nevertheless, the deviation from the original reading might have been caused by *râd* denoting future and thus making perfect sense in the passage adduced. Yet it is sometimes idle to speculate on deviations from the correct reading.

17 J. Blau, *Syntax des palästinensischen Bauerndialekts von Bîr-Zêt,* Walldorf-Hessen 1960.

18 W. Marçais–A. Guîga, *Textes arabes de Takroûna, II, Glossaire...,* Paris 1958–61.

19 In some cases it is difficult to say whether the verb of volition has lost its volitive sense or is being used metaphorically (cf. *supra* Zamaksharî's *Kashshâf,* who adduces cases in which personification is the central issue; v. C. Reinhardt, *Ein arabischer Dialekt gesprochen in Oman und Zanzibar,* Berlin 1894, p. 15, who speaks of a knife which does not want to cut, but also of rain which does not agree to fall; in the latter case, imminence, rather than personification, seems *prima facie* to be the central issue).

presumably mirrors the influence of these dialectal verbs of volition used as markers of the future.

8.1. S. Skoss, *Kitâb jâmi al-alfâẓ... of David... al-Fâsî,* I, New Haven 1936, p. 254, 145 ff. *wa-mâ kân li-l-'infâ ya'qubh(û) mêm mithl u-bhi'artâ hârâ' mi-q-qirbêkhâ... wa-lâ 'alâ mâ tawahham ba'ḍ al-'aghbiyâ 'anna lô təbha'arû 'esh la tunfû an-nâr min buyût-kum wa-hâdhâ fâsid min al-lugha wal-ma'nạ. 'ammâ min al-lugha fa-kamâ dhakarnâ 'anna kull bi'ûr 'infâ yatba'h(û) mêm fa-kân yurîd yaqûl lô təbha'ªrû 'esh mikkol môshəbhôtêkhem* "and when (*bi 'er*) is used in the sense of removal, it is followed by *min,* like 'you shall remove wickedness from the midst of you' ... and it is not as some stupid people have imagined that 'you shall not *b'r* fire' means 'you shall not remove fire from your houses,' because this is wrong from the point of view of language and meaning. As to language, it is as we have mentioned that every *b'r* in the sense of removal is followed by *min.* Therefore it [Scripture] SHOULD have said..." exhibits *'arâd* in the sense of necessity. As a matter of fact, the development of "volition" to denote necessity is well-attested in modern Arabic dialects (v. the overall view offered by Marçais-Guîga, p. 711, §11, who quotes additional literature; further, e.g., M. Cohen, *Le parler arabe des Juifs d'Alger*, Paris 1912, p. 253; G. Boris, *Lexique de parler arabe des Marazig,* Paris 1958, *s.v. ḥbb*). In some cases, to be sure, this transition may be due to special conditions, as in the case of *bidd-* (v. also *Bîr Zêt*, p. 148, Grotzfeld, p. 89) to blend with *min kull budd/bidd* "there is no escape > necessarily" (v. M. Feghali, *Syntaxe des parlers arabes actuels du Liban,* Paris 1928, p. 65)[20] or in that of *ḥabb* to the influence of the passive (v. Marçais-Guîga, *loc. cit.*). Again, it is impossible to know whether *'arâda* has developed to denote necessity in genuine Middle Arabic or whether it rather represents a dialectal word, in which this development has occurred.[21]

20 Even Dozy, *s.v.* ***budd***, confused ***budd*** with ***bidd***; yet *s.v.* ***wadd*** he rectified the error.

21 J. C. Greenfield, ***Biblica,*** 45 (1964), 532, translated the Syriac *byad'âṯâ ṣḇâ dnehwê ṣmîd* as "he should have occupied himself with knowledge." In this case, the passage would exhibit a similar transition of *ṣḇa* to denote necessity. Yet one *may* simply translate "he (originally) had wanted to occupy himself with knowledge."

MIDRASH AS DEEP PESHAT

W. G. Braude

Many years ago, I studied the Book of Amos with Moses Buttenwieser, a very gifted and imaginative man. One of the students in the class had Rabbinic training, and from time to time dared draw upon his knowledge to interpret a verse in a manner which differed from the Professor's. Whereupon Professor Buttenwieser, glowering, would respond in his Alsatian accent: "Ah, z-z-zat is Midrash," his way of consigning the differing interpretation to an exegetical guillotine. In more recent years, at a small gathering in another institution, a distinguished exegete of the modern school was holding forth on a passage in Scripture and I dared cite a Rabbinic interpretation which differed from the guru's. He did not even let me finish – his revulsion was all but physical.

The two men I have spoken of are committed to a scientism which presumes to be the sole trustee of the true understanding of Scripture, and as such are vehemently intolerant of any approach other than theirs. But these two men, it should be said in their behalf, knew Hebrew, knew it well.

There are others whose knowledge of Hebrew is limited and whose grasp of Rabbinic texts is even more greatly limited, yet these are more Papal than the Pope in the days when the Pope was a Pope. Thus Professor Hans Jakob Polotzky told me that Holtzmann, translator of the Mishnah into German, insisted on reading אל תרבה שיחה עם האשה. באשתו אמרו קל. וחומר באשת חברו. When a young Jew spoke up and said: "But Herr Professor, קל וחומר is a technical term, the units of which may not be separated," Professor Holtzmann thought a while and then dismissed the challenger as being guilty of *Rabbinische Spitzsinnigkeit.*

The charge of *Spitzsinnigkeit* against anything Rabbinic may well go back to Baruch Spinoza, whom Simon Rawidowicz calls "the first Peshat-Jew of modern times." Rawidowicz goes on to say that Spinoza's preference of peshat was "stimulated not only by his reaction against the Jewish tradition of *interpretatio,* but also – and decisively – by the new mathematico-mechanical outlook, which was the basis for his philosophy at large" (*Studies in Jewish Thought,* Philadelphia 1974, p. 67).

Now the men who minted Midrashim, whatever interpretation they came up with, frequently insisted: מקרא אני דורש (TB Yoma 76a, Ta'an. 5b, Ket. 11a and elsewhere). In matters pertaining to Halakah decided upon by R. Meir, R. Judah, Hillel the Elder, R. Joshua b. Ḳorḥah and R. Jose, each of them was reported as היה דורש לשון הדיוט, that he sought the meaning of common terms of speech or writing (TB BM 104a–b). The quest in each case was peshat, the plain meaning of the common term used.

And scholars, men like Isaiah Hurwitz, Yehudah Loew of Prague, Ephraim Zalman Margulies, Zeeb Wolf Einhorn, David Luria, the Malbim and others who studied חז״ל, sought to unravel the line of thought which men who minted Midrashim followed in explaining Scripture's meaning. Generally, these scholars see in Midrashim peshat, deep peshat, but nevertheless peshat. Yet, like the Midrashim themselves, what these interpreters of Midrash say is derogated as *Spitzsinnigkeit,* because traditional interpreters of Midrash deny the mathematico-mechanical outlook, because they believe in revelation and hence in the polyphony of a text.

Their critics, on the other hand, followers of a mechanico-mathematical outlook, set out with the premise that a text has only a single meaning and that no other meaning is possible.

I suppose critics of Midrash in the main do not fault the mind or knowledge of חז״ל or of the great commentators on חז״ל. But many moderns are so busy with their own notions – to demonstrate polemics where there ain't none, to impart theories irrelevant to Scripture or to Midrash, or are in such a hurry to publish that they do not even take the time to learn to read and comprehend the texts they say they are using. But perhaps worst of all is the notion that a word, a phrase, a verse, a text is limited to a single meaning. פלשתים עליך ישראל: Philistines of a new kind – men of bare unilinear peshat or no peshat at all, seeing both Scripture and חז״ל as a kind of gibberish – are abroad, O Israel.

A friend, who studied with one of the modern exponents of peshat, told of the following experience. The professor offered a certain reading of a passage, and the student recalled that in a preceding year the same professor had offered a different reading of the particular passage and the student cited it. Whereupon the professor exploded: "Nonsense." Now the professor I refer to is a great scholar; but his reaction, I would respectfully say, rests on several false premises. False premise No. 1: we moderns really know Hebrew – in any event, we know it better than חז״ל. False premise No. 2: we have the means to recover the intent of the writer of Scripture. False premise No. 3: a great text such as Scripture, which even those who do not believe in revelation will admit that it indeed is, has one meaning, and one meaning only.

The fact is that there are שבעים פנים לתורה. The word of God or, if you will, the word of the great men responsible for Scripture, speaks in many tones to men in different moods; and if by procrustean analogues to ancient languages Scripture is reduced to mini-size and mini-tone, it becomes חוכא ואטלולא, a joke, as indeed happened to the Book of Psalms in the Anchor Series, linked as it was largely to Ugaritic, as though מאוגרית and the like תצא תורה.

Peshat is important, dealing as it does with the physical substratum of Scripture. Both חז״ל and their interpreters were always aware of peshat, however they defined it. But חז״ל also knew that, in Lee Hall's words, "no human response lacks a vast associative network of values, beliefs, thoughts, conscience, and consciousness." Midrash or deep peshat deals with more than one nexus and more than one connotation of a word or a phrase, reaching into the entirety of human experience and Jewish tradition. Moreover, Midrash copes with the structure of a passage seemingly disparate and discovers its underlying and richly significant unity. In every passage Midrash captures overtones of spirit, overtones which are the ultimate concern of the Redactor or of the redactors who wrought and preserved the text. And make no mistake about it, an author's intention, even in a work in mathematics, must be known precisely if the work is to be deciphered. Thus a distinguished mathematician whom I know finds an eighteenth century treatise on geometry by Fagnana de Fagnani obscure. Though the mathematics is simple, the author's point of view, my friend says, has been lost over the generations, and consequently the underlying theme of the symbols is likewise lost. How then can the plain-meaning-of-text men, latter-day followers of Spinoza who affirm that מאוגרית or the like תצא תורה, be so certain of the point of view of the author or authors of Scripture, so sure of it that they rule out as nonsense all opinions other than their own, which they happen to hold at a particular time? How can they be so certain of their own understanding of Scripture that they are prone to guillotine חז״ל with a contemptuous "z-z-zat is Midrash," or dismiss it as *Rabbinische Spitzsinnigkeit?*

In all fairness to a man like Moses Buttenwieser, whom I admired, may I add that the Spinozistic approach to the text *is* a way, revealing to us some facets of Scripture's meaning; but it is not the only way, certainly not *the* way. The royal way is Midrash, which is sensitive to the polyphony of – the multiplicity of meaning in – a text.

The Rabbinic works I have dealt with invariably seek peshat, deep peshat, a few examples of which I shall set forth.

First the clause ויתנו עליו את הנזר ואת העדות (II Chron. 23:11) which occurs in the account of the crowning of Joash as king of Judah. The clause precedes

וימליכו אתו וימשחהו יהוידע ובניו ויאמרו יחי המלך (*ibid.*). The meaning of נזר is clear enough. But העדות, as evident from its varying renditions, is difficult. AV, English Revised, American Revised, American, and New Catholic translate: "And put upon him the crown and *gave him* the testimony." JV has: "They put upon him the crown and the insignia." Yehoash, following JV, has זיי האבן אנגעטאן אויף אים די קרוין און די [קיניגלאכע] צייכנס. By the adjective קיניגלאכע, "royal," Yehoash tells us what the insignia were; James Moffatt, following de Vaux, and Montgomery (2 Chronicles, *The Anchor Bible,* New York 1965, p. 130) define עדות as *"royal bracelets."* By relating עדות to עדי, "ornaments," Buber proposes *schmuck*. Ronald Knox says, "the pledge that went with it." One wonders how a child of six or seven can take a pledge. The Jerusalem Bible has "imposed the law on him." The New English renders: "handed him the warrant." Finally, in the Anchor Bible, Jacob M. Myers translates "[delivered to him] the royal stipulations" which, in a note, he explains were "the rules governing [the king's] position in relation to Yahweh and the people." The document "would [thus, according to Myers] signify the terms of the kingship under which the monarch would rule" (*ibid.*, p. 130, note 11).

Into this chorus of disaccord as to what the peshat of עדות is, may I bring in deep peshat via Rab and Rashi, peshat associated with an ancient tradition, namely, that the crown of the house of David, about to be put upon the head of the six-year old Joash, had a unique feature: "a golden rod, passing through it from front to back, fitted into a cleft or indentation in the skull – a characteristic peculiarity of some in the House of David.[1] Only he whom the crown fitted was deemed worthy to be king" (TB Sanh. 21b and Av. Zara 44a). Rab thus takes הנזר והעדות to be a hendiadys: "They put upon Joash the crown as evidence of his descent." In defining עדות as evidence of Davidic descent, Rab addressed himself to a question most relevant. The child – so Jehoiada, his savior and patron, maintained – was of the stock of David. But how was Jehoiada to counter the argument that Athaliah had in fact murdered all the male survivors of the House of David and that he, Jehoiada, was merely attempting to palm off a foundling as scion of royalty? By placing the crown upon the child's head and showing that it fit, Jehoiada gained the assent of the people. It was only then that he was able to proclaim Joash king, to anoint him and to shout "God save the king."

Now, in the context, what Rab says has psychological validity and is as peshat-worthy as any of the other renditions of עדות.

1 If the lip and the chin of the Hapsburgs are distinctive, why not the skull of the House of David?

But by definition a man like Rab is charged with credulity, fantasy, *Spitzsinnigkeit*, or all three. If what Rab said were found on a sherd, smudged, partly legible, in a language barely understood, and indited by an anonymous scribe, whose credentials for trustworthiness were completely unknown, it would command the instant attention of what in self-serving fashion is known as "the scholarly world." But unless proved otherwise a man like Rab is deemed guilty of credulity, fantasy, *Spitzsinnigkeit*, or a crime calling for the guillotine, homiletics.

May I now turn to a passage in Midrash where the polyphony of nuance is all but celebrated. In this passage a difficult verse in Proverbs will incidentally be rendered more or less in the form in which it will appear in the New Jewish Version, a work surely dedicated to peshat.

Here is the passage:

והארץ היתה תוהו וגו׳. ר׳ ברכיה פתח גם במעלליו יתנכר נער אם זך ואם ישר פעלו (משלי כ, יא). אמר ר׳ ברכיה עד היא פַגה אָפֶקָת כּוּבַיָה. מה שעתיד להתנבות עליה ראיתי את הארץ והנה תהו (ירמיה ד, כג) (בראשית רבה ב, א; מהד׳ תיאודור־אלבק עמ׳ 14—15).

In the Soncino Translation (London and Bournemouth 1951), p. 15, H. Freedman and M. Simon render the passage as follows:

> NOW THE EARTH WAS UNFORMED AND VOID, AND DARKNESS WAS UPON THE FACE OF THE DEEP; AND THE SPIRIT OF GOD HOVERED OVER THE FACE OF THE WATERS (1, 2). R. Berekiah quoted: *Even a child is known by his doings, whether his work be pure, and whether it be right* (Prov. XX, 11). Said R. Berekiah: While she [the earth] was as yet immature [in her infancy], she produced thorns; and so the prophet was one day destined to prophesy of her, *I beheld the earth, and, lo, it was waste and void* (Jer. IV, 23).

The difficulty with this translation is that nothing in the verse in Genesis suggests any relationship with the verse in Proverbs which R. Berechiah quotes to begin his discourse. Moreover, the conclusion R. Berechiah draws does not follow at all from the verse in Proverbs. As for what the prophet was one day destined to prophesy, his words seem like a kite fluttering without any direction.

In the *Encyclopedia of Biblical Interpretation* (Menahem M. Kasher [New York 1953], p. 16), Harry Freedman translates the text somewhat differently:

> NOW THE EARTH WAS UNFORMED AND VOID. R. Berekiah quoted: *Even a child is known by his doings* (Prov. 20:11). While the earth was as yet in her infancy she produced thorns; and so the prophet was one day destined to prophesy of her, *I beheld the earth, and, lo, it was waste and void* (Jer. 4:23).

Here Freedman does provide a link between *the earth was unformed and void* and *even a child is known by his doings*. But the trouble with this translation is that he amputates the verse in Proverbs, quoting only its first part and omitting *whether his work be pure, and whether it be right,* the part which contradicts the very point he apparently endeavors to make, namely that already in its infancy the earth produced "nothing but spiritual thorns." The phrase "nothing but spiritual thorns," may I add, is taken from Freedman's own note, a phrase which is characteristic of modern preachers, but not of men of Midrash who eschew pious generalities and zero in on a specific target.

Before offering another translation of the passage in Genesis Rabbah, I would note that the phrase תהו ובהו remains a philological conundrum, and its sundry explanations form a minor תהו ובהו. One may indeed say, as playfully suggested in Rabbinic literature, תוהה "there is wonderment," בו הוא "what it is or what it means in truth."

Proverbs 20:11 is another conundrum. The Septuagint seems to have a different reading. Alexander Gordon in the American translation suggests: "Even a child is known by his deeds, according as his conduct is crooked or straight," apparently changing זך "pure" into זר "crooked." Moffatt has: "Even a child is known by what he does, as he behaves well or ill." The New English reads: "Again a young man is known by his actions, whether his conduct is innocent or guilty." Both seem to change ישר into רשע, which one renders "ill" and the other "guilty." All take יתנכר to mean "is known." Among the Jewish commentators I consulted, only two, Gersonides (1288–1344), and *Meṣudat Dawid* (18th century), take יתנכר in the sense of "feign," "pretend," or "dissemble."

Now I come to the proposed reading of the passage in Genesis Rabbah:

> From the beginning, the inhabitants of the earth [were such dissemblers that they] *set one to wonder as to what their true nature was* (Gen. 1:2).[2] And so R. Berechiah began his discourse with the verse *Though his actions appear to be innocent and proper, even a child may in fact dissemble in his behavior* (Prov. 20:11).[3] Accordingly, R. Berechiah went on to say: At the very beginning, mankind was like a young fig tree which even before it bore fruit put forth thorns. Hence in prophetic vision it was to be said, *I looked at [the inhabitants of] the earth, and they set one to wonder [as to what their true nature was]* (Jer 4:23).[4]

2 JV: *Now the earth was unformed and void.*

3 NJV: *A child may be dissembling in his behavior, even though his actions be innocent and proper.*

4 JV *I beheld the earth, and, lo, it was waste and void.*

The proposed reading of the verse in Proverbs provides a meaningful link with the verse preceding it, which denounces "One weight here, another there, here one measure and there another" (Jerusalem Bible). Even so, directly after Jeremiah said: "Clever are they to do wrong, to do right they don't know how" (John Bright in the Anchor Bible), he went on to say, "I looked at the earth, and, seeing so much תהו, dissembling, I wondered what it was in truth."

In this passage R. Berechiah responds to the clash in overtones between בראשית ברא אלהים את השמים ואת הארץ, an assertion of order, and והארץ היתה תהו ובהו, a description of chaos. To explain the perplexing juxtaposition, R. Berechiah, citing Prov. 20:11 and Jer. 4:13, concludes by way of deep peshat that from the very beginning of time, pretense, dissembling, and hypocrisy account for the world's chaos and undoing.

To conclude. The *sensus literalis,* literal peshat, is a will o' the wisp, something of a chimera. Even when designating specific items in present usage, it is often difficult to match in two languages the terms meant to designate such items, unless these items, as well as the specific operations by which they are manufactured or in which they are utilized, are actually shown to the eye. This is one of the reasons, I am told, that a German-English dictionary intended for use in the jewelry trade did not see the light of day. If such difficulties are encountered in an area where the precision of terms used is constantly checked in the give-and-take of trade, how can the literal-peshat men draw their dogmatic conclusions as to the meaning of specific words in Scripture on the basis of so-called analogues in cognate languages, languages which one will readily admit are hardly known?

But to return to the main argument, *sensus literalis* all but denies the polyphony of Scripture. Midrash listens to it and with exuberant love articulates it. Midrashic texts themselves echo Scripture's polyphony. Accordingly, men who render Rabbinic texts literally – and such men act like devout Catholics who have just gone through their novenas – men who render Rabbinic texts literally produce utter nonsense. In passing, may I say that Rabbinic texts so rendered appear in publications whose author or authors vaunt themselves as setting forth the Rabbinic world *denudata.* What such authors actually perpetrate is חילול השם.

To be understood, every text in Scripture must go through the alembic of a mind. If the mind of a particular interpreter belongs to an avowed or unavowed disciple of Spinoza, such a disciple, bemused by Spinoza's geometric method, will flatter himself that each interpretation of his – even if it contradicts the preceding one – is *the* truth. Such men often dispense not *sensus literalis*, but – forgive the barbarism – *nonsensus literalis.*

"All Midrash," my friend Leon Nemoy wrote in a letter, "has more than one entrance-way. You cannot follow more than one of them – others may, and hopefully, will enter through other gates and driveways. It takes an artist to construct a literary document with a dozen entrance-ways, all of them leading to the same house of righteousness. The Midrashic authors were artists."

Surely Scripture, whether its author was an artist or, as I would say *the* Artist, provides a thousand and more entrance-ways for the man whose heart is alert and whose eyes are open to peshat's unending depths.

TWO UNRECOGNIZED CASES OF *TALḤIN*

N. M. Bronznick

1. שמה ושרקה

This phrase, a favorite of Jeremiah in depicting the sorry state of a place (18:16; 19:8, 25:9,18; 29:18; 51:37), is generally treated as an ellipsis. Hence, most modern translators feel compelled to supply such words as "thing"[1] or "object of"[2] or "scene of"[3] or "spectacle of"[4] in resolving the elliptical meaning of the phrase, "[I shall make it] an astonishment[5] and a hissing."

There is no gainsaying this interpretation since the phrase also appears frequently in a verbal form, ישם וישרק, e.g., Jer. 19:8; 49:17, in which case the meaning is unquestionably, "he will be astonished (or, horrified) and hiss." What has not been recognized, however, is that this phrase in its nominal form is amphibolic, resulting in a peculiar type of paronomasia. It contains two distinct denotations, one of which represents the primary intent the author aims to convey, while the other one represents the author's secondary intent, both of which, however, are appropriate to the context and are present in the author's mind. This rhetorical device, termed by the medieval Arab rhetoricians as *Talḥin* or *Tawriya,* is often employed in the Bible, though not always noticed by the commentators.[6]

There is no need to demonstrate that שמה, besides the denotation of "astonishment" (or "horror"), also has the meaning of "desolation." This is self-evident from many contexts, and it is so recorded in all the lexica. In fact,

1 *The Interpreter's Bible,* Jer. 19:8; *The Jerusalem Bible,* Jer. 51:37.

2 *The New English Translation,* Oxford and Cambridge 1970, Jer. 19:8.

3 *Idem,* Jer. 51:37.

4 *Anchor Bible,* Jer. 28:18.

5 Cf. medieval Hebrew commentaries, e.g., Rashi and Radak to Jer. 18:16; Gesenius—Robinson (Boston 1885), s.v.; Fuerst—Davidson, s.v.; *ICC* and *Jerusalem Bible* to Ps. 46:9. The contemporary lexica, however, prefer rendering שמה as "horror."

6 Cf. R. Gordis, *The Book of God and Man,* Chicago 1965, p. 347.

"being desolate" is the basic sense of the stem שמם from which the noun שמה in both its senses is derived.

Similarly, שרקה, besides denoting "whistling" or "hissing," also denotes "hollowness" or "emptiness," with the latter being its essential semantic denotation. This is evidenced from Syriac, where the verb שרק means "to be hollow" or "empty," from which the abstract noun שרקותא, with the meaning of "emptiness," is derived. Only in the Afel form does this verb mean "to whistle" or "to hiss," which indicates that its basic meaning is that of "being empty" or "hollow."[7]

This basic meaning seems to be present in the phrase עֹבְדֵי פשתים שריקות (Isa. 19:9). If its parallel ארגים חוֹרָי (*ibid.*) is to be rendered as "weavers of network," as done by many interpreters,[8] then the rendering of this phrase as "workers of combed flax" or "workers in fine flax", although lexically tenable, is contra-indicated by the need for synonymous parallelism called for in the passage. To establish proper synonymity, שריקות should be rendered, based on the meaning of hollowness of the stem שרק, as "perforations," i.e., nets. Thus שריקות and חורי are truly synonymous, as required by the context, each having reference to a particular type of fishing net[9].

The semantic relationship between the meanings of "hollowness" and "whistling," both contained in the stem שרק, derives from the fact that whistling is produced by thrusting air through a hollowed-out object such as a reed. That words for hollowness and whistling may be paronymous is attested by the verb צפר, whose meaning in both Arabic and Aramaic is "to whistle," but also has in Arabic the additional meaning of "being empty." In fact, this stem with the denotation of "emptiness" entered from the Arabic, via medieval Latin, into the modern European languages, in such forms as the English cipher or the French chiffre, as a mathematical term for zero.[10]

7 In this connection, the verb סרק, which denotes "emptiness" in both Aramaic and Syriac, is to be considered as a cognate of the Syriac שרק.

8 Cf. Rashi and Radak *ad loc.*, and King James Version *ad loc.*

9 Since vv. 8 and 10 deal with the lack of fishing, the interpretation of v. 9 proposed here commends itself as it, too, has reference to fishing, thus making for continuity. However, all the other interpretations, according to which v. 9 deals with the disappearance of all kinds of flax or cotton, cause an abrupt break in the continuity of the three verses. According to these interpretations, v. 9 should have logically followed vv. 6 and 7, which deal with the withering of vegetation.

10 Cf. H. H. Rowley, "The Semantic Sources of Cipher and its Cognates," *ZAW, Beihefte* 66 (1936), 177–90. In this connection reference should be made to the Tannaitic term ציפר נפש which, according to certain views, refers to the windpipe (cf. Ben-Yehuda, p. 5591) For other views, cf. H. Yalon, *Pirkei Lashon*, Jerusalem 1971, pp. 145–46.

Hollowness or emptiness as the elemental denotation of שרק will also account for the meaning of "swallowing" or "sipping" or "sucking," which this verb has in Arabic as well as in Syriac, for emptying is the efficient cause of these acts. Sipping is effectuated by sucking air in, thus creating a vacuum, which facilitates the passing of the liquid to be swallowed. Viewed from this perspective, there is a close affinity between the denotation of "whistling," which this verb has in Hebrew, and the denotation of "sipping," which this verb has in Arabic. Both are produced by the selfsame process of creating a vacuum, the former by thrusting air out, the latter through the reciprocal act of drawing or sucking air in. Interestingly enough, in Syriac this verb serves with both of these correlative denotations, "whistling" as well as "sipping," thus tending to prove their semantic kinship.

With "desolation" being the essential meaning of שמם, as noted by all lexicographers, and "emptiness" being the essential meaning of שרק as demonstrated above, the treatment of שמה ושרקה as a case of *Talḥin* becomes irresistibly compelling in its appeal. Thus, the prophet makes use of this phrase for its double-edged effect, deftly depicting at the same time the devastation as well as the disgrace resulting therefrom.[11]

The question that needs to be resolved is whether the meaning of "desolation and emptiness" is to be taken as its primary intent, or the meaning of being the object of "astonishment and hissing" is to be retained as its primary intent. Needless to state, etymology cannot serve us as a guide in determining which of the meanings is to be taken as the primary intent of an author. As long as a stem has, in fact, more than one meaning, an author is fully at liberty to choose any one of them for his primary intent, even if it be semantically secondary in meaning. To resolve this question, the context must in each instance be consulted. For the phrase under discussion, suffice it, for the purpose of illustration, to analyze briefly three instances.

In Jer. 29:18, where the stress is laid on the "horror... curse... and disgrace" in the devastation, or in Jer. 19:8, where the phrase in question is expatiated on by the verbs ישם וישרק, "he will be astonished and hiss," the primary intent of שמה ושרקה should be taken as "being the object of astonishment and hissing."

11 The stem שאה has the denotations of "being desolate," "making noise" and, in the reflexive, of "wondering," which have baffled lexicologists as to their interconnection. However, as seen from שרק and שמם, both wondering and sound-making are associated with emptiness. Astonishment is characterized by the vacuous gaze or empty thought, and sound is produced by air being thrust through an empty space. The latter idea seems to be contained in the verse "in the waste of the howling wilderness" (Deut. 32:10).

In the case of Jer. 51:37, however, where the phrase in question is expanded by מאין יושב, "without inhabitant," "desolation and emptiness" seems obviously to be its primary intent.[12]

In any case, this phrase should be treated on each level as a unit, either in the sense of "desolation and emptiness" or "astonishment and hissing." Its meaning should not be jumbled, as done by some interpreters,[13] resulting in a mixed metaphor that needlessly mars the rhetorical effect of *Talḥin* contained in the phrase.

2. בקרת תהיה

This phrase (Lev. 19:20), relating to the disposition of the case of the "bondmaid designated for a man" who cohabited with another man, has been a *crux interpretum* of long standing. It has been variously rendered: "there shall be an investigation";[14] "there shall be a punishment,"[15] with the nature of the punishment left unspecified; "there shall be a lashing";[16] "there shall be a monetary payment for damages."[17]

While exegetically one or the other of these interpretations may be preferable, they are semantically all equally tenable. However, regardless of whichever interpretation one might opt for, the term בקרת has yet another denotation that is at least secondarily implied in the phrase under consideration. This will help

12 That שרקה does not have "hissing" as its sole denotation is evident from Jer. 18:16, where the reading, according to the *ketib*, is שרוקת. Appearing in the form of a passive participle, with the antecedent feminine noun "land" as its subject (cf. Mandelkern's Concordance, *ad loc.*), its sense would be extremely strained if we were to apply to it the denotation of "hissing." It does, however, make excellent sense with the denotation of "emptiness," resulting in the meaningful phrase "emptied forever."

R. P. Gordon's conjecture that the targumic rendering of שרוקים (Zech. 1:8) as קוחין, or קחחין in one of the several other variant readings, should be emended to קרוחין, with the meaning of "white-spotted" ("An Inner Targumic Corruption," *VT*, 25 [1975], 217), is now reinforced. The meaning of "white-spotted" for שרוקים derives from its essential denotation of "emptiness," as can be seen from the stems אור, בקר, חור, נהר, נקד with which I intend to deal in a separate study. Suffice it to mention that English provides an instructive analogue in "blank," meaning both "white" and "empty." This is also reflected in the Hebrew term שדה לבן (M. Shevi. 2, 1) "a white field," i.e., a treeless field.

13 E. g., "I will make this city a desolation, a derision..." (*The Jerusalem Bible,* Jer. 19:8).

14 *The Chicago Bible;* similarly, "inquiry" in *The Interpreter's Bible.*

15 E. g., Koehler-Baumgartner s.v.; Saadiah Gaon rendered it by the Arabic מחדודה, which J. Kafaḥ in his *Perushei R. Saadiah Gaon Al ha-Torah,* p. 105, correctly renders "punishment" against Ben-Yehuda, p. 601, who wrongly renders it "lashed."

16 TB Ker. 11a.

17. This summarizes the interpretation of E. A. Speiser in his "Leviticus and the Critics," *Y. Kaufmann Jubilee Volume,* p. 36.

in properly placing this law in its legal setting, the Holiness Code (Lev. chaps. 19, 20), wherein the penalties for illicit sexual relations are promulgated.

It is the consensus of the lexica, on the strength of the Arabic as well as on internal evidence, that the primary denotation of the stem בקר is "to split," "to break up." From this meaning is derived the noun for dawn, i.e., daybreak, a semantic transition witnessed in the Aramaic קרץ. From this is also derived the noun for cattle, the animals employed in plowing, i.e., in breaking up the soil.

With "splitting" as the primary denotation of בקר, the Tannaitic rendering of בקרת as "lashing," which has been a puzzle to many,[18] has indeed a sound semantic basis. Lashing, required by the Halakha to be administered with full force on the naked body,[19] will frequently result in bruises and lacerations.[20] Such being the case, it is metonymically justifiable to render בקרת as "lashing" since bruises, i.e., breaking up the skin, are the natural result of lashing. This nexus is also present in מצליף, one of the talmudic words for lashing,[21] the denotations of whose stem in Syriac are "to split," "to wound" and "to beat."[22]

That the rabbis were aware of the true primary meaning of בקר is apparent from their interpretation of לבקר (Prov. 20:25) to mean: פנקסו נפתחת, "his account book is opened."[23] The wording of this interpretation strongly indicates that the rabbis are playing on the essential meaning of לבקר, which is "splitting," an act akin to that of "opening."

From this primary denotation are derived the extended meanings "to view" (II Kings 16:15; Ps. 27:4) and "to supervise" (Ezek. 34:11,12), as these acts are performed by keeping the eyes open, a semantic transition attested in the stem פקח.[24] By extending the primary meaning in a somewhat different direction we obtain the meanings "to sift" and "to investigate," since these acts are effectuated by breaking up a conglomerate, separating it into its constituent

18 Cf. Ibn Janaḥ, *Sefer ha-Shorashim,* p. 74; Ibn Ezra to Lev. 19:20. The Amoraic rationalizations (TB Ker. 11a) are in the nature of homiletical interpretations, as noted by Ibn Ezra *loc. cit.;* Saadia Gaon's explanation, quoted by Kimḥi, *Sefer ha-Shorashim,* p. 46, belongs to the realm of popular etymology.

19 M. Mak. 3, 13.

20 Cf. Mid. Tannaim = Mid. ha-Gadol to Deut. 25:3.

21 Cf. TB Zev. 38a, and parallels.

22 Cf. Syriac lexica; cf. Ben-Yehuda, p. 5505, n. 5. Similarly in Mandaic, Drower and Macuch, *A Mandaic Dictionary,* p. 395.

23 TJ Ned. 1, 1, 36d; cf. TB Ned. 22a. In a parallel source (Gen. R. 81:1, ed. Theodor-Albeck, p. 968), the phrase reads נתבקרה פנקסו, which tends to prove that the two are interchangeable. Cf. Syriac פצל, which means "to split" as well as "to open a book." See Payne Smith, *A Compendious Syriac Dictionary,* p. 454.

24 Cf. Jastrow, p. 1208.

parts. This semantic transition is clearly illustrated by the stem בדק, whose primary meaning is "to crack."[25]

From this vantage point, those who render בקרת as "investigation" would do better rendering it by the English technical term "trial." For בקרת, in this sense, is truly the semantic equivalent of "trial," which is derived from the verb "to try," in French "trier," with the meaning "to sift," "to separate."

Finally, we may now proceed to demonstrate that the semantic compass of בקר also includes a hitherto unrecognized denotation. This stem is a close semantic cognate of the Arabic فجر, as it covers a similar semantic range. Both share the same primary meaning and, in one nominal form, they have the identical meaning "daybreak." They also have in common the meaning of "licentiousness." This can be seen from the targumic rendering פוחזים (Jud. 9:4) as בקרין, according to the reading cited by Kimḥi *ad loc.*,[26] which he correctly explains to mean "licentious men" by associating this noun with the Hebrew מבקיר and הבקר, of which מפקיר and הפקר are the respective variants. It is worth nothing that the targumic rendering has support in the Syriac, where the stem פחז means "to be voluptuous," "to be licentious."[27]

But the Arabic فجر also has the denotation of "fornication." This sense may well solve the well-known crux ובפגרי מלכיהם במותם (Ezek. 43:7).[28] Taking into consideration that the Aramaic פגר has a similar primary meaning as its Arabic cognate,[29] it becomes even more reasonable to render the above phrase "...and by the fornications of their kings in[30] their high places." This interpretation is exegetically attractive, as it comports with the fact that fornication was associated with the "high places" as attested elsewhere in Ezekiel (16:24,25,31). The semantic kinship between "splitting" and "fornication" also exists in the stem פרד. This stem, whose basic meaning is "to break apart," is used with the sense of "fornication" in Hos. 4:14, and perhaps also in Prov. 18:1. Similarly, the stem חרש, "to plow," i.e., to break up the soil,

25 Cf. J. C. Greenfield, "Lexicographical Notes," *HUCA*, 29 (1958), 221, 222; S. Lieberman, "Forgotten Meanings," *Leshonenu*, 32 (1968), 89–102. Cf. Targ. J., Jud. 14:18

26 Cf. Targ. J., Jer. 23:32.

27 Cf. Syriac lexica; cf. Ben Sira 19:2; 23:8 and Segal's notes in his edition, pp. 115, 138, where he shows this use in midrashic Hebrew.

28 For a review of the literature on this phrase, see B. W. Barrick, "The Funerary Character of 'High Places' in Ancient Palestine: A Reassessment," *VT*, 25 (1975), 569–95.

29 "Splitting" may be the primary meaning of the Hebrew cognate as well, as evidenced in Gen. 15:11, where פגרים is the equivalent of בתרים "cuts," "pieces." Cf. Targ. O. thereto, and note variants; cf. Targ. Y. and Neofiti thereto.

30 The elision of the preposition ב before a noun beginning with this consonant is attested in many instances, e.g., Gen. 24:23; Mic. 6:10.

is used in midrashic Hebrew for having sexual intercourse.[31]

In view of the cumulative evidence pointing to the semantic nexus between the denotation of "splitting" and that of "fornication," it is not unreasonable to conjecture that the semantic range of בקר includes the latter denotation as well. There is only a small step from the concept of general licentiousness, included in its semantic range, to the specific form of fornication, which will thus make the Hebrew בקר the close semantic cognate of the Arabic فجر that it truly is.[32]

Thus the phrase under consideration should be interpreted as follows: "There shall be an investigation" (or "a trial," or "a punishment," or "a lashing," or "a monetary payment," whichever is preferable) with the added connotation, by way of *Talḥin*, that "it shall be treated as a case of mere fornication."[33] The implication is that it should not be treated as a case of true adultery for the reason, supplied further on in the verse itself, that the bondmaid has not been freed and, therefore, her "designation for a man" does not constitute a legally valid marriage.

This interpretation commends itself for the following reason. In the section of Leviticus in which this law is found, in addition to naming the penalty for each particular illicit sexual act, in virtually every instance the severity of each sin is characterized either by a descriptive phrase (e.g., 19:11,18,19) or by a specific epithet such as זמה (19:29; 20:14), תבל (20:12), תועבה (20:13), חסד (20:17), נדה (20:21). Only in the case of the bondmaid, while the required atonement is indeed prescribed, no characterization of the nature of the sin is offered. However, this missing characterization is now admirably filled with the proposed denotation of בקרת as a technical term for "fornication," employed in this instance at least in a secondary sense.

---

31 TJ Yev. 1,1, 2b; Gen. R. 85:4, p. 1037; 98:4, p. 1253.

32 Cf. TB Yev. 61b; TB Git. 13a. This will lend greater credence to the opinion that ביקרותיך (Ps. 45:10) means "your concubines," a view cited by Ibn Ezra thereto and accepted by Ben-Yehuda s.v. It should not appear strange to us that a substantive for "concubine" should be derived from a stem meaning "fornication," as such is also reflected in the case of שגל (see Koehler-Baumagartner s.v.). Cf. also דרוכא, the Syriac substantive for "concubine" that is derived from דרך.

33 Ibn Janaḥ, *loc. cit.*, and Nachmanides to Lev. 19:20 already anticipated the connection of בקרת with הבקר/הפקר, but their respective interpretations differ from the one proposed here. Ibn Janaḥ interprets the phrase to mean "she shall be freed [from capital punishment]"; Nachmanides interprets the verse rather awkwardly to read that, although the bondmaid has been designated for a man, she is not considered duly married, but "she should be considered his freeloving woman."

PRAYERS FROM THE GENIZA FOR FATIMID CALIPHS, THE HEAD OF THE JERUSALEM YESHIVA, THE JEWISH COMMUNITY AND THE LOCAL CONGREGATION

S. D. Goitein

Public prayers for the welfare of the rulers under whose protection Jews lived are as old as the establishment of the Second Commonwealth. The very edict of the Persian king Cyrus which ordered the restoration of the Temple of Jerusalem contains these words: "So that they may offer sacrifices of sweet savor to the God of Heaven and pray for the life of the King and his sons" (Ezra 6:10). This implies that the prayer for the king expressed the acknowledgment on the part of the Jews that they regarded themselves as his subjects. The Aramaic papyri related to the Jewish military colony of Elephantine betray the same expressions of allegiance to the Persian government.[1] This practice clearly continued within the empires succeeding the ancient Iranian kingdom and also survived the difficulties caused by Roman emperor-worship.[2]

In Talmudic and early Islamic times we hear little, if anything, about this custom, although its existence is presupposed in the Mishna.[3] As far as the Geniza period is concerned, I discussed the matter in my book *A Mediterranean Society, the Jewish Communities of the Arab World,* with a reference to Jacob Katz, *Exclusiveness and Tolerance*.[4] The students of Jewish

1 A. H. Sayce and A. E. Cowley, *Aramaic Papyri discovered at Assuan,* London 1906, nos. 30, 32, 38. See S. W. Baron, *A Social and Religious History of the Jews,* New York 1952, I, p. 353, n. 37.

2 For this matter cf. Baron, *op. cit.* pp. 244/5, 404.

3 "Pray for the welfare of the government because were it not for the fear it inspires every man would swallow his neighbor alive" (M. Avot 3, 2).

4 S. D. Goitein, *A Mediterranean Society,* II, Berkeley 1971, p. 351; J. Katz, *Bēn Yehudim le-Goyim,* Jerusalem 1960, p. 60, n. 15. See also Seligman Baer's commentary on the Prayer book, *'Avodat Yisrael,* 1937 (reprint), p. 231.

liturgy are particularly disturbed by the fact that the text of the prayer, the *ha-nōtēn teshū'ā*, seems to be absent from the classical sources of Jewish law and ritual. The reason for this absence will become evident through the facts provided in the following: since the public prayer for the authorities, whether gentile or Jewish, possessed a practical aspect, namely, demonstration of the community's allegiance, it had to be adapted to the circumstances and formulated accordingly.

In view of this situation, it is fortunate that the Cairo Geniza has provided us with two examples of such public prayers, the first being very detailed and comprising invocations for a caliph, a head of the Jerusalem yeshiva (then also the head of the Jewish community in the Fatimid period) and the Jewish community at large, as well as the local congregation. The second piece contains only the prayer for the caliph. The first text was discovered and put at my disposal by my eminent friend, Professor Shalom Spiegel of the Jewish Theological Seminary of America, New York, in July 1959.[5] I copied and translated the text immediately, but hesitated to publish it, because the very form of the document, namely the numerous abbreviations found in it, induced me to assume that other such prayers might be found in the Geniza. However, it was only in summer 1971, when I was working on the identification of the documentary material preserved in the Mosseri Collection of Geniza fragments, that the second piece turned up. Experience has taught me that once you have two examples of the same type, a third may be found soon. Fortunately, quite a number of competent scholars are now at work in Geniza research; therefore I believe it is advisable not to tarry any longer with the publication of what is in hand; hopefully, the texts edited below will be helpful to colleagues in the identification of similar material. I take the jubilee of Dr. Leon Nemoy, that indefatigable veteran of Judaeo-Arabic studies, who has earned the gratitude of all students of Judaism, as an auspicious opportunity for this publication. May he be blessed with all the good wishes expressed in these prayers.

Since the Friday public service in the mosques contained a kind of sermon declaring the congregation's allegiance to the incumbent ruler and his family, it might appear natural that a corresponding demand was made from the members of the minority religions. A charter, issued by the Abbasid caliph al-Muktafī of Baghdad in the year 1138, at the installation of the *catholicos* or

5 When we both worked in the Anderson Room for manuscripts and rare books of the University Library, Cambridge, England. That room has been meanwhile replaced by a number of other structures. But the largeness of that beautiful place was conducive to scholarly cooperation.

head of the Nestorian Church, concludes with these words: "Set up prayers and invocations for the Commander of the Faithful as a token of your gratitude and a sign of your allegiance." It has been rightly concluded that the same "sign of allegiance" was expected or demanded from the Jewish Exilarch, the *Rosh ha-Gola*.[6]

Yet, one wonders whether the *date* of the *catholicos* patent has not something to do with its content. The 1120's–1130's were the time of the largest expansion of the Crusaders' conquests. Edessa, a fortified city situated in the heart of Mesopotamia and as near to Baghdad as to Jerusalem, was then in their hands. Under such circumstances it might be expected that the Muslim rulers, whether in Baghdad or in Cairo, became a bit more watchful as to the reliability of their non-Muslim subjects. In other words, the ancient institution of the prayer for the government, which had perhaps fallen somewhat into desuetude among Christians and Jews under Islam, was now strictly enforced. This impression seems to be confirmed by the dates of the Geniza finds discussed in this paper.[7]

The first document is dedicated to the Fatimid caliph *al-Āmir bi-aḥkām Allāh* ("He who orders the fulfillment of God's commandments"), who ruled Egypt and its region during the years 1101–1131, and to the Gaon Maṣlīaḥ b. Solomon ha-Kohen, head of the Jerusalem yeshiva, or Jewish high council, which then had its seat in Cairo.[8] Maṣlīaḥ was recognized as head of the Jewish community of the Fatimid state in 1127. Thus our document must have been

6 See Baron, *op. cit.* (n. 1 above), V, pp. 6 and 293, n. 2.

7 The Christians and Jews did not represent a military threat. Therefore the Muslim government could permit itself, in normal times, not to care what they did in their churches and synagogues. The Muslims, however, often revolted against their rulers (already the third caliph, Othman, was openly attacked while speaking from the pulpit in the mosque of Medina and was soon afterwards assassinated). Therefore the Muslim "sermon of allegiance" during the solemn Friday service soon became an obligatory element of the religious ritual. The Christians were dangerous only as a potential fifth column, and it was common in Islam to impose on all non-Muslims, including the Jews, the same obligations and restrictions.

8 S. Lane-Poole, *A History of Egypt in the Middle Ages,* London 1914, p. 162 (I do not agree with Lane-Poole's translation of the Caliph's title).
About Maṣlīaḥ see, for the time being, J. Mann, *The Jews in Egypt and Palestine under the Fatimid Caliphs,* New York 1970 (reprint), especially I, pp. 220–221 (on both pages, 1027–1038 is a misprint for 1127–1138); II, 274–277. The Geniza is very rich in material on this period. I am happy to learn that Dr. Mark R. Cohen, who has so successfully treated the preceding period of Egyptian and Palestinian Jewish history, that of the Nagid Mevōrākh and his family, is taking up a study of the stewardship of Maṣlīaḥ. For the meaning of the term *yeshiva* in those days and the position of the Palestinian Gaon, see *A Mediterranean Society,* II, pp. 5–17.

written between 1127 and 1131.[9] The second piece, as stated before, contains solely the prayer for the caliph, namely, al-Āmir's successor, *al-Ḥāfiẓ li-dīn Allāh* ("the Guardian of the Religion of God"), who ruled during the years 1131–1149.[10] Thus, the two documents are almost contemporary with the installation of the leader of the Nestorian Church of Baghdad in 1138 and, as long as no evidence to the contrary is found, the surmise that this coincidence was not fortuitous, and that it is to be explained by the encroachment of the Crusaders, might be upheld.

Moreover, a definite progress in government supervision is to be observed from the first to the second Geniza document. The prayer over al-Āmir is in Hebrew and styled in rather general terms. The second is in Arabic and composed of Muslim religious phrases which – *prima facie* – no Jewish dignitary would have introduced into a synagogue service. This, too, seems to indicate that our documents reflect a newly aroused interest of the Muslim governments in the declarations of allegiance of their non-Muslim subjects.

My statement that the first prayer is written in Hebrew needs a slight qualification: the two first words are in Aramaic: *umeṣalliyīn anan*, "And we pray." This, I assume, was in the Sassanid and early Islamic periods the beginning of the prayer for the government. Similarly, the prayer for the Gaon starts with four Aramaic words, "To the good memory of those whose souls are at rest," an indication that the prayer for the leader of the community was introduced by a memorial service for his forefathers not only in Geniza times, but centuries before.[11]

When was the prayer for the caliph recited? Perhaps every Saturday morning, but this is doubtful. On the free space and on the reverse side of the first document liturgical compositions destined to be chanted on the Day of Atonement are written. Therefore, I assume that the elaborate prayer contained in that document was recited on the most festive occasion of the year, the eve of the Day of Atonement, as is still common practice in the Oriental and Sefaradi (but not the Ashkenazi) congregations.

I shall now provide the text and translation of the prayers, followed by a few considerations which they evoke. The prayer for Maṣlīaḥ's ancestors and

9 See the data in Mann, *op. cit*, II, p. 274. There are more.

10 Lane-Poole, *op. cit.* (n. 8 above), p. 166.

11 The institution of the memorial services in Geniza times is treated in the third volume of my *A Mediterranean Society*, subtitled "The Family," 1978, pp. 4–6. For bibliographical hints to memorial lists, see *A Mediterranean Society*, II, p. 554, nn. 28–31.

relatives included in the first document needs some preliminary discussion. J. Mann, *Jews in Palestine and Egypt, etc.,* II, pp. 62–63, edited three such lists concerning Maṣlīaḥ's family, and there is no doubt that those lists, too, were used for memorial services. Mann's list A is practically identical with the genealogy provided in our document, except that there, between the seventh and eighth forefathers of Maṣlīaḥ mentioned in our prayer, a Gaon named Solomon is inserted.[12] The first ancestor known by name was an Elijah Gaon, but another head of a yeshiva seems to have preceded him, whose name had not been preserved. Thus three (or four) ancestors of Maṣlīaḥ had been heads of a yeshiva in Iraq-Babylonia *(yeshiva shel gola)*; after them one, Mordechai, obviously had not obtained any office. With him we are already on solid historical ground. The family had meanwhile emigrated to Palestine; Yehōsēf (for Joseph), Mordechai's son, had become president of the court of the Jerusalem yeshiva, and his son Solomon, followed (after an interval of about

12 For easier orientation, Maṣlīaḥ's genealogy according to TS NS 110, f. 26, the first document edited here, and British Museum Or 5549 (J. Mann, *op. cit.* [n. 8 above], II, pp. 62–63) are reproduced:

	An anonymous Gaon	
	Elijah	head of a Babylonian yeshiva
	(Solomon)	head of a Babylonian yeshiva
	Menaḥem	head of a Babylonian yeshiva
	Mordechai	held no office
	Yehōsēf	president of the court of the (Palestinian) yeshiva
	Solomon	Gaon head of the Palestinian yeshiva
Yehosef, president of court	Elijah	Gaon head of the Palestinian yeshiva
Evyathar Gaon (Tyre)	Solomon	Gaon (Damascus)
Elijah the Fourth	Maṣlīaḥ	(Cairo)

Zadok the Fifth — Azarya the Fifth — Uzziel

See n. 28, below.

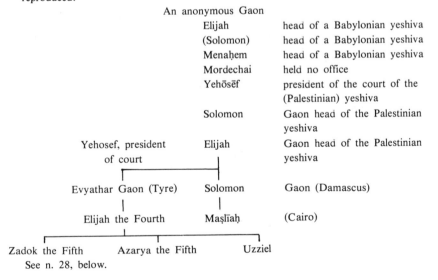

forty years) by his son Elijah and, later, his grandson Evyathar, was the first of three Gaons presiding over the Palestinian yeshiva in Jerusalem, and, as of 1072 approximately, in Tyre on the Lebanese coast. Evyathar's brother Solomon headed a yeshiva in Damascus and the latter's son, the Gaon Maṣlīaḥ, obtained in 1127 the *reshūt* as generally recognized head of the Jews of Egypt and its region.

Evyathar and his nephew Maṣlīaḥ had bad luck with their sons. Elijah, Evyathar's son, died after having attained only the rank of "fourth" in the Palestinian yeshiva. He is listed as such in Mann, *Jews etc.*, II, p. 63, A, and in our document in a postscript. There was a good reason for this addition. Maṣlīaḥ had two sons, but both must have died before our prayer was written, for it is entirely out of question that his sons should have been omitted from the good wishes for life and welfare, had they been alive at that time.[13] The only possible successors of Maṣlīaḥ in his family were the sons of his first cousin, Elijah the Fourth, wherefore they are enumerated in the postscript. I have not seen their names in another source.

The first document edited below is preserved in one of the boxes of the New Series of the Taylor-Schechter Collection of the University Library, Cambridge.[14]

תפילה ציבורית על הח׳ליף אלאָמִר בִּאַחְכַּאם אללה, על אבותיו של הגאון מצליח בן שלמה הכהן, על מצליח עצמו, ועל כל קהל ישראל

TS NS 110, f.26

1 בשׁ(מך) רחׄ(מנא)

נשיא בני קדר מולאנא وسيدنا الامام

2 ומצליין אנן לחיי אדוננו המׄ(לך) הגׄ(דול) אלאמאם

3 אלאמר באחׄ(כאם) אללה אמיר אלמוׄ(מנין) ובניו זרע המׄ(לוכה)

4 וכל בני המלׄ(וכה) העוזרים למלׄ(ך) מאהבה והעושׄ(ים)

5 מלחׄ(מה) לפׄ(ניו) מאׄ(ויביו) המׄ(קום) בׄ(רוך) הׄ(וא) יעזרם ויעזרנו יכניע

6 קמיהם וקמינו יתן בלבותם לעשות טובה עמׄ(נו)

7 ועם כל עמו בית ישׄ(ראל) ואמׄ(רו) אמן

8 דוכרן טב לניחי נפשׄ(הון) לזכר גאוני ישראל וראש[י

9 ישיבותי/ה/ם ואבות בתי דיניהם וחכמיהם

13 On Maṣlīaḥ's two sons of tender age, see Mann, *op. cit* (n. 8 above), I, p. 221; II, p. 274, section 1.

14 Parentheses show the parts of a word or sentence which are not written out in the original but alluded to by a dot over the last letter written before the omitted parts. Brackets include words or parts of words destroyed in the original. Slanted strokes indicate that a letter is written above a line. Pairs of slanted strokes refer to words written above the line.

אדיריהם אשר נהגו שררה בעם יי׳ צבאות
כהוגן וכשורה //עד// כ(בוד) ג(דולת) ק(דושת) מ֯(רנו) ור֯(בנו) אדו֯(ננו) גאו֯(ננו)
וכגק מ֯ור֯ אדנ(נו) אליהו הכהן ראש היש֯(יבה) שלגולה ז״ל
וכ]גֹק מר֯ור֯ אדו֯ [מנח]ם הכהן [ראש ישיבה] שלגולה ז״ל
וכֹגֹק מ֯ור֯ אדו֯ מרדכי כהנא רבא ז״ל
וכֹגֹק מור יהוסף הכהן הצדיק בית דין צדק ז״ל
וכֹגֹק מ֯ור֯ אדו֯ שלמה ראש ישי֯(בת) גאון יעקב ז״ל
ושני חמודיו יהוסף הכ(הן) הצדיק אב ב(ית) ד(ין) ש֯(ל) יש֯(ראל) ז״ל
וכֹגֹק מ֯ור֯ אדו֯ אליהו ראש ישיבת גאון יעקב ז״ל
וכֹגֹק מ֯ור֯ אדו֯ אביתר הכהן ראש יש֯ [גאון יעקב ז״ל
זכ֯(ר) חס֯(יד) זכ֯(ר) ישר זכר ענו זכר שפל רוח
]כֹגֹק מ֯ור֯[
שלמ]ה ה[כהן
] ביעקב הקדוש והט֯(הור) מטה [
] נחמד במ֯(לון)* נחשק במשכנות מבט֯(חים)
תהא] מנו֯(חתו) שאנ[נות] תהי עמידתו בקרוב ילוה עליו
הש֯(לום) ועל מש֯(כבו) יהי שלום והחיים והש֯(לום) והכבוד
ו]ארי֯(כות) היָמ֯(ים) וְמלאוי כל משאל ומזל גבוה וכללי
הברכות הערו֯(כות) והנ[נ]אָמ֯(ות) על יד כל נביא וחוזה כולם
י]חוּלו על ראש כֹגֹק מ֯ור֯ אדו֯ גאו֯ מצליח הכהן
הגדול מאחיו ראש ישיבת גאון יע֯(קב) המכובד והמיו֯(קר)
האלהים יברכהו ירוממ֯(הו) יגדלהו ינסיכהו יעזרהו
יאמצהו וְיַאֲרִיךְ ימָ[יו] בטוב ושנותיו בנעימים
יתמיד ממשלתו ע[ד] ביאת הממשלה הראשו֯(נה)
ממ[ ] בימיו תושע יהודה
ויש֯(ראל) ישכון לבטח וגַ[ם י]כתירהו בכתר עוז מלפ֯(ניו)
ו]יתן חִנו בעיני המלכות ובעיני השרים
ו]בעיני כל רואיו גם יברך אלהינו את כל ⟦ראשי ישראל⟧
ישראל //וראשיהם// וחכמיהם ודייניהם וחביריהם ונקובי
השם שבהם אשר במקום הזה ובכל

עמודה ב׳

מקומות מושבותם אשר נדו שמה
בגלותם וגלו ממקום חמדתם ושכנו
בארץ לא להם במזרח ובמערב בצפון
ובים ישרוק לקבצינו יקצר צרתינו
יקיים נואם אשרקה להם ואקבצם כי פדי֯(תים)

* ההשלמה לפי יעקב מאן, טקסטס, ב, 211.

יראה בענינו יזכר לנו ברית אבותינו להועילינו(!)
לקיים וזכרתי להם ברית ראשו(נים) אש(ר) הוצ(אתי) או(תם) מא(רץ)
מצ(רים) לעיני הגו(ים) אני י׳ אלהיהם יושיענו תשועת
עול(ם) לקיים נואם יש(ראל) נושע בי׳ וג׳ ויברך
אלהינו בכל הברכות הנאמות מפי כל נב[יא
וחוזה את כלל הקהל הק(דוש) הזה מגדולם ועד
קטנם האלהים יברכם ישמ(רם) יעז(רם) יענם טר[ם
יקראוהו יקיים עליהם קרא דכתיב והיה
טרם יקראו ואני אע(נם) חברים לכל יש(ראל) ואמ(רו) אמ[ן

(הפיסקה הבאה, שורות 15—19, מקומה בשורה 26 של העמוד הקודם אחרי המלים "יהי שלום" ולפני "והחיים והשלום", אך עיין ההסבר להלן.)

וחמודו כגק מרנו ורבנו אדו אליהו הרביעי בחבו(רה)
זכר צדיק (לברכה) ושלשת חמודיו צדוק
הכהן החמישי וכגק מר ורבנו עזריה
הכהן החמישי ואחיו עוזיאל הכהן
סגן הכהנים והחיים והשלום

TS NS Box 110, f. 26

In (Your name, o) Me(rciful).

And we pray for the life of our lord, the g(reat) k(ing), // the prince of the sons of Kedar,[15] our master and lord, the Imām[16] // al-Āmir bī'aḥ(kām) Allāh, the Commander of the F(aithful) and for his sons, the r(oyal family), and all persons of his e(ntourage), who serve the k(ing) out of love and wa(ge) w(ar) f(or him) against his e(nemies). May G(od) – m(ay He be) p(raised) – help them and help us; may He subdue their foes and ours; and may He fill their hearts with kindness t(owards us) and towards all His people, the house of Is(rael), and let us s(ay) Amen.

Blessed be the memory of those whose souls rest in peace, namely, the Gaons of Israel, the heads of their yeshivas, their chief judges, their scholars and public leaders, who have ruled over the people of the Lord of Hosts in fairness and integrity prior to our present lord and Gaon, namely...[17]

15 Name of a bedouin tribe mentioned in the Bible (e.g., Ps. 120:5, Cant. 1:5), designating Arabs or Muslims in medieval Hebrew.

16 Literally, leader (in prayer), one of the official titles of the caliph. The two last words are written in Arabic letters for the simple reason that these take less room than the Hebrew ones. The writer had forgotten these words and could not otherwise squeeze them in. Not unusual.

17 Here follow the names of Maṣlīaḥ's forefathers and other members of his family, discussed before. While the names of the more remote ancestors are followed merely by the words "of

And may life, p(eace) and honor, longevity and fulfillment of all wishes, an auspicious star[18] and all of the blessings pr(onounced) by the prophets be granted to his h(onor), g(reatness), and h(oliness), (our) m(aster and) t(eacher), our lord and Gaon Maṣlīaḥ, the High Priest, the head of the yeshiva "Geon Ya'aqov," the honored and revered. May God bless him and make him great[19] ...may He prolong his rule until the coming of the f(irst) kingdom.[20] In his time Judah will be saved and Israel dwell securely.[21] May God crown him with a crown of might. May He grant that he find favor in the eyes of the king and of the great and of all that see him.

May our God bless also all Israel, // its heads,[22] // scholars, judges, learned men and notables,[23] here and in all the settlements to which they have fled in their exile, when they were forced to leave the land of their love and dwell in countries not theirs, in East and West, North and South.[24] May He call out to gather us in and shorten our sufferings, to fulfill that which is written...[25]

May our God bless everyone in this h(oly) congregation, old and young, with all the blessings pronounced by the prophets; may He bless, k(eep) and h(elp) them, and may He answer them, before they call, as it is written, "Before they call, I shall answer them,"[26] together with all Is(rael),[27] and let us s(ay) Amen.

Here follows the postscript concerning Maṣlīaḥ's cousin Elijah the Fourth and his three sons which, the writer indicates, should be inserted immediately before

blessed memory," Solomon, Maṣlīaḥ's father, receives a special prayer asking for God's grace, and the granting of peace and quick resurrection.

18 Astrology and astronomy were accepted as scientific truth. But God, of course, arranged the stars at his wish (Ps. 8:4).

19 Another five similar wishes, especially for a long and pleasant life, as before.

20 Namely that of King David, which is identical with that of the Messiah. This is a quotation from Mic. 4:8.

21 Jer. 23:6.

22 A reference to persons from the house of the Babylonian Exilarchs, who styled themselves Rosh Gola. See the Comments.

23 Literally, those that bear a title. Actually any Jewish person of consequence bore one or several honorific by-names, *laqab* in Arabic, *shēm* in Hebrew, conferred on him by a Gaon or any other Jewish authority. Those connected with the court (as officials, physicians, conveyors) also received Arabic titles.

24 "South" is rendered by *yām* as in Ps. 107:3. See my *Bible Studies*, Tel-Aviv 1963 (in Heb.), p. 160.

25 Quoting Zech. 10:8, Lev. 26:45, and Jer. 45:17.

26 Isa. 65:24.

27 This translates *ḥavērīm le-khol yisrā'ēl*, which is probably the original and correct form of the phrase *ḥavērīm kol yisrael* in the prayer on the Sabbath preceding a New Moon.

the blessings for Maṣlīaḥ. To be sure, Elijah was the son of Evyathar, who is mentioned seven lines before, not of Solomon, Maṣlīaḥ's father. But such misleading references are the rule in memorial lists rather than the exception. These lists were not written for us, or indeed for any reader, but the cantor who would recite them jotted them down in order to support his memory. He was, of course, familiar with the relatives of his Gaon.[28]

Comments

The prayer for the caliph surprises one by the simplicity of its wording, as compared with the profuse blessings showered on the head of the yeshiva. There is an additional twist in that section of the prayer: "May He help them *and us,* may He subdue their foes *and ours,* etc." The caliph deserves to be included in a Jewish public prayer in his role as protector of the community.

To be sure, the prayer for the head of the yeshiva had a long history behind it. The prayer for the Gaon Joshia (ca. 1015), also found in the Geniza, is clearly an adaptation of an earlier, Aramaic, version.[29]

Secondly, the prayer for the Jewish people at large and, in particular, its leaders, is remarkable for its anonymity. No mention is made of a Rosh Gola. Perhaps no one was in office, i.e., was officially recognized by the government, at that time. I assume this, because in the rather detailed report on messianic troubles in Baghdad in 1121 (published by myself) no mention is made of one, while other Jewish notables represented the community at the court.[30] On the other hand, in or around 1134 a Persian Jew, claiming to be a cousin of the Rosh Gola and of royal blood, visited the Jewish communities of Yemen and was recognized by them as their religious leader, while the prayer for Maṣlīaḥ, which had been in vogue there before, was discontinued.[31] Thus the prayer for

28 The two first sons both bear the title "Fifth." This can be explained only by the assumption that the firstborn had died and the second received his title. In this case, however, a blessing over the dead would have been obligatory. I guess the scribe erred and the second son was "Sixth" or "Seventh."

29 Mosseri L—199, ed. J. Mann, *op. cit.* (n. 8 above), p. 439 = *HUCA*, 3 (1926), 265. The phrase *meḥawwēr lewushēnū*, "he who makes our clothing white," *ibid.*, l. 7, is a patent Aramaism.

30 "A Report on Messianic Troubles in Baghdad in 1120—21," *JQR*, 43 (1952), 57—76.

31 See my paper "Yemenite Jewry between the Egyptian Gaonate and the Rosh ha-Gola of Babylonia," *Sinai,* 33 (1953), 225—237 (in Heb.). New material on this affair has been found meanwhile, and a number of statements made in that article must now be revised. See my book, *Ha-Tēmānīm*, Jerusalem 1982, ch. 3.

Kelal Israel was phrased in the most general terms so that no one should be offended.

Finally, an intense messianic spirit pervades the entire document. Each of the sections (for the Gaon, the community at large and the local congregation) concludes with Bible quotations proclaiming the good tidings of the ingathering of the people and the re-establishment of the ancient kingdom.[32]

Under these circumstances it is not surprising that the government wished to streamline the communal prayers of the non-Muslim in line with Islamic concepts. The text, of course in Arabic, provided by it, was short. It was to be followed by a prayer in Hebrew comparable to one read above.

תפילה על הח׳ליף אל־חאפץ̇ לדין אללה

Mosseri L—62

1 צלואת אללה וברכאתה
2 ונ/ו/אמי זכו/א/תה ואפצל
3 תחיאתה וסלאמה עלי
4 מולאנא וסידנא אלאמאם
5 אלחאפץ̇ לדין אללה
(שוליים) אמיר אלמומנין

Mosseri L-62

(May) the prayer of God and His blessings,[33] His ever-growing benefactions, His greetings and call of Peace (be) upon our lord and master, the Imām al-Ḥāfiẓ li-dīn Allāh, the Commander of the Faithful.

The text is in Hebrew characters, but was probably dictated to a Jewish cantor by a Muslim official.

32 It is remarkable that none of the three sections expresses the expectation of the erection of the Temple, which is normally connected with messianic expectations.

33 The Bible reader is reminded of Ps. 72:15: "May He always pray for him [the King] and all day long bless him." The standing Islamic blessing for the Prophet Muhammad is: "May God pray for him and greet him with Peace." The Fatimid caliphs, who pretended to be Muhammad's descendants, claimed the same blessing for themselves.

WORD PLAY AS A CONTRARY ELEMENT IN THE POEMS OF AVRAHAM SHLONSKY

L. S. GOLD

This paper originally appeared as a chapter of the author's doctoral dissertation, *Contrary Clues in the Original Hebrew Poems of Avraham Shlonsky*.[1] The intent was to examine different manifestations of contrariness in the poet's work in order to demonstrate that contrariness is a basic element of Shlonsky's poetics. This contrariness is explained in the dissertation as a means of enabling the Hebrew language to function poetically under a new set of circumstances, foremost of which was the spreading use of Hebrew as a spoken language.[2] The term "contrary clues" is used by E. H. Gombrich in his analysis of Cubism in painting.[3] The present writer has taken great pains to avoid confusing poetry with painting. Nevertheless, enough of an analogy exists between the phenomenon Gombrich describes in painting and the contrary elements pervasive throughout Shlonsky's poetry to justify borrowing the term. Those citations used to locate Shlonsky's poems that contain volume and page number refer to the collected poems, שירים, issued in five volumes in 1971 by Sifriyat Po'alim and Mif'ale Neyar Ḥadera as part of the ten-volume set כתבים.

* * *

Pun and rhyme both grow out of the homophonic accident. If rhyme is primarily metrical, if its main function is organizational in that it marks the end of lines and, together with rhythm, works toward the establishment of a sound pattern, it also "limits meaning by asking us to consider suddenly the

1 New York University, 1975. Copyright by the author. Xerox University Microfilms no. 76–10, 172.

2 Roman Jakobson, in *Style in Language*, ed. T. A. Sebeok (Cambridge, Mass., 1960), p. 356, states: "The set (*Einstellung*) toward the MESSAGE as such, focus on the message for its own sake, is the POETIC function of language... This function, by promoting the palpability of signs, deepens the fundamental dichotomy of signs and objects."

3 E. H. Gombrich, *Art and Illusion* (Princeton, N.J., 1972), p. 282.

connection of two things whose sound shapes happen to be resemblant."[4] It is in this lexical function, in arousing "the surprise that we feel in observing the curious cooperation in sound the two disparate words have in common," that rhyme approaches pun. Chatman explains: "One function of this surprise, as I understand it, is to fix or cement the meaning in a more unified and aesthetically satisfied way than could occur by mere juxtaposition." Chatman's observations on surprise serving to fix or cement meaning are seconded by Foss's reflections on "simultaneity of coincidence." Foss states: "Knowledge makes us see that simultaneity was merely an experimental statement, and replaces it by a lawful unity."[5] The justification of the pun or the rhyme in the poem as a whole, the function of the device in its larger setting, leads to the cementing of meaning or the lawful unity which replaces simultaneity.

Barbara Herrnstein Smith has described pun as "a linguistic structure that creates expectations in terms of which the different meanings of the homonym have equal appropriateness. Their witty effect arises from the consequent havoc they play with the reader's expectations, simultaneously fulfilling and surprising them. The effectiveness of a pun obviously depends upon its context; a list of homonyms is not witty."[6] We shall examine here a spectrum of word play, ranging from examples which conform to Smith's strict description of pun to rhyme situations where Chatman's remarks on lexical function of rhyme are applicable. It follows that, because the pun depends on different possible interpretations of the same set of sounds in a given context, it is in the nature of puns to provoke metalinguinal activity, that is, checking up on the "the code" itself.[7]

Let us take the first examples of pun from "non-serious" Shlonsky, from his children's classic עלילות מיקי־מהו.[8] Note that the dialogue is supposedly spoken over the telephone. This creates an illusion of total dependence on the language "code," since no visual reinforcement of the message is possible. The purpose is mainly to amuse. The game is built on the fact that hippo, as in hippopotamus, sounds like הִיא פֹּה, which means: "She is here." This is followed by a

4 S. Chatman, "Comparing Metrical Styles," in *Style in Language*, ed. T. A. Sebeok (Cambridge, Mass., 1960), p. 153.

5 M. Foss, *Symbol and Metaphor in Human Experience*, Lincoln, Nebr., 1964, p. 51.

6 Barbara Herrnstein Smith, *Poetic Closure; A Study of How Poems End* (Chicago 1968), p. 166.

7 See R. Jakobson, "Closing Statement: Linguistics and Poetics," in *Style in Language*, p. 356.

8 אברהם שלונסקי, ספר עלילות מיקי־מהו (מרחביה 1947). A comparison with Kornei Chukovsky's *Telefon* would show both Shlonsky's indebtedness to Chukovsky and the originality of Shlonsky's treatment of the material. A recent English adaptation of Chukovsky's poem by William Jay Smith was published as *The Telephone* by Delacorte Press / Seymour Lawrence in 1977.

subordinate coincidence, the resemblance between מְפֻטָּם, stuffed or fattened up, and the penult and antepenult of hippopotamus, and the fact that this animal's appearance can justly be described as "stuffed" or "fattened up." As for הַכְּנוּפְיָה הַתַּנִּינִית in the fifth line, it will be recalled that Miki (Mickey?) has just gotten off the phone with the crocodiles of the Nile who, stricken with malaria, have called from Egypt to order a ton of quinine.

"מַה שָּׁם? מִי שָׁם? מִי הַפַּעַם?"

"הִיפּוֹ מִמִּצְרַיִם!"

"הִיא פֹּה? מִי פֹּה? מָה? מִצְרַיִם??
בְּוַדַּאי כְּבָר שׁוּב צָרָה עִם
הַכְּנוּפְיָה הַתַּנִּינִית
אִם מְצַלְצְלִים שֵׁנִית".

"לֹא אָסוֹן, וְלֹא צָרָה פֹּה,
וְשׁוּם פֶּגַע לֹא קָרָה פֹּה,
לֹא תַּנִּין הוּא, וְלֹא תַּן, —
זֶהוּ הִיפּוֹ הַקָּטָן!"

"מִי פֹּה?"
"הִיפּוֹ!"

"אֵיזֶה הִיפּוֹ?
וְסוֹף־סוֹף זֶה הוּא, אוֹ הִיא??"
"זֶה אֲנִי פֹּה... כלוֹמֶר: הִיפּוֹ...
כְּלוֹמֶר: הוּא פֹּה... הוּא־הַא־הִי...

הִיפּוֹ, הוּפּוֹ — הֶמְפּוּטָם,
הֵם פֹּה צֶמֶד־חֶמֶד,
זוּג מִבֵּית הִיפּוֹפּוֹטָם,
פִּירְמָה מְפֻרְסֶמֶת".

(עלילות מיקי־מהו, ע' 86—87)

This gives Shlonsky full rein to play with pronouns:

מי, מה, אני, הוא, היא, הם (הֶמְפּוּטָם)

and the Aramaic הא, and he does so to hilarious effect.

Another of many humorous instances of pun in the same work is found on page 137. Here Shlonsky actually makes use of an ancient midrashic exegetical technique, that of splitting a bisyllabic or multisyllabic word into its parts and, by giving the meaning of the components, creating a folk-etymological explanation for the whole. Thus Shlonsky "explains" פַּרְפָּר (butterfly) as twice פר (bull):

פִּט שׁוֹאֶלֶת:

(What *par* is not a *par,*	אֵיזֶה פָּר אֵינֶנּוּ פָּר,
Even though it has in it double *par*?)	אַף־כִּי יֵשׁ בּוֹ כֶּפֶל פָּר?

פּוּט מֵשִׁיב:

(The butterfly!)	הַפַּרְפָּר!

The game continues with a question about what a פרה (cow) of this kind would be, and elicits the reply: פרת־משה רבנו (a ladybug, literally: cow of Moses our Master):

פִּט שׁוֹאֶלֶת:

וּפָרָה כָּזֹאת? עֲנֵנוּ!

פּוּט מֵשִׁיב:

כֵּן! פָּרַת־מֹשֶׁה־רַבֵּנוּ!

Incidentally, the names of the characters, פִּט and פּוּט are the two syllables of פִּטְפּוּט, chatter, prattle.

Pun and word play occur in the "serious" poetry as well. It is difficult to organize the examples strictly according to underlying principle since, in a given poem, several kinds of word play may occur, and these must be discussed in context. In such cases we shall try to group material according to the most important play on words in the poem. A simple kind of pun is built on true homonyms, two words which sound exactly alike, but have different meanings. Such a pair is להתנצל על — להתנצל את, where the difference in meaning is conveyed by the particle. There are also words which sound almost alike but differ only slightly מְעָנָיו — מַעֲנָיו. Related to this is the shorter word whose sounds are entirely contained in the larger שוטה — שוט. The use of a grammatical ending may cause these to become true homonyms שוטו — שוטו. In all of these examples the coincidence is one of sound only. No semantic relationship is immediately apparent. A connection on the level of meaning is created only within the context of the poem.

However, in another instance of a short word contained in a longer one, גֹּבַהּ — גב, a semantic opposition (though the words are not antonyms) between depth and height is apparent, even without reference to the poetic context. Other pairs linked by a "double bond," one of sound and of meaning, whether like or unlike, are the following: רם — תהם, שכלונו — שכללונו, ירנה — יתרונן, מעל — מַעַל.

Another kind of word play which will be discussed is based on the substitution of something novel for something expected in a conventional formula. The expected element may either be stated in the poem, as with הֲרֵי אַתְּ מְקֻדֶּשֶׁת לִי — הֲרֵי אַתְּ מְגֻדֶּשֶׁת לִי or it may be implied by the context:

[מַצִּילִים אֶת נַפְשָׁם פֶּן תָּמוּת] — מַצִּילִים אֶת נַפְשָׁם פֶּן תִּמּוֹט
[וְגַס בָּהֶם לִבִּי] — וְגַס בָּהֶם נִיבִי

Some instances, and these may also exhibit characteristics of other groups described above, have in common the resemblance of a foreign word to a Hebrew word. A poem about Paris alludes to הַחֵן הַמְּפֹרָז. The adjective reproduces the consonants of פריז, Paris, since *p* and *f* are allophones in Hebrew. The pair עוֹטֶה לוֹ — אוֹתֶלוֹ would be perfect homonyms but for the subtle matter of word juncture. In לונה — לונה, Garcia Llorca's Spanish *luna* matches the Hebrew imperative stay, abide, לונה, which is then modulated into לו נע, if only he wandered, and this involves an opposite area of meaning. Finally, two examples will be discussed which are so complex that they are best described as compositions based, in the one case on the theme *TA* and in the other, on the sounds OLU, OLELA. These two poems may also be described as onomatopoeic approximations of a train and a *hora*, respectively.

The verse below contains a play on two possible meanings of the *hitpa'el* construction התנצל. With the preposition על, it means "to apologize for." With the direct object particle את, it means "to strip oneself of" (vol. 5, p. 14):

Line no.	Rhymeme			no. of syllables
1	ha-ÓT	(a)	וְזֶה הָאוֹת:	4
2	ve-giDYÁM	(b)	גְּדוֹלִים שׁוֹכְחִים אֶת עַרְשָׁם וְגִדְיָם	12
3	miXTÁM	(c)	עֲבָרִים נִקְטָפִים כְּבָרָק שֶׁל מִכְתָּם	12
4	eDYÁM	(b)	מִתְנַצְּלִים אֶת עֶדְיָם	6
5	XeT'ÁM	(c)	מִתְנַצְּלִים עַל חֶטְאָם	6
6	timÓT	(a)	מַצִּילִים אֶת נַפְשָׁם פֶּן תִּמּוֹט.	9

The first line: "And this is the sign:" establishes an "end of days" mood. The ערשם וגדים, which the great forget, being an allusion to a well-known Jewish lullaby, are associated with the wholesomeness of childhood.[9]

9 Ruth Rubin transcribes and translates the words of the lullaby "Unter Dem Kind's Vigele" in her *Treasury of Jewish Folksong* (New York 1950), pp. 16–17, as follows:

1 Unter dem kind's vigele	1 Under baby's cradle here
Shteyt a klor-vays tsigele.	There's an all-white nanny, dear.
Dos tsigele z'geforn handlen	Nanny's come to bring the baby

The imagery of the third line is stunning. "Past" is normally an abstraction. Using it in the plural, עברים, imparts to it a concrete quality. The verb נקטפים, are plucked or picked, sustains the concretization. This unusual configuration is then compared to something. But the comparison is disturbing. Instead of resolving the problematic "pasts are plucked" by anchoring it to something familiar, the poet compares it to yet another provocative amalgam of concrete and abstract, "like the flash of an aphorism." This is very contrary. The syntax suggests clarification: A is being done like B. But the content leads from one perplexity to another. Is the aphorism presented as something deadly, a kind of lightning, or is the flash softened by being no more than the flash of an aphorism? Actually both things occur.

Lines 2 and 3 begin with a subject-verb construction. Lines 4, 5 and 6 begin with a verb. The subject of these three verbs may be either גדולים or עברים. The repetition of מתנצלים, which here constitutes the word play, is resolved into מצילים, the *hif'il* construction of a different but similar-looking root נצל.

The rhyme is more than the *abcbca* that it appears to be. The AM syllable appears at the end of both the *b* and the *c* rhymeme; but, because it is a morphological ending (except in מכתם) and Shlonsky meets the morphological norm in rhyme, it does not constitute a sufficient rhymeme. Nevertheless, the repetition of AM at the end of four successive lines makes פן תמוט seem a very sharp contrast and, at the same time, very final. Hearing the clause מצילים את נפשם followed by the conjunction פן one might expect a form of the verb למות to occur. It may be present subliminally and, if so, the actual תמוט, realized

Rozhinkes mit mandlen. Rozhinkes mit mandlen iz zeyer zis. Mayn kind vet zayn gezunt un frish.	Almond nuts and raisin candy. Raisins and nuts are a special treat. Baby will grow up healthy and sweet.
2 Gezunt iz di beste schoyre. Mayn kind vet lernen Toyre. Toyre vet er lernen. S'forim vet er shraybn. A guter un a frumer Vet er im yirtseshem blaybn.	2 Healthy's better far than wealthy. Baby will grow up a scholar. A scholar of the Torah will he be, A writer too, of holy writs. A good man and a pious, God willing, that's what he will be.

Another version is found in *A Treasury of Jewish Folklore,* edited by Nathan Ausubel (New York 1948), p. 684. Shlonsky plays with these lyrics in his "נאם השוטה" (vol. 1, p. 204), where the subject of the poem sings a lullaby to his mother:

תַּחַת עֶרְשֵׂךְ עוֹמֵד גְּדִי
גּוֹעֶה הוּא — וְלֹא בִּכְדִי
הָיָה לוֹ לִזְרָא דִּשְׁאֵךְ
וְהַתְּבוּנָה — לְקַדִּישֵׁךְ.

גְּדִי לֹא יֵלֵךְ לִקְנוֹת סְחוֹרָה
וְקַדִּישֵׁךְ — לִלְמֹד תּוֹרָה
הַגְּדִי יֵלֵךְ לִמְצֹא גְדִיָּה
וְקַדִּישֵׁךְ — אֶל הַשְּׁקִיעָה.

against an imagined תמות, would constitute a play on words.

The following poem, third in the cycle "שירי השוט והשוטה" (vol. 5, p. 46), contains several examples of word play. The combination השוט והשוטה, the rod and the fool, is based on Shlonsky's translation of King Lear, act 1, scene 4, where Lear warns the fool: "שים לב, בחור! יש שוט לגו שוטים". The English says: "Take heed, sirrah; the whip." The pairing שוטה — שוט is therefore Shlonsky's own.

הַשּׁוֹט וְהַשּׁוֹטֶה. תְּמוֹ שֶׁל מְחֻצָּף!
זֶה עֹנֶשׁ הַכִּפָּה שֶׁהוּא עוֹטֶה לוֹ.
כִּי לֹא רַק סַנְשׁוֹ וְקִישׁוֹט חָבְרוּ יַחְדָּיו
גַּם יָגוֹ וְאוֹתֶלוֹ.

וּמֶלֶךְ בִּמְסִבּוֹ. וּבְסוֹד הַפַּיִט
חִדּוּד הַפִּיפִיּוֹת שֶׁל לֵץ הַבַּיִת.
וְכֵפֶל צַחֲקָם שֶׁל חֶצְרוֹנָיו:
עַל מְעַנָּיו שֶׁל הַשּׁוֹטֶה וּמַעֲנָיו.

זֶה מֶלֶךְ וְשׁוֹטוֹ.
זֶה מֶלֶךְ בְּשׁוֹטוֹ.
זֶה הַשַּׁרְבִיט
הַבֶּצַע
הָעָרְמָה —
וְהַשּׁוֹטֶה הַמִּתְנַצֵּחַ עַד חָרְמָה.

The principal pun is השוט והשוטה. Although the two are not exact homonyms, they differ only in that the longer member, which completely includes the shorter, contains one additional sound. The meanings, forced into joint consideration by the resemblance of sounds, the whip and the fool, inform the whole poem. At the beginning of the third stanza, the use of a grammatical ending aligns the two members of the pun even more:

ZE MELEX vEŠOTO
ZE MELEX bEŠOTO

(This is a king and his fool/This is a king and his whip)
This is supported by a secondary pun:

וְכֵפֶל צַחֲקָם שֶׁל חֶצְרוֹנָיו: / עַל מְעַנָּיו שֶׁל הַשּׁוֹטֶה וּמַעֲנָיו.

Through the duplicity of the courtiers' laughter, a coupling is established between the fool's tormentors and his replies. But the fool, under cover of poetry, is sharpening his two-edged sword. The pun עוטה לו — אותלו, homonyms but for word juncture, links the Iago – Othello pair to the combination of whip and fool, making Iago and Othello a sinister realization of the whip and fool relationship, as opposed to the more benign pair Sancho and Quixote. Note also that the rhyme ha-ŠOT – kiŠOT links Sancho and Quixote to the whip and the fool. Finally, the last line seems to present the fool with a qualified victory over the whip by intimating that he will go on arguing to the bitter end.

A pair of words similar to השוט והשוטה is גֹּב וְגֹבַהּ. In both pairs the longer word includes the shorter one and is longer by one sound only. In the second case, however, a semantic opposition, expressed as pit and height, is apparent. The enigmatic "הוא בא" (vol. 5, p. 71–72), in which this occurs, uses word play at several points to support the series of oppositions upon which it is built.

אֵיכָה שִׁכְּלוּנוּ שִׁכְלְלוּנוּ.
הֶעֱשִׁירוּנוּ עֹשֶׁר מַר...

The pair ŠIkLUNU – ŠIxleLUNU, both in the pi῾el construction (they have made us bereaved, they have improved us), is introduced by the word איכה, the opening formula of the Book of Lamentations. This bears out the allusion in the last two lines of the preceding (fifth) stanza וְשִׁיר־שִׁירֶיךָ שָׁר קֹהֶלֶת / בְּהִי־וְהֶגֶה שֶׁל אֵיכָה (And your Song of Songs Koheleth sings / With the alas and moan of Lamentations). The second line of the sixth stanza ...העשירונו עשר מר (They have enriched us with bitter riches...) is an elaboration upon the idea of the pun, tying together, as it does, material improvement and bereavement.

The next pun (p. 72) is built on לונה לונה, probably borrowed from Garcia Llorca.[10] While in Hebrew it has nothing to do with the moon, there is still a residual suggestion of moon underlying this sequence. In the first instance it means "abide, stay:" הוֹ סוֹד כָּמוּס! הוֹ לוּנָה לוּנָה! (Oh well-kept secret! Oh stay stay!). It then becomes לו נע (if only... roamed about): לוּ נָע עַד נֶצַח הַזַּמָּר (May the singer roam evermore) and is finally resolved as לוּ נע לוּ נד, based on the language of Gen. 4:12: a fugitive and a wanderer in the earth:

לוּ נָע לוּ נָד הַזֶּמֶר סֶלָה / קָשׁוּב לְרוֹם וּתְהוֹם־רַבָּה

(May the melody wander and roam – Selah / Attentive to height and great abyss). The pair לו נע — לונה contains the opposition between staying and wandering, so that the ear does not expect to make the transition: — לונה לונה לו נע לו נד. The passage is also marked by a rhythmic change occasioned by the difference in stress between לוּנה and לו נע́:

10 Federico Garcia Llorca, "Romance de la Luna, Luna," in *Obras Completas* (11th ed., Madrid 1966), pp. 425–426.

הוֹ סוֹד כָּמוּס! הוֹ לוּנָה לוּנָה!
לוּ נָע עַד נֶצַח הַזֶּמֶר.

The pattern of sound modulation: lúna→ lúna→ lu ná'→ lu nád, serves as the vehicle for a complete turnabout in meaning. The assonance of לרום — תהום, which stand for the opposites height – abyss, in the line following ...לוּ נָע לוּ נָד, comes close to being a pun, and this confirms what has gone before.

These puns or pun-like devices are only part of the structure of oppositions in this poem. Some completely non-homonymic pairs are: קול מִקֶּדֶם — קול מִשְׁנֶה מִקֵּץ־יָמִים, למנצח — את נשמת, קצר־יד — כל יכול, דוּקְרָב הַקֹּדֶשׁ — וְהַחוֹל, דוּשִׂיחַ־עַד בֵּין רוּם — למטה, הֵן וְלָאו. These oppose days of yore with the end of days, impotence with omnipotence, sacred with profane, again height and depth, and positive – negative. In the third stanza on page 71 allusion is made to a crown of thorns (זֶה סוֹד עֲטֶרֶת וְקוֹצֶיהָ) with all the contrariness that image suggests.

Another instance of a "double bond," that is, a pair of words of like sound and opposing areas of meaning, occurs in the poem "הצו הכפול" (vol. 5, p. 190), which plays on the similarity between מֹעַל (lifting, raising) and מַעַל (treachery, fraud). While these words are not true opposites, it is the opposition of their positive and negative moral connotations which is emphasized by the coincidence of sound:

— דַּבֵּר אָדָם דַּבֵּר
כִּי מֹעַל בַּוִּדּוּי.

— הַחְרֵשׁ אָדָם הַחְרֵשׁ
כִּי מַעַל בַּוִּדּוּי.

גַּם מֹעַל — וְאֵין־רֵעַ.
גַּם מַעַל — וְאֵין־לֵב.
גַּם הַדּוֹבֵר גּוֹרֵעַ.
גַּם הַמַּחְרִישׁ כּוֹזֵב.

וּכְשֶׁאֲנִי אוֹמֵר: "דַּבֵּר!"
כַּוָּנָתִי לַדּוּמִיָּה
שֶׁאֵין כָּמוֹהָ נוֹף שֶׁל סְעָרוֹת.

וּכְשֶׁאֲנִי אוֹמֵר: "הַחְרֵשׁ!"
כַּוָּנָתִי לְמַאֲגַר כָּל הַמִּלִּים
הַמִּתְקַדְּשׁוֹת לְיִחוּדָן בַּזִּוּוּגִים
שֶׁבְּכֹחוֹ בִּלְבַד אִלּוּף כָּל סוֹרְרוֹת הַנֶּפֶשׁ.

— הַחְרֵשׁ אָדָם הַחְרֵשׁ.
— דַּבֵּר אָדָם דַּבֵּר.

This provides a good example of contrary clues at work in a poem. The doubleness of the command to which the title refers is given in the first four lines: " – Speak, Man, speak / For there is uplift in confession. / Keep silent, Man, keep silent / For there is treachery in confession." The construction of these two utterances is exactly parallel, the only varied elements being the repeated commands דבר and החרש, and the close-sounding מֹעַל and מַעַל. These latter, which are not strict semantic opposites, are forced into opposition by their respective relationships to דבר and החרש. The formula דבר אדם is reminiscent of biblical prophecy. ודוי remains constant, so that both good and bad are ascribed to it. The lines of the next stanza are cemented by the repetition of the initial גם and by end rhyme. The positive מֹעַל is now associated with friendlessness. The negative מַעַל is linked with heartlessness. The speaker detracts. The silent one deceives. Both sides of the equation are shown to be negative. Now the speaker "clarifies" the meaning of his commands. By "Speak" he refers to that silence "as which no landscape is so stormy." By "Keep silent" he means "the store of all the words which consecrate themselves to their singularity (but יחוד is also associated with יחד, together) in pairings in whose power alone (the ending of בכחו seems to refer to מאגר) lies the taming of all the shrews of the soul." סורר is actually rebellious, but אלוף הסוררת is the "Taming of the Shrew." And then the commands are repeated in reverse order from the beginning of the poem. In the stanza which begins ...וכשאני there is no true rhyme. The first and fourth lines end in the same two sounds EŠ, but in one case the syllable is stressed, while in the other it is not. The second and third lines end on the plural ending IM. SEʿaROT at the end of the previous stanza and SorEROT have certain sounds in common. The lines contain eight, twelve and fourteen syllables respectively and the rhythm is somewhat freer than in many of the other stanzas discussed. In addition to all the balances and contrasts of speech and silence, מעל and מעל, etc., the utterance

...מאגר כל המלים
המתקדשות ליחודן בזווגים
שבכחו בלבד אלוף כל סוררות הנפש

seems to have special relevance to our theme. It appears to indicate that the contrary clues being sought and discussed in this study are not a trivial matter, but lie at the heart of this poetry.

Another doubly bound pair, יְרָקָה — יְתְרוֹנָן occurs in "אדם וחידותיו" (vol. 5, p. 54). It is not as central to the poem, however, as is מֹעַל — מַעַל to "הצו הכפול."

The main play on words in "אדם וחידותיו" belongs to the group of convential formulae used in a new and disconcerting way. Here the formula is the type of alphabetic acrostic which appears in hymns such as "אדיר הוא", "אין אדיר" and "כי לו נאה" (although in the latter two the ב is represented by בחור):

אדיר, ברוך, גדול, דגול, הדור.

In this sequence גדול and דגול contain the same letters, though the first two are inverted and the second vowel is slightly different. Shlonsky exploits the גדול — דגול affinity by the way he places them in his poem:

אָדָם וְחִידוֹתָיו

כִּי יָפוּ חִידוֹתָיו מִפִּתְרוֹנָן
וּפָעֳלוֹ — בְּגִידָה בְּשׁוֹגֵג וּמִדַּעַת —
יִרְנֶה עָלָיו קוֹלוֹ וְלֹא יִתְרוֹנָן
וּמָרוֹם פְּרִי הָעֵץ מִלָּגַעַת.

הַקָּרוֹב לְחָמְדוֹ וְרָחוֹק מִלְּקְטוֹף!
כְּשׁוּעָל אֶל מוּל גֶּדֶר הַכֶּרֶם.
יְקַלֵּל "בְּאֻשִׁים!" הַמֵּרִיעַ "כִּי טוֹב!" —
זוֹ נִקְמַת הַכְּלוֹת — בַּטֶּרֶם.

עַל־כֵּן יֹאהַב חַיִּים בְּעוֹדָן אַגָּדוֹת
וּבְטֶרֶם מַכְאוֹבִים וָכַעַשׂ.
כִּי אַדִּיר הוּא לִבְדּוֹת
כִּי בָּרוּךְ הוּא לִבְדּוֹת
כִּי גָדוֹל
כִּי דָגוּל
כִּי הָדוּר הוּא לִבְדּוֹת —
וְעָנִי וְאֶבְיוֹן מִמַּעַשׂ.

All the positive qualities stated in the alphabetical chain of adjectives are made to apply to the infinitive לבדות (to fabricate, to make up a story). Attention is called to the דגול — גדול pair, which are parallels, by their position, each almost alone in a line, as opposed to the two preceding lines and the line following, where the formula הוא לבדות is repeated. A discontinuous rhyme is achieved in which the main norm, that of matching the last stressed vowel, is not quite met, but almost: KI GADóL – KI DAGúL. The basic thrust of the poem, that man's riddles are more beautiful than their solutions, is finally balanced by the thought that fabrication, which is mighty, blessed, great, etc., is devoid of deed. There is a play on the words ירנה (will rattle or clank) and יתרונן (will sing with joy), both of which contain *resh nun* in their roots and have to do with making sound. But against these similarities the difference between an unpleasant and a pleasant noise is thrown into relief. It is assumed that the endings of עליו, ופעלו, חידותיו refer to the אדם of the title. The image of the fox and the grapes appears in the second stanza, and the opposition between desire and ability to reach is stated הַקָּרוֹב לְחָמְדוֹ וְרָחוֹק מִלְּקְטוֹף and וּמָרוֹם פְּרִי הָעֵץ מִלְּגַעַת.

The fox-like exclamations are expressed in Jewish terms: באושים (Isa. 5:2, 4) and כי טוב (Ps. 118, 136). Their opposition is echoed by the בטרם — הככלות of the next line. Finally, life is described in two contrasting ways: בעודן אגדות and בטרם מכאובים וכעש. Both are descriptions of a state of innocence, one in positive terms, the other in negative terms.

Another example where the poet plays with a conventional formula is the poem "הרי את" (vol. 4, p. 33). The pun is based on the words spoken by the bridegroom as he places the ring on the bride's finger: הרי את מקֻדשת לי... (Behold, you are consecrated unto me...). At one point in the poem the *kuf* in מקֻדשת changes to *gimel* to produce מגֻדשת (abundant, overflowing):

1. עֶרְיָה הִיא — מְקֻטֶּרֶת אֵד וְזֶבֶל.
2. תּוֹבַעַת וְנוֹשֶׁפֶת אֶת חֻמָּהּ.
3. שָׂדֶה — וּמְנַחִירֶיהָ טַל וְהֶבֶל.
4. כַּלָּה — בְּהִינוּמָהּ. וְיִחוּמָהּ.

5. מַה פֶּרַע שְׂעָרָהּ וּמַה צֶּמַח.
6. נָכוֹנוּ רְגָבֶיהָ לְהַדְשִׁיא.
7. וַיּוֹשֶׁט לָהּ אֶת פֶּלַח הַיָּרֵחַ
8. הָעֶרֶב כְּטַבַּעַת־קִדּוּשִׁין.

9. הֲרֵי אַתְּ מְקֻדֶּשֶׁת לִי בְּדֶשֶׁא
10. בְּרַחַשׁ שַׂרְעַפּוֹת וְדַרְדָּרִים
11. הֲרֵי אַתְּ מְזֻבֶּלֶת לִי בְּדֶשֶׁן
12. בְּגֶלֶל שֶׁל צֹאנִים וַעֲדָרִים.

13. נוֹבַבְתְּ לִי בַּשִּׁבֹּלֶת וּבַשַּׁיִת.
14. שׁוֹבַבְתְּ לִי חֲרוּלִים וְגִבְעוֹלִים.
15. יָבוֹאוּ יִבְעָלוּךְ חוֹרְשַׁיִךְ
16. וְזֶרַע בָּךְ יָקִימוּ לְיבוּלִים.

17. יִחַמְתְּ לִי וָאָבוֹאָה אֶל הַקֹּדֶשׁ.
18. רְחַמְתִּי בָּךְ הַמְּתֹם וְהָרְוָיָה.
19. הֲרֵי אַתְּ מְגֻדֶּשֶׁת לִי בְּגֹדֶשׁ
20. שָׂדֶה לְעֵת דּוֹדִים. הַלְלוּ־יָהּ!

The את of the title, the female to whom the modifiers of line 1 apply and who is the subject of תובעת ונושפת (demanding and exhaling) in line 2, is revealed in the third line as שדה (field). The personification is supported by the ascribing to her of nostrils. Her role is explicitly established at the beginning of the fourth line by the appositive כלה (bride). The sexuality of the mood is projected in the first stanza by עריה (nakedness, especially as applying to the genitals), מקֻטרת (smoking, as incense, hence, perfumed), תובעת (demanding), ונושפת את חֻמה (exhaling her warmth), ויחומה (in a state of sexual excitation as applicable to a female animal, in heat). The syntax at the beginning of line 1 is not adjective-pronoun, but noun-pronoun; not "Naked is she" but "Nakedness is she." While both are perfectly acceptable in Hebrew, the construction chosen by the poet heightens the sense of identity between the two members of this grammatical equation. עֲרֻמה היא might have left room for the implication the "she is other things as well," but עריה היא tends to suggest that the nakedness is all.

Since this is clearly a paean to earthiness and fertility some of the word combinations exhibit a deliberate *grossiereté*: thus the prominence given to זבל (manure) as a source of perfume, placed in a rhyming position at the end of the very first line and in the ...הרי את מזֻבלת of line 11. The pair בהינומה ויחומה (in her bridal veil and in heat), combining human romance and a shade of modesty with blunt animal sexuality, also belongs to this category. In addition to the obvious end rhyme of the stanza, the words bE-hInUMÁ – vE-yIxUMÁ play an interesting music against one another.

The subject of the verb ויושט in line 7 is הערב at the beginning of line 8. The marriage symbolism is sustained in the second stanza by the image of the evening holding forth a silver moon to her (the field) as a wedding ring. The "ceremony" begins in line 9 with the first four words of the traditional formula spoken by the bridegroom as he places the ring on the bride's forefinger. This marks a turning point. The field, first referred to in the third person, is from now on addressed directly in the second person. The fifth word, however, is not the expected בטבעת but בדשא, thus: "Behold, you are consecrated unto me with green grass." Within the line a rhyme has been established between mekuDEŠET and be-DEŠE. There is also a very rich pattern of sound repetition between lines 9 and 11:

HAREY AT MEkUdEŠET LI BE-DÉŠE
HAREY AT MEzUbELET LI BE-DÉŠEn

As in the first stanza, a positive value is assigned here to things considered negative in ordinary discourse: דרדרים (thistles) and גלל (droppings, dung). The syntactic parallel between lines 9/10 and 11/12, reinforced by the rich orchestration of lines 9 and 11, creates an equality between the sentences:

"Behold, you are consecrated unto me with green grass / With the rustle of branches and thistles" and "Behold, you are manured unto me with fertilizer / With the droppings of sheep and flocks." מקֻדשת and מזֻבלת are both feminine singular *beynoni* forms of the *pu'al* construction. The entire מזבלת... בגלל... sequence has been made esthetically acceptable here, first, by being placed after הרי את מקֻדשת..., second, by the close syntactic parallel between lines 9/10 and 11/12, and, third, by the morphological parallel between מקֻדשת and מזֻבלת.

The initial rhyme of lines 13 and 14 provides relief from the predominance of the *segol* in the third stanza. The pair nOVAVT LI – šOVAVT LI (You have flourished for me – You have seduced me) again sets up an equation against which are counterpoised the positive (שבלת – ear of grain) negative (שית – thornbush) of line 13 and the negative (חרולים – nettles) positive (גבעולים – stalks) of line 14. In other words, your grain and your thorns are equally dear to me. The pairing in line 13 is reinforced by the *shin* alliteration and in line 14 by the sound repetition xaruLÍM ve-giv'oLÍM.

In line 15 the ploughmen are depicted as having sexual intercourse (although בעל may also mean rule over) with the field. The following line speaks of the seed they implant for their harvest. The effectiveness of this metaphor is somewhat diminished by its obviousness. Men working the land do, in a sense, assert their mastery over it and, of course, they do sow seeds after ploughing.

The narrator describes his answering of the field's sexual call in terms of "entering the Holy Temple." The קדש at the end of the seventeenth line thus serves as preparation for the pun to follow in the nineteenth, where the הרי את theme is recapitulated with *gimel* substituted for *kuf*, yielding: "Behold, you are bountiful unto me with bounty / Field at the lovers' season. Halleluyah!" Aside from the fact that everything in the poem points to Spring, the phrase לעת דודים may also be an oblique reference to the Song of Songs, read at Passover. The restatement of the theme and of the word שדה work toward closure, which is finally achieved with "Halleluyah," a closural word in a number of Psalms.

Another play on words based on the occurrence of an unexpected substitution in a standard idiom is found in the poem "כתב־יד של סבא" (vol. 4, pp. 132–134). The speaker – and here the speaker of the poem is extremely close to Shlonsky the poet – speaks of his grandfather's generation of Hebrew writers as the generation of stutterings. But the talk of these powerless predecessors only seemed meaningless and naive. In reality, nobody knew as they did to create idioms out of naught:

אָהַבְתִּי הַמְּלִיצוֹת שֶׁל דּוֹר הַגִּמְגּוּמִים.
קוֹדְמַי קְצָרֵי־הַיָּד! הֵן רַק לְמַרְאִית־עַיִן

הָיָה אָז לַהַגְּכֶם אֵין־שַׁחַר וְתָמִים.
מִי עוֹד כָּמֹכֶם יָדַע לִבְרֹא נִיבִים מֵאָיִן!

Elsewhere the poet makes fun of the vagueness of their figures of speech: "מִין־פֶּרַח וּמִין־עֵץ". In the final stanza the word נִיבִי is substituted for לִבִּי in a well-known expression. The idiomatic גס בהם לבי would mean "I have become too familiar with them." But Shlonsky's invention וְגַס בָּהֶם נִיבִי seems to indicate that "My poetic expression has grown stale":

הַיּוֹם כָּל פְּרָט וּפְרָט אֲנִי נוֹקֵב בְּשֵׁם
וְגַס בָּהֶם נִיבִי:
לֹא רָז לֹא דֶרֶךְ־אֶרֶץ!
אַךְ נַפְתּוּלֵי־אֱנוֹשׁ — רְאֵה כִּי אֲמַשֵּׁם
בִּמְלִיצוֹתֶיךָ סָב
בְּחָרְזְךָ בְּקֶרֶץ.

Incidentally, in employing קרץ — ארץ Shlonsky pokes gentle fun at a kind of rhyme favored by the דור הגמגומים, the generation of stammerings, to which his grandfather belonged.

Shlonsky is known as a creator of neologisms. In the following example, a new word is created through the same kind of substitution we have been discussing. When a word was required for moving pictures, the roots ראה, to see, and נוע, to move, were combined to form רְאִינוֹעַ (with the addition of sound, this became קולנוע). In the second poem of the cycle שעות שרופות Shlonsky joins תבונה, intelligence, understanding, reason, wisdom, to נוע, and achieves תבונע, literally, moving reason: אֶל אֵיזֶה חוֹף אֲרוּר־מָנוֹחַ / גּוּשֵׁי בָּתִּים / שָׁטִים שָׁטִים / כְּצִי הָרַעְיוֹנוֹת הַנִּבְעָתִים / שֶׁנֶּעֶקְרוּ מֵעֹגֶן הַתְּבוּנֹעַ (vol. 3, p. 86). Contrary to what might be expected, it is the terribly abstract "fleet of terrified ideas that have come loose from the anchor of the תבונע" that is used to illustrate the concrete "flocks of houses." Furthermore, it is unusual that a word containing a root meaning to move should be thought of as an anchor, whose normal function is to prevent movement.

In two examples of word play already discussed, a factor underlying the homophonic coincidence is the resemblance of a foreign word or combination to something Hebrew. We have seen this in עוטה לו — אותלו, Othello and "he wraps himself in" or "he puts on," and לונה לונה, luna (moon in Spanish) and "abide, stay." Things of this sort are scattered throughout Shlonsky's work. Thus, the Eiffel Tower, *La Tour Eiffel*, is called טוּר עֹפֶל, Hill of Ophel, a hill near Jerusalem which was fortified in antiquity (vol. 2, p. 102).

Sections of the poem "רכבת" (vol. 2, pp. 104–107) are such an amalgam or rhyme, rhythm, alliteration and lexical meaning that the terms "pun" or "word play" fail to do justice to the complexity of the structure at hand. In the stanza reproduced below, the syllable TA figures prominently, appearing in: תָּא־תָּא־תָּא (compartment-compartment-compartment), טְאטֵאתָ (you have been swept away), תִּעְתַּעְתָּ (you have lead astray, deceived), לְמַטָּה (down), אַתְּ אַתָּה (you, you – feminine singular, masculine singular).

וְאַחַר:
עוּף עָיַפְתִּי.
אַךְ נוֹשֶׁפֶת הָרַכֶּבֶת שֵׁן חוֹרֶקֶת וְשׁוֹקֶקֶת:
הָלְאָה שֶׁקֶט! הָלְאָה שֶׁקֶט!
וּמְשַׁקְשֶׁקֶת: תָּא־תָּא־תָּא!
וְטוֹרְדִים פַּסִּים: טְאטֵאתָ!
וְטוֹרְדִים פַּסִּים: תִּעְתַּעְתָּ!
וְטוֹרְדִים פַּסִּים: לְמַטָּה
רַק לְמַטָּה
אַתְּ אַתָּה!

The TA reappears in the seventh stanza of the poem:

ma TA'ITA	מָה: טָעִיתָ?
Te'oT TA'ITA	תְּעוֹת תָּעִיתָ:
derex rusya-poLIn-LITA	דֶּרֶךְ רוּסְיָה־פּוֹלִין־לִיטָא.
TA. Te'eh. Te'i. Te'u.	תָּא. טְעֵה. טְעִי. טְעוּ.
ve-ATA?	וְעַתָּה?

The elements at play are טעית (you have made a mistake), תעית (you have gone astray), ליטא (Lithuania), תא (compartment) and עתה (now). The use of the infinitive תעות at the beginning of the second line and ועתה in the fifth create a syncopation, since the lines with which these alternate all begin on stressed syllables. The passage from תא to a conjugation of טעה in the imperative is a harbinger of things to come.

The eighth stanza begins with "ועתה", as if to reply to the "ועתה?" which precedes it. The first three lines rhyme on the feminine ITA rhymeme: אֲלִיטָה, תַּבִּיטָה, אַשְׁקִיטָה. The stanza ends with the fourth line: וְאִם הֻכֹּת — אֻכַּת עַתָּה!. The line ends on TA, as do the other lines in the stanza; but, since the stress here comes on the last syllable, this does not constitute an end rhyme. There is a remarkable internal orchestration, however, HUKóT UKáT, in which the stressed vowels do not match, but most other sounds are shared. This combination is made up of the *huf'al* infinitive of נכה, "to be beaten," and the first person singular future of the *huf'al* construction of the semantically close כתת, "to be routed, crushed." This yields, more or less, "If I am beaten I shall be crushed." Also, the combination ukAT ATA almost reproduces the sounds TA-TA-TA, which have appeared earlier in the poem as תא־תא־תא and are about to appear as טע־טע־טע (Plant! Plant! Plant! – this may also mean to pitch a tent or to establish something).

The ninth stanza begins with the restatement of an earlier, rather onomatopoetic "train" formula, in which the *segol* and the consonants Š, K, T figure prominently:

אַף נוֹשֶׁפֶת הָרַכֶּבֶת שֵׁן חוֹרֶקֶת וְשׁוֹקֶקֶת:
הָלְאָה שֶׁקֶט! הָלְאָה שֶׁקֶט!
וּמְשַׁקְשֶׁקֶת:

ax noŠEfET ha-rakEvET ŠEn xorEKET ve-ŠoKEKET
hal'a ŠEKET hal'a ŠEKET
um-ŠaKŠEKET:

The effect, of course, is the opposite of ŠEKET (silence). Some of the meanings brought together by these sounds are: blows, train, cog, grinds, moves to and fro, silence (but the poem says "Away with silence!" or "Down with silence!") and rumbles.

Suddenly, the stanza shifts into the mode of TA. Again, one may regard this as onomatopoetic if one thinks of the train's whistle sounding:

al TITA!	אַל תִּטַּע!
al TiTA! lo eT ATA	אַל תִּטַּע! לֹא עֵת עַתָּה.
TA! TA! TA! ki eT ATA	טַע! טַע! טַע! כִּי עֵת עַתָּה.
al TiTA!	אַל תִּטַּע!
TA! TA! TA!	טַע! טַע! טַע!
TA!	טַע!

This is simply a sequence of contradictory commands: Don't plant! Don't plant! It's not time now. Plant! Plant! Plant! For it is time now, etc. In the next stanza, the first three lines begin אל תטע. This is balanced by the affirmative command of the fourth and last line:

AL TITA – VANI tArAFTI	אַל תִּטַּע — וַאֲנִי טָרַפְתִּי!
AL TITA – VANI ArAFTI	אַל תִּטַּע — וַאֲנִי עָרַפְתִּי!
AL TITA – VANI AyAFTI	אַל תִּטַּע — וַאֲנִי עָיַפְתִּי!
	וְהַלֵּב בִּי: טַע! טַע! טַע!

The orchestration of the first three lines is very rich, partly because all three follow the same syntactic formula: Don't plant — for I have... The chain טרפתי — ערפתי — עיפתי — means: I have preyed upon or mixed up, I have broken the neck or decapitated, I have grown weary: This stanza is concluded by a repetition of the TA-TA-TA theme.

The next three lines present a rhythmic relief, which provides respite after what has gone before and furnishes a necessary lull in tension before the strident climax. From the strongly binary, heavily-accented beat of what has preceded we pass on to three ternary lines which have an almost "singing" quality. It is as if the chugging of the locomotive gave way to a waltz:

אַךְ צוֹלֵעַ תְּמוֹלְי הַגִּבֵּן הַקָּרוּחַ:
עוֹד מְאוּם לֹא נָתַתָּ וְלָמָּה תָּנוּחַ?
וְטוֹרְדִים גַּלְגַּלִּים עִם פַּסִּים וְעִם רוּחַ:

The rhyme kaRÚAX — RÚAX with the support of the exact but less rich tanÚAX, is less demanding than the rhymes both of the preceding stanza and the one to follow. It is less demanding because, being less rich and thus farther from homonymy, the ear has to strain less to catch meanings. Indeed, the ear alone could not possibly catch all the meanings. How could it distinguish between תא־תא־תא and טע! טע! טע!? In poetry as dense as most of this, eye, ear and mind must all strain to catch meanings. The three-line stanza at hand therefore permits a moment of relaxation.

The climactic last stanza is the remarkable product of rhythm, rhyme and meaning, realized chiefly through the grammatical exercise of conjugation. The roots chosen, and the morphological endings of the past tense selected, sustain the play on the syllable TA. The final verb, מות (to die), has not been used previously in the poem. We have been prepared for it phonologically and semantically, but it has been saved for the end (vol. 2, p. 107):

מְאוּם לֹא תַּתִּי
לֹא נָתַתָּ
לֹא נָתַנּוּ
לֹא נָתַתְּ
סְתָם טְאטֵאתָ
סתָם תִּעְתַּעְתָּ
סְתָם לְמַטָּה
רַק לְמַטָּה
כֹּל גָּמַעְתִּי

מַתִּי מַתָּ
מַתְנוּ מַתֶּם
מֵתוּ
מָת.

At the core of the stanza lie three pun elements, טאטאת, תעתעת, למטה, used earlier in the poem. Here each is introduced by סתם, whose repetition suggests that all of the turmoil described is without purpose. The conjugation which forms the first part of the stanza's "sandwich" construction is introduced by a series of negatives: מאום לא — לא — לא — לא. The word גמעתי includes within it and thus prefigures the sounds of מתי, which sets into action the concluding chain.

Before ending this discussion of word play we shall examine one more piece which, like "רכבת", is part of the section לך לך in the Collected Poems. This is the third poem in the cycle "קרועים אנו" (vol. 2, p. 111). If the whole of "רכבת" is suggestive of the chugging of a locomotive, this poem is clearly a *hora*:

	No. of syllables		Line no.
NIThOLÉLA	4	נִתְהוֹלֵלָה	1
NITxOLÉLA	4	נִתְחוֹלֵלָה	2
NIšTOLELA	4	נִשְׁתּוֹלֵלָה	3
amen sÉLA	4	אָמֵן סֶלָה!	4
bisxarxORET	4	בִּסְחַרְחֹרֶת	5
lev šikORET	4	לֵב שִׁכֹּרֶת	6
kacipORET	4	כַּצִּפֹּרֶת	7
el ha-eš	3	אֶל הָאֵשׁ.	8
MI ŠEyEš LO	4	מִי שֶׁיֵּשׁ לוֹ	9
MI ŠE-EN LO	4	מִי שֶׁאֵין לוֹ	10
petax et pihu	4	פְּתַח אֶת פִּיהוּ	11
yayin tEN LO	4	יַיִן תֵּן לוֹ.	12
hOLU xOLU	4	הִלּוּ חִלּוּ	13
tsaʿar gOLU	4	צַעַר גִּלּוּ	14
halleluya	4	הַלְלוּיָהּ	15
lev yaxef	3	לֵב יָחֵף!	16

Here, the specific verb form and the use of related roots help create the rhyme. Lines 1–3 consist of verbs in the first person plural future of the *hitpoḷel* construction. The meanings are mutually reinforcing: Let's go wild / Let's whirl / Let's be boisterous. The fourth line, while it does not adhere to this pattern, still makes an exact, if less rich, rhyme with lines 1–3. The use of Amen Selah in this context seems deliberately naughty, but nothing more. The verbs of lines 1 and 2 are used again in line 13 in the plural imperative of the *kal* construction. The שלל root of line 3 will not lend itself to this kind of transformation, so that the poet has chosen another verb which will sustain the OLU rhyme, and yield צער גלו (banish sorrow), which makes sense.

Line 8, which does not participate in the rhyme of lines 5–7, is echoed in line 16: EL hA-Eš – LEv yAxEf, and the v of לב is close to the f of יחף. Both sounds are produced in the same way. The former is voiced; the latter is not. Also, there is repetition of sounds between ha-EŠ of line 8 and ŠE-yEŠ of line 9. Lines 9 and 10 rhyme and are syntactic parallels. And line 12 rhymes with 10. Finally, "Halleluya" in line 15, which is not rhymed, nevertheless contains the LU syllable which is part of the rhymeme in lines 13 and 14.

* * *

The examples given here, though relatively few in number, represent something characteristic of Shlonsky's poetry. Pun and word play are related to rhyme and alliteration in that all deal with homophony. Homophony, with the ambiguity to which it gives rise, is generally avoided in prose. In poetry, and particularly in Shlonsky's poetry, it abounds. This means that conundrums are constantly being presented to the ear. The ear cannot interpret all the sounds it has detected without deliberate effort and, in some cases, without the visual reinforcement of the printed message. Consider the most extreme example discussed here: TA-TA-TA. Prose aims at clarity. This kind of poetry, it would at first seem, aims at confusion. By pushing homophony to the limit the poet demands concentration of his audience and forces upon them the realization that this is other than ordinary, prosaic discourse. He does not abandon signification altogether. The sounds can be deciphered. Rather, he focuses on the message for its own sake. To paraphrase Jakobson, he is promoting the palpability of signs, deepening the fundamental dichotomy of signs and objects. And this is basic to making the language function poetically.

A HAPAX LEGOMENON: ממשק חרול

J. C. GREENFIELD

The general intent of Zephaniah 2:9, b–c is clear:

כִּי מוֹאָב כִּסְדֹם תִּהְיֶה וּבְנֵי עַמּוֹן כַּעֲמֹרָה
מִמְשַׁק חָרוּל וּמִכְרֵה־מֶלַח וּשְׁמָמָה עַד עוֹלָם

Ammon and Moab will be as desolate as Sodom and Gomorrah, their land will be infertile and eternally desolate.[1] A consensus has developed among modern translators for the difficult phrase ממשק חרול ומכרה־מלח, which is now usually rendered: "a land possessed by nettles and salt pits" (RSV) or "a field of nettles and a salt pit" (NEB). The source for these translations is not to be found in the early versions such as the LXX, Vulgate or Peshitta, which differed among themselves (see below), but rather in the comments of the medieval lexicographers and commentators such as Abraham ibn Ezra and R. David Kimchi.

The word that proved the most troublesome in this phrase is ממשק, a hapax legomenon for which a suitable explanation has not been offered. The LXX *Damaskòs eklelimméne,* etc. bears witness to a text similar to ממשק חרול but eludes interpretation.[2] The Vulgate's *siccitas spinarum* shows that it grasped the meaning of *ḥārūl* but was baffled by *mimšaq*. The Peshitta's *dĕ'itḥablat neṣbathen* "whose plants were destroyed" may best be explained as a context translation. As far as the second part of the phrase, מכרה־מלח, is concerned, the LXX *thēmonia hálōnos* and the Vulgate's *acervi salis* point to the same text as that of the MT, but the hapax *mikreh* is taken as being from a root *krh* "to pile up," as G. R. Driver has noted.[3] Most medieval commentators and lexicographers refer *mimšaq* to *ben-mešeq bētī* (Gen. 15:2), which is not very helpful.

1 This passage is discussed in detail by G. Gerlemen, *Zephanja, textkritisch und literarisch untersucht* (Lund 1942), pp. 37–39. I have not seen any serious discussion of this passage subsequent to this.

2 Cf. Gerlemen, p. 38.

3 G. R. Driver, *Journal of Theological Studies,* 1940, p. 173.

The translation that offers a clue to the meaning of ממשק is the Targum. Its משמט מלוחין ומחפורין דמלח matches the usual translation found in the medieval commentators for the last three words of the phrase, and indeed may have been influential in establishing the consensus that later emerged, the major differences being that *mikreh* was interpreted as a plural "pits" – based on the context – and that *ḥārūl* was taken as *mallūḥīn* "saltwort," which is a possible interpretation of *ḥārūl*, although elsewhere the Targum translates the same noun as *hīgē* "thorns" (Job 30:7). But of real interest, and unique among the ancient translations, is the choice of משמט for ממשק. The verb שמט must mean "picking, removing" here; this is a rare use of the verb *šmṭ* in Aramaic, but it is attested in both Mishnaic Hebrew and Babylonian Aramaic. In Mishnaic Hebrew it is used for cutting away and removing vines under certain conditions: מוותרין ומשמטין בקנים (Tosef. Shevi. 1, 7, ed. Lieberman, p. 167; TJ Shevi. 2,2, 33c),[4] while in Babylonian Aramaic it is used for picking fruit (BB 28b) or plucking flax (Ned. 48b).

This use of *šmṭ* is not unique to Aramaic and Mishnaic Hebrew but is already found in Akkadian. The use of *šamāṭu* for harvesting was commented on some years ago by the late Hildegard and Julius Lewy in discussing the *ḫamuštum ša tašmīṭim* of the Old Assyrian calendar.[5] They noted that *šamāṭu* was a synonym of *qatāpu* "to pluck." The material for this verb and related nouns is now amply assembled by von Soden.[6] The verb *šamaṭu* was used for the removal and gathering of leaves, branches and dates; the usage for dates seems to be the most widely attested. The משמט מלוחין of the Targum would then be a place for the harvesting of saltwort or the like.[7]

One may properly ask how the Targum derived this meaning from ממשק חרול or, specifically, משמט for ממשק. I believe that the answer may be found in the simple displacing of the diacritical point of משק from the right side of the *shin* to its left side, thus producing a *śin*. The noun *mimśāq* would then be a *nomen loci* from the root *mśq*. The root appears normally as מסק in Mishnaic Hebrew. The shift שׂ > ס is standard, and may be easily seen in words found in both Biblical and Mishnaic Hebrew (e.g., סחט/שׂחט ;סיד/שׂיד). In Mishnaic Hebrew מסק is part of the technical vocabulary of agriculture and is of relatively frequent usage. Its precise meaning is "to pluck, pull olives" in

4 Cf. *Tosefta kifshutah*, vol. 2 (New York 1955), p. 490.

5 *HUCA*, XVII (1942–43), 54, n. 234.

6 *Akkadisches Handwörterbuch*, p. 1155, s.v. *šamāṭu*; *ibid.*, 1159, s.v. *šamṭu*, where a thorn plant with that name is listed.

7 The translation *mallūḥīn* for *ḥārūl* may be influenced by Job 30:4, הַקֹּטְפִים מַלּוּחַ עֲלֵי־שִׂיחַ.

harvesting them.[8] It is often found in the sources with other verbs with specialized use for the harvesting of particular produce: בצר for grapes, קצר for cereals, ארה for figs, גדר for dates, etc.[9] The noun מסיק *masiq* "olive harvest" is also well attested; cf. זמיר, חריש, בציר, קציר, אסיף for the *qatil* form frequent in agricultural activities. The verb מסק/משק is not found in any of the Aramaic dialects but Arabic *mašaqa* is recorded with the meaning "to remove leaves." Dozy records the expression *mašaqa-lwarqa ʿani-ššigri* "effeuiller, ôter les feuilles."[10] Some lexicographers report that it is peculiar to the dialect of Syria and Palestine. The *ša* of the Arabic root would fit well with the *śin* of מֹשׂק assumed in this paper. The verb *šmṭ*, noted above, as used in the various Semitic languages, may serve to demonstrate that the same root may be variously used while remaining in the same basic semantic range; the same is true for *mśq/msq*. The Targum recognized in ממשק a form of the familiar root מסק; at a later date, perhaps under the influence of מֹשׂק, it was pointed ממֹשׂק.

The phrase מִמְשַׁק חָרוּל means, then, a place for harvesting nettles (or, if you wish, a plant like the saltwort). It fits well with מִכְרֵה־מֶלַח, a place for "mining " salt — that is, salt pits. The verse means that Ammon and Moab will be eternally destroyed and will remain a place unfit for agricultural activity. Thorns and salt are both used as traditional imagery of unproductive land due to a curse or catastrophe. The Hebrew Bible uses קוץ ודרדר (Gen. 3:16, Hos. 10:8); קוץ ושמיר (Isa. 32:13); and שמיר ושית (Isa. 5:6, 7:23—24). The same is true of salt מלח, used for land with high alkaline content (Deut. 29:22, Jer. 17:6, Ps. 107:34). Salt has no seed (*kīma ṭabtu zēra la išû*) and the sowing of salt was used symbolically to insure infertility.[11] The biblical example is Shechem (Jud. 9:45) while that of Carthage was known in the ancient world.

One may turn to the curse formulae of the Babylonian boundary stones, the *kudurru,* for excellent parallels to Zeph. 2:9:

1) *ugāršu lirḫiṣma kīmû urqīti idrānu*
kīmû ᵈNisaba *puquttu liḫnub*
"May (Adad) inundate his field, let alkali grow there instead of green vegetation, thistles instead of cereals" (BBSt. No 7, ii 33).

8 Cf. I. Löw, *Die Flora der Juden,* 2, p. 288; F. Goldmann, *Der Oelbau in Palästina zur Zeit der Mischnah* (Pressburg 1907), pp. 19—21.

9 E. g., Tosef. Shab. 9, 17. The verb נקף is used for gleaning olives; a distinction is made between the verbs in Ḥal. 3,9.

10 R. Dozy, *Supplement aux dictionnaires arabes* (Leiden 1881), II, 594b.

11 Cf. D. R. Hillers, *Treaty Curses and the Old Testament Prophets* (Rome 1964), p. 23, and the literature quoted in n. 32; M. Weinfeld, *Deuteronomy and the Deuteronomic School* (Oxford 1972), pp. 110—112; and J. A. Fitzmyer, *The Aramaic Inscriptions of Sefire* (Rome 1967), p. 53, for Sefire I 36 and the parallels and literature quoted there.

2) *kīmû uṭṭati lardâ kīmû mê idrāna lišabši*
"May (Adad) produce there nard-grass instead of barley, alkali instead of water" (BBSt. No. 9, ii 13).[12]

The fear of salinity and barrenness was widespread throughout the ancient Near East. It was the prophet's wish that Moab and Ammon become ממשק חרול ומכרה־מלח, fit only for harvesting thorns and salt, and thus eternally desolate like Sodom and Gomorrah.[13]

12 Cf. *CAD,* 'I/J', p. 9, s.v. *idrānu;* 'L', p. 103, s.v. *lardû.*
13 For Jer. 48:9 a contemporary oracle on Moab cf. W. L. Moran, *Biblica*, 39 (1958), 69–71.

THE LEGEND OF THE WANDERING JEW IN HUNGARY: TWO GERMAN TEXTS

A. Scheiber

Two decades ago I showed the path taken by the legend of the Wandering Jew in Hungary in folklore, in popular literature, and in literature proper.[1] I pointed out that it is found in Hungarian as early as 1704, and we know that it appeared in popular literature by 1848.[2] Further traces of it in folklore have been found since.[3] A German version was noted in Pozsony (Bratislava):[4]

"Auf der Schloss-Strasse in Pressburg, oberhalb der in morgenländischem Stil erbauten schönen Synagoge der Orthodoxen, war eine berühmte Weinhandlung und an der Ecke des Hauses stand ein Randstein. Auf diesem sah einmal eine Frau einen sehr alten Juden sitzen, der so mager war, wie eine Zaunlatte und der so traurig in die Welt blickte, dass einem das Herz weh tat. Mitleid erweckten auch das langelockige Haar, der schöne, weisse Vollbart, der ihm über die Brust hing, und dann der alte schäbige Kaftan. Dazu hatte er noch einen gequälten Gesichtsausdruck, der auf ein unruhiges Gewissen schliessen liess.

"Als der Wirt – ein alter Jude – diesen armen Menschen sah, bedauerte er ihn und brachte ihm ein Stück schönes, weisses Brot und einen Krug Wasser dazu. Als er ihm das geben wollte, stand der Sitzende auf und lief davon. Es war *der ewige Jude,* der Jesus Christus auf dem Weg nach Golgotha bei seinem Hause nicht hatte ausruhen lassen, und nun ruhelos bis zum letzten Tage herumirren muss."

1 A. Scheiber, *Midwest Folklore,* 4 (1954), 221–235; *idem, ibid.*, 6 (1956), 155–158; G.K. Anderson, *The Legend of the Wandering Jew*, Providence 1965, pp. 68, 99, 279, 417–418.

2 A. Scheiber, *Folklór és tárgytörténet,* I, Budapest 1974, pp. 168–171.

3 L. Kálmány Legacy in the Hungarian Ethnographical Museum, Budapest (EA 2801); S. Bálint, *Karácsony, húsvét, pünkösd*, Budapest 1973, pp. 250–251; *idem, Tombácz János meséi*, Budapest 1975, pp. 547–550, no. 20; I. Nagy, *Népi Kultúra – Népi Társadalom*, XIII Budapest 1982 (in press).

4 K. Benyovszky, *Sagenhaftes aus Alt-Pressburg,* Bratislava–Pressburg 1932, p. 112.

Now an occasional newspaper in German has been found in the National Széchényi Library in Budapest: "Einzig wahre weder vor- noch nachgedruckte Darstellung der wirklichen 48ten grossen Versammlung der Spatzen und anderer Vögel in Buda-Pest... Abgelauscht von E. März. Druck von Adolf Müller" (Signature: 9602. quart. Széch.).[5]

Three versions of the legend appear on pages 1—2. The ending leads to the conclusion that this Wandering Jew is antisemitism:

"Der ewige Jude. Die Fabel von einem seit Christi Kreuzigung bis zum jüngsten Tage in der Welt herumlaufenden und niemals sterbenden Juden hat sich in vielen Ländern von Europa ausgebreitet, die Erzählung ist aber nicht vollkommen übereinstimmend, wie bei allen Legenden. Die eine ist diese: Als Christus zum Tode geführt wurde, so wollte er, von der Last des Kreuzes ermüdet, nahe bei dem Thore, vor dem Hause eines Schuhmachers, namens Ahasveros, ein wenig ausruhen; dieser aber sprang herbei und stiess ihn fort. Christus wendete sich um und sagte: 'Ich will hier ruhen, du aber sollst gehen, bis ich wieder komme.' Und von dieser Zeit an hatte er keine Ruhe mehr, sondern musste beständig herumwandern. — Die andere Erzählung ist diese, wie sie Mathias Parisiensis, ein Mönch aus dem 13. Jahrhunderte, vorträgt: Da Christus aus dem Richthause des Pilatus zum Tode geführt wurde, so stiess ihn der Thürhüter, mit Namen Cartofilus, mit der Faust von hinten zu und sagte: 'Geh, Jesu, geschwind; was säumst du?' Christus sah ihn ernsthaft an und sagte: 'Ich gehe, du aber sollst warten, bis ich komme.' Und dieser Mensch lebt noch, geht von einem Orte zum anderen, und bringt seine Zeit in beständiger Furcht zu, bis Christus zum Weltgericht erscheinen wird. Eine dritte Erzählung setzt noch hinzu: Dieser herumwandernde Jude werde alle hundert Jahre tödtlich krank, werde aber doch wieder gesund, und bekomme seine vorige Gestalt wieder, und daher komme es, dass er nach so vielen hundert Jahren nicht viel älter aussehe, als ein Mann von 70 Jahren. — So viel ist aus verschiedenen Legenden bekannt. Kein einziger von den alten Schriftstellern gedenkt mit einer einzigen Silbe einer solchen Geschichte; der erste, der etwas davon sagt, ist ein Mönch aus dem dreizehnten Jahrhundert, wo man weiss, dass die Welt mit frommen Andichtungen bis zum Eckel angefüllt war. Indessen hat sich diese Geschichte so weit ausgebreitet, dass es sogar zum Sprichworte geworden ist, — er läuft herum wie der ewige Jude.[6] Es fehlte nicht

5 Now in possession of the Hungarian National Archives, Budapest.

6 E. Dal — R. Edelmann, *Fund og Forskning,* 12 (1965), 31—46; A Scheiber, *Acta Orientalia Hungarica,* 27 (1973), 393—394; H. Lixfeld, *Enzyklopädie des Märchens,* I, Berlin—New York 1975, p. 227; S. Shunami, *Bibliography of Jewish Bibliographies,* Jerusalem 1975, p. 72, no. 5117; *ibid.,* p. 323, no. 6613; A. Scheiber, *Fabula,* 17 (1976), 81.

an Personen, die diesen ewigen Juden wirklich wollten gesehen haben, allein wenn man ihr Zeugnis nach den Gesetzen der historischen Glaubwürdigkeit untersucht, so findet sich, dass ein und der andere Betrüger sich dieses Märchens mögen bedient haben, um den guten und einfältigen Leuten aufzubinden, dieser oder jener sei der herumwandernde Jude. – Völlig unwahr ist jedoch diese Legende auch nicht; es gibt einen ewigen Juden, der fast in ganz Europa, mit Ausnahme Frankreichs, herumwandert, in jedem Säculum tödtlich krank, aber wieder gesund wird, und seine vorige Gestalt wieder bekommt: dieser ewige Jude ist, leider, der – Judenhass."

With this contribution I wish to honor Professor L. Nemoy, the outstanding scholar of Karaite studies, to whom I am obliged for almost four decades of correspondence.[7] May Providence grant him many further fruitful years in the service of Jewish scholarship!

7 A. Scheiber, *Jubilee Volume in Honour of Professor Bernhard Heller*, Budapest 1941, Hebrew Part, p. 102; reprinted: *Judah ben Elijah Hadassi Eshkol Ha-Kofer*, ed. L. Nemoy, Westmead 1971.

THE LADY ON HER THRONE AND HER URSINE ATTENDANTS*

E. J. WIESENBERG

בישישים חכמה וארך ימים תבונה (איוב יב, יב)

In the goodly company of a great many of his other admirers, I have always read with sustained interest Leon Nemoy's writings on Karaitica. My personal acquaintance with him dates from our correspondence in 1959–60 over my "Appendix to Maimonides' Sanctification of the New Moon," contributed to the volume of Maimonides' ***Book of Seasons*** in the Yale Judaica Series, of which he was then – and happily, still is – the General Editor. Our association was the greatest possible pleasure to me. He carefully scrutinized each and every item in my contribution, not infrequently detected flaws, whether in typing slips or lack of clarity in presentation, and offered valuable suggestions. This notwithstanding, he self-effacingly remarked in his preface to the volume concerned that in the matter of my "Appendix," mainly on the background to "Sanctification" on the the basis of mathematical astronomy – about which he knew nothing – he had left everything to me; as great a departure from strict veracity as has ever been prompted by humility.

One of his letters, full of meat as usual, reached me whilst I was laid up with 'flu. In order to avoid delay, I drafted my reply in bed and dictated it to our eldest daughter Naomi. The letter had to be handwritten as no typewriter was available at that time. It was therefore stated in the letter that it was being dictated to her. In our subsequent fairly long correspondence over my "Appendix," Leon Nemoy with his inimitable charm never omitted in any of his letters to append his courtesies to "good Miss Naomi." It is therefore doubly pleasurable to me to be able to make my contribution to the *Festschrift* honoring Leon Nemoy's eightieth birthday, in the form of an article on an aspect of rabbinic literature which has a bearing on mathematical astronomy and moreover has a title involving a leading lady.

* The following sigla have been used: B.M. = British Museum; Decl. = declination; lat. = latitude; N. = North; N.P. = North Pole; N.P.D. = North Polar Distance; tr. = translation. Works of reference: ***Almagest*** = ***Claudii Ptolemaei Megale Syntaxis***, II, ed. J.L.

I

The constellation *Cassiopeia* is the 10th in Ptolemy's Catalogue of 1022 stars,[1] in its Arabic version by Zakaria Ibn Maḥmud Kazwini[2] and in its brief *résumé* in the rabbinic code of laws ***sui generis Ṣedah la-Darekh*** by R. Menahem b. Aaron Ibn Zeraḥ (d. 1385).[3] The 13 stars in *Cassiopeia* visible to the naked eye, specified in Greek and Arabic by Ptolemy and Kazwini, respectively, and briefly stated in Hebrew by Ibn Zeraḥ,[4] are distributed in the sky in a manner that suggested to the fancy of the ancients the outlines of the figure of a woman reclining on her chair.[5] She was said to represent the Ethiopian queen Cassiopeia – or Cass*ie*peia, with some other variations both in the spelling of

Heiberg (Leipzig 1898–1903; reprinted 1940); figures enclosed in brackets refer to the German tr. by Karl Manitius (Leipzig 1912–3; reprinted 1963 with corrections by Otto Neugebauer); Azulai = R. H.Y.D. Azulai, ***Shem ha-Gedolim,*** I, ed. Y. E. Ben-Jacob (Vienna 1864); BL = H. Bauer and P. Leander, ***Historische Grammatik d. Hebräischen Sprache des A.T.,*** I (Halle 1922; reprinted Hildesheim 1962); Boss's *Catalogue* = L. Boss, *Preliminary General Catalogue of 6188 Stars*, etc. (Washington 1910); Dunkin = E. Dunkin, *The Midnight Sky* (London 1869); *EJ(E)* = *Encyclopaedia Judaica* in English (Jerusalem 1971); *EJ(G)* = *Idem* in German (Berlin 1927); GK = Gesenius-Kautzsch, *Hebrew Grammar* (corrected 2nd English ed., Oxford 1966); *HDB* = *Hastings' Dictionary of the Bible,* 8th impression (Edinburgh and New York 1906); Ideler = L. Ideler, *Untersuchung über den Ursprung u. die Bedeutung der Sternnamen* (Berlin 1809), containing the Arabic original and annotated tr. of a work on the stars by Zakariah Ibn Maḥmud Kazwini (fl. 1260) – figures enclosed in brackets refer to the original; *JE* = *Jewish Encyclopaedia* (New York 1916); *KaL* = R. Jonah Ibn Janaḥ, *Kitâb al-Luma'*, ed. J. Derenbourg (Paris 1886); Kunitzsch = P. Kunitzsch, *Arabische Sternnamen in Europa* (Wiesbaden 1959); Malter = H. Malter, *Life and Works of Saadia Gaon* (Philadelphia 1921); Maunder = E. W. Maunder, *Astronomy without a Telescope* (London 1902); PW = Pauly-Wissowa; Smart = W.M. Smart, *Text-Book on Spherical Astronomy* (5th ed., Cambridge 1965); *SR* = *Sefer ha-Riqmah*, R. Judah Ibn Tibbon's tr. of *KaL*, ed. M. Wilensky (2nd ed., Jerusalem 1963/4); Webb = T.W. Webb, *Celestial Objects for Common Telescopes,* Vol. II, *The Stars,* ed. M. W. Mayall (New York 1962); *YJS* = *Yale Judaica Series.*

References to page numbers are sometimes amplified, indicating the number of the line after a colon (:), with an asterisk (*) whenever the lines are counted from the end of the page, e.g., p. 36:5 = page 36, line 5; p. 36:5* = page 36, line 5 from end.

Parts of this paper were included in a lecture delivered at a session of the Winter Meeting of the Society for Old Testament Studies (= SOTS) in London on January 2, 1975.

1 *Almagest*, pp. 38–169, esp. pp. 60–63 and 168–169 (pp. 32–64, esp. 38 and 64).

2 Ideler, *passim*, esp. pp. 80:24 ff (382:14 ff).

3 Pt. 1, Sect. 1, ch. 27, ed. pr. (Ferrara 1554), p. 22b = p. 34b in ed. N. H. Herzog (Warsaw 1880). The title is modeled on Gen. 42:25 (with two parallels).

4 *Almagest,* pp. 60–63 (38); Ideler, pp. 80:24 ff; Ibn Zeraḥ, *loc. cit.*

5 See, *inter alia, Almagest, ibid.*, for the designations of some of the stars concerned, referring partly to the woman and partly to her chair or throne.

her name and in her habitat[6] – who boasted that she (or, according to another version, her daughter Andromeda) was more beautiful than the nymphs of the sea. As a punishment for this *hubris*, her land was devastated by a sea monster. By way of vicarious atonement, her husband Cepheus had Andromeda chained to a rock and exposed to the monster. She was liberated by the gallant Perseus, who subsequently married her. After their deaths, the whole illustrious group – Cassiopeia, Andromeda, Cepheus and Perseus, as well as the latter's winged horse Pegasus – were translated to the Northern sky; whilst the monster, the constellation *Cetus* (= Κῆτος), was placed in the distant Southern hemisphere. The reclining figure – ἡ τοῦ θρόνου in Greek – suggested to the Arabs the name *dhât al-kursî* (literally, "she with [or 'of'] the throne").[7] This is rendered by Ibn Zeraḥ in *Ṣedah la-Darekh* as **היושבת על הכסא** (= she that sits on the chair or throne).

The modern equivalents of these names are "the Lady in her Chair," "...on her Throne,"[8] or "the [vacant] Chair." The latter has led to the facetious observation: "The constellation is thought to represent either the queen herself or her chair, a flattering alternative."[9] The fact of the matter is that it is neither flattery to the chair nor an insult to the lady, but due to a genuine misunderstanding of the Arabic name, seeing that not all astronomers are fully acquainted with the linguistic aspects of the designation of the objects of their studies. As an illustration of another misunderstanding, of a somewhat more serious nature than this, the observation *sic hebraice vocavit Aben Ezra* – viz. "Ibn Ezra uses this Hebrew name [for *Cassiopeia*]" i.e., the above Arabic name, which was clearly written in Hebrew characters, **ד̇את אלכרסי**, and therefore referred to as Hebrew instead of Judaeo-Arabic – was misunderstood

6 See PW, pp. 2315-32 where, according to a widespread version of the myth, she is the queen of the "Phoenician" (evidently pre-Israelite) town of Joppa. This version, however, is stated not to have any connection with the stars. The original name of the constellation – as given by Ptolemy, *Almagest, loc. cit.* – is Κασσιεπεια, with ε. Regarding the etymological origin of the name *Cassiopeia*, which does not seem to have been discussed in the sources, it has been suggested by Dr. Marcus Schalimtzek that it may derive from **כסא**, the Hebrew for "chair" or "throne"; a very plausible derivation in view of the Semitic – possibly even Phoenician (i.e., linguistically quasi-Hebrew) – background of the story.

7 According to Kazwini – see Ideler, *loc. cit.* – this name designates the constellation *Cassiopeia* in its entirety; whilst Kunitzsch, p. 198, restricts it, on the authority of other Arab astronomical writers, to the designation of δ *Cas.* = *rukbat dhât al-kursî.* Usage evidently varied from author to author.

8 Maunder, pp. 16:21–22 and 35:28–29.

9 Dunkin, p. 150:14–15; also p. 30a:10–12 in H.A. Rey, *A New Way to See the Stars* (London 1966).

by an astronomer of note, who will best remain nameless, to mean that *Cassiopeia* is named in Hebrew "Aben Ezra." This sent him on a wild goose chase for a meaning of either of the two Hebrew words אבן (= stone) and עזרה (= help) in any way suitable for use as the designation of Queen Cassiopeia.[10] A nodding acquaintance with the third part of R. Jacob b. Asher's *'Arba'ah Ṭurim* and the biblical background to its title might, perhaps, have led him to an interesting solution of his problem.

II

The five brightest stars in the constellation are designated on the star maps as α, β, γ, δ and ε *Cassiopeiae* (= *Cas.*). All clearly visible to the naked eye without any effort, they suggest to the star-gazer the scrawl of a W, of a capital M in the Greek or Latin alphabet, or a capital ***Sigma*** (= Σ) in the Greek alphabet or of its mirror image, depending on the position of ***Cassiopeia*** in the sky. An illustration of this may be seen in Figs. 1–4. These have been chosen from among 12 diagrams showing the most prominent stars in the three principal Northern circumpolar constellations – as seen in the London sky, weather permitting, at midnight in intervals of about 30–31 days from January to December – in the chapter named "The Great Star Clock in the North"[11] in Maunder's popular book on astronomy (which is very useful to the naked-eye observer). These are ***Cassiopeia***, with the above-mentioned five stars, ***Ursa Maior*** (= the Great Bear) with seven stars and ***Ursa Minor*** (= the Little Bear) with three stars. Among the latter there is a bright star in the tail of the Little Bear, named α *Ursae Minoris* (= *U. Mi.*) or ***Polaris*** (= the Polar Star) by reason of its present closeness to the celestial North Pole.[12]

10 See Ideler, p. 81:22 ff, who ridicules the misinterpretation of the observation, which he quotes from [Joseph Juste] Scaliger, ***Notes on M. Manilius' Astronomicon***, etc. (Leyden 1600), p. 477. Scaliger does not specify his source. He may be mistaken, as there appears to be no trace of any reference by Ibn Ezra to ***Cassiopeia*** as דאת אלכרסי or by any other name.

11 Maunder, pp. 12–28. Our Figs. 1–4 are, respectively, Maunder's Figs. 4 (p. 22), 10 (p. 25), 1 (p. 18) and 7 (p. 24). As for the dates and hours at which the constellations concerned are seen in the position indicated, see columns I, IV, VII and X in the chart, *ibid.*, p. 21. Equally profitable is the ***All Year Round Celestial Clock*** in Rey, *loc. cit* (n. 9 above), pp. 120–121.

12 According to data in Boss's ***Catalogue***, No. 325 on pp. 14–16 and 252, ***Polaris*** moved from Decl. 88°14′24″.53 N. (with N.P.D. of 1°45′35″.47) at 1800 C.E. to Decl. 88°46′49″ N. (with N.P.D. of 1°13′11″) at 1900 C.E. and to Decl. 88°54′10″.94 N. (with N.P.D. of 1°5′49″.06) at 1925 C.E. These changes in Declination (and also in Right Ascension) are, of course, due to the Precession of the Equinoxes. See Sec. IV below and nn. 60, 66 and 71; regarding the star nearest the N.P., see. n. 14 and also Section V below and n. 93.

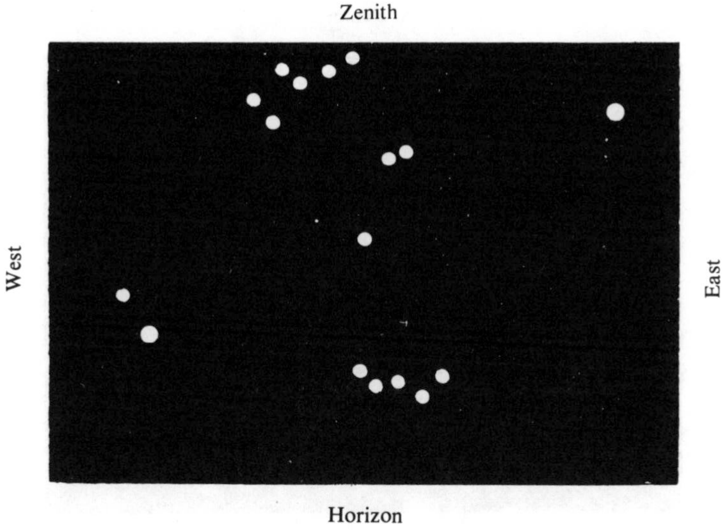

Fig. 1. Looking north at midnight on April 15

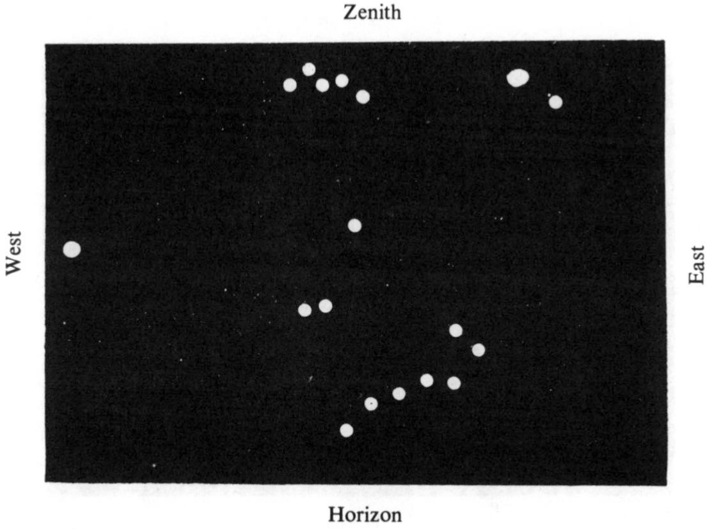

Fig. 2. Looking north at midnight on October 14

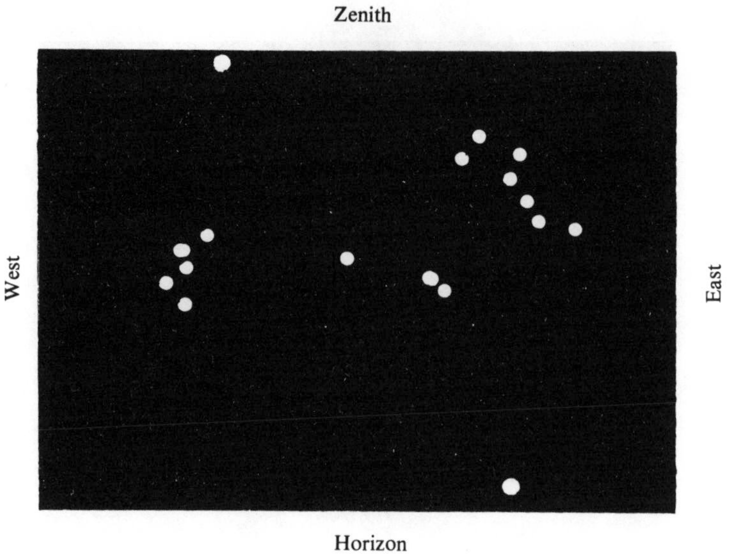

Fig. 3. Looking north at midnight on January 13

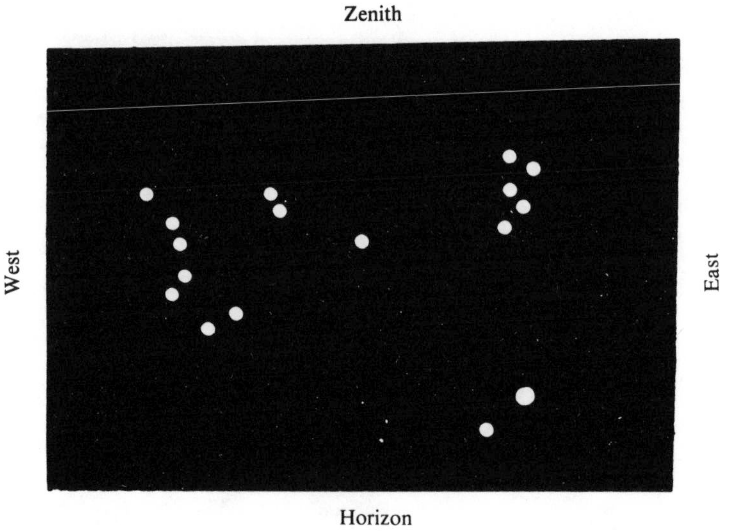

Fig. 4. Looking north at midnight on July 15

Actually, *Ursa Minor* consists of seven stars and *Ursa Maior* of 27, all visible to the naked eye. These are likewise specified in the respective Catalogues of Ptolemy and Kazwini[13] and briefly referred to by Ibn Zeraḥ;[14] four fainter stars are added in the former and 20 in the latter. The aforementioned 15 brilliant stars – three in the Little Bear, named α, β and γ *U. Mi.*; seven in the Great Bear, named α, β, γ, δ, ε, ζ and η *Ursae Maioris* (= *U. Ma.*); and five in *Cassiopeia*, named as already stated α, β, γ, δ and ε *Cas.* – are clearly marked in Fig. 5, likewise taken from Maunder's book.[15]

They will be clearer still, even to readers who have not had the time to study the mathematical principles required to understand figures and diagrams in works on astronomy, from the photograph, reproduced in Fig. 6, of the London sky at midnight on October 15 at it appears to an observer looking north.[16] Figures and photographs of this kind – and, to some extent, also simplified diagrams such as those reproduced above – should enable the novice to locate *Cassiopeia* without difficulty: (1) A straight line through β and α *U. Ma.* (= "the Pointers" or "the two hind wheels of the Wagon") in the most conspicuous group of the seven stars in the Great Bear, bearing slightly to the right and about 5 times as long as the distance from β *U. Ma.* to α *U. Ma.*, leads to *Polaris* (= α *U. Mi.*) in the Little Bear. (2) A straight line from η *U. Ma.* (the point at the end of the "Shaft" of the "Wagon"), extended via *Polaris,* leads to the W of the five prominent stars in *Cassiopeia.*

At this stage, it behoves us to note that these stars are also known as *kaff ath-thurayyâ al-yumnâ al-mabsûṭa* = "The outstretched right hand of the *Pleiades*."[17] The latter are a cluster of rather faint stars – nevertheless conspicuous by reason of their nestling so close together – in the zodiacal constellation *Taurus*, whereof six (formerly seven) are visible to the naked eye.[18]

13 *Almagest*, pp. 38–43 (32–33); Ideler, pp. 3–32 (375–378), with 29 stars in *U. Ma.*

14 *Loc. cit.* (n. 3 above) The brief עיש ובניה וכוכביה שבעה in ed. Ferrara – expanded into הצורה הראשונה היא קרובה אל הקוטב הצפוני היא עיש ובניה ואחרים קראוה הדוב הקטן וכו׳ in ed. Sabbionetta (1567) and subsequent editions – clearly refers to *U. Mi.*, as is evident from הצורה השניה הדוב הגדול וכו׳ in all the editions. On the confusion of the two Bears in the modern exposition of rabbinic texts, see Section V below. In Ibn Zeraḥ's list *U. Ma.* consists of only 17 stars.

15 Maunder, p. 27. See also the more detailed Star Map No. 1 in *ibid.* p. 33, reproduced as our Fig. 7, in which the outlines of the various constellations are mapped out differently.

16 Taken from Dunkin, p. 76.

17 Kunitzsch, p. 152:14 ff; see also *ibid.*, p. 144:18 ff.

18 See Star Map No. 7 in Maunder, p. 71, reproduced as our Fig. 8. At the upper end of its central region, just beneath the Roman numerals II – XXIII (marking Hour Angles), is the essential part of *Cassiopeia* with four of the five bright stars forming the W (i.e., α, β, γ and δ *Cas.*; ε *Cas.*, situated outside the upper limit of the map, is not shown). At the center of the

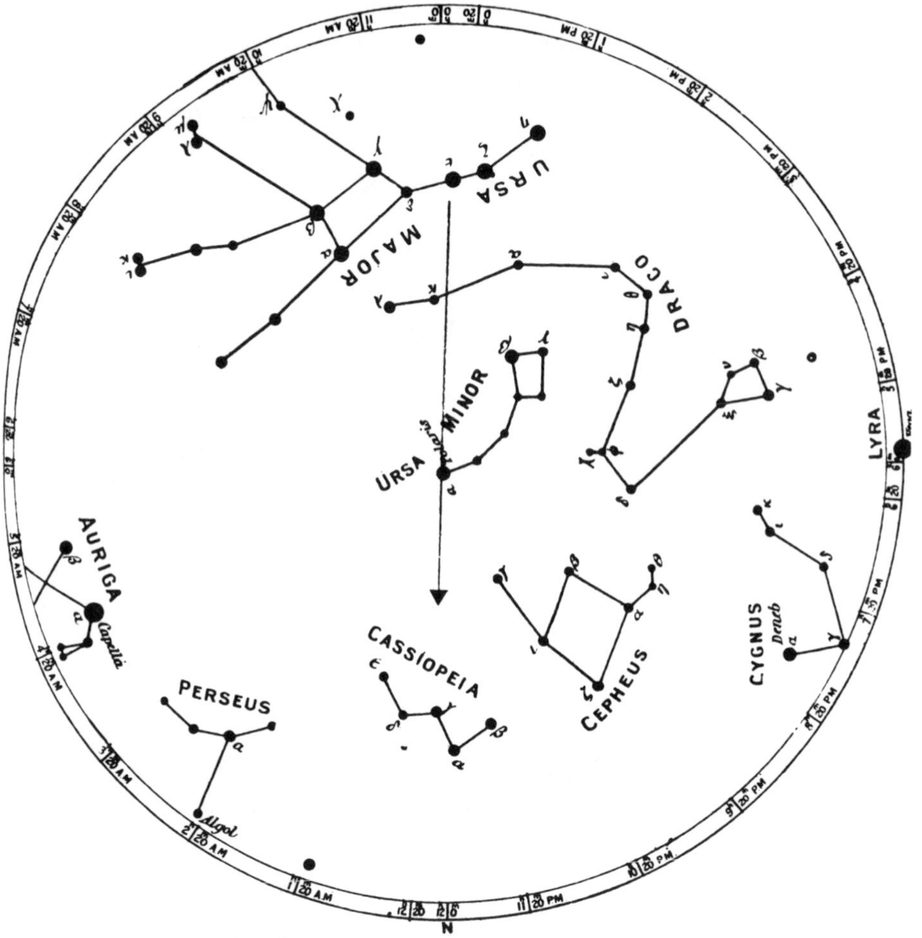

Fig. 5. The chief circumpolar stars, midnight April 1.
Starting from ε *Ursae Maioris* (the star in the Great Bear's tail nearest the root) and crossing the celestial North Pole (next to α *Ursae Minoris*), we find on the further side of the Pole five stars in the shape of a W, the principal stars of the constellation *Cassiopeia*, the "Lady on her Throne"; see the arrow in the figure (adapted from Maunder, p. 27).

extreme left of the map (astride the curve of the Ecliptic) is the essential part of *Taurus*, in whose right corner the *Pleiades* are clearly marked, though they are reduced – because of the small scale of the map – to a small cluster, showing only five of their seven stars. As is evident to any observer of the stars (and shown quite clearly in this map), the *Pleiades* are seen by the human eye as an object much smaller than the W of the five bright stars in *Cassiopeia*. Moreover, as is likewise evident from this map, the angular distance from the *Pleiades* to the W is quite considerable. Hence it requires quite a stretch of the imagination to see, with Arab fancy, the *Pleiades* and the W as the head and hand, respectively, of the same

Fig. 6. The Midnight Sky at London, looking North, October 15

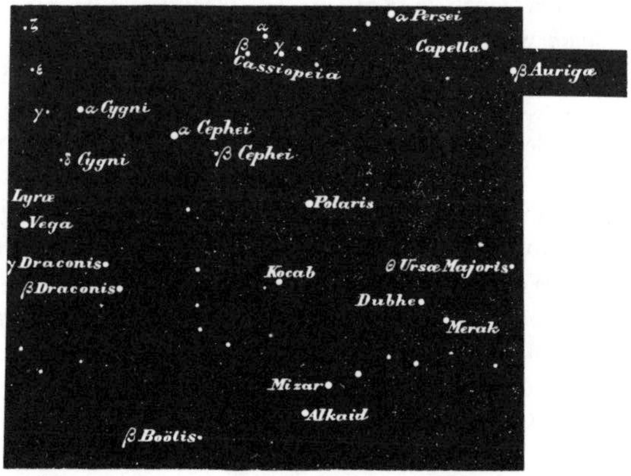

Index map

Identified with the biblical *Kîmah*[19] in some of the Greek and Latin versions,[20] as well as by R. Saʿadya Ga'on,[21] Ibn Janaḥ[22] and Ibn Ezra,[23] they figure in

feminine figure. But so do a great many other shapes which widespread popular fancy sees represented by one or another of the constellations.

Regarding the number of stars in the *Pleiades,* see Ibn Ezra to Amos 5:8, quoted in n. 23 below; also Maunder, p. 103:15–25, and Webb, p. 230:10–17. Those observable by telescope are counted in their hundreds; there is a remarkable anticipation of this in TB Ber. 58b, near end: מאי כימה... כמאה כוכבי.

19 Amos 5:8; Job 9:9, 38:31.

20 Symmachos and Theodotion to Amos 5:8; Vetus Latina and Vulgate to Job 9:9, and also LXX *ibid.*, except for the the reversed order of the three names; LXX, Aquila, Vetus Latina and Vulgate, *ibid.* 38:31. The name *Pleiades (*Πλειάδες) is the plural of Πλειάς, etymologically connected with πλέω (= to sail, swim, float) or with πλεών (the comparative of πολύς = much); see *HDB* III, 895:9* ff and the unabridged *Greek-English Lexicon* of Liddell and Scott, p. 1414b.

21 He renders כימה as אלתֿריّא in Job 9:9, 38:31 in his Arabic version of Job with commentary, ed. B.Z. Bacher (Paris 1899); see also the French tr. by J. and H. Derenbourg of the version, the editor's annotated Hebrew tr. of the commentary, and ed. J. Qafaḥ (Jerusalem 1972/3). The same is true of כימה in Amos 5:8 in an anonymous annotated Arabic version of the Minor Prophets in the Bodleian Ms. Neub. 181 (Hunt 206) – held to be based mainly on Saʿadya Ga'on's exegetical methods – of which Joel and Amos were published by Dezsö Klein as a doctoral dissertation with Introduction and Notes, mainly linguistic, in Hungarian: *Joél és Ámosz próféták könyveinek arab fordítása névtelen szerzötöl* (= *An Anonymous Writer's Arabic Translation of the Prophetical Books of Joel and Amos;* Budapest 1897). Regarding the manuscript referred to, see Malter, p. 318:27. The aforementioned rendering is printed on p. 23:4* of Klein's publication, a copy of which was kindly sent me by Professor A. Scheiber, Director of the Jewish Theological Seminary of Hungary. The name *thurayyâ*, only superficially similar to *thaur* (= Bull = *Taurus* in the zodiac), derives from the two related roots *tharâ* and *thariya* (= to increase in numbers, to become wealthy), as pointed out by Ideler, p. 146:16 ff; see also Kunitzsch, p. 55 n.1. Hence its etymology is similar to that of the above-mentioned Hebrew and Greek counterparts.

22 In the rendering of *Kîmah* in *Sefer ha-Shorashim* s.v. כים as אלתֿריّא, which reverts to the first explanation by Ibn Janaḥ in *KaL*, p. 279:19 ff (= *SR*, p. 294:17 ff). For his identification of *Kîmah* with אלפרקדאן, see n. 96 below.

23 In quotations from earlier authorities (קדמונינו and הקדמונים, respectively) in his comment on Amos 5:8: "*Kîmah* stands for six stars in the tail of *Aries* and the head of *Taurus*, which, although small, are visible (כימה הוא זנב טלה... ו׳ כוכבים נראים אף על פי שהם קטנים) and in his comment on Job 38:31: *"Kîmah* stands for seven small stars at the end of *Aries*, of which six are visible" (כימה הם ז׳ כוכבים... והנראים הם ששה). He is evidently referring to the same stars in his treatise on the astrolabe, *Kelî Neḥosheth* (Königsberg 1845), p. 33:6 ff, with ראש האשה = ראס אלמראה (= the Woman's Head) which he says is at 2°38′ from the end of *Aries* (this is the probable meaning of his dictum הוא במזל טלה שני מעלות שלושים ושמונה דקים). This does not quite tally with Fig. 8, in which the *Pleiades* are placed within *Taurus*, at some distance from the border between *Taurus* and *Aries*; neither does it conform to Ibn Ezra's own view (see above) that the *Pleiades* are on the border between *Aries* and *Taurus*. However, as

Greek mythology as the seven daughters of Atlas, who were placed among the stars in order to escape the hunter Orion's designs on their virginity.[24] This has a Jewish pendant in the legend about the maid ***Isṭahar,*** who was placed among the stars of ***Kîmah*** as a reward for her constancy in denying the advances of ***Shemḥazai.***[25] To the Arabs, the ***Pleiades*** appear as a single woman, her right hand stretched out and visible in ***Cassiopeia,*** the five stars of the W representing the tips of the five fingers. The star at the right end of the W, designated by the prosaic β *Cas*. in the catalogues,[26] has a more romantic name in Arabic: *al-kaff al-khaḍîb* = "The hand dyed [with *ḥenna*]."[27] It has been suggested that this was originally the name of the entire group of five stars, Arab fancy regarding them as the five nails painted with *ḥenna* at the ends of the fingers on the outstretched right hand of the woman whose face is represented by the ***Pleiades***.[28]

III

At first glance, it seems that any thought about Cassiopeia is quite as far from any aspect of Hebraic or Judaic lore as the above-mentioned five stars are from the solar system and from our humble abode on the sun's "third planet" Earth. However, there is evidence – which appears to have so far escaped scholars'

conventional lines of this kind have been subject to considerable variations, there is no doubt that Ibn Ezra is referring to the ***Pleiades***. The authority he follows (as does Kimḥi with אמרו ז״ל in his comment on Amos 5:8) is probably TB Ber. 58b, near end, where his *Vorlage* evidently read מאי כימה – instead of מאי עש in the extant text – a variant also evident in Rashi ad BM 106b s.v. עד זמן and ad R.ha-Sh. 11b s.v. ואזדו, in Tos *ibid.* s.v. יום and in a great many other early authorities. Rejecting the identification of the ***Pleiades*** with ***Kîmah***, Ibn Ezra ultimately identifies the latter with "a large star in the Ecliptic, north of its intersection with the Equator" (בפאת שמאל מגלגל הנוטה...), in his comment to Job 9:9, and supplements this with the description: "a large star named the Left Eye of the Bull" (כוכב גדול יקרא עין השור השמאלי...), ad *ibid.* 38:31, which stands for α *Tauri*, also known by its Arabic name *Aldabaran* (the westernized form of *ad-dabarân*), as clearly stated in his *Kelî Neḥosheth*, p. 31:22. Further discussion of this question is outside the scope of the present paper.

24 See PW, s.v. Atlas, pp. 2120–2122.

25 *Yalquṭ* No. 44, ed. Frankfort-Main (1687–1709), p. 12b:5* ff = ed. Jerusalem (1959/60), p. 24b:31 ff.

26 E.g., *Almagest*, pp. 60–61 (p. 38); also Boss's ***Catalogue***, pp. 2–3, No. 12; see also our Figs. 5 and 7.

27 Kunitzsch, p. 152:16 ff; also p. 66:1 ff.

28 Ideler, p. 84:16–85:3. See also Ibn Ezra's reference to "The Woman's Head" in his treatise on the astrolabe, *loc. cit.* (n. 23 above).

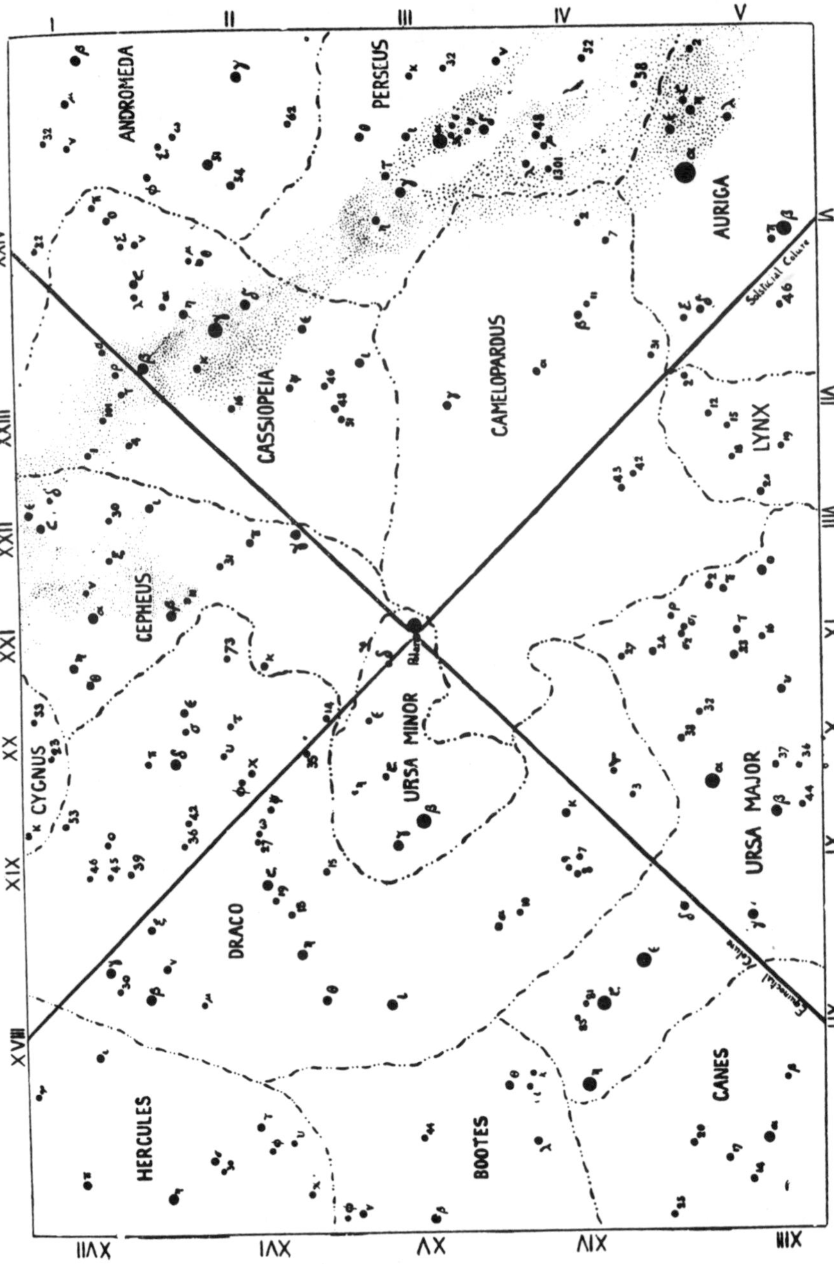

Fig. 7. The north circumpolar region

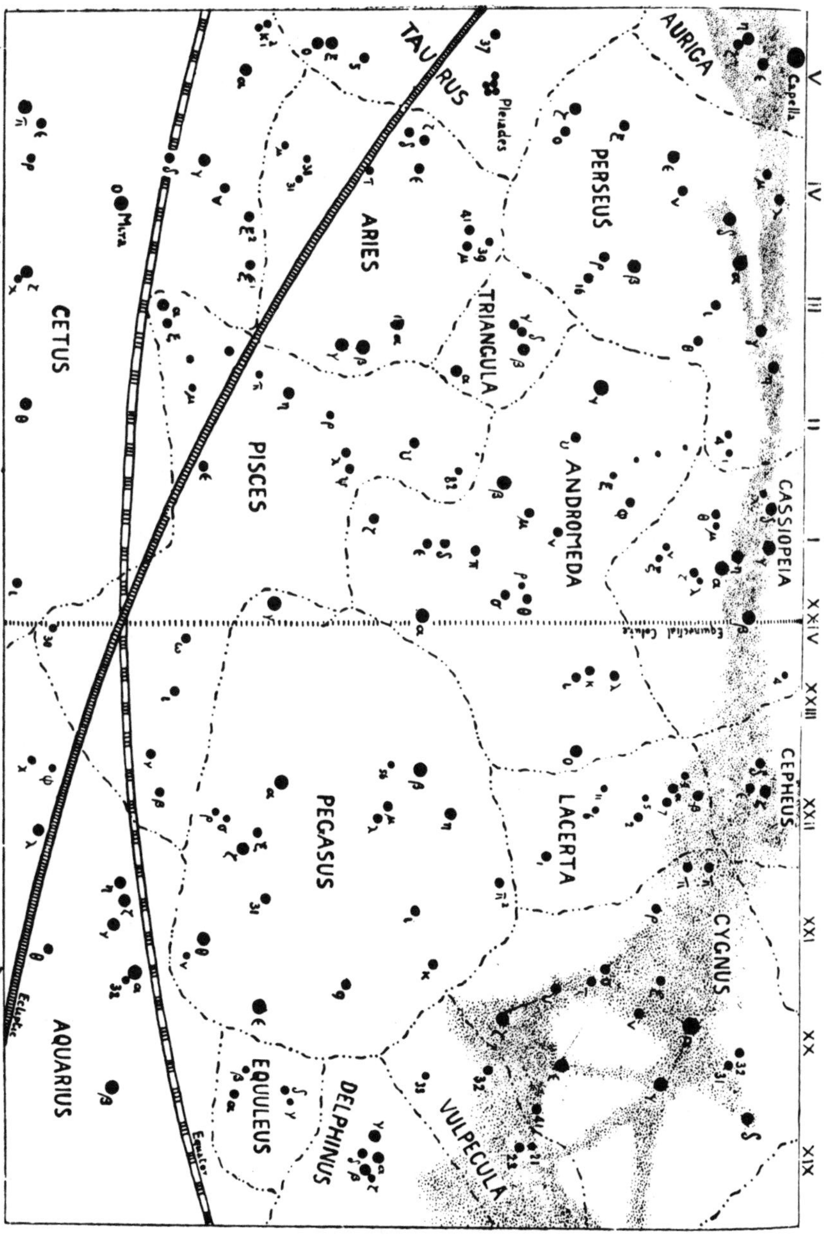

Fig. 8. The region of the royal family

attention – that these stars are not outside the range of rabbinic thought, albeit they are associated with ideas that bear no resemblance to the Greek myth of the boastful Ethiopian queen. They may, in fact, be referred to in a biblical text presenting a dialogue between God and Zion (Isa. 49:14 ff). Zion is portrayed as a wife, forsaken and forgotten by her husband, bemoaning her lot. The divine reply is (*ibid.* v. 16): "Behold, I have graven thee *upon the palms of my hands*, thy walls are continually before me." In the renderings of most of the ancient versions – such as ...כדעל ידין את ציירא קדמי... (= ...on the hands, as it were, art thou depicted...) in the Targum, *...in manibus meis descripsi te...* in the Vulgate, and the more specific ...על פסא דאידי רשמתיכי (= upon *the palm of* my hand...) in the Peshiṭto – the phrase is understood in the sense of a boldly anthropomorphic metaphor: "God has, as it were, Zion engraved on his two hands. Hence he can never forget her sad plight." Rashi, Ibn Ezra and Kimḥi, followed by a great many modern commentators,[29] likewise take the phrase in this sense. Modern commentators differ as to whether it is the name or the image of Zion that is said to be engraved. Some of them[30] claim support for the latter from the Septuagint rendering,... ἐζωγράφηκά σου τὰ τείχη[31] καὶ ἐνώπιόν μου εἶ διὰ παντός, which they say presupposes the Hebrew *Vorlage* ...חקותי חומותיך| נגדי [את] תמיד = "...I have graven thy walls upon my hands, before me art thou continually." Actually that *Vorlage* is far from being proved. It is equally plausible that the Septuagint rendering is due to the Hebrew original having been dictated to the translator who heard – or thought to have heard – ...חקותיחומותיך... (= *...ḥaqqôthîḥômôthayikh...*), with assimilation of כף רפה (= *kh*) to חי"ת (= *ḥ*), as common in the *Sandhi* pronunciation of Hebrew,[32] and neglect of the doubling of the חי"ת[33] instead of the correct חקותיך חומותיך (= *ḥaqqothikh ḥomotayikh*). It is also possible that the translator took חומותיך as

29 See, *inter alia*, the comments *ad loc.* in A. Dillman, *Commentary on Isaiah*, ed. R. Kittel (Leipzig 1898), p. 430; also those of E. J. Kissane (Dublin 1941–43) and of R.B.Y. Scott in *The Interpreter's Bible* (New York 1956); to which many more could be added.

30 See Dillman-Kittel, *loc. cit.* The image of the walls, evidently on the basis of the supposed *Vorlage* of the LXX, is also said to be engraved upon the hands in J. Skinner's comment *ad loc.* in the *Cambridge Bible for Schools* (1902). The same appears to be the basis of the rather free rendering in the *New English Bible.*

31 The slight textual variants in LXX$^{\aleph AQ}$ do not make any difference whatever to the meaning of the phrase. For the sigla "ℵAQ," see the prefaces to Vol. I (pp. vii–viii, xx–xxiii) and Vol. III (pp. vii–ix) of H.B. Swete's 3rd ed. of the LXX (Cambridge 1901).

32 On *Sandhi* see BL, p. 199, n. 1; the phonetic phenomenon concerned was already anticipated by Ibn Janaḥ in *KaL*, pp. 236–238 (= *SR*, pp. 251–254).

33 In keeping with the Massoretic pointing of Biblical Hebrew, in which this guttural never has the *daghesh forte*. One may perhaps also take into consideration the pronunciation of חקותיכומותיך by way of the change, by assimilation, of ךח into ככ (see GK, 19 f and n. 1

being in apposition to the suffix ך——,[34] i.e., as the object of the verb חקותי. According to this second alternative, the previously mentioned claim remains substantially correct; viz., that the Septuagint rendering, though not incompatible with the Massoretic Text, presupposes the engraving of the image of the walls of Zion.

However, a case can be made for the idea that these interpretations allude to the selfsame figure: the walls of Jerusalem — stylized from the real shape of their battlements with merlons and embrasures, viz. ...⎍⎍... — were likened in shape to a capital M or W. The latter is nearly identical with the shape of the letter *Shin* in the Palaeo-Hebrew script, the initial of Jerusalem's ancient name שלם.[35] Neither is it greatly dissimilar from the Palaeo-Hebrew

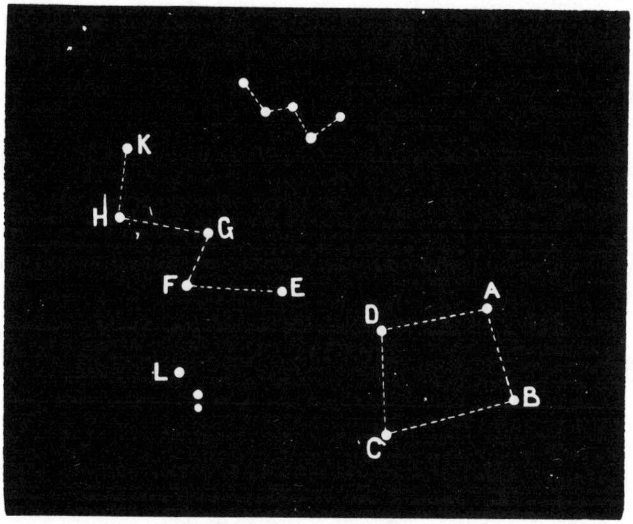

Fig. 9. The greater "W" and the "Square":
A — β *Pegasi*; B — α *Peg.*, C — γ *Peg.*; D — α *Andromedae*; E — β *And.*, F — β *Trianguli*; G — γ *And.*; H — β *Persei*; K — α *Persei*; L — α *Arietis*

ibid., and also BL 15a-b and 52u) — or of כף רפה replacing חי"ת — and the ungrammatical suppression of *daghesh forte* (כ̄ instead of ככ = כּ). Both these phonetic phenomena are among the characteristic features of Spoken Israeli Hebrew (= SIH) which, although often referred to as "Sefaradi," is mainly *Ashkenazic* in phonetic structure; see W. Weinberg, *Journal of Semitic Studies*, 11 (1966) 46 (1.3—1.3.2.) and 53 (3.1.2.3, near end), on the complete disappearance of *daghesh forte* from SIH and the replacement of חי"ת (= ḥ) by כ̄ (= kh).

34 For instances of this kind of apposition, see GK 131m.

35 Cf. Gen. 14:18, Ps. 76:3; see also Josephus, *Antiquities* I, x, 2 and *War* VI, x, 1 = Loeb Classical Library: *Josephus* IV, pp. 88—89 (*Ant.* I, 180); III, pp. 500—503 (*War* VI,

Ṣâdê, the initial of ציון, the speaker in Isa. 49:14 to whom על כפים חקותיך (*ibid.* v. 16) is addressed. This is particularly true if, in order to complete the shaft of the Palaeo-Hebrew *Ṣâdê*, the line from ε *Cas.* to δ *Cas.* is continued to the luminous star α *And.* or, with a slight curve, toward one of the two appreciably nearer points β *And.* or γ *And.* in the contiguous constellation *Andromeda*; i.e., to one of the points marked *G, E* and *D* in Fig. 9.[36]

With כפים in its literal sense, this resembles the popular notion, often heard in Eastern Europe, that when the palms are half folded the lines inside them combine into the shape of the capital M, which conveys the saddening *M[emento] M[ori]* = "Remember, thou must die."[37]

On the other hand, if כפים is thought of as synonymous with the sky or with something in the sky, one is at once reminded of the W-like shape of the five principal stars in *Cassiopeia* and especially of their Arabic name *al-kaff* (= the Hand). An interpretation of כפים in this or in a similar sense is traceable from at least as early as the age of Rashi (1040–1105) and has even been attributed to R. Saʿadya Ga'on (892–942).[38] In his commentary on Isaiah, Rashi quotes from an anonymous source (ד״א = דבר אחר) that על כפים (*ibid.* 49:16) stands for מעל ענני הכבוד (= that which is above the clouds of glory), like על כפים in Job 36:32. This probably refers to the sky. It is in fact explicitly stated in Rashi's commentary on Lamentations, likewise quoting an anonymous source (ד״א), that אל כפים (*ibid.* 3:41) – parallel to בשמים in the second half of that verse and therefore quasi-synonymous with it – stands for אל העננים אל [ה]שמים, adducing in support of this Job 36:32, and also I Kings 18:44, where a little cloud (עב קטנה) is likened to a man's hand (כף איש).

The same two texts are adduced in Rashi's commentary on Job[39] in support of כפים (*ibid.* 36:32) in the sense of clouds. In their respective commentaries on

438–439); cf. also *ibid.*, V, pp. 392–395 (*Ant.* VII, 67–68) and n. *a ibid.*, I, pp. 232–233 (*Against Apion* I, 74).

36 From Maunder, p. 79; see also Fig. 8.

37 This phrase "rang a bell" to several members of the staff of the Department of Classics, University College, London, yet none of them could help me trace any ancient or medieval source in which it occurs.

38 Regarding the date of his birth see Malter, pp. 421 ff; also *EJ(E)*, XIV, col. 543.

39 Regarding the authenticity of this commentary, see the note in the editions ad Job 40:20: עד כאן יסד רש״י וכו׳; also the remark עיין איוב סי׳ ח׳ אמר שם פירש רש״י in Heilprin, *Seder ha-Doroth*, ed. pr. (Karlsruhe 1769), p. 177a, s.v. רי״ש near end, quoted and criticized by Azulai, p. 74c s.v. רש״י פירש; the correction of ח׳ to מ׳ in ed. Naphtali Maskil le'Ethan, III, p. 93b (Warsaw 1878–82; reprinted Jerusalem 1955/6). See also Isaac Maarsen on Rashi's commentaries to Proverbs and Job, *MGWJ*, 83 (New Series Vol. 47, 1939; reprinted Tübingen 1963), 442–456, on the basis of sundry manuscripts and old editions (specified on p. 445, n. 12, *ibid.*), who is inclined to the view of L. Donath (*ibid.*, 443–444) that the

Isaiah, Ibn Ezra (1092–1167) and Kimḥi (1160–1235)[40] quote the same interpretation, in respect of כפים (*ibid.* 49:16), in the name of R. Saʿadya Ga'on.[41] This is contrary to the rendering of the crucial על כפים חקותיך (*ibid.*) as וכאנך עלי אלכפין רסמתך – fairly close to the aforementioned targumic rendering (*ibid.*) – in the Ga'on's Arabic version of Isaiah.[42] It is also at variance with אל כפים in Job 36:32, rendered ועלי אעמאלהם (= and because of their deeds) in his Arabic version of Job, with the comment קולה על כפים... מענאה על מעשה כפים (= מה שאמר על כ'... טעמו על מ' כ'), i.e., "hands" in this context denote the "deeds of human hands,"[43] an interpretation quoted in Rashi (*ibid.*) as ורבותינו אמרו וכו'. It is likewise at variance with the rendering of the same אל כפים as מע כפינא (= עם כַּפֵּינוּ = with our hands), akin to Rashi's first and Ibn Ezra's second interpretation (*ibid.*), in an Arabic version of Lamentations held to be the work of the Ga'on.[44] All this notwithstanding, the attribution to the Ga'on appears to be correct, as it is supported by his Arabic version of the Pentateuch,[45] where כַּפִּי (= my hand) in Ex. 33:22–23 is rendered סחאבי (= my cloud). That cloud is evidently related somehow to the cloud associated with the revelation of the Divine Glory,[46] which is apparently also alluded to in the phrase ענני הכבוד in Rashi to Isa. 49:16 (quoted above). Consequently, it cannot be a mere condensation of vapors in the atmosphere, like עננים in other contexts. In particular, the rendering of the crucial על כפים

commentary to Job was written in Rashi's old age, did not receive his finishing touches and contains additions by his pupils. Be that as it may, the crucial comment on Job 36:32 – not mentioned in Maarsen's list of passages in which later additions have to be reckoned with (*ibid.*, 448–449) – appears to be an authentic comment by Rashi himself.

40 Kimḥi repeats this in his *Mikhlol* s.v. כפף. Not so כפים in that sense in Lam. 3:41 in his commentary *ibid.*, which is his own and not quoted in the Ga'on's name; *contra* Steinschneider in his *Catalogue of the Bodleian*, p. 2189, line 8 from below, quoted thence by Malter, p. 324, lines 11 ff from below. Moreover, it is contrary to the Arabic rendering of Lam. 3:41 in a manuscript held to be the Ga'on's version; see n. 44 below.

41 אמר הגאון... (*ibid.*) refers to the Ga'on Saʿadya, as is evident from the quotations so introduced in Ibn Ezra's commentary on the Pentateuch *passim* from Gen. 1:2–3 s.v. תהו and ויאמר, etc., all of which tally with the renderings in the Ga'on's Arabic version, ed. J. Derenbourg (Paris 1893).

42 Ed. J. and M. Derenbourg (Paris 1896); see also n. 5 *ad loc.*

43 See his note *ad loc.* in ed. Bacher (see n. 21 above), quoting as a parallel Joel 2:6, where he explains קבצו פארור in the sense of קבצו שחור פארור. The wording of this note in ed. Qafaḥ (see n. 21 above) is rather different, but the meaning is the same.

44 In B.M. Ms. Or. 2375, col. 191c, attributed to R. Saʿadya Ga'on in G. Margoliouth, *Catalogue of the Hebrew and Samaritan MSS in the B.M.* (reprinted London 1965), I, p. 112a.

45 *Loc. cit.* in n. 41 above; see also nn. 1–10 *ad loc.*

46 Cf. Ex. 40:34 ff and parallels.

חקותיך as עננים would be pointless if it stood for physical clouds, which are symbols of transient rather than permanent shapes.[47] Hence, כפים, whenever it is said to stand for the clouds – whether derived from the כִּפָּה overhead,[48] i.e., כיפת הרקיע (= the heavenly arch, the sky),[49] or from phrases like ימיני טפחה שמים (Isa. 48:13)[50] and ושמים בזרת תכן (*ibid.* 40:12) – leads again to כפים in the sense of the sky.

The image of the universe above man's earthly abode as a superstructure of canopies above canopies, the clouds forming the lowest canopy, is met with in cultures widely separated in space and time. It is therefore not surprising that the above quasi-synonymity of "cloud" with "sky" has parallels in languages other than Hebrew. The Latin *nebula* (= "mist" or "vapor") is used by astronomers as a technical term for distant celestial objects outside the galaxy of which our sun, with its planets and their satellites, is but a small part.[51] The German *Himmelbett* stands for a "four-poster" with a canopy as the counterpart of the celestial vault. The English "ceiling" is held to derive from *ciel,* the French for "heaven." The Hungarian *mennyezet* (= ceiling) derives from *menny* (the shorter form of *mennyország*), which is synonymous with *ég*, the Hungarian for "heaven." Many more examples could easily be added.

כפים = עננים = שמים is in fact clearly presupposed in the interpretation of כפים, alongside its literal sense, in an *Aggadah*, based on Isa. 49:16,[52] and quoted in the name of R. Berechiah, a Palestinian *Amora* of the fourth generation who flourished at the beginning of the 4th century C.E.,[53] as follows: "... the Assembly of Israel... said before Him: 'Oh, Master of the universe, set me as a seal upon thy heart, as a seal upon thine arm.'[54] Thereupon, the Holy

47 Cf. Hos. 6:4, 13:3 and Job 7:9; also the successive facetious comparisons of a cloud to the shapes of a camel, a weasel and a whale in Hamlet, Act III, Sc. ii.

48 As per the second suggestion in R. David Altschuhler's מצודת ציון ad Job 36:32, already anticipated in Kimḥi's *Mikhlol* s.v. כפף.

49 Cf. TB BB 25b and parallels.

50 See Ibn Ezra *ad loc.*: שמדד השמים בטפח; also Kimḥi, *ibid.*: תכן אותם בטפחו.

51 Cf. Webb, pp. 21–23, concerning "The Great Nebula in Andromeda," the most famous object of this kind; also *ibid., passim*, for other nebulae. The definition "distant stars... outside solar system," in the *Concise Oxford Dictionary* (5th ed., 1966), p. 805a, is not quite accurate.

52 TB Ta'an. 4a. See also Cant. Rabbah 8:5 and its parallels in *Pesiqta de R. Kahana*, ed. B. Mandelbaum (New York 1962), I, p. 292, also referred to in *Yalquṭ* No. 333 and in *'Aggadath Bereshith*, ch. 42 (p. 55 in ed. Lublin 1883).

53 See *JE*, III, pp. 52–53; *EJ(G)*, IV, cols. 181–182; *EJ(E)*, IV, col. 596.

54 Cant. 8:6, whose interpretation here is in keeping with the rabbinic view of Canticles, as a whole, as an allegory symbolizing the relationship between God and His chosen people Israel in terms of the love between groom and bride.

One Blessed be He said to her: 'Oh, my daughter, thou requirest of me something that is sometimes seen and sometimes not seen, but I shall make for thee something that is always seen; as it is said (Isa. 49:16), I have graven thee upon the palms of my hands.'" In the commentary attributed to Rashi,[55] s.v. **פעמים** *ad loc.*, this is expounded as follows: "When a person is undressed his arm is seen and so is the region of his heart, but they are not seen when he is dressed; whilst the palm, like the hand, is seen at all times." In the second explanation, quoted in the name of the commentator's teacher (= **רבי**),[56] the sign engraved **על כפים** is said to be a sign in the sky (**על השמים**),[57] in the shape of a human figure on a throne (**צורת אדם שהוא בכסא**), in the sense of **אל כפים** in Lamentations 3:41.

In view of the close similarity of this phrase to Ibn Zeraḥ's aforesaid **היושבת על הכסא** as the designation of *Cassiopeia*, "The Lady on her Throne," there is no doubt whatever that this phrase likewise alludes to that constellation. The more so as the Arabic names *kaff ath-thurayyâ al-yumnâ al-mabsûṭa* and *al-kaff al-khaḍîb*[58] of β *Cas.* and/or of all the five prominent stars α, β, γ, δ and ε in *Cassiopeia* bear a striking resemblance to **כפים** in Hebrew.

Why then, is she referred to as **אדם**, not as **אשה**, the usual Hebrew term for "woman"? It is possibly sheer delicacy that the image on the throne, said to be always exposed to sight, is not explicitly referred to as the image of a woman. In addition, the crucial phrase **צורת אדם וכו'** may be due in part to the impact of **כתפארת אדם לשבת בית** in Isa. 44:13, a phrase which the Targum renders **כתושבחת אתתא וכו'**, referring to the "*fair* sex." Nor is it altogether impossible that the likeness of the appearance of a man upon the likeness of a throne in Ezek. 1:26, symbolizing the divine presence, likewise contributed to **צורת אדם שהוא בכסא**, ousting the image of Cassiopeia, the *Lady* on her Throne.

55 Its authenticity was already questioned in R. Jacob Emden's *Mishneh Leḥem*, according to the testimony of Azulai, p. 75c, s.v. הרב הנז[כר] במשנה לחם הוסיף; I have been unable to trace this in the ed. pr. of that work, a supplement to Emden's *Leḥem Shamayim* (Wandsbeck 1727/8). Substantial arguments against authenticity were raised in L. Zunz, *Gottesdienstliche Vorträge*, 2nd ed. (Frankfort-Main 1892), pp. 46 n. *b*, 68 n. *d*, 96 n. *b*, 398 n. *a* (line 18 from end). The subject is discussed at length in I.H. Weiss, *Dor Dor we-Doreshav* (New York – Berlin 1923/4), IV, pp. 330–33.

56 Of course, his identity depends on that of the commentator.

57 The omission of על suggested in הגהות הב"ח *ad loc.*, n. 7, seems unnecessary.

58 See end of Section II above and nn. 17 and 27–28 *ibid.*

IV

It is very tempting to assume that the phrase "... something that is *always seen*..." (דבר שנראה לעולם) in the above-mentioned *Aggadah* of R. Berechiah is what prompted the unknown commentator on *Ta'anith* to interpret the *Aggadah* in the sense of a specific allusion to *Cassiopeia*, a group of circumpolar stars which never sets below the horizon and therefore remains in sight throughout all nights of the year; and also that the allusion is in fact within the purview of the plain meaning of R. Berechiah's phrase and even of the scriptural phrase על כפים חקותיך on which he was commenting.

The attractiveness of this assumption is enhanced by the fact that in the present century the five stars α, β, γ, δ and ε *Cas.* are indeed circumpolar not only at the latitude of London (ca. lat. 51°30′N.) but also at the much lower latitude of the northernmost region of Galilee (ca. lat. 33°30′N.). This is evident from the mean position of α *Cas.*, the southernmost of the five stars concerned, which has been calculated at Decl. 55°59.′3N. and Decl. 56°33′N. at the respective epochs 1900 C.E.[59] and 2000 C.E.,[60] which correspond to the N.P.D.'s 34°00.′7 and 33°27′, since Northern declinations are complementary to N.P.D.'s Hence, since the local altitude of the celestial North Pole corresponds everywhere on the earth's surface to the geographical latitude of the place concerned, the star α *Cas.* and *a fortiori* the more northerly stars β, γ, δ and ε *Cas.* are circumpolar in the current century at all locations of geographical latitude not lower than lat. 34°00.′7N. Adding the effect of horizontal refraction, which makes the apparent Zenith Distance of a celestial body 35′ less than its true Zenith Distance,[61] all the five principal stars of *Cassiopeia* – including the southernmost, α *Cas.* – are in the current century circumpolar stars, never disappearing at night (by setting below the horizon) at Northern geographical latitudes not lower than 33°26′. As stated, this includes the extreme north of Galilee.

We may recall now that, at one stage of the Arabs' stellar nomenclature, the individual star β *Cas.* was specifically named *al-kaff al-khaḍîb* (= the Painted Hand).[62] That star, at Decl. 59°10′N. (= N.P.D. 30°50′) at 2000 C.E., is closer to the celestial North Pole than α *Cas.* – at Decl. 56°33′N. (= N.P.D. 33°27′) at 2000 C.E., as stated above – but farther from it than γ *Cas.* at Decl. 60°43′N. (= N.P.D. 29°17′) at 2000 C.E.;[63] or δ and ε *Cas.*, whose N.P.D.'s

59 See Maunder, p. 264. For a more precise figure see n. 64 below.

60 See Webb, p. 286a. The changing of the position is due to the precession of the equinoxes (see n. 12 above); see also n. 66 below.

61 See Smart, pp. 58–72, esp. p. 69.

62 See end of Section II above and nn. 27–28 *ibid.*

63 See Webb, pp. 285a and 286a.

are also smaller than that of β *Cas*. Hence, in respect of β *Cas*., which is more appropriately referred to as כפים than α *Cas*. – as also, *a fortiori*, in respect of γ, δ and ε *Cas*.[64] – the circumpolarity of *Cassiopeia* extends southwards to lat. 30°50′N. and, by reason of the above-mentioned effect of horizontal refraction, even as far south as lat. 30°15′N. This includes not only the whole of Galilee but also most of the area of the modern State of Israel, as far south as the region of the Southern *Negev*, substantially beyond El Arish at lat. 31°4′N. (= the *Rhinocorura* or *Rhinocolura* of the ancients),[65] yet not quite as far south as Eilath, at lat. 29°30′N.

For all its attractiveness, however, this interpretation of דבר שנראה לעולם cannot be accepted without very substantial modification, because of the well-known continuous changes in the Declinations of α, β, γ, δ and ε *Cas*. and in their complementary N.P.D.'s – on a par with those of all other stars and with corresponding changes in most of their other coordinates – due to the precession of the equinoxes.[66] If one neglects other factors, whose effects appear to be negligible and therefore need not be taken into account – such as

64 The declinations of all the five principal stars in *Cassiopeia* at 1900 C.E. are given in Boss's *Catalogue* as follows: α *Cas*. at 55°59′20″.15 N. (No. 135, pp. 6–7; more precise than Maunder's ...59.′3 quoted in n. 59 above); β *Cas*. at 58°35′53.″45 N. (No. 12, pp. 2–3); γ *Cas*. at 60°10′31″ N. (No. 199, pp. 8–9); δ *Cas*. at 59°42′56.″03 N. (No. 314, pp. 14–15); ε *Cas*. at 63°10′39.″51 N. (No. 419, pp. 18–19). These correspond to the following N.P.D.'s: α *Cas*. at 34°0′39.″85, β *Cas*. at 31°24′6.″55, γ *Cas*. at 29°49′29″, δ *Cas*. at 30°17′3.″97 and ε *Cas*. at 26°49′20.″09.

65 See P. Ferrarius and M. A. Baudrand, *Lexicon Geographicum* (Paris 1670), p. 129b; see also *HDB*, I, p. 667b, s.v. Egypt, River of.

66 See Smart, pp. 228–47; especially pp. 240 ff. As for references to the precession in exegetical and halakhic works among the rabbinic sources – as distinct from rabbinic writers' works on astronomy – note Ibn Ezra to Amos 5:8, estimating it at about 1°30′ in 100 years, and Maimonides at "the rate of the sun's daily motion (= 0°59′8.″33) in about 70 years"; see Hil. Yesodey ha-Torah 3:7 (where והירח in the editions, absent in the manuscripts, is due to a scribal error), Hil. Qiddush ha-Ḥodesh 12:1; English tr. by S. Gandz (*YJS*, XI, 1956). p. 45, also the notes of Gandz and O. Neugebauer, *ibid*., pp. 99 and 148, and my correction of the latter (*YJS*, XIV, 1961), pp. 581–2. Whilst the above two figures are explicitly stated to be approximations only, the precise figure of $51^{ii}26^{iii}$ per annum is given in Ibn Ezra's treatise on the astrolabe, *loc. cit*. (n. 23 above), p. 31:9–12. This corresponds to $1°0^{i}0^{ii}20^{iii}$ in 70 years, which is less close to Maimonides' figure of $59^{i}8.^{ii}33$ than to his alternative approximation, 1° in 70 years (the figure usually quoted in the name of Albategni *alias* Albatani [fl. 877 C.E.], probably likewise meant only as an approximation). Further, $51^{ii}26^{iii}$ p.a. corresponds to $1°25^{i}43^{ii}20^{iii}$ in 100 years, as against Ibn Ezra's own approximate 1°30′ in the above-mentioned comment on Amos 5:8. His precise figure, although rather in excess of modern estimates (see Smart, p. 238: 50.″2564 at 1900 C.E. + 0.″000222 p.a.), compares quite favorably with other medieval astronomers' estimates.

aberration, the annual parallax, nutation, the secular diminution of the obliquity,[67] the proper motion of the stars[68] and the variations in the rate of the Earth's rotation and in the position of its axis on the surface[69] – it appears that in 1200–1300 C.E., the probable period of the anonymous commentator on *Taʿanith*, the W-shaped group of five stars in *Cassiopeia*, circumpolar in his presumed habitat France (as far south as, say, Marseilles at lat. 43°17′N.), was not circumpolar at Jerusalem (lat. 31°47′N.), let alone in 300–350 C.E., the generation of R. Berechiah,[70] and *a fortiori* in 600–500 B.C.E., the century of the Babylonian Exile, which forms the background to Isa. 49:14–21.[71] This appears to lead to the inescapable conclusion that a Palestinian homilist's

67 See Smart, pp. 178 ff (esp. pp. 182–4), pp. 217 ff, 231 ff.

68 *Ibid.*, pp. 249 ff. The respective annual rates of the proper motion of α and γ *Cas.* are negligible (0.″062 and 0.″030), whilst those of β and δ *Cas.* and especially of ε *Cas.* (0.″561, 0.″306 and 1.″24, respectively) do, of course, add up quite considerably in the course of many centuries; provided that appreciable portions of them are in Declination (which is not clarified in my source: Charles Whyte, *The Constellations and Their History* [London 1928], pp. 165–6).

69 See W. H. Munk and G.J.F. Macdonald, *The Rotation of the Earth* (Cambridge 1966), *passim*. Violent changes in that position – as in the wild theory of I. Velikovsky in *Worlds in Collision* (London 1950), *passim*, without reliable evidence in recorded history – have not been considered here.

70 See Section III above and n. 53 *ibid.*

71 The declinations of α, β, γ, δ and ε *Cas.* are readily calculable (see Smart, p. 40, near end) from their latitudes and longitudes in the *Almagest*, p. 38 (60), at the epoch of Ptolemy (130 C.E.); or, as is held by the consensus of scholars, from their longitudinal counterparts at the epoch of Hipparchus (135 B.C.E.) by subtracting 2°40′ – which Ptolemy is assumed to have added (by reason of his wrong estimate of the Precession) to Hipparchus' values of longitude. Calculation shows the Decl. of α *Cas.* to be 45°59′51″ N. at 130 C.E. or, more correctly, 44°52′20″ N. at 135 B.C.E. These figures correspond approximately to the respective N.P.D.'s 44° and 45°, which exceed the N.P.D. of α *Cas.* at 1900 C.E. – about 34° (see n. 64 above) – by about 10° and 11°, respectively. There is a similar rate of about 10° lower Decl. N. (= 10° greater N.P.D.) in the case of β, γ, δ and ε *Cas.*; i.e. at the epoch of Ptolemy or of Hipparchus, the approximate N.P.D.'s of β, γ, δ and ε *Cas.* were 41°, 40°, 41° and 37°, respectively. Hence, none of the five stars in the W of *Cassiopeia* could have been circumpolar in Jerusalem (lat. 31°47′ N.) at 135 B.C.E. (let alone 600–500 B.C.E.). It is also fairly safe to assume that none of them was circumpolar in Jerusalem at 300–350 C.E. Neither is any of them – with the possible exception of ε *Cas.* – likely to have been circumpolar in Jerusalem at 1200–1300 C.E. There can be no doubt, however, that in that century they were already circumpolar in the South of France and *a fortiori* in higher Northern latitudes. One reaches these conclusions by plausible interpolations of the N.P.D values of α, β, γ, δ and ε *Cas.* at 300–350 C.E. and at 1200–1300 C.E. between their approximate N.P.D.'s 45°, 41°, 40°, 41° and 37° at 135 B.C.E., as shown above, and their counterparts 34°, 31½°, 30°, 30¼° and 27° at 1900 according to Boss's *Catalogue* (n. 64 above).

allusion with the words דבר שנראה לעולם to the W in *Cassiopeia* as a group of circumpolar stars is impossible on astronomical grounds at Pseudo-Rashi's epoch no less than at R. Berechiah's. Hence, Pseudo-Rashi's identification of על כפים in the sense of על שמים with צורת אדם שהוא בכסא – which distinctly points to *Cassiopeia*, as has been shown – would seem to evince not only an ignorance of the precessional displacements of the stars but also the mistaken belief that conditions for star-gazing in his country were the same as in R. Berechiah's habitat further south. Hence, either R. Berechiah's homily does not allude to *Cassiopeia* at all, or the allusion is in no way connected with the crucial phrase דבר שנראה לעולם.

On second thoughts, however, לעולם may not have been meant in its strictly literal sense of "always" but in its wider sense of "most of the time." This may be compared with the wider sense of its counterpart תמיד in Biblical Hebrew with regard to the shewbread[72] and other sacrificial ritualia,[73] the presence of each of which, by its very nature, was intermittent; the sole exception was the perpetual fire on the altar of the burnt offerings (Lev. 6:6). In this sense, לעולם is quite correct as a description of the visibility of *Cassiopeia* at Jerusalem's lat. 31°47′N. in 300–350 C.E. and *a fortiori* in 1200–1300 C.E., the respective epochs of R. Berechiah and of the anonymous commentator on *Ta'anith*. Indeed, even at the earlier of those two epochs each of the five stars concerned, whose N.P.D.'s can be calculated by interpolation from their respective counterparts 45°, 41°, 40°, 41° and 37° at 135 B.C.E., was above Jerusalem's horizon for part of the night (varying in length in accordance with the season) throughout the year, as their Northern Declinations – which can again be calculated from their approximate counterparts 45°, 49°, 50°, 49° and 53° at 135 B.C.E. – exceed the sun's maximum Northern Declination (about $23\frac{1}{2}$°) by so much that at Jerusalem's latitude the intervals from their rising to their setting very appreciably exceed the interval from sunrise to sunset, even at the summer solstice when daytime is at its longest.[74] Hence, at the two epochs mentioned, each of our five stars was necessarily above the Jerusalem horizon for some of the night throughout the year, even in midsummer when the night is shortest, in the interval from the end of the evening twilight to the beginning of the morning

72 Ex. 25:29, Lev. 24:8, Num. 4:7; cf. the observation of R. José in M. Men. 11, 7: אפילו אלו נוטלין ואלו מניחין אף זו היתה תמיד and its exposition in TB Men. 99b.

73 E.g., the Perpetual Light (Ex. 27:20, Lev. 24:2–4), the Daily Burnt Offerings (Ex. 29:38, Num. 28:3,6) and parallels; etc.

74 The intervals concerned are determined by the solar and respective sidereal Hour Angles at rising and setting; see Smart, pp. 47 and 52, for their computation. Our statement concerning the N.P.D.'s and Northern Declinations of the five stars in question at 300–350 B.C.E. is based on the calculations in n. 71 above.

twilight.[75] This was probably true even at earlier epochs, including the epoch of the Babylonian Exile (600–500 B.C.E). It is, in fact, probable that the Northern Declinations of the five stars concerned are always greater than the sun's maximum Northern Declination.[76] Hence, in this modified sense of the crucial phrase, R. Berechiah's interpretation of על כפים חקותיך in Isa. 49:16 as a reference to דבר שנראה לעולם is more than a mere homily; i.e., the scriptural phrase may in fact allude to the Lady on her Throne as a celestial object not completely out of sight during any night of the year.

Moreover, there is yet another consideration that necessitates the wider interpretation of לעולם with respect to the visibility of circumpolar stars (say, of the W in *Cassiopeia* at the present epoch). In fact, the strictly literal sense of the phrase is inadmissible in regard to the fixed stars observed at any place on the Earth's surface subject to normal atmospheric limitations on star-gazing: apart from the moon and some of the planets (in some of their phases), no celestial object is visible in the sky during those parts of the twilight when the sun is only a few degrees below the horizon,[77] and *a fortiori* in daytime when the sun is above the horizon.[78] Thus, the suggestion that על כפים חקותיך could allude to the W in *Cassiopeia* at the latitude of Jerusalem at the epoch of R. Berechiah or of the Babylonian Exile is as unobjectionable on astronomical grounds as is the analogous suggestion in relation to the latitude of Pseudo-Rashi's habitat and his epoch.

There still remains the difficulty that, in R. Berechiah's homily, the "heart" and the "arm" (על לבך... על זרועך), as objects at times seen and at times not seen (דבר שפעמים נראה ופעמים אינו נראה), are said to be in contrast to the "palms" (על כפים) as objects always in sight (דבר שנראה לעולם). If *Cassiopeia* was not continually in sight in the homilist's habitat at his epoch, as has been demonstrated, it is odd that the W in *Cassiopeia* should have been equated with דבר שנראה לעולם rather than with דבר שפעמים נראה. The likely solution of this

75 In the present context these terms are used in the sense of the minimum depression of the sun at which the stars concerned become visible. This minimum varies from star to star in accordance with its position and intensity of light. Regarding some of the stars in *Cassiopeia*, see Webb, p. 72, n. 1. As is well known, the length of the interval entailed is subject to further variations due to season, geographical latitude and atmospheric conditions.

76 Precise calculation of the perennial visibility of these stars at all epochs entails – in addition to the factors already mentioned – computation of the precessional effects on their Right Ascensions (by the formula in Smart, p. 40) and Declinations (by another formula, *ibid.*, p. 40).

77 For the variations of its minimum, see n. 75 above.

78 The statement in Webb, p. 248, that *Polaris* in *U. Mi.* "...has been perceived *by day*" clearly refers to telescope observation. However, conditions are appreciably different in the rarefied atmosphere of high mountain tops.

difficulty is as follows. R. Berechiah must have reasoned, with a not illegitimate degree of homiletical licence, that the pendant to על לבך... על זרועך was not *Cassiopeia* – which, at the geographical latitude in question, is never out of sight for more than about 17–18 hours, from dawn till the next nightfall or from some time before dawn till some time after the next nightfall – but rather the moon or any of the planets near their respective conjunctions with the sun, or any of the stars or groups of stars in the belt of the zodiac, each of which is completely out of sight for several consecutive nights of the year.

Concerning one such group, the conspicuous asterism of the *Pleiades*, we have the testimony, quoted in the name of the expert Hesiod,[79] that it is out of sight for 40 days every year – i.e., 40 ***nights***, since in *daytime* it is *always* out of sight. Hesiod is generally dated to the 8th century B.C.E.; he is said to have been born in the village of Ascra in Boeotia and to have lived most of his life in the city of Orchomenos in the same country;[80] these locations are at lat. 38°21′N. and lat. 38°30′N., respectively.[81] He must have referred to conditions prevailing at his own places of observation, with the *Pleiades* rather closer to the Equator[82] than at present (at Decl. 24°N., approximately).[83] The interval he mentions was not appreciably different at the latitude of Jerusalem (31°47′N.) at R. Berechiah's epoch (300–350 C.E.),[84] when the *Pleiades* had a somewhat more northerly Declination, closer to the present one. All this applies, of course, to other fixed stars at comparable Declinations. The corresponding respective periods of the planets' total invisibility are subject to great variations, owing to their varied rates of elongation from the sun near their times of conjunction with it.[85] On the whole, these daily rates are less than the fixed stars' daily rate of elongation (= the sun's daily rate of motion, which is slightly less than 1°).[86] Hence the planets' respective periods of invisibility exceed those of the fixed stars in the belt of the zodiac. As for the moon – whose mean daily elongation

79 See Maunder, p. 103:1–5.

80 See the standard reference works on classical antiquity, *inter alia*, W. Smith, *A Smaller Classical Dictionary* (London 1910), pp. 261–2, s.v HESIODUS; with reference to editions of Hesiod's works in the Greek original and in English.

81 See S. Butler, *Atlas of Ancient and Classical Geography* (London 1910), Map. No. 11.

82 Since its Declination, like that of all stars, varies continuously owing to the precession of the equinoxes.

83 See Webb, p. 230:18–19, regarding the star *Alcyon* within this asterism.

84 See Section III above and n. 53, *ibid.*

85 A synopsis of these rates may be obtained from diagrams of the planets' orbits in Plates XXVII and XXVIII in "Astronomy" in the *Encyclopaedia Britannica*, 9th ed., Vol. II, facing p. 782.

86 See n. 66 above.

is about 12°[87] – its corresponding period of invisibility, near its conjunction with the sun (named the "true" *Molad* in rabbinic works on the calendar),[88] is very much shorter. Occurring once a month and extending from the last sighting of the waning moon – shortly before sunrise on one of the last days of the month[89] – till the first sighting of the new crescent shortly after sunset, it mostly exceeds 60 hours (= three days and the intervening two nights).[90] The rarity of the shorter period of about 38 hours only (= two days and the one intervening night) appears to be reflected in the hesitant report by witnesses, confessing their doubt as to what their eyes had seen, which led to the conflict between Rabban Gamaliel and R. Joḥanan b. Nuri recorded in the Mishnah.[91]

By contrast, the five stars in the W of *Cassiopeia* were not out of sight throughout any night of the year at R. Berechiah's epoch or at still earlier epochs, being above the horizon very much longer than the sun on the longest day of the year. Hence, Pseudo-Rashi's explanation that R. Berechiah's linking of **על כפים** with **דבר שנראה לעולם** alludes to *Cassiopeia* is quite plausible. Nevertheless, there remains a speculative element in this explanation. It may well have been prompted by the constant sight of *Cassiopeia*, which was circumpolar in Pseudo-Rashi's habitat at his epoch night after night, despite the flaw in the inference therefrom. With all this hanging in the balance, in a manner of speaking, the decisive factor would seem to be that the interpretation of **כפים** in the sense of **שמים** predates Pseudo-Rashi and, as has been stated,[92] probably also the Arabic names *al-kaff al-khaḍîb* and *kaff ath-thurayyâ* (pendants to the Hebrew **כפים**) of the five stars of the W in *Cassiopeia*.

87 See *YJS*, XI, p. 137, top. This value arises from the moon's and sun's respective mean daily rates of motion; i.e., 13°10′35″ minus 59′8″ as given *ibid.*, pp. 65:1–2 and 47:2–4.

88 *Inter alia, ibid.*, p. 33:3 ff = Maimonides, Hil. Qiddush ha-Ḥodesh, 7:7. For the identity of מולד with קיבוץ, see *ibid.*, 6:2 = *YJS*, XI, p. 27:6–7.

89 See M. Yoma 3,2, with Maimonides' comment *ad loc.* =... **עד כדון דהוה סיפיה** in TJ *ad loc.*, as pointed out by the standard commentators *ad ibid.*

90 See *YJS*, XI, pp. 136–140. For further discussion of the variations of the interval from the true conjunction till the first visibility, see also my "Appendix" in *YJS*, XIV, pp. 584–592.

91 M. R. ha-Sh. 2,8a. Though this is at variance with the standard commentators' explanation of this passage, it obviates the need to assume that the sighting [of the waning moon] in the morning was but imagination on the witnesses' part. Accordingly, "in the morning" is not the morning of the same day as of the ensuing "in the evening," but the morning of the last day of the month, the ensuing day being sanctified on the basis of the sighting of the new crescent at its end: after sunset but before the coming out of the stars (as per the Mishnah, *ibid.*, 3, 1). Furthermore, **שש שעות** in TJ *ad loc.*, and also **חצות** in TB, *ibid.*, 20b, must denote not "midday" but "midnight."

92 End of Section II above; see also nn. 17 and 28 *ibid.*

V

Of the constellations in the neighborhood of *Cassiopeia*, the Little Bear and the Great Bear were described at some length in Section II of this paper, in connection with the diagrams and the figure showing the location of *Cassiopeia*. Both these constellations attracted the Jews' attention at an early date, far more than did *Cassiopeia*; the Little Bear because of its usefulness in orientation, for navigational and other purposes, since the celestial North Pole has been close to one or another of its seven stars throughout recorded history;[93] the Great Bear because of the conspicuousness of its seven brilliant principal stars, α, β, γ, δ, ε, ζ and η *Ursae Maioris*, which are collectively known by a great many popular names, such as "The Plough," "The Dipper," "The Wagon," etc.,[94] and each of which also has its own individual name in Arabic.[95]

עש and **עיש על בניה** in Job 9:9 and 38:32, whatever their original meaning, were identified in the majority of early rabbinic sources with the Little Bear or with some of its seven stars.[96] In presentations of the rabbinic interpretation of the aforementioned biblical terms by modern scholars (especially their presentation of Ibn Ezra's view on this subject), as well as of other rabbinic dicta, the Little Bear is frequently confused with the Great Bear. Very prominent among these scholars is the noted Italian astronomer Giovanni Virginio Schiaparelli, in his admirable *Astronomy in the Old Testament*. The exposition of rabbinic dicta anent the Great Bear and the Little Bear, the familiar configurations of stars fairly close to *Cassiopeia* and useful aids in locating her in the sky as described above, is in a way related to the foregoing exposition of *Cassiopeia* in rabbinic sources. It is nonetheless beyond the scope of the present paper.

93 Concerning α *U. Mi.* as the nearest star to the celestial North Pole, see n. 12 above; concerning β and γ *U. Mi.* see n. 96 below.

94 See Maunder, pp. 22–23, and other popular books on astronomy.

95 See Ideler, p. 22:23 ff; Kunitzsch, pp. 158:31 ff (for α *U. Ma.*) , 135:27 ff (for β *U. Ma.*), 192:25 ff (for γ *U. Ma.*) , 178:26 ff (for δ *U. Ma.*), 121:27 ff (for ε *U. Ma.*), 186:31 ff (for ζ *U. Ma.*), 123:10 ff and 150:9–11 (for η *U. Ma.*); also Dunkin, p. 165.

96 *Inter alios*, Ibn Zeraḥ, *loc. cit.*, identifying **עיש ובניה** with the seven stars of *U. Mi.* (see n. 14 above) and Ibn Janah in *KaL*, p. 279:19 ff (= *SR*, p. 294:17 ff), locating **עש** *alias* **עיש** in the region of the celestial North Pole next to ***Kîmah***, which he ultimately identified with **אלפרקדאן** = The Two Calves = β and γ *U. Mi.*; see Ideler, pp. 3:10 ff (375:8), 12:8 ff, Kunitzsch, p. 192:36 ff; and also Lane's Arabic Dictionary s.v. *farqad*.

HEBREW IN ARABIC SCRIPT – QIRQISĀNĪ'S VIEW

H. BEN-SHAMMAI

The peculiarity of the Karaite Bible texts written in Arabic characters, as well as of Karaite Judaeo-Arabic texts written in the same script, within the framework of Judaeo-Arabic, has been noticed and dealt with for several decades.[1] Some of the problems evolved in the course of the study of these texts, such as their origin in place and time or the scope of their circulation, could however be solved in the light of one chapter in Qirqisānī's *al-Anwār wa-'l-marāqib*. To the man whose labor has made this voluminous source accessible to the scholarly world an attempted study of that chapter is hereby presented.

The text in question is chapter (*bāb*) 35, in the fifth part (*maqāla*, article) of *al-Anwār*.[2] To be sure, this particular chapter has already been edited and published, with some short comments, by S. Poznański.[3] His edition was based on a single manuscript (preserved in the British Museum).[4] In the following translation Nemoy's division into numbered sections has been retained, while the page numbers of his edition are given in brackets.

1 Cf. the recent thorough review, with numerous references, by J. Blau, *Emergence and Linguistic Background of Judaeo-Arabic,* Jerusalem 1981², pp. 38–44; 226.

2 Ed. by L. Nemoy (in 5 vols.), New York 1939–1945, pp. 553–555.
A revised edition, with many variants and extensive linguistic references has been prepared by J. Blau (ed.), *Judaeo-Arabic Literature – Selected Texts (Max Schloessinger Memorial Series*, Texts 4), Jerusalem 1980, pp. 47–51. This edition was made accessible to me only while reading proof-sheets of this paper. It was therefore impossible to consider it appropriately in the footnotes.

3 "Aus Qirqisâni's Kitâb al-'anwâr wa'l-marâqib," in G.E. Kohut (ed.), *Semitic Studies in Memory of Alexander Kohut,* Berlin 1897, pp. 435–456. Poznański's comments on this chapter are on pp. 439–440 and the text on pp. 453–456.

4 This fact apparently caused several misreadings in Poznański's edition. There are, however, a couple of instances in which Poznański's text appears to be preferable.

TRANSLATION

Chapter 35 [p. 553, 1.9]
On reading any non-Hebrew script on the Sabbath Day

1. This also is among the things which a group of our co-religionists[5] has forbidden, without firm proof. With regard to that (prohibition) I say: The words[6] and nouns have actually been formed in order to indicate notions, which are notions of things, and in order to serve as means by which the things are to be known and pointed out. The same applies to the scripts and letters; they have actually been formed as signs and symbols which indicate speech, which (in its turn) is the movement of the tongue, the lips and all (other) organs of speech.[7] (Accordingly) when it says in the Hebrew text of Scripture: *ānōḵī aḏōnāy elohēḵa*,[8] the[9] written composition is a sign and symbol which indicates that its meaning in the language of the Arabs is *anā al-rabb ilāhuka* [= I am the Lord, thy God]; and also, when we see these four figures, namely *ANKY*, and we know where[10] the place is from which each figure is (articulated), from the mouth and the organs (of speech), we[11] pronounce[12] *ānōḵī*. In the same manner, when we substitute each of these four (Hebrew) letters by a different symbol and figure which indicate it, we put for (Hebrew) *A* that figure which (indicates) *A* for the Arabs, and for the figure which is Hebrew *N* that figure which is Arabic *N*, or other symbols and figures in other scripts.

2. If we are permitted on the Sabbath Day to utter in the language of the Arabs *anā al-rabb ilāhuka*, to indicate the meaning of *ānōḵī aḏōnāy elōhēḵa*,

5 *aṣḥābunā* refers usually to co-religionists in the strictest sense, viz. the Karaites. In the 12th century the Karaite Judah Hadassi mentions in his *Eškōl hakkōfer*, Gozlow 1836, alphabet 145, letter *zayin* (fol. 55c), the prohibition on studying "foreign" writings (or anything) except the Torah.

6 *lughāt* may also be translated as "forms," "expressions," or even "idioms."

7 *lahawāt* does not seem to indicate here a particular organ, i.e., the uvula.

8 Exodus 20:2.

9 The apodosis of *iḏā* is preceded by *wa* (see J. Blau, *A Grammar of Mediaeval Judaeo-Arabic* [in Hebrew], Jerusalem 1980^2, §307.a).

10 The manuscripts have *an*, which should probably be read *ayna*.

11 The apodosis of *iḏā* is preceded by *fa* (cf. Blau, *op.cit.*, §301, where this *fa* precedes the imperfect in accordance with classical Arabic, whereas here it precedes the perfect and is therefore "redundant"). See also Blau, *op. cit.*, p. 329 (add. to p. 191).

12 *faqulnā* (cf. end of section 4). Nemoy has after this word *bi-'l-'arabī*, missing in Poznański, whose version here appears to be preferable. Transliteration into Arabic script (this is the subject matter of the section, not Arabic pronunciation) is discussed in the next sentence.

and (surely) that is not prohibited, in the same way when we see this (Arabic) figure [p. 554] *ANḪY* which indicates that other [Hebrew] figure *ANKY*, we are not forbidden to read it, and (surely) this is permitted. Or, (conversely,) if it is prohibited to look at this (Arabic) figure, namely *ANḪY*,[13] and to read it on the Sabbath Day, then the utterance *anā al-rabb ilāhuka* is prohibited as well. (Moreover) if it is prohibited to read the Arabic script on the Sabbath Day, be it in the Hebrew language or in the Arabic language, namely a commentary on Scripture or a study of it, then (any) speech on the Sabbath Day in the Arabic language (used) in a commentary on Scripture or its study is prohibited as well. (But) if[14] speech in the Arabic language, or (any) other language, is not forbidden on Sabbath Day for any need which (might) arise on that day then, by the same token, reading of the Arabic script, and (any) other script, is not forbidden for the purpose of (Biblical) commentary, study and the like.

3. If one of them[15] argues: Are we not permitted to speak and converse on the Sabbath in the Arabic language and other languages about that which we eat and drink, and to relate that which happened before the Sabbath which is not of the nature of Biblical commentary and study? If so, are we permitted to read these things when they are written in a non-Hebrew script? If you[16] claim that this is permitted, your opinion is (to be considered as) dissent from (the true) religion. And if you claim that this is not permitted, then you have made a distinction between speaking in a non-Hebrew language and reading that which is written in (that language). We shall (refute their argument and) say: Those subjects about which it is not permitted to read in a non-Hebrew script, like relating what we eat and drink, and conversing about that which has happened and which will happen, namely those subjects which are not of the nature of Scripture commentary and study, are not permitted to be read about even if written in the Hebrew language. Had it been permitted to read this when written in the Hebrew script, it would have been permitted to read it in (all) other scripts (as well). Our distinction is only between speaking and reading writings of those (things) which are distinguished in the manner which we have explained.[17] Our argument is (therefore) firmly proven.

4. We shall argue furthermore: If we had clothes and dishes which we had to

13 Poznański reads here "to look at this figure, namely the Arabic figure" (*bi-ṣūrat al-ʿarab* [ms. *al-ʿarabī*]). This reading may seem less ambiguous than Nemoy's.

14 *in* in the text might be understood as "since."

15 Those who forbid reading non-Hebrew script on the Sabbath.

16 I.e. Qirqisānī.

17 The difference is thus determined by content, not by script or language.

use on the Sabbath, and others which we did not use on the Sabbath, we would be permitted to have a sign on that which we wanted to use on the Sabbath, so that when we saw that sign we would be able to distinguish between that which we wanted to use on the Sabbath and that which we did not. From that sign we (could) make an inference with regard to that which we wanted, talk about[18] it and use it. In the same manner, since the letters of Arabic, and other scripts (as well), are but symbols of the language, as we have already explained, it is not prohibited to look at them on the Sabbath Day, so as to know what they indicate, concerning reading or commentary, and to pronounce them and speak about them.

5. In order to refute them[19] we shall raise the argument of the vowel-signs and the accents.[20] These are not (part) of the Hebrew script, but signs marking the quality of recitation and intonation. Accordingly,[21] they are forced to forbid one to look at them or to employ them on the Sabbath. One of them did in fact claim that since the Sabbath Day is holy, we are not permitted to read on that day any script but that which has been written in holiness; and that is the Hebrew script, to the exclusion of (any) other (script). Accordingly, he will be forced to the same conclusion concerning speech [p. 555] and concerning[22] all that which we utilize, such as clothes, utensils etc.

6. One of them advanced another argument, saying that since Scripture says, "Thou shalt rest,"[23] every action and every movement have been prohibited, except that for which there exists elsewhere an (explicit) proof of its permissibility.[24] Since there exists an (explicit) proof for the permission to read the books[25] of Scripture[26] in these Hebrew letters, namely the verse, "This book

18 This word (*fa-nuḫbiru*) is actually the crux of the hypothesis. In Ms. Br. Mus. (= Poznański) this word was amended (by a different hand?) into *fa-nujīz*.

19 See note 15.

20 In the text *bi-'l-simānāt wa-'l-ṭa'amīn*, for which see Blau, *Emergence*, pp. 139, 163, 164; see also below n. 48a.

21 Nemoy has *wa-innahu* instead of Classical (= Poznański's) *fa-innahu*, cf. Blau, *op. cit.*, p. 96.

22 In the text *wa-fī*. However, it would seem preferable to read *fī* instead, and to translate "speech about all that," etc.

23 Exodus 23:12; 34:21.

24 The explicit proof, *dalīl*, required by Qirqisānī's adversary, is of course a Biblical verse.

25 So Nemoy (*kutub*); Poznański "book" (*kitāb*) which, if accepted, could mean the Pentateuch only (cf. note 28 below).

26 Qirqisānī's usual term for "Scripture" is *al-kitāb*. Here he has *al-tanzīl*, a typical Qur'ānic term, e.g., Qur'ān 41:2; cf. S. Pinsker, *Liqqūtey Qadmōniyyōt*, Vienna 1860, II, p. 131; Blau, *op. cit.*, p. 159.

of the law shall not depart out of thy mouth,"[27] and (since) there is no proof (for the permission) of any other (fashion of reading), we are not permitted to read anything but that for which we have an (explicit) proof, excluding everything else. Had we raised against him an argument like (his own) concerning Hebrew speech, it would have taken a long time before he (could) find the (pertinent) passage (in Scripture). It follows therefore from his argument that he is not permitted to speak on the Sabbath except in the Hebrew language, since it is speech in the Hebrew language, excluding (any) other (language), which is permitted by an explicit proof. However, we shall leave this (question). We would (rather) ask him about that which is written in Hebrew script (but) in a different language, whether Arabic or any other: "Is it permitted to read it?" If he permits it, we will demand that he provide the proof for his (permission). Surely, he will not find it, for the existing proof applies only to the permissibility of reading that which is written in Hebrew letters (and) in the Hebrew language, to the exclusion of everything else. Furthermore, according to his reasoning, he will be forced not to permit the reading of any book of science[28] or commentary, even though it is written in the Hebrew language, since an (explicit) proof for permission exists only with regard to the reading of the Torah, and that is in the verse, "This book of the law shall not depart out of thy mouth."

COMMENTS

A. The prohibition quoted at the beginning of this chapter in the name of "a group of our co-religionists" is of a general character. It is only through Qirqisānī's refutation that the reader gathers that the prohibition could refer to Hebrew in Arabic characters. Qirqisānī bases his refutation on a short exposition of his theory on the nature of individual letters and of script, namely that individual letters are merely symbols of phonetic entities, inasmuch as written words, i.e. combinations of such symbols, are no more than symbols of notions and ideas[28a] (section 1, and cf. below, comment D). Qirqisānī

27 Joshua 1:8.

28 *'ulūm*, might also be rendered as "philosophy" or "theology." It is not clear, however, whether Qirqisānī wants to force his adversary to admit the exclusion of the Prophets and Hagiographa from the permitted reading, thus limiting it to the Pentateuch only. The seventh and last section of this chapter has not been translated, being an introduction to the next chapter.

28a It may be of some interest to quote here Saadia's opinion in his *Commentary on Sefer Yezira* (ed. Y. Qāfiḥ, Jerusalem 1972, p. 48,17–49,4 = ed. M. Lambert, Paris 1891, p. 22,15–23,2), that things exist in four forms (or: modes, *ma'ānī*): in essence, in thought, in

strengthens this argument in section 4 by equating letters to any other kind of symbol or sign used to mark the distinctive character of a given object, and which enable us to express this distinction. Referring back to section 1, this leads to the following conclusions:

a. In Qirqisānī's time and district, there was an established custom of transliterating Biblical texts, including the Pentateuch, into Arabic characters.[29]

speech and in script. "Two amongst them are variable, namely script and speech. Thus we observe (that) languages and scripts differ from each other. Nevertheless, although they are variable, the notions *(al-ma'ānī)* are not liable to any change". A similar opinion is quoted in a Mu'tazilite context by Shahrastānī, *Nihāyat al-iqdām fī 'ilm al-kalām*, ed. A. Guillaume, Oxford 1934, p. 323, 5–10, English translation, p. 107, and see n. 1 there (the example is *allāh*, the name of God, with its equivalents in other languages).
Saadia's opinion probably reflects Aristotle's view in *De Interpretatione*, 16a, 5–8 (Engl. transl. by E. M. Edghill, in W.D. Ross [ed.], *The Works of Aristotle, Translated into English*, vol. 1): "Just as all men have not the same writing, so all men have not the same speech sounds, but the mental experiences which these directly symbolize, are the same for all, as also are those things of which our experiences are the images." It seems that Saadia's "notions" *(ma'ānī)* stand for both the mental experience ("thought" in Saadia's opening statement) and things of which the mental experience is the image (Saadia's "essence"). It is interesting that in the Arabic translation of Aristotle's text, as presented in al-Fārābī's *Commentary on De Interpretatione* (ed. W. Kutsch – S. Marrow², Beyrouth 1971), p. 27, 23, the "things of which our mental experiences are images" are glossed by the phrase *wa-hiya al-ma'ānī.*

Qirqisānī's exposition seems to be related not only to Aristotle's view but also to Al-Fārābī's following comments. It is not unlikely that these Comments were known to Qirqisānī. Commenting on Aristotle's statement 16a, 1–4, al-Fārābī says (p. 25, 7–9): "Spoken words (or: articulations, *alfāẓ*) indicate that they are common symbols (*'alāmāt*). When they are heard, the thing which they symbolize actually comes to one's mind *(khaṭara bi-bāl al-insān)*." On the function of words as reminders he says (p. 25, 9–10): "Words are like other symbols which man forms in order to remind him what he needs to remember." On the relation between things, speech and script al-Fārābī makes two statements. The first (p. 25, 13–14): "Aristotle's intention in this statement was to inform us about the mode in which spoken words indicate the intelligibles which are in the soul, and that this mode is similar to that by which script indicates spoken words." In the second, more detailed statement, al-Fārābī comments on 16a, 6–8 (p. 28, 6–11): "Aristotle did not have to mention here the relation of the intelligibles to the things existing outside the soul. He had to mention but the relation of the intelligibles to articulations or vice versa. Doing so, he informed us as to which is the mode by which spoken words serve as indicators and that it is similar to the mode by which script indicates spoken words. Script indicates spoken words by two Modes: 1) Like reminding symbols *(dalālāt 'alāmāt al-tadhkira)*. 2) By convention *(istilāh)*. This is common to all parts of logic." It is more than likely that al-Fārābī's views are represented in other Jewish works as well. The subject deserves a more detailed consideration.

29 This has already been pointed out by Poznański (see above note 3), who rightly based his

b. At the same time and in the same district, there existed at least one Judaeo-Arabic translation of the Bible (or, perhaps, the Pentateuch). This translation was not necessarily the Saadian, and might have been of Karaite origin.[30] From the beginning of section 2, it may be gathered that this translation was publicly recited along with the weekly portion of the Pentateuch. This conclusion is, however, outside the scope of the present paper.

The importance of the information leading to the first conclusion lies in the fact that it determines the origins, in time and place, of the custom of writing Hebrew in Arabic script. In the British Museum there are about twenty manuscripts containing Biblical texts (with or without translations and commentaries) which are written in that fashion,[31] and several more manuscripts of different contents.[32] Only one of these manuscripts, Or. 2554, has a colophon detailing when and where it was copied, namely in Ramle ("For the library [*ḫizāna*] of Abū 'l-Faraj Ya'qūb"), in 395 A.H. (= 1004/5 C.E.).[33] Other manuscripts in the same collection are apparently from the same hand[34]

conclusion on his close acquaintance with several Karaite manuscripts written in this manner. He has also pointed to the use of Hebrew vowel-marks and accents in these texts, as is borne out by section 5.

30 Cf. M. Zucker, *Rav Saadya Gaon's Translation of the Torah* (in Hebrew), New York 1959, pp. 1–7.

31 See R. Hoerning, *Six Karaite Manuscripts... in the British Museum,* London 1889, where twenty are described briefly, and six are dealt with in detail.

32 Such as large fragments of Qirqisānī's *al-Anwār;* cf. Poznański, *loc. cit* and also his "Die Qirqisani Handschriften im British Museum," *Festschrift Steinschneider,* Leipzig 1896, pp. 195–218. Cf. also *Bulletin of the School of Oriental and African Studies,* 38 (1975), 126–130 for examples of commentaries, prayerbooks, Books of Law, etc. Manuscripts of the same kind are also to be found amongst the Karaite manuscripts in the libraries of Cambridge University and the Jewish Theological Seminary in New York, and most probably also in the Firkovitch Collection in Leningrad, unfortunately inaccessible to most students. It is worthy of note that there are Karaite manuscripts in which Arabic only is written in Arabic characters, whereas Hebrew words and phrases are written in square characters (cf. Blau, *Emergence,* pp. 152–153), such as Br. Mus., Or. 2557, fols. 1–12, published by H. Hirschfeld in his *Quirqisānī Studies* (*Jews' College Publications,* no. 6) London 1918. See *Emergence*[2], p. 243 (to p. 152). Another example for a text in Arabic script is ms. Bodl. Heb. e. 76 (*Catalogue*, no. 2861), fol. 7–8 (exegetical Halachic of Rabbanite origin?); and for a text with alternating scripts Bodl. Heb. f. 103, being a Karaite(?) commentary on Gen. 6:2.

33 See no. 301 in G. Margoliouth's *Catalogue*. The datings of the rest of these manuscripts (cf. Hoerning, *op. cit.*, pp. v–ix) are but conjectures; one would tend to question late datings such as thirteenth-fourteenth century.

34 Or. 2548, described *ibid.*, no. 279.

or the same school of scribes. This could have led to the conclusion that this custom did in fact emanate from, and was current amongst, limited Karaite circles in Palestine, or in Ramle in particular.[35]

Qirqisānī wrote his *al-Anwār* in the fourth decade of the tenth century, apparently in Mesopotamia.[36] Writing Hebrew in Arabic script, as reflected in this book, was already an accepted custom, to the extent that it had met with legal opposition from some Karaite lawyers. These developments must have taken at least a few decades before Qirqisānī's discussion, which brings us to the end of the ninth century. The Karaite settlements in Palestine were just in their beginnings at that period.[37]

These considerations lead to the conclusion that the custom of writing Hebrew in Arabic characters is indeed part of the cultural history of Karaism from its earliest period in its oldest stronghold – Mesopotamia.[38] Thus, the Palestinian manuscrips are no more than one stage in that history, and not the last one. There are six autograph manuscripts written by the eleventh century

35 Cf. Blau, *Emergence*, p. 42–43, and Poznański, *loc. cit.* (see above note 3) who believed that the Karaites adopted the Arabic script in some areas ("manchen Gegenden").
Prof. Blau has recently drawn my attention to a private letter written in Arabic characters by a Rabbanite dignitary, from Ramle (ca. 1040 C.E.). The letter was published by S. D. Goitein, "Arabic Documents on the Palestinian Gaonate," *Eretz-Yisrael*, 10, pp. 106–113 (in Hebrew), and reprinted in his *Palestinian Jewry in Early Islamic and Crusader Times*, Jerusalem 1980, pp. 60–69. This document may be of some consequence with respect to Ramle. Notwithstanding, the proportion of such documents in relation to the entire Judaeo-Arabic documentary material of Rabbanite origin remains limited.

36 For the date see L. Nemoy, "Kirkisani," *Encyclopaedia Judaica,* 10, coll. 1047–1048. The place where *al-Anwār* was completed can only be conjectured. Qirqisānī was a native of Upper Mesopotamia, and most probably stayed in Baghdad. He also mentions conversations with Christian priests in Upper Mesopotamia.

37 Cf., e.g., Z. Ankori, *Karaites in Byzantium,* New York 1959, pp. 21 ff.
On the chronology of the Karaite settlement in Jerusalem see also "A Fragment of Daniel al-Qūmisī's Commentary on Daniel as a Source for the History of Eretz-Israel," *Shalem*, III (1981), pp. 295–307 (in Hebrew).

38 It is therefore difficult to see a necessary connection between that custom and any specific social layer amongst the Karaites; cf. L. Nemoy, "Anan ben David," *Semitic Studies in Memory of Immanuel Löw*, Budapest 1947, pp. 245–246, n. 36 (repr. in P. Birnbaum [ed.], *Karaite Studies,* New York 1971, p. 315, n. 36). Concerning the geographical origin of that custom, there is some interest in the fact that part of the manuscripts under discussion had been acquired in Hīt (in the valley of the Euphrates), as Hoerning relates in his Introduction, *op. cit.*, p. v. About the Karaite community in Hīt through the ages see A. Ben-Jacob, *A History of the Jews in Iraq* (in Hebrew), Jerusalem 1965, pp. 318–320. Yet, this evidence is not very decisive, as the manuscripts could have travelled with their owners.

Karaite scholar ʿAlī b. Sulaymān.[39] Five of them are written in Arabic script,[40] including a commentary on Genesis. Most of them were written in Egypt. Accordingly, writing Hebrew in Arabic script was common to Karaites in their main centers in the Arabic-speaking world[41] for at least three centuries.

B. The phenomenon of a non-Muslim sect adopting the Arabic script in copying their most hallowed books is indeed unique in the history of Arabic script. Adoption of that script followed, in most cases, conversion to Islam, or could have, in some cases, coincided with conversion.

Karaite texts known so far do not seem to furnish any information which could explain this unique phenomenon. Qirqisānī's text, translated above, is aimed at its justification. Consequently, modern students have been compelled to base their explanations on indirect information and various assumptions. Poznański[42] suggested that the Karaites adopted the Arabic script for the sake of convenience. His suggestion might sound plausible with regard to monolingual texts, such as Biblical texts not accompanied by any translation or commentary. Yet it is hard to see the convenience of shifting from one language to another in the same script, sometimes twice in one line. The search for convenience would rather bring about a change of script wherever the language changed, so that words in the two different languages are discernible at first sight.[43] Blau suggested[44] that "These manuscripts... reveal an absorption into Arab culture on an extraordinary scale." This suggestion, too, might be

39 On these manuscripts see A. Ya. Borisov in *Palestinskii Sbornik*, 9 (1962), 109—114. Four of them are preserved in the Firkovitch Collection, Leningrad. According to Borisov's article (which, apparently, escaped the notice of the editors of *Encyclopaedia Judaica*, 1, col. 632, who therefore omitted facts concerning ʿAlī's biography, and also adhered to the erroneous dating "c. 1200"), the period of ʿAlī's literary activity stretched over 49 years (1045—1093 C.E.), most of them spent in Tinnis, the rest in Fusṭāṭ.

40 Firkovitch II, Jud. Arab. 4419 is apparently in square characters, cf. Borisov, *ibid.*, p. 112.

41 For the views held by Karaites outside the Arabic-speaking world see below, note 49.

42 *Loc. cit.* (see note 3) ; cf. his rejection of H. Hirschfeld's theory that the Karaite scribes used Arabic script in order to make it impossible for Rabbanites to read Karaite books. Cf. also Blau, *Emergence*, pp. 40—41.

43 Cf. *idem, ibid.*, pp. 152—153, 161 n. 5.

44 *Ibid.*, pp. 43—44, cf. his rejection (in n. 5) of another theory of H. Hirschfeld, regarding the adoption of Arabic script as a result of the Karaites' defeat by Saadia, and cf. above comment A.

Concerning Blau's suggestion see also H. Ben-Shammai, "The Attitude of Some Early Karaites Towards Islam," to be published in I. Twersky (ed.), *Studies in Medieval Jewish History and Literature* (Harvard Univ. Press).

satisfactory for the pure Hebrew Biblical texts, but it seems less convincing for the Arabic texts, in which a relatively high proportion of Hebrew elements is interwoven. These Hebrew elements belong to various fields, such as Biblical quotations, grammatical terms, legal terms, liturgy, words of general use and nature (e.g., *gālūt, berāḵa, qelāla, ṣaddīq, rāšā'*), and also to different stages in the history of Hebrew, namely Biblical Hebrew and Mishnaic Hebrew.[45] Karaite authors, while integrating the Hebrew elements into their Arabic style, must have presupposed a close acquaintance with the Hebrew language and culture on the part of their readers. In any event, Qirqisānī cannot be described as absorbed into Arab culture, but rather as being well-versed, and having a keen interest, in many branches and fields of knowledge.

One could suggest various other explanations for the phenomenon of Hebrew in Arabic script, but it seems that no explanation can be properly sustained in the present state of knowledge of Karaite sources. This cannot be done until new, decisive evidence comes to light.

C. In section 6 a reference is made to "that which is written in Hebrew script (but) in a different language, whether Arabic or any other." This reference appears to constitute clear evidence that Judaeo-Arabic works, written in Hebrew characters, were circulating in Qirqisānī's period and district. The works referred to are not necessarily of Karaite origin. Karaite-dated works of this kind, both books and documents, are not known before the eleventh century.[46] On the other hand, we know from numerous quotations from Saadia by Qirqisānī and other tenth century Karaites, that they already had access to Saadia's writings in his lifetime. These and similar Rabbanite works were probably in Qirqisānī's mind.[47]

The wording "or any other" in the above-mentioned reference is too vague to

45 Long quotations from Talmudic literature transliterated into Arabic characters are to be found, for example, in works by Qirqisānī and Yeshu'a b. Judah.

46 And even then are quite rare, e.g., Mss. A, O and P of Qirqisānī's *al-Anwār* (see Nemoy's edition, vol. V, pp. 09, 011–012), or Yūsuf el-Baṣīr's *al-Muḥtawī*, Ms. Kaufmann (Budapest) 280, copied in Jerusalem, Ḏū al-Qa'da 411 A.H. (= 1021 C.E.; cf. the brief description in the catalogue by Weisz, Frankfurt a.M. 1906, p. 100) or Cambridge Univ. T-S. 8.106 – a letter written about 1040 C.E. in Damascus by a Karaite dignitary (published by Y. Eliash, *Sefunot,* 2 [1958], 20–21; cf. S.D. Goitein, *Mediterranean Society,* I, p. 410 n. 3).

47 Cf. Blau, *op. cit.*, pp. 38–41. Salmon b. Yeruḥīm, in his commentary on Lamentations (chap. I, ed. by E. Feuerstein, Krakau 1898), 1:8 (*ibid.*, p. xxix) enumerates "reading of foreign (*barrānī*) books" as one of the transgressions of the Sabbath committed by Jews (Rabbanites?) in his time (the middle of the 10th century).

permit any conclusions as to whether a theoretical possibility is indicated or a fact of life, namely anything written in Hebrew characters in a language other than Arabic, like Judaeo-Persian.

D. Attention should be drawn to Qirqisānī's interesting theory of script and language (summed up above, comment A). According to this theory, script (including vowel-signs and accents) as such is devoid of any value or holiness. But Qirqisānī goes further by implicitly denying the holiness of the Hebrew language. Language is no more than a tool to express notions and ideas. The idea of God's unity, as expressed in Hebrew in the first Commandment, can be expressed equally in Arabic. Qirqisānī's theory rejects not only the ancient Rabbinic approach to Hebrew as "The Holy Language" (*lešōn haqqōdeš*)[48], but also a similar, formal, Karaite approach, which apparently gained currency in Qirqisānī's time.[48a] It is not surprising to find that kind of formal approach amongst Karaites. It is Qirqisānī's approach which is somewhat surprising. He unequivocally indicates his opinion that it is the content of any expression

48 It is needless to quote here the numerous references in Rabbinic literature to that idea (including the ascription to Moses of Massoretic traditions about accents, etc.). Suffice it to remark that the term *lešōn haqqōdeš* is already well-established in Tanaitic literature (e.g., Mishna Sōṭa 2,7; *Mekiltā*, Yitrō, 2,9, p. 238 in Horovitz-Rabin edition) and that the notion of the Holy Language was fully adopted and systematically elaborated by Medieval Jewish thinkers, such as Judah Halevi, *Kuzari*, III, 28—34. Even Ibn Quraysh (about 900 C.E.) the pioneer of comparative lexicography, speaks of Hebrew as *lešōn haqqōdeš* in the Introduction to his *Epistle*, see Bargès-Goldberg edition, Paris 1857, p. 2, ll. 16—17 (Hebrew translation by M. Katz, Tel-Aviv 1952, pp. 3—4 of the text); and cf. A. S. Halkin, "The Medieval Jewish Attitude Towards Hebrew," in A. Altman (ed.), *Biblical and Other Studies*, Cambridge, Mass., 1963, p. 241, and, concerning the accents, M. H. Goshen-Gottstein, "The Rise of the Tiberian Bible Text," *ibid.*, pp. 96—97 and especially n. 60.
[For a revised edition of the passage quoted from the *Epistle* by Ibn Quraysh see J. Blau, *Judaeo-Arabic Literature* (see n. 2 above), p. 89, ll. 3, 31.]

48a *Lešōn haqqōdeš*, spoken already by Adam, is mentioned in a fragment of a Karaite Hebrew commentary on Genesis, ascribed by J. Mann to Daniel al-Qūmisī; see the text in *JQR* (NS), 15 (1924/5), 373, 7—9 (and *ibid.*, n. 56 for Rabbinic parallels). Several references to this idea and its ramifications may be found in Hadassi's *Eškōl hakkōfer*: in alphabet 173, letter *'ayin* (fol. 70a), Adam is described as the first transmitter of "the Holy Language of our God" along with its script, vowels and accents. According to alphabet 163, letter *wāw* (fol. 60c) = 173, letter *samek* (fol. 70a), the script on the Tablets of the Law had vowels and accents, otherwise it would have been impossible to understand it. In what may be called Hadassi's "Ten Principles of Faith," he counts (alphabet 33, letter *'ayin*, fol. 21c-d) as the sixth Principle: the obligation to comprehend the language of the Torah, which is "the language of our God."

which matters and not its form. Consequently, a Hebrew expression dealing with everyday life is not holy, whereas an Arabic expression dealing with Biblical exegesis or religious speculation is (to some extent?) holy.[49]

However, Qirqisānī does not completely deny the prestige of Hebrew. Evidence to this effect is furnished by a section of the introduction to his Commentary on the non-legal parts of the Pentateuch.[50] In that section[51] he emphasizes that Hebrew is the language in which God addressed Adam and all other prophets; many etymologies of common nouns and proper names in Aramaic and Arabic go back to Hebrew and therefore Hebrew was the first language and is the oldest one; with the appearance of the Messiah Hebrew will prevail again. There Qirqisānī seems to be disputing with an adversary who claims seniority for Aramaic, but there is no hint as to the holiness of either Hebrew or Aramaic. In that respect Qirqisānī's opinions in both places do not contradict each other.

49 Thus, Qirqisānī rejected the view maintained by Benjamin Nahāwendī; "It is not appropriate [or permitted, *yajūz*] for us [= the Karaites?] to speak among ourselves in a language other than Hebrew," quoted by Qirqisānī, *Anwār*, VI. 25, p. 645 in Nemoy's edition. Qirqisānī's main concern in that chapter is to refute the view that oaths (using the name of God) are valid only when pronounced in Hebrew. Qirqisānī holds that the names of God in any language (e.g., Allāh) can validate an oath. (About the opinions of Muslim doctors on oaths taken by Jews cf. I. Goldziher, "Mélanges Judéo-arabes, XIII: Les serments des Juifs," *REJ*, 45 [1902], 1–8.) A few decades later Salmon b. Yeruḥīm, commenting on Lamentations 1:8 (see n. 47), p. xxxi, says: "How many sins do we commit mingling with the gentiles and following their ways, aiming at learning their language, along with its grammar. We spend (our) Dirhems in order to learn it; at the same time we give up the knowledge of the Holy Language (*lešōn haqqōdeš*) and the study of the Lord's Commandments."

50 Published by H. Hirschfeld (see above note 32).

51 *Ibid.*, pp. 44–45, translated by L. Nemoy, *Karaite Anthology*, pp. 61–63.

THE EGYPTIAN KARAITE COMMUNITY IN THE LATE NINETEENTH CENTURY

W. M. Brinner

Among Leon Nemoy's many great contributions to scholarship are his Karaite studies, dealing primarily with the early period of the history of that group. It is hoped that this paper, although dealing with a much later period, namely, the late nineteenth century, may be found worthy of inclusion in a volume dedicated to his honor.

A notoriously difficult aspect of ancient and medieval historical studies – especially those concerning the Near East – has been the question of the reliability of population statistics given by historians, chroniclers, travelers and other writers, where corroborative evidence such as birth, marriage or death records are lacking. Not only did writers inflate population figures in order to add dramatic emphasis to the magnitude of natural disasters such as plagues and earthquakes, but, motivated by political or religious zeal, they used such statistics to increase the glory of a military victory or the terrors of a persecution. Thus, for example, we have no reliable statistics to help us trace what must have been a rather dramatic decline in the Jewish population in countries like Egypt and Iraq from the pre-Islamic period to the beginnings of the modern era.[1]

Egypt's very ancient Jewish community consisted of three distinct entities in medieval times: Rabbanite Jews, Karaites and Samaritans.[2] The latter group had disappeared from Egypt by about the fifteenth century, while the Karaites declined in both numbers and importance. In a recent work on the Jews of Egypt in the nineteenth century, for example, only a few brief references to them are to be found.[3] Nevertheless, both they and the Rabbanites, though greatly diminished in numbers, retained their identity down to the present, being

1 Cf. the estimate of 1,000,000 Jews each in Egypt and in Babylonia in classical times, S. Baron, *A Social and Religious History of the Jews,* New York 1952, I, p. 170.

2 Cf. al-Qalqashandī, *Ṣubḥ al-a'shā*, Cairo 1913–19, XI, pp. 385 ff.

3 J. M. Landau, *Ha-yehudim be-miṣraim ba-me'ah ha-tesha'-'esreh*, Jerusalem 1967.

constantly replenished – especially in the case of the Rabbanites – by immigrants from the Middle East, North Africa and Europe. Indeed, the population of Egyptian Jewry had reached a new high of almost 100,000 when the circumstances of the Middle East conflict after 1948 caused a second Exodus of Jews from Egypt and reduced the community, both Rabbanite and Karaite, to a total of no more than a few hundred souls.

We are here concerned with trying to establish the number of Karaites in Egypt in the last quarter of the nineteenth century. Despite the immigration mentioned above, the size of the Egyptian Jewish community at the beginning of the nineteenth century was very small, one estimate from 1830 numbering no more than 5,000 in a population of somewhat over 2,000,000.[4] Of this small number, the bulk – some 4,000 or more – lived in Cairo.[5] With the general growth of Egypt's population since the middle of the nineteenth century, the number of Jews increased too, aided after 1880 by immigration from Russia and other parts of Eastern Europe. By 1907 the Jewish population was over 38,000[6] – a figure which presumably includes the Karaites, who were often lumped together with the Rabbanites in speaking of Egyptian Jewry.

According to the *Encyclopaedia Judaica*, the Karaite community in 1932 numbered "approximately 2,000... outside Russia, in Poland..., Constantinople, Jerusalem, Cairo, and Hit (on the Euphrates)."[7] It estimates that in 1970 there were 7,000 Karaites in Israel, many of them formerly resident in Egypt and other Arab lands.[8] Some years before, the late President of Israel, Itzhak Ben-Zvi, had estimated that there were 3,000 Karaites "in the East" – meaning primarily Egypt, Iraq and Constantinople.[9]

Bearing in mind what has been said about the reliability of statistical information in historical works, it is most welcome to find a document that can serve as the basis for a more reliable estimate of the size and make-up of the Karaite community than any previously available material. Such a document is to be found in the Judah L. Magnes Memorial Museum – The Jewish Museum of the West – located in Berkeley, California, which recently acquired a small collection of Karaite books from Egypt, some handwritten, others printed. This collection numbers some 46 items, mostly dating from the eighteenth and nineteenth centuries.[10] While examining one of these books, a handwritten copy

4 E. W. Lane, *The Manners and Customs of the Modern Egyptians*, London 1944, p. 23.

5 *Ibid.*

6 *American Jewish Year Book*, Philadelphia 1921, XXI, p. 602.

7 *Encyclopaedia Judaica*, Jerusalem 1971, X, col. 776.

8 *Op. cit.*, col. 777.

9 I. Ben-Zvi, *The Exiled and the Redeemed,* Philadelphia 1957, p. 157.

10 At the time of writing the material was uncatalogued; temporary numbers had been assigned.

of the ritual for the festival of Shavuʻot,[11] I found on the last few pages, which had been left blank by the copyist of the prayerbook, a list of over two hundred male Karaites in Cairo in the year 5635/1875.

It is proposed to present here the names in the list in Hebrew and in English transcription, with a translation of the accompanying introductory and explanatory material. This will be followed by an interpretation of the list as a source for estimating the Karaite population of Cairo, as well as a discussion of the names themselves.

TRANSLATION AND TRANSCRIPTION OF THE HEBREW TEXT

(The Karaite Community)

These are the names of the males living in Cairo (Miṣrayim)[12] who are married and are householders, each man (with) his wife and children; Priests,[13] Levites[14] and Israelites,[15] except for widows, divorcees and bachelors. (They are) the Karaite community – may their Rock and Redeemer guard over them! – as of the New Moon of Nisan, 5635 (1875).[16]

(These are) the names of the Priests who are here:

	Name	Family	
1)	Abraham ben Joseph (g)[17]	Aṣlān[18]	אברהם ב׳ יוסף ג׳ אצלאן
2)	Abraham ben Jacob	Aṣlān	אברהם ב׳ יעקב אצלאן

11 This volume bears the temporary number KC 21.

12 Miṣrayim is taken here to have the same ambiguous connotation as the Arabic Miṣr, which is used both for Cairo and for Egypt as a whole. As the former usage is more common it is translated thus here. Cf. the modern usage in note 36 below.

13 *Kohanim,* descendants of the ancient Temple priesthood recognized among Rabbanite Jews, Karaites and Samaritans as well. As such they retain certain largely vestigial ritual functions and are subject to the special regulations regarding marriage, purity and the like, to which the ancient priests were subject.

14 *Leviyim*, the musicians and servants in the ancient Temple. No special significance attaches to Levitical descent in present-day Judaism, except that Levites are entitled to be called to the reading of the Torah after the Kohanim and are required to prepare the Kohanim for the blessing of the congregation.

15 *Yisre'elim*, the rest of the Jewish community; those of nonpriestly and non-Levitical descent.

16 In the Rabbanite calendar this was equivalent to April 6, 1875. The Karaite calendar, however, occasionally differs from the Rabbanite by a day or two.

17 An abbreviation for *gadol*, "big, old," i.e., the elder. Used in this list to indicate a difference in generations between two men bearing the same name and patronymic.

18 This name seems to be derived from the Arabic root *'ṣl*, meaning basically "root, base, foot

3)	Abraham ben Joseph (q)[19]	Aṣlān	אברהם ב׳ יוסף ק׳ אצלאן
4)	Elijah b.k.r[20] Ḥayyim	Aṣlān	אליהו בכ״ר חיים אצלאן
5)	Elijah b.k.r. Jacob	Aṣlān	אליהו בכ״ר יעקב אצלאן
6)	Elijah b.k.r. Moses	Aṣlān	אליהו בכ״ר משה אצלאן
7)	Barukh b.k.r. Joseph	Aṣlān	ברוך בכ״ר יוסף אצלאן
8)	Barukh b.k.r. Moses	Aṣlān	ברוך בכ״ר משה אצלאן
9)	Bekhor b.k.r. Ḥayyim	Elazar	בכור בכ״ר חיים אלעזר
10)	Ḥayyim b.k.r. Judah	Aṣlān	חיים בכ״ר יהודה אצלאן
11)	Ḥayyim b.k.r. Moses	Aṣlān	חיים בכ״ר משה אצלאן
12)	Joseph b.k.r. Ḥayyim	Aṣlān	יוסף בכ״ר חיים אצלאן
13)	Judah b.k.r. Ḥayyim	Aṣlān	יהודה בכ״ר חיים אצלאן
14)	Farag Yeshuʿah[21] b. Moses	Aṣlān	פרג ישועה ב׳ משה אצלאן
15)	Farag Yeshuʿah b. Jacob	Aṣlān	פרג ישועה ב׳ יעקב אצלאן
16)	Moses b.k.r. Joseph	Aṣlān	משה בכ״ר יוסף אצלאן

The number of Priests is sixteen.[22]

(These are) the names of the Levites who are here:

	Name	**Family**	
1)	Abraham b. Moses	Maṣliaḥ	אברהם ב׳ משה מצליח
2)	Abraham b. Nissīm	Garbūʿa	אברהם ב׳ נסים גרבוע
3)	Abraham b. Joseph	Levi	אברהם ב׳ יוסף לוי

(of a mountain)," with derivatives meaning "of good extraction (*ibn aṣl*) or well-born." The form *aṣlān* itself does not occur in the dictionaries. In Hebrew the basic root meaning is "to separate from, impart from one's spirit, inspire" and the derivative *aṣīl* means "honored, noble, important." Again the form *aṣlān* does not occur, although the pattern is found in both Arabic and Hebrew. Since the name is usually found among Kohanim, it may indeed have the basic meaning of "honored, well-born." See, however, the special meaning of *aṣl* found in medieval Judeo-Arabic usage in Genizah documents, where it means "title to property," in which case this might mean "property holder." Cf. M. Gil, *Documents of the Jewish Pious Foundations from the Cairo Geniza* (Publications of the Diaspora Research Institute, vol. 12), Leiden 1976, pp. 10, 23, 40, 41, and document 66.

19 An abbreviation for *qaṭan*, "little, young." Cf. note 17.

20 Probably an abbreviation for *ben kevodo, rav...*, or *ben kevod ha-rav*. In either case, an indication of respect. Why it is used with some names and not with others is not clear from the text.

21 A couplet consisting of a Hebrew and an Arabic name with the same or similar meaning. The Arabic *faraj* (here the Egyptian pronunciation *farag* is followed, especially since Hebrew has no *j* sound) means "deliverance, salvation," as does Hebrew *yeshuʿah*. Cf. below, Khiḍr Elijah, and Ṣāliḥ Maṣliaḥ.

22 Note the difference in numbers of Priests, Levites and Israelites: 16, 37 and 115 respectively. All the priests but one bear the family name Aṣlān, which still occurs among present-day Egyptian Karaites, although the family name Kohen is also found today.

4)	Elijah b.k.r. Abraham	Dimashqī	אליהו בכ"ר אברהם דמשקי
5)	Elijah b.k.r. Abraham	Maṣliaḥ	אליהו בכ"ר אברהם מצליח
6)	David b.k.r. Obadiah	Dimashqī	דויד בכ"ר עובדיה דמשקי
7)	David b.k.r. Joseph	Sofer	דויד בכ"ר יוסף סופר
8)	Zechariah b.k.r. Joseph	Levi	זכריה בכ"ר יוסף לוי
9)	Ḥayyim b.k.r. Elijah	Levi	חיים בכ"ר אליהו לוי
10)	Joseph b.k.r. Farag Yeshuʻah	Darwīsh	יוסף בכ"ר פרג ישועה דרויש
11)	Joseph b.k.r. Abraham	Maṣliaḥ	יוסף בכ"ר אברהם מצליח
12)	Joseph b.k.r. Abraham	Dimashqī	יוסף בכ"ר אברהם דמשקי
13)	Joseph b.k.r. Moses	Maṣliaḥ	יוסף בכ"ר משה מצליח
14)	Joseph b.k.r. Jacob	Kaḥḥālah	יוסף בכ"ר יעקב כחאלה
15)	Joseph b.k.r. Elijah	Qayyis	יוסף בכ"ר אליהו קייס
16)	Joseph b.k.r. Moses	Qarpī	יוסף בכ"ר משה קרפי
17)	Isaac b.k.r. Elijah	Levi	יצחק בכ"ר אליהו לוי
18)	Isaac b.k.r. Abraham	Dimashqī	יצחק בכ"ר אברהם דמשקי
19)	Isaac b.k.r. Yeshuʻah	Maṣliaḥ	יצחק בכ"ר ישועה מצליח
20)	Jacob b.k.r. Elijah	Levi	יעקב בכ"ר אליהו לוי
21)	Jacob b.k.r. Moses	Maṣliaḥ	יעקב בכ"ר משה מצליח
22)	Jacob b.k.r. Joseph	Maṣliaḥ	יעקב בכ"ר יוסף מצליח
23)	Jacob b.k.r. Solomon	Kaḥḥālah	יעקב בכ"ר שלמה כחאלה
24)	Jacob b.k.r. Joseph	Kaḥḥālah	יעקב בכ"ר יוסף כחאלה
25)	Khiḍr Elijah b. Abraham	Gindī	חצ̇ר אליהו ב' אברהם ג̇נדי
26)	Moses b.k.r. Elijah Khiḍr	Saḥābu	משה בכ"ר אליהו חצ̇ר סחאבו
27)	Moses b.k.r. Jacob	Levi	משה בכ"ר יעקב לוי
28)	Moses b.k.r. Solomon	Kaḥḥālah	משה בכ"ר שלמה כחאלה
29)	Moses b.k.r. Abraham	Maṣliaḥ	משה בכ"ר אברהם מצליח
30)	Nissīm b.k.r. Abraham	Garbūʻa	נסים בכ"ר אברהם גרבוע
31)	Farag Yeshuʻah b. David	Darwīsh	פרג ישועה ב' דויד דרויש
32)	Farag Yeshuʻah b.k.r. Jacob	Maṣliaḥ	פרג ישועה בכ"ר יעקב מצליח
33)	Farag Yeshuʻah b. Moses	Shakūshī	פרג ישועה ב' משה שכושי
34)	Ṣāliḥ Maṣliaḥ b. Jacob	Maṣliaḥ	צאליח מצליח ב' יעקב מצליח
35)	Sasson b.k.r. Jacob	Kaḥḥālah	ששון בכ"ר יעקב כחאלה
36)	Solomon b.k.r. Yeshuʻah	Sirgānī	שלמה בכ"ר ישועה סירגאני
37)	Solomon b.k.r. Jacob	Kaḥḥālah	שלמה בכ"ר יעקב כחאלה

The number of Levites is thirty seven.[23]

23 The 37 Levites bear only 13 family names, 4 of which — Maṣliaḥ (10), Levi (6), Kaḥḥālah (6), and Dimashqī (4) — account for 22 individuals.

And these are the names of the Israelites who are here:

1)	Abraham b.k.r. Yeshuʿah	Sirgānī	אברהם בכ״ר ישועה סירגאני
2)	Abraham b.k.r. Joseph	Menasheh	אברהם בכ״ר יוסף מנשה
3)	Abraham b.k.r. David	Rūmiyah	אברהם בכ״ר דויד רומיה
4)	Abraham b.k.r. Isaac	Bamīyah	אברהם בכ״ר יצחק במייה
5)	Abraham b.k.r. Moses	ʿŪziel	אברהם בכ״ר משה עוזיאל
6)	Abraham b.k.r. Yomtov	Aṣlān	אברהם בכ״ר יום טוב אצלאן
7)	Abraham b.k.r. Joseph	ʿŪziel	אברהם בכ״ר יוסף עוזיאל
8)	Abraham b.k.r. Moses	ʿŪziel	אברהם בכ״ר משה עוזיאל
9)	Elijah b.k.r. Solomon	Nasī	אליהו בכ״ר שלמה נשיא
10)	Elijah b.k.r. Elisha	Ṣaʿīr	אליהו בכ״ר אלישע צעיר
11)	Elijah b.k.r. Solomon	Ṣaʿīr	אליהו בכ״ר שלמה צעיר
12)	Elijah b.k.r. Joseph	Nakkash	אליהו בכ״ר יוסף נכש
13)	Elijah b.k.r. Abraham	Marzūq	אליהו בכ״ר אברהם מרזוק
14)	Elijah b.k.r. Moses (g)	Aqraʿ	אליהו בכ״ר משה ג׳ אקרע
15)	Elijah b.k.r. Moses (q)	Aqraʿ	אליהו בכ״ר משה ק׳ אקרע
16)	Elijah b.k.r. Moses	Sirgānī	אליהו בכ״ר משה סרגאני
17)	Aaron b.k.r. Elijah	Aqraʿ	אהרון בכ״ר אליהו אקרע
18)	Ayyūb (Job) b.k.r. Moses	Shammāsh	איוב בכ״ר משה שמאש
19)	Elisha b.k.r. Elijah (g)	Ṣaʿīr	אלישע בכ״ר אליהו ג׳ צעיר
20)	Elisha b.k.r. Joseph	Menasheh	אלישע בכ״ר יוסף מנשה
21)	Elisha b.k.r. Elijah (q)	Ṣaʿīr	אלישע בכ״ר אליהו ק׳ צעיר
22)	Elisha b.k.r. Elisha	Ṣaʿīr	אלישע בכ״ר אלישע צעיר
23)	Barukh b.k.r. Joseph	Masʿūdah	ברוך בכ״ר יוסף מסעודה
24)	Barukh b.k.r. Elijah	Masʿūdah	ברוך בכ״ר אליהו מסעודה
25)	Barukh b.k.r. Elijah	Gāmīl[24]	ברוך בכ״ר אליהו גאמיל
26)	David b.k.r. Isaac	Ṣaʿīr	דויד בכ״ר יצחק צעיר
27)	David b.k.r. Marzūq	Dabbāḥ	דויד בכ״ר מרזוק דבאח
28)	David b.k.r. Elijah	ʿŪziel	דויד בכ״ר אליהו עוזיאל
29)	David b.k.r. Elijah	Masʿūdah	דויד בכ״ר אליהו מסעודה
30)	David b.k.r. Elijah	Nasī	דויד בכ״ר אליהו נשיא
31)	David b.k.r. Jacob	Rūmiyah	דויד בכ״ר יעקב רומיה
32)	Hayyim b.k.r. Yefet	Dimashqī	חיים בכ״ר יפת דמשקי
33)	Joseph b.k.r. Isaac	Ṣaʿīr	יוסף בכ״ר יצחק צעיר
34)	Joseph b.k.r. Elijah	Ṣaʿīr	יוסף בכ״ר אליהו צעיר
35)	Joseph b.k.r. Abraham	Ḥayyinah	יוסף בכ״ר אברהם חיינה
36)	Joseph b.k.r. Moses	Ḥayyinah	יוסף בכ״ר משה חיינה

24 Probably a miswriting of Arabic *jamīl/gamīl* "beautiful, handsome."

37)	Joseph b.k.r. Joseph	Menasheh	יוסף בכ"ר יוסף מנשה
38)	Joseph b.k.r. Obadiah	Dimashqī	יוסף בכ"ר עובדיה דמשקי
39)	Joseph b.k.r. Yeshu'ah	Dimashqī	יוסף בכ"ר ישועה דמשקי
40)	Joseph b.k.r. Abraham	Marzūq	יוסף בכ"ר אברהם מרזוק
41)	Joseph b.k.r. Yefet	Dimashqī	יוסף בכ"ר יפת דמשקי
42)	Joseph b.k.r. Mordecai	Ḥayyinah	יוסף בכ"ר מרדכי חיינה
43)	Joseph b.k.r. Yomtov	Aṣlān	יוסף בכ"ר יום טוב אצלאן
44)	Joseph b.k.r. Elijah	Ṭaḥḥān	יוסף בכ"ר אליהו טחאן
45)	Joseph b.k.r. Nissīm	Dabbāḥ	יוסף בכ"ר נסים דבאח
46)	Joseph b.k.r. Barukh	Mas'ūdah	יוסף בכ"ר ברוך מסעודה
47)	Joseph b.k.r. Nissīm	Tufāḥī	יוסף בכ"ר נסים תופאחי
48)	Joseph b.k.r. Solomon	Mas'ūdah	יוסף בכ"ר שלמה מסעודה
49)	Joseph b.k.r. Abraham	Ṭawīl	יוסף בכ"ר אברהם טויל
50)	Joseph b.k.r. Elijah	Khāfīs[25]	יוסף בכ"ר אליהו כֹאפיס
51)	Joseph b.k.r. Moses	'Ūziel	יוסף בכ"ר משה עוזיאל
52)	Joseph b.k.r. Yeshu'ah	Sirgānī	יוסף בכ"ר ישועה סרגאני
53)	Isaac b.k.r. Joseph	Ṣa'īr	יצחק בכ"ר יוסף צעיר
54)	Isaac b.k.r. Yefet	Dimashqī	יצחק בכ"ר יפת דמשקי
55)	Judah b.k.r. Ḥayyim	Yomtov	יהודה בכ"ר חיים יום טוב
56)	Jacob b.k.r. Yefet	Dimashqī	יעקב בכ"ר יפת דמשקי
57)	Jacob b.k.r. Moses (g)	'Ūziel	יעקב בכ"ר משה ג' עוזיאל
58)	Jacob b.k.r. Moses	Ḥayyinah	יעקב בכ"ר משה חיינה
59)	Jacob b.k.r. Moses	Shammāsh	יעקב בכ"ר משה שמאש
60)	Jacob b.k.r. Moses	Aqra'	יעקב בכ"ר משה אקרע
61)	Jacob b.k.r. Moses (q)	Ḥayyinah	יעקב בכ"ר משה ק' חיינה
62)	Khiḍr Elijah[26] b. Joseph	Ṭanānī	חצֹר אליהו ב' יוסף טנאני
63)	Khiḍr Elijah b. Joseph	Sirgānī	חצֹר אליהו ב' יוסף סרגאני
64)	Khiḍr Elijah b. Joseph	Mas'ūdah	חצֹר אליהו ב' יוסף מסעודה
65)	Khiḍr Elijah b. Joseph	'Ūziel	חצֹר אליהו ב' יוסף עוזיאל
66)	Khiḍr Elijah b. Joseph	Ṭaḥḥān	חצֹר אליהו ב' יוסף טחאן
67)	Khiḍr Elijah b. Solomon	Gāmīl	חצֹר אליהו ב' שלמה גאמיל
68)	Khiḍr Elijah b. Josiah	Qarīmī	חצֹר אליהו ב' יושייהו קרימי
69)	Moses b.k.r. Elijah	Khīrānah	משה בכ"ר אליהו כיראנה
70)	Moses b.k.r. Yeshu'ah	Naggār	משה בכ"ר ישועה נגאר

25 Perhaps a misspelling of Arabic *ḥāfiẓ* "memorizer," often given by Muslims as a title of respect to one who has memorized the entire Koran. Perhaps used similarly in a specifically Jewish context. Occurs as personal name in the journal *al-Kalīm*, cf. n. 34.

26 Also read Khaḍir, the Muslim figure equivalent in pious folklore to Elijah, especially in connection with the working of wonders.

71)	Moses b.k.r. Solomon	Mas'ūdah	משה בכ״ר שלמה מסעודה
72)	Moses b.k.r. Elijah	Aqra'	משה בכ״ר אליהו אקרע
73)	Moses b.k.r. Abraham	Ṭawīl	משה בכ״ר אברהם טויל
74)	Moses b.k.r. Jacob	Shammāsh	משה בכ״ר יעקב שמאש
75)	Moses b.k.r. Ḥayyim	Fairūz	משה בכ״ר חיים פירוז
76)	Moses b.k.r. Elijah	Mas'ūdah	משה בכ״ר אליהו מסעודה
77)	Moses b.k.r. Abraham	Mas'ūdah	משה בכ״ר אברהם מסעודה
78)	Moses b.k.r. Abraham	Marzūq	משה בכ״ר אברהם מרזוק
79)	Moses b.k.r. Joseph	'Ūziel	משה בכ״ר יוסף עוזיאל
80)	Moses b.k.r. Joseph	Dimashqī	משה בכ״ר יוסף דמשקי
81)	Moses b.k.r. David	Dabbāḥ	משה בכ״ר דויד דבאח
82)	Moses b.k.r. Ḥasdael	Bamrah	משה בכ״ר חסדאל במרה
83)	Moses b.k.r. Nissīm	Khāfis[27]	משה בכ״ר נסים כֿאפס
84)	Moses b.k.r. Elijah	Ṭaḥḥān	משה בכ״ר אליהו טחאן
85)	Mordecai b.k.r. Joseph	Ḥayyinah	מרדכי בכ״ר יוסף חיינה
86)	Marzūq b.k.r. Jacob	Dimashqī	מרזוק בכ״ר יעקב דמשקי
87)	Nissīm b.k.r. Joseph	Tufāḥī	נסים בכ״ר יוסף תופאחי
88)	Nissīm b.k.r. Abraham	Dabbāḥ	נסים בכ״ר אברהם דבאח
89)	Nissīm b.k.r. Abraham	Garbū'a	נסים בכ״ר אברהם גרבוע
90)	Sa'adiah b.k.r. David	Dabbāḥ	סעדיה בכ״ר דויד דבאח
91)	Sa'adiah b.k.r. Jacob	Ḥayyinah	סעדיה בכ״ר יעקב חיינה
92)	Sa'adiah b.k.r. Joseph	Tūfāḥī	סעדיה בכ״ר יוסף תופאחי
93)	Sa'adiah b.k.r. Isaac	Hannah	סעדיה בכ״ר יצחק הנה
94)	Obadiah b.k.r. Yeshu'ah	Dimashqī	עובדיה בכ״ר ישועה דמשקי
95)	Obadiah b.k.r. Joseph	Dimashqī	עובדיה בכ״ר יוסף דמשקי
96)	Obadiah b.k.r. Elijah	Gāmīl	עובדיה בכ״ר אליהו גאמיל
97)	Farag Yeshu'ah b. Joseph	Ṣa'īr	פרג ישועה ב׳ יוסף צעיר
98)	Farag Yeshu'ah b. Joseph	Menasheh	פרג ישועה ב׳ יוסף מנשה
99)	Farag Yeshu'ah b. Obadiah	Dimashqī	פרג ישועה ב׳ עובדיה דמשקי
100)	Farag Yeshu'ah b. Yeshu'ah	Bandaq	פרג ישועה ב׳ ישועה בנדק
101)	Farag Yeshu'ah b. Abraham	Mas'ūdah	פרג ישועה ב׳ אברהם מסעודה
102)	Farag Yeshu'ah b. Elijah	Khāfīs	פרג ישועה ב׳ אליהו כֿאפיס
103)	Farag Yeshu'ah b. Mordecai	Ḥayyinah	פרג ישועה ב׳ מרדכי חיינה
104)	Farag Yeshu'ah b. Eliah	Ḥayyinah	פרג ישועה ב׳ אליהו חיינה
105)	Farag Yeshu'ah b. Moses	'Ūziel	פרג ישועה ב׳ משה עוזיאל
106)	Farag Yeshu'ah b. Yeshu'ah	Sirgānī	פרג ישועה ב׳ ישועה סרגאני
107)	Farag Yeshu'ah b. David	Dabbāḥ	פרג ישועה ב׳ דויד דבאח
108)	Farag Yeshu'ah b. Elijah	Mas'ūdah	פרג ישועה ב׳ אליהו מסעודה

27 Cf. note 25. Note the difference in spelling in this instance.

109)	Solomon b.k.r. Moses	Mas'ūdah	שלמה בכ״ר משה מסעודה
110)	Solomon b.k.r. Jacob	Kaḥḥālah	שלמה בכ״ר יעקב כחאלה
111)	Solomon b.k.r. Sa'adiah	Ḥayyinah	שלמה בכ״ר סעדיה חיינה
112)	Solomon b.k.r. Elijah	Nūnū	שלמה בכ״ר אליהו נונו
113)	Solomon b.k.r. Elijah	Ṣa'īr	שלמה בכ״ר אליהו צעיר
114)	Solomon b.k.r. Elisha	Ṣa'īr	שלמה בכ״ר אלישע צעיר
115)	Solomon b.k.r. Yeshu'ah	Shabī'a[28]	שלמה בכ״ר ישועה שבייע

The number of Israelites is one hundred and fifteen, of Priests sixteen, of Levites thirty seven. Altogether, householders (whether) Priests, Levites (or) Israelites are two (!) hundred and sixty seven, one hundred eight (!) and sixty[29] besides the bachelors, widowers, widows, divorcees and others.

These are the names of the men, householders, married to two women.[30]

1)	Isaac b.k.r. Joseph	Ṣa'īr	יצחק בכ״ר יוסף צעיר
2)	Elijah b.k.r. Joseph	Mas'ūdah	אליהו בכ״ר יוסף מסעודה
3)	Barukh b.k.r. Joseph	Mas'ūdah	ברוך בכ״ר יוסף מסעודה
4)	Obadiah b.k.r. Yeshu'ah	Dimashqī	עובדיה בכ״ר ישועה דמשקי
5)	David b.k.r. Obadiah	Dimashqī	דויד בכ״ר עובדיה דמשקי
6)	Sa'adiah ben Jacob	Ḥayyinah	סעדיה ב׳ יעקב חיינה
7)	Joseph ben Solomon	Mas'ūdah	יוסף ב׳ שלמה מסעודה
8)	Jacob b.k.r. Joseph	Kaḥḥālah	יעקב ב׳ יוסף כחאלה
9)	Jacob b.k.r. Moses	Shammāsh	יעקב ב׳ משה שמאש
10)	Sa'adiah b.k.r. Isaac	Hannah	סעדיה ב׳ יצחק הנה
11)	Joseph b.k.r. Isaac	Ṣa'īr	יוסף בכ״ר יצחק צעיר

All the men married to two women are eleven householders.

We shall also begin to write the names of bachelors in need of the (wedding) canopy from the age of fifteen[31] and over:

1)	Elijah ben Jacob Marzūq	Dimashqī	אליהו ב׳ יעקב מרזוק דמשקי
2)	Elijah ben Joseph	Naggār	אליהו ב׳ יוסף נגאר
3)	Elijah ben Joseph	Marzūq	אליהו ב׳ יוסף מרזוק
4)	Elijah ben Joseph	Dimashqī	אליהו ב׳ יוסף דמשקי
5)	Abraham ben Joseph	Dimashqī	אברהם ב׳ יוסף דמשקי

28 Or perhaps Shubay'a.

29 The correct number is 167. Note the error made in each instance here.

30 Bigamy has been practised by some non-European Jews down till the present time; cf. "Bigamy," *Encyclopaedia Judaica,* IV, cols. 985 ff.

31 Presumably the age of majority required for marriage, although thirteen is recognized as such by Rabbanite Jews.

6)	Abraham ben Jacob	Kaḥḥālah	אברהם ב׳ יעקב כחאלה
7)	Abraham ben Yeshuʿah	Sirgānī	אברהם ב׳ ישועה סרגאני
8)	Abraham ben Solomon	Zamūrudī	אברהם ב׳ שלמה זמורדי
9)	Abraham ben Jacob	Shammāsh	אברהם ב׳ יעקב שמאש
10)	Abraham ben Joseph	Gindī	אברהם ב׳ יוסף גנדי
11)	Abraham ben Solomon	Dimashqī	אברהם ב׳ שלמה דמשקי
12)	Abraham ben Joseph	Marzūq	אברהם ב׳ יוסף מרזוק
13)	Abraham ben Ḥayyim	Levi	אברהם ב׳ חיים לוי
14)	David b.k.r. Jacob	Kaḥḥālah	דויד בכ״ר יעקב כחאלה
15)	David b.k.r. Moses	Maṣliaḥ	דויד בכ״ר משה מצליח
16)	David b.k.r. Joseph	Dabbāḥ	דויד בכ״ר יוסף דבאח
17)	Zakītū ben Elijah	Ṣaʿīr	זכיתו ב׳ אליהו צעיר
18)	Zakītū ben Elisha	Ṣaʿīr	זכיתו ב׳ אלישע צעיר
19)	Ḥayyim ben Elijah	Qayyis	חיים ב׳ אליהו קייס
20)	Ḥayyim ben Joseph	Maṣliaḥ	חיים ב׳ יוסף מצליח
21)	Joseph ben Judah	Aṣlān	יוסף ב׳ יהודה אצלאן
22)	Joseph ben Saʿadiah	Tūfāḥī	יוסף ב׳ סעדיה תופאחי
23)	Joseph ben Abraham	Dabbāḥ	יוסף ב׳ אברהם דבאח
24)	Joseph ben Jacob	Shammāsh	יוסף ב׳ יעקב שמאש
25)	Joseph ben Ḥayyim	Fairūz	יוסף ב׳ חיים פירוז
26)	Joseph ben Ḥayyim	Ṣaʿīr	יוסף ב׳ חיים צעיר
27)	Joseph ben Moses	Masʿūdah	יוסף ב׳ משה מסעודה
28)	Jacob ben Joseph	Darwīsh	יעקב ב׳ יוסף דרויש
29)	Jacob ben Simon	ʿŪziel	יעקב ב׳ שמעון עוזיאל
30)	Jacob ben Joseph	Sofer	יעקב ב׳ יוסף סופר
31)	Jacob ben Joseph	Dimashqī	יעקב ב׳ יוסף דמשקי
32)	Isaac ben Yeshuʿah	Naggār	יצחק ב׳ ישועה נגאר
33)	Isaac ben Barukh	Masʿūdah	יצחק ב׳ ברוך מסעודה
34)	Mordecai ben David	Darwīsh	מרדכי ב׳ דויד דרויש
35)	Manṣūr ben Solomon	Kaḥḥālah	מנצור ב׳ שלמה כחאלה
36)	Moses ben Elijah	ʿŪziel	משה ב׳ אליהו עוזיאל
37)	Saʿadiah ben Nissīm	Tūfāḥī	סעדיה ב׳ נסים תופאחי
38)	Salīm ben Elijah (g)	Ṣaʿīr	סלים ב׳ אליהו ג׳ צעיר
39)	Salīm ben Elijah (q)	Ṣaʿīr	סלים ב׳ אליהו ק׳ צעיר
40)	Sulīmān ben Abraham	Barbar	סולימאן ב׳ אברהם ברבר
41)	Farag ben Abraham	Gindī	פרג ב׳ אברהם גנדי
42)	Farag ben Saʿadiah	Tufāḥī	פרג ב׳ סעדיה תופאחי
43)	Farag ben Joseph	ʿŪziel	פרג ב׳ יוסף עוזיאל
44)	Farag ben Joseph	Kaḥḥālah	פרג ב׳ יוסף כחאלה
45)	Farag ben Joseph	Dimashqī	פרג ב׳ יוסף דמשקי

46)	Faḍlallāh ben Moses	Ḥasdael	פצלאלה ב׳ משה חסדאל
47)	Solomon ben Joseph	Mas'ūdáh	שלמה ב׳ יוסף מסעודה
48)	Solomon ben Elijah	Mas'ūdah	שלמה ב׳ אליהו מסעודה
49)	Solomon ben Joseph	Sirgānī	שלמה ב׳ יוסף סרגאני

The list ends here without comment.[32] It seems complete in the sense that Solomon would normally be one of the last names in Hebrew alphabetical order. The scribe may, however, have intended to list other categories of individuals such as widowers, widows and divorcees, referred to at the beginning of the list.

If we examine the numbers given here we may arrive at certain tentative conclusions about the size of the Karaite community.

Priests (Kohanim) – heads of households only	16
Levites – heads of households only	37
Israelites – heads of households only	115
number of households	168
of which there were two-wife households	10
men with monogamous households	158

There were, therefore, 316 married adults in monogamous households and 33 in bigamous households (10 men double-listed and one appearing only in the list of two-wife households, hence 11 × 3). To this we may add the 49 bachelors over the age of 15, to reach a more-or-less certain total of 398 adult males and married women. This does not include the following categories: widows, widowers, divorcees and marriageable women above the age of 15. The existence of people in some of these categories may be assumed not only from the scribe's statements but also from the occurrence, in the list of bachelors, of family names not found in the other lists, indicating that they might have been orphans residing with widowed mothers. We may guess that the number of adults in the categories of widows, widowers, divorcees and marriageable women would add perhaps 50 persons to the list of adults. This rather firm estimated total of ca. 400–430 adults, when supplemented with estimates of the children in each family, would give us a total which falls well within the range of 1000–1200 which might be guessed from other sources as the size of the Karaite community in Cairo in 1875.[33]

32 The purpose of the list and its intended use are not clear. It is almost certainly not intended as a census – which is prohibited by Karaite law. If complete – and bearing the names of males only – it would seem to be intended for some type of synagogue use, e.g., a list of those who could be counted for a quorum, called to the Torah, etc.

33 See *Jewish Encyclopedia*, New York 1903, V, p. 70, where two figures are given: 100

NAMES IN THE LIST

The names, both personal and family, are of some interest. Almost all of the personal names in both generations given are of Biblical or other traditional Jewish origin. Where Arabic names occur they are generally in couplets with Hebrew names, where each name translates or otherwise complements the other, e.g., Farag Yeshuʿah, Khiḍr Elijah, or Ṣāliḥ Maṣliaḥ.[34] The few occurrences of purely Arabic names are Marzūq, Manṣūr (i.e., Elazar, Ezra, or the like), Salīm and Faḍlallāh. In one instance Sulīmān (Sulaymān) is used instead of Solomon (Shelomo), and there are two instances of the unusual name Zakītū. Otherwise the personal names lean heavily towards Abraham, Isaac, Jacob, Joseph, Moses, Solomon and Elijah, with other Biblical names such as Aaron, Job, Barukh, Elisha, Judah, Josiah, Obadiah and Mordecai occurring with much less frequency. Among non-Biblical names in Hebrew, Ḥayyim occurs quite often, Yomtov less frequently, while names such as Saʿadiah, Nissim and Bekhor remind us that this is not a European Jewish community and Yefet, rarely found among Rabbanite Jews, that this is a Karaite community.

It is in the realm of family names that the influence of the Arabic-speaking environment is most strongly evidenced. As may be expected, some family names were probably once the personal names of an earlier ancestor, as in the case of the Menasheh and Yomtov families. Including these two names, there are only nine that can be clearly identified as Hebrew in origin, the other seven being Levi, Maṣliaḥ, Sofer, ʿUziel, Nasī, Ḥasdael and Ṣaʿīr. The last-mentioned name is actually uncertain, since the Hebrew rendering can be interpreted either as the Hebrew Ṣaʿīr (lit. "young") or as the Arabic Ṣaghīr (lit. "small").

Surprisingly, only a small group of *nisba* or gentilic names occur, of which not all can be traced to a known place, the one clear exception being Dimashqī (Damascene). The others are Qarpī, Shakūshī, Sirgānī, Ṭanānī, Qarīmī, Gindī, Tūfāḥī and Zamūrudī.

Of the remaining names a few are clearly either patronymics or matronymics, such as Marzūq, Masʿūdah or Fairūz, while others like Rumiyah, Bamiyah, Ḥayyinah, Khīrānah, Bamrah, Hannah and Nūnū, may be matronymics. Certain names were descriptive adjectives, probably attached to a forebear and continued through the generations, as is the case with many European Jewish family names, e.g., Ṭawīl, Jamīl (generally written Gāmīl),

Karaites in 1841 according to Jost's "Annalen" and 1000 in 1900 according to E.N. Adler. On p. 67 of the same volume, "Eben Sappir" is quoted as saying that there were 150 Karaite *families* in Cairo, presumably around 1860 when the author visited Egypt.

34 Cf. note 20 above.

Ṣaʿīr. A few are names of professions or occupations, such as Shammāsh (sexton), Kaḥḥālah (oculist), Ṭaḥḥān (miller), Naggār (carpenter) and the like. At least one is an animal name, Garbūʿa (jerboa), in a form found in Maghrebi Arabic.

In the Magnes Museum there are also several issues of a now defunct Arabic-language organ of the Karaites of Egypt, dating back to the 1940s.[35] In the issue of 1 April 1947 (9 Nisan 5707) there is a list of sixty members of the community[36] and it is interesting to note that twenty of the family names in that list also occur in the 1875 list.[37] The main difference in both the personal and family names is the stronger evidence of Arabization. e.g., Shammās instead of Shammāsh, al-Tūfāḥī, etc., and the appearance of French personal names — for women as well as for men.[38]

Like the Rabbanite Jews of Egypt, the Karaites — except for a handful — have left and found homes elsewhere, in many cases in Israel. For them this list restores the memories of parents and grandparents. Otherwise it is of value in providing us with hitherto unavailable information about the size and composition of this ancient community.

35 The Arabic title is *al-Kalīm* and it bears the French subtitle Revue Israélite Caraïme. The issue cited is No. 52 in the third year of publication, pp. 6–10.

36 This occurs in the annual report of the "Association de Bienfaissance pour le Mariage des Pauvres Javnes (!) Filles Israélite Caraïme du Caire" (Ḥevrat ʿEzrat Zivvug ha-ʿAniyot la-Yisre'elim ha-Qara'im be-Miṣrayim).

37 These are the following:

Aṣlān	Gamīl/Jamīl	al-Nasī	Ṭaḥḥān
Dabbāḥ	Levi	Nissīm	al-Ṭanānī
Darwīsh	Marzūq	Nūnū	Ṭawīl
Fairūz	Masʿūdah	Shammās	al-Tūfāḥī
Ḥayyinah	Menasheh	al-Sirgānī	ʿUziel

38 Jacques, Maurice, Michel, Renée, Regina, Giacomo, are some of the European (mainly French) names while Fu'ād, Murād, ʿAbd al-ʿAzīz, Tawfīq, are among the Arabic names used.

ואלה שמות האנשים הגרים בחצרים השייכים נשים ובעלי בתים
איש ואשתו ובנו כהנים לוים וישראלים חוץ מטפם ואלמנות
וגרושות ובחורים עדית בני מקרא יצ"ו והיה בר"ח ניסן ש' התרל"ה

שמות הכהנים הנמצאים מספר שמותם משפחתם

מספר שמותם משפחתם

א אברהם ב' יוסף נ' אצלאן
א אברהם ב' יעקב אצלאן
א אברהם ב' יוסף ן' אצלאן
א שלמה בכ"ר חיים אצלאן
א שלמה בכ"ר יעקב אצלאן
א שלמה בכ"ר משה אצלאן
א ברוך בכ"ר יוסף אצלאן
א ברוך בכ"ר משה אצלאן
א בכור בכ"ר יוסף שעמור
א חיים בכ"ר יהודה אצלאן
א חיים בכ"ר משה אצלאן
א יוסף בכ"ר משה אצלאן
א יהודה בכ"ר חיים אצלאן
א פרג ישועה ב' משה אצלאן
א פרג ישועה ב' יעקב אצלאן
א משה בכ"ר יוסף אצלאן

כלל מספר הכהנים שש עשר

שמות הלוים הנמצאים

מספר שמותם משפחתם

א אברהם ב' משה שלוש
א אברהם ב' נסים ערבוע
א אברהם ב' יוסף לוי

א שלמה בכ"ר אברהם דמשקי
א שלמה בכ"ר אברהם מצליח
א דויד בכ"ר שמריה דמשקי
א דויד בכ"ר יוסף קוכר
א זכריה בכ"ר יוסף לוי
א חיים בכ"ר שלמה לוי
א יוסף בכ"ר פרג ישועה דרויש
א יוסף בכ"ר אברהם מצליח
א יוסף בכ"ר אברהם דמשקי
א יוסף בכ"ר משה מצליח
א יוסף בכ"ר יעקב כמאלה
א יוסף בכ"ר שלמה קייס
א יוסף בכ"ר משה קרסי
א יצחק בכ"ר שלמה לוי
א יצחק בכ"ר אברהם דמשקי
א יצחק בכ"ר ישועה מצליח
א יעקב בכ"ר שלמה לוי
א יעקב בכ"ר משה מצליח
א יעקב בכ"ר יוסף מצליח
א יעקב בכ"ר שלמה כמאלה
א יעקב בכ"ר יוסף כמאלה
א בכ"ר שלמה ב' אברהם בגדדי
א משה בכ"ר שלמה בכ"ר סמאבו

מספר שמותם משפחתם
א משה בכ"ר יעקב לוי
א משה בכ"ר שלמה כחאלה
א משה בכ"ר אברהם מצליח
א נסים בכר אברהם נרבוע
א מר ישועה ב' דויד דרויש
א מר ישועה בכר יעקב מצליח
א מר ישועה ב משה שפועי
א צליח מצליח ב' יעקב מצליח
א שמעון בכ"ר יעקב כחאלה
א שלמה בכ"ר ישועה סירגאני
א שלמה בכ"ר יעקב כחאלה
לז מספר הלוים שלשים ~~ששה~~ ושבעה
ואלה שמות הישראלים הנמצאים
מספר שמותם משפחתם
[illegible]
א אברהם בכר יוסף מנשה
א אברהם בכ"ר דויד רומיה
א אברהם בכר יצחק במייה
א אברהם בכ"ר משה עוזיל
א אברהם בכ"ר [illegible] אבלון
א אברהם בכ"ר יוסף עוזיל
א אברהם בכ"ר משה עוזיל
א אליהו בכ"ר שלמה נשיא
א אליהו בכ"ר אלישע צעיר
א אליהו בכ"ר שלמה צעיר
א אליהו בכ"ר יוסף נכש
א אליהו בכ"ר אברהם מרזוק
א אליהו בכ"ר משה ב' אקרע
א אליהו בכ"ר משה ק' אקרע

מספר שמותם משפחתם
א אליהו בכ"ר משה סירגאני
א אהרן בכ"ר אליהו אקרש
א איוב בכ"ר משה שמאש
א אלישע בכ"ר אליהו נ"ע צעיר
א אלישע בכ"ר יוסף מנשה
א אלישע בכ"ר אליהו ק' צעיר
א אלישע בכ"ר אלישע צעיר
א ברוך בכ"ר יוסף מסעודי
א ברוך בכ"ר אליהו מסעודי
א ברוך בכ"ר אליהו נחמיל
א דויד בכ"ר יצחק צעיר
א דויד בכ"ר מבשר דבאח
א דויד בכר אליהו עוזיל
א דויד בכ"ר אליהו מסעודי
א דויד בכ"ר אליהו נשיא
א דויד בכ"ר יעקב רומיה
א חייס בכ"ר יפת דמשקי
~~א יוסף בכ"ר יעקב מצליח~~
א יוסף בכר יצחק צעיר
א יוסף בכ"ר אליהו צעיר
א יוסף בכ"ר אברהם חיינה
א יוסף בכ"ר משה חיינה
א יוסף בכ"ר יוסף מנשה
א יוסף בכ"ר עובדיה דמשקי
א יוסף בכ"ר ישועה דמשקי
א יוסף בכ"ר אברהם מרזוק

מספר שמותם משפחתם

א יוסף בכ"ר יפת דמשקי
א יוסף בכ"ר מרדכי חיינה
א יוסף בכ"ר יום טוב גלגלן
א יוסף בכ"ר אליהו עמאן
א יוסף בכ"ר נסים דבאח
א יוסף בכ"ר ברוך מסעודה
א יוסף בכ"ר נסים תולאתי
א יוסף בכ"ר שלמה מסעודה
א יוסף בכ"ר אברהם טוול
א יוסף בכ"ר אליהו כלפים
א יוסף בכ"ר משה עוזיאל
א יוסף בכ"ר יהושע פירנאני
א יצחק בכ"ר יוסף לציר
א יצחק בכ"ר יפת דמשקי
א יהודה בכ"ר חיים יום טוב
א יעקב בכ"ר יפת דמשקי
א יעקב בכ"ר משה ן' עוזיאל
א יעקב בכ"ר משה חיינה
א יעקב בכ"ר משה שמאש
א יעקב בכ"ר משה מקדש
א יעקב בכ"ר משה ן' חיינה
א כמ"ר אליהו ב' יוסף שמאני
א כמ"ר אליהו ב' יוסף פירנאני
א כמ"ר אליהו ב' יוסף מסעודה
א כמ"ר אליהו ב' יוסף עוזיאל
א כמ"ר אליהו ב' יוסף עמאן
[illegible]

מספר שמותם משפחתם

א כמ"ר אליהו ב' שלמה נמאני
א כמ"ר אליהו ב' יהושע קרימי
א משה בכ"ר אליהו ן' פירנאני
א משה בכ"ר יהושע נגאר
א משה בכ"ר שלמה מסעודה
א משה בכ"ר אליהו מקדש
א משה בכ"ר אברהם טוול
א משה בכ"ר יעקב שמאש
א משה בכ"ר חיים פירון
א משה בכ"ר אליהו מסעודה
א משה בכ"ר אברהם מסעודה
א משה בכ"ר אברהם מירדוך
א משה בכ"ר יוסף עוזיאל
א משה בכ"ר יוסף דמשקי
א משה בכ"ר דוד דבאח
א משה בכ"ר מסעוד בחיה
א משה בכ"ר נסים כלפים
א משה בכ"ר אליהו עמאן
א מרדכי בכ"ר יוסף חיינה
א מרדוך בכ"ר יעקב דמשקי
א נסים בכ"ר יוסף תולאתי
א נסים בכ"ר אברהם דבאח
א נסים בכ"ר אברהם ערבוע
א סעדיה בכ"ר דוד דבאח
א סעדיה בכ"ר יעקב חיינה
א סעדיה בכ"ר יוסף תולאתי
א סעדיה בכ"ר יצחק הנה

מספר שמותם משפחתם

א עובדיה בכ״ר ישועה דמשקי
א עובדיה בכ״ר יוסף דמשקי
א עובדיה בכ״ר טיאן נעמאן
א פרג ישועה ב׳ יוסף לציר
א פרג ישועה ב׳ יוסף מנשה
א פרג ישועה ב׳ עובדיה דמשקי
א פרג ישועה ב׳ ישועה בנים
א פרג ישועה ב׳ אברהם מקשורה
א פרג ישועה ב׳ טיאן כהנים
א פרג ישועה ב׳ מרדכי חיונה
א פרג ישועה ב׳ טיאן חיונה
א פרג ישועה ב׳ משה עזיאל
א פרג ישועה ב׳ ישועה סירנעי
א פרג ישועה ב׳ דוד רבאח
א פרג ישועה ב׳ טיאן מקשורה
א שלמה בכ״ר משה מקשורה
א שלמה בכ״ר יעקב כחלה
א שלמה בכ״ר סעדיה חיונה
א שלמה בכ״ר טיאן נונו
א שלמה בכ״ר טיאן לציר
א שלמה ב׳ טיאן לישע לציר
א שלמה בכ״ר ישועה שבייע

וחמשה
ק״ה מספר הישראלים חלה
עשר והלוים ושלשים הכל
בעלי בתים כהנים לוים
וישראלים קטן ... ושנים
מלבד הבחורים והנשים וה
והאלמנות והנערות ותולדותם

ואלה שמות הנשיאים בני ישראל
שהם נשים בעלי ביתים

א יצחק בכ״ר יוסף לציר
א טיאן בכ״ר יוסף מקשורה
א ברוך בכ״ר יוסף מקשורה
א עובדיה ב׳ ישועה דמשקי
א דוד בכ״ר עובדיה דמשקי
א סעדיה ב׳ יעקב חיונה
א יוסף ב׳ שלמה מקשורה
א יעקב ב׳ יוסף כחלה
א יעקב ב׳ משה שמאע
א סעדיה ב׳ יצחק הנה
א יוסף בכ״ר יצחק לציר

יא כל הנשים הנשואים שהי
נשים אחד עשר בעלי ביתים
וגם נתחיל לכתוב שמות
הבחורים הנערכים לחופה
מבן חמש עשרה שנה ומעלה

א טיאן ב׳ יעקב מרואן דמשקי
א טיאן ב׳ יוסף נעמאן
א טיאן ב׳ יוסף מרקוץ
א טיאן ב׳ יוסף דמשקי
א אברהם ב׳ יוסף דמשקי
א אברהם ב׳ יעקב כחלה
א אברהם ב׳ ישועה קירקוני
א אברהם ב׳ שלמה מקורה
א אברהם ב׳ יעקב שמאע
א אברהם ב׳ יוסף נגרי
א אברהם ב׳ שלמה דמשקי
א אברהם ב׳ יוסף מרקוץ
א אברהם ב׳ חיים מכעתך
א דוד בכ״ר יעקב כחלה
א דוד בכ״ר משה מלוך

א דוד בכ׳ר יוסף רבאח

א זכיתו ב׳ שאול צעיר
א זכיתו ב׳ ישוע צעיר
א חיים ב׳ שאול קייס

א חיים ב׳ יוסף מצליח

א יוסף ב׳ יהודה גזלאן

א יוסף ב׳ סעדיה תופאח
א יוסף ב׳ אברהם רבאח
א יוסף ב׳ יעקב שמאש

א יוסף ב׳ חיים טירון

א יוסף ב׳ חיים צעיר

א יוסף ב׳ משה מסעודה
א יעקב בן יוסף דרויש
א יעקב ב׳ שמעון טוקיש

א יעקב ב׳ יוסף קוכר

א יעקב ב׳ יוסף רמעקי

א יצחק ב׳ ישועה נגאר

א יצחק ב׳ ברוך מסעודה

א מרדכי ב׳ דוד דרויש

א מנצור ב׳ שלמה כחלה

א משה ב׳ שאול טוקיאל

א סעדיה ב׳ נסים תופאחי

א סלים ב׳ שאול ז׳ צעיר

א סלים ב׳ שאול ק׳ לטיף

א פלחאן ב׳ אברהם צרבר
א טרנ ב׳ סעדיה תופאח

א טרנ ב׳ יוסף טוקיאל

א טרנ ב׳ יוסף כחלה

א טרנ ב׳ יוסף רמעקי

א פצלה ב׳ משה חמרש

א שלמה ב׳ יוסף מסעודה

א שלמה ב׳ שאול מסעודה

א שלמה ב יוסף סירגאני

A KARAITE CREED*

A. S. HALKIN

Rabbi Israel ben Samuel the Maghrebi, a fourteenth-century Karaite scholar, is known by the sobriquet *ha-Dayyān*, since he was a judge of the Karaite community, and lived in Cairo from 1306 to 1313.[1] He was the teacher of Japhet ben Zair, a well-known physician in Cairo.[2]

Rabbi Israel compiled a code of Karaite law.[3] According to Pinsker,[4] he adopted a more lenient position than had prevailed in the policy of *rikkūbh*, a complicated system of forbidden marriages, based on the principle that man and woman become one in marriage and consequently the near or distant relatives forbidden to each of them are forbidden to both. This led to a situation where it would prove difficult for a Karaite to find a mate in his town. Rabbi Israel's reform resulted in a departure from a practice which had obtained among Karaites for some 600 years.[5] The known Karaite scholar Rabbi Samuel the Maghrebi criticizes, in his chapter dealing with incestuous marriages, the unreasonable complications and difficulties imposed by a number of Karaite scholars because of their system of *rikkūbh*, and speaks praisefully of a few learned men who disapproved of these extremists, among

* This study is presented to Dr. Leon Nemoy in recognition of the important contributions he has made to the understanding of the Karaite movement. His edition of Ḳirḳisāni's *al-Anwār wal-Marāḳib* (1940–43), and his *Karaite Anthology* (1952), not to mention articles of his in this field, entitle him to high standing among students of Karaism.

1 Steinschneider, *Arabische Literatur der Juden,* par. 184 (pp. 243–4). Neubauer, *Aus der Petersburger Bibliothek,* 24, reports that our author's work on incestuous relations is dated 1257, yet in the printed edition of *Hilkhot Sheḥīṭā* (Vienna 1836) the date of composition is given as 1306. If both dates are to be accepted, Rabbi Israel must have reached old age before he passed away.

2 Steinschneider, *loc. cit.*, par. 185. He composed a ספר המצוות. It should be added that the Karaite scholar Samuel al-Maghrebi was also a disciple of Israel ha-Dayyan.

3 Cf. Pinsker *Liḳḳūṭē Ḳadmōniōt,* 176 ff.

4 *Loc. cit.,* 177.

5 *Ibid.*

them our Rabbi Israel.[6] He is also credited with a work on ritual slaughter[7] and with some poetical compositions.[8] In addition, he is said to have authored some other works.[9]

His creed, originally in Arabic, is to be found in manuscript form in several libraries[10] and is also available in a Hebrew version. Some questions arise in connection with this creed. It is surprising that there is no reference in it to the Messiah or to an age of bliss in the life of the Jewish community. It seems likely that the expectation of the Messiah found in later works[11] came in under the influence of the Jewish belief.[12] It is also interesting to note that the fifth article of faith, the central position of Jerusalem, does not occur in later formulations of the creed, although these contain ten and not six points.[13] It is, however, true that a few of the beliefs which the later compilations list as separate items are subsumed by our author in his more limited statement. It should be added that our author's position on God, like that of his successors, is reminiscent of the satement of Maimonides in his *Mishne Torah*.[14] This cannot be the place to examine the affinities between the Rabbanite and Karaite fundamentals of faith, but even without detailed analysis it is evident that the historical portions drawn from the Bible are common to both groups, and the more doctrinal articles, Revelation and the Day of Judgment, were probably part of the Jew's world of belief even before the schism occurred.

The Arabic text was edited and published by Ernst Mainz in 1953.[15] A few

6 In his *Murshid*, ch. 9: והדברים היותר ראויים להסמך עליהם מאלה הנזכרים כולם הם דברי ר׳ ישראל הדיין ז״ל לפי שהוא אֶמֶת אמתיות לא אִמְתָּם מי שקדם לו ודקדק בזה אל התכלית האפשרית יותר מזולתו מן הקודמים לו.

7 *Murshid,* ch. 7, cited in Neubauer, *loc. cit.,* 117, note xix.

8 Pinsker, *loc. cit.,* 176 bottom.

9 Steinschneider, *ibid.*

10 *Ibid.* In Hebrew it is called ספר האמונות or ששת האמנות. Neubauer, *ibid.,* lists the six Articles.

11 Elijah Bashyazi in his *Adderet Eliyahu* counts as the tenth article (p. 175, col. l) the certain coming of the Messiah. So also אפריון עשה by Solomon ben Aharon of Troki (in Neubauer, *loc. cit.,* p. י״ז) lists the arrival of the Messiah as article 9 and the resurrection as article 10.

12 Aharon ben Eliyāhu of Nicomedia (1300–1369) in his philosophic work *Eẓ Ḥayyim* (ch. III) discusses various eschatological beliefs. He seems to prefer the expectation of a resurrection for the Jewish people and a period of the gathering of the exiles (p. 203), but there is no intensity of feeling as in the Rabbanite writings; see also his comments in the commentary on the Torah to Deut. 30:1–6. Moses ibn Ezra (c. 1055–c.1140) in his ספר הדיונים והעיונים, 270–1, charges the Karaites with not expecting the Messianic period (in my note I asserted that they believed in the coming of the Messiah, but this was evidently at a later date).

13 It is true that the *ḳibla* was important in Karaite thinking; cf. notes to the fifth article, but only our author lists it as a fundamental belief.

14 See the notes to article l.

15 *Proceedings of the American Academy for Jewish Research*, 22, pp. 55–63. Dr Mainz wrote an introduction to the text in which he raised the above-mentioned problems, with solutions

variants in the manuscript in my possession[16] hardly warrant its republication.[17] The translation with its explanatory notes will, I hope, make it accessible to a public different from, if not larger than, the readers of the original.

other than those provided here.

16 British Museum, Or. 2528, I (Catalogue, II, 188). I wish to thank the authorities of the Museum for sending me the photostats.

17 Here are a few of the more significant variants: F2r l. 4: הואה כל for הוא הכל; l. 18: אלמנשט for אלמשפי; f4r, l. 3: אלחמא for אלסמא; l. 17: אג̇ מעין אמין for אג̇מעין; f 4v l. 7; כלמה כלמה for כלמה; l. 10: תנסך̇ for תפסך̇; l. 18: אלעדלה for לעדלה; f6r, l. 2: אלמכ̇סרה for אלמכארה.

First Article: The Belief in His Lordship

It is the duty of every Israelite to believe that He possesses the total universe, the heavens and what is in them, the earth and what is upon it, the seas and what is contained in them, the hills and their valleys.[1] One Creator, magnified be His illustriousness, He has no beginning and no end. No one triumphs over Him, no one coerces Him. He has no above that would set Him below, no below that would set Him above, no sides that would bind Him, and no directions that would define Him.[2] He wanted that what He willed be, and it came to be,[3] and He brought it forth not in time, not in space. He produced the created objects from non-existence,[4] He is different from them by His pre-existence. He is alive, immortal;[5] enduring, imperishable; self-sufficient, not needy; generous, not miserly; wise, not ignorant; He comprehends in His knowledge all the knowables, past and present and what they include. All existence is in need of Him, and its reliance in its entirety is upon Him. He is not multiplied by the multiplication of His attributes,[6] and He is neither increased nor decreased in His essence. He is not apprehended by the five senses, and He is much beyond taste and touch.[7]

It cannot be said of Him that He is accident or substance, and He does not flush before the sense so that He becomes apparent. He neither sleeps so that He wakes, nor is He overcome so that He is coerced. He is not a body nor a faculty within a body. His name is Allah, and how magnificent a name it is![8] Obedience does not benefit Him, nor does disobedience hurt Him.[9] He hears prayer, accepts repentance, reduces pitfalls, relieves faults, spares from misfortune, saves from false steps. He is trustworthy in His promise, keeping

1 Cf. Hil. Yesodei Ha-Torah 1, 1: וכל הנמצאים משמים וארץ ומה שביניהם לא נמצאו אלא מאמתת המצאו.

2 *Ibid.* 1, 11: ...לא חיבור ולא פירוד לא מקום ולא מדה לא עליה ולא ירידה לא ימין ולא שמאל ולא פנים ולא אחור ולא ישיבה ולא עמידה ואינו מצוי בזמן עד שיהיה לו ראשית ואחרית ומנין שנים ואינו משתנה שאין לו דבר שיגרום לו שנוי ואין לו לא מות ולא חיים כחיי הגוף החי ולא סכלות ולא חכמה כחכמת האיש החכם...

3 A common conception of the ontological argument, expressed in the Arabic word *Kun*; Ḳur'ān 2, 111; 3, 41, and elsewhere.

4 This is the belief in *creatio ex nihilo* (יש מאין).

5 In the Arabic text we have a series of pairs, a statement and the negation of its opposite.

6 He touches here on the issue of the attributes and their effect on God's unity, a major snaggy problem in medieval theological writings.

7 It is surprising that, after mentioning the five senses, he singles out taste and touch. Was it the need of the rhyme?

8 Obviously, he has the Tetragrammaton in mind, yet he strangely gives His Islamic name.

9 Reminiscent of the Hebrew expression, Job 35:7—8, and the formulation of this belief in צדוק הדין.

the covenant; kind, provident, ruler, judge, most merciful among the merciful, protecting the right of the wronged from the wrongdoer. He compensates the patient and those in pain. In His judgment there is no injustice, and His commandments and prohibitions are not affected by corruption. It is He Who kills,[10] makes alive, causes sickness and heals, causes privation and provides wealth.

There is no God but He, before Whose glorious and beautiful magnificence and perfection one is to prostrate oneself. The chiefs honor Him, and mouths speak in praise of Him and of His freedom from imperfection. There is no grace but His grace. Be He blessed and sanctified, lauded and knelt to, adored and elevated above all imperfection, and greeted with Joy. Be He mighty and glorious, and His resplendent name exalted for ever and ever. We pray to Him, that He protect us from sin and missteps in this world and the next, and that He not count us among those who stray from the truth. Amen. Amen.

Second Article: The Belief in the Apostleship

It is that one must believe that the absolutely perfect of the human species[11] in moral character, in intellect and in mind, in discernment, in nobility, in humility, in glory and in majesty is the master, the noble, the honorable, the eminent, the model of the prophets and of the messengers, the foremost among the ancients and the moderns. All that fill the earth are agreed about the validity of his truthfulness and the confirmation of his miracles,[12] and all the prophets bear witness that the Great Lord spoke to him, and his God called him to give a revelation to him among the highest of the high. Among his miracles is the turning of the rod into a serpent and back to its natural state,[13] and making the hand white and restoring it.[14] Also the proofs he did and the wonders performed in the ten terrifying plagues that he inflicted upon Pharaoh time and again.[15] Then he split the boisterous sea,[16] and made water rush from the rock in

10 Cf. Deut. 32:39; I Sam. 2:6

11 The lavish praise and characterization are in line with the efforts of Jewish writers in the Middle Ages to emulate the growing conversion of Muhammad into a supernatural being. In view of the large field of agreement between Judaism and Islam on matters such as God, His attributes, revelation, reward and punishment, the need to emphasize the uniqueness of the messenger and the eternity of the revealed book was felt to be most imperative.

12 This claim is unqualifiedly true. The first prophet and recipient of a revelation, he was recognized as great and his tradition as true by Christians and Muslims, not to mention our prophets who came after Moses.

13 Ex. 4: 3–4.

14 *Ibid.* 6–7. Cf. Saadia's rendering, ultimately based on the Targum of מצׂרעת: חַוְּרָא.

15 *Loc. cit.* chs. 7–10, 12.

16 *Loc. cit.* 14:15–28.

waves.[17] He healed disease,[18] and by his hand he made the manna come down[19] and the quails,[20] and by raising his hands the giants were defeated,[21] and by his high rank the victorious kings were humbled.[22] God addressed him face to face on Mount Sinai,[23] and light from God shone on his noble face.[24] He was given by the most high Lord the tablets of rare precious stone, on which the word of God was written.[25] He interceded for the disobedient.[26] He saw the retinues of the Holy Presence coming and going.[27] He surpassed all the prophets in might and glory as the sun surpasses the moon when it inclines, because he preceded and led them, and their commands revolve around him.[28] He is our lord and our model, the crown of our head and the pole of our tent; our link with our Worshipped One, and the master of our Law. He is our lord Moses son of Amram who spoke the words of God, exalted be He. Peace upon him and on his noble forbears, lord of the day of judgment. Praise to God, Lord of the universe. Amen.

Third Article: The Belief in the Prophets and the Emissaries that came before, with and after him

It is for him to believe that he is a true prophet, of whomever the reliable books speak regarding the veracity of his prophecy – whether he lived before him, like our chiefs Abraham, Isaac and Jacob our patriarchs, peace be upon them, of whom it was said: "Do not touch my anointed ones and do not harm my prophets";[29] or was his contemporary, like our chief Aaron, our chiefs Eleazar, Phineas, Joshua, and the seventy elders, peace be upon them; or lived after him, like our chiefs Samuel of Ramah, Elijah, Elisha, Isaiah, Jeremiah, Ezekiel, Daniel and his companions, peace be upon them – to whom miracles occurred, and testimony was brought by them through wonders and signs. Such was the

17 *Loc. cit.* 17:5–7.
18 *Loc. cit.* 15:22–26.
19 *Loc. cit.* 16:14–15.
20 *Loc. cit.* 16:13 and also Num. 11:31–32.
21 Ex. 17:8–13
22 The subjugation of Siḥon the Ammonite and Og king of Bashan, Num. 21:21–35.
23 Ex. 33:11.
24 *Loc. cit.* 34:29–30.
25 *Loc. cit.* 31:18.
26 *Loc. cit.* 32:11–14.
27 Ps. 68:18–19.
28 The task of the prophets, according to the traditional view, was to urge the people to follow the teachings of Moses. See, e.g., Mal. 3:22.
29 Ps. 105:15. Jewish exegetes also apply this verse to the patriarchs; see Kimḥi, Meiri *ad loc.*

stopping of the sun and moon for Joshua,[30] and the checking of the plague by our chief with the firepan.[31] The chief Elijah walked in the water,[32] fire came down for his protection,[33] he restored to life the son of the Ṣarfit,[34] had rain come down with his prayer,[35] and blessing dwelt with the woman who afforded him hospitality.[36] Elisha also walked in the water,[37] lifted the head of the pickaxe from the river,[38] restored the life of the son of the Shunamite.[39] Every one of the prophets was distinguished by wonders and miracles, a recitation of which would be too long, but their trustworthiness has come down by tradition; there is no doubt of that and no skepticism can affect it. All of them follow the Law of our master Moses son of Amram, father of the prophets, proclaim and establish its truth, learn and act in conformity with it. No law and no religion will issue from any of them;[40] they establish the truth of their loyalty by their veracity. Peace of God be upon all of them. Amen. Praise to God, Lord of the universe.

Fourth Article: The Belief in the Revealed Book

It is that the pure, sanctified, highly-esteemed Law, called Torah – may He magnify and glorify it in the hearts of all people, as the prophet foretold:[41] "It pleases the Lord for His vindication to magnify the Torah and glorify it" – is the one dictated to our master Moses, peace be upon him, by the supreme Reader,[42] without an intermediary,[43] word by word and letter by letter, accurate in its letters and words, eloquent, clear; there is no contradiction in it, and no doubt can affect it; pure truth, a perfect Law. Its precepts are just. It will never be abrogated and at no time annulled.[44] Its tradition through an unbroken chain of transmission is authentic, and its validity through an unbroken chain of

30 Josh. 10:12–13.
31 Num. 17:11–12.
32 II Kings 2:8.
33 *Loc. cit.* 1:10–12.
34 I Kings 17:17–22.
35 *Loc. cit.* 18:20 sqq.
36 *Loc. cit.* 17:14–16.
37 Cf. note 32 above.
38 II Kings 6:5–7.
39 *Loc. cit.* 4:18–37.
40 This is the categorical denial of the possibility of abrogation of Moses' law and its replacement by another. Islam, without questioning the validity of the law of Moses before the time of Muhammad, teaches its abrogation since his appearance.
41 Isa. 42:21.
42 Cf. BB 15a: עד כאן הקב״ה אומר ומשה אומר וכותב.
43 Cf. Num. 12:8.
44 Cf. note 40 above.

generations is established.[45] It is in five books. The intellects agree with its meanings, and confirm them as true. The rest of the multitudes heard its precepts, and rendered them honor. Thanks to its rank, it grants the licence to slaughter beasts,[46] because of the loftiness of His judgments which reveals to just intellects and minds what its wisdom contains and the justice which is inherent in it.

The wisdom which penetrates it no book can compare with, and no sensible person can challenge,[47] as was said[48] – glorious is He Who said – "No weapon formed against you shall succeed, and any tongue that contends with you at law you will defeat; this is the lot of the servants of the Lord, and their triumph through Me, says the Lord."

The Fifth Article: The Belief in the Ḳibla[49]

It is [his duty] to believe that the great, highly-honored and esteemed *ḳibla* – may God restore it to its majesty, excellence and superiority – is the upland, chosen from the rest of the inhabited world for the glorious light of the holy Presence to dwell in it. He declared to our master Solomon:[50] "I have now chosen and consecrated this house in which to put My name forever; My eyes and My heart shall be there for all time." It is [the place] which is prescribed for us to face in prayer,[51] and in the rituals of slaughter[52] and circumcision.[53] We even lay our deceased to face it above ground and below it. It is the place of which it is said:[54] "Look to his habitation and go there." It is the place to which all of the peoples will return to pray, as was said[55] – glory be to the One Who said it – "For My house shall be called a house of prayer for all people."

45 *Tawātur* is the Islamic term to denote an unbroken chain of tradition.

46 It is somewhat surprising that this license to eat meat ritually was singled out from all the precepts. Possibly there is something wrong with the text. Yet it may be an example of the doctrinal importance ascribed to *Sheḥīṭa*, which was regarded cardinal enough to result in the compilation of numerous tracts on the theme.

47 Cf. the Jewish attitude: מי איכא מידי דכתיבי בכתובי דלא רמיזי באוריתא "Is there anything written in the Hagiographa which is not written in the Torah?" (Ta'an. 9a).

48 Isa. 54:17.

49 The name for the direction to Mecca in Islam, which is the position assumed by the worshipper during prayer. Our author employs the same term to designate Jerusalem, towards which Rabbanites and Karaites face during divine services.

50 I Kings 9:3. The first two words ועתה בחרתי are not in the text. It is the consequence of citing from memory.

51 See הדבור החמשי, ענין תפלה, גן עדן (Gozlow, 1866, f. 69.4).

52 *Loc. cit.*, פרק ששה עשר, ענין שחיטה (f. 92c towards the top).

53 I have found no parallel to this.

54 Deut. 12:5.

55 Isa. 56:7.

The Sixth Article: The Belief in the Day of Judgment

It is to be believed that the time of Promise[56] is inescapable. It means the restoration of the dead to the state they were in during their lifetime,[57] by the return of their spirits to them, and their resurrection from their graves to the surface of the earth, and the return of the bodies to the state they were in formerly, even from the depth of the sea and from inside the dark caves and valleys. For it is said:[58] "The Lord said: I will retrieve from Bashan, I will retrieve from the depths of the sea." It will mean the delivery of them entirely and summarily,[59] every one of them in conformity with what he had done, obedience or disobedience, and the scrutiny of his works before Him, and the calculation of joy or distress to him for it. He whose works were good will be translated to Paradise, to take what his heart desires of the great gains, joined to eternal, unceasing honor and respect. Woe and alas to those whose works were not good; they are translated to the house of punishment, to humiliation and insult, to prolonged torture, and they will be subjected to privation and to pain which cannot be comprehended, forever and ever, without surcease. Thus it is written of the wicked:[60] "Their worms shall not die, nor their fire be quenched, and they shall be a horror to all flesh." Of the righteous it is written:[61] "And you shall again distinguish between the righteous and the wicked, between him who served God and him who served Him not." We pray to Him for pardon and forgiveness, mercy and atonement and safety in this world and the next. Amen and Shalom.

The six articles of faith are completed.

56 The word in Arabic which means promise is probably a mistake for **מעאד** return, restoration.

57 See **העקר השמיני, אדרת אליהו**, f. 85c. Our author is evidently discussing the second of the two resurrections listed by the **אדרת אליהו**.

58 Ps 68:23.

59 Clearly, our author has the last judgment in mind; see *loc. cit.* (note 57 above), f. 86a *passim*.

60 Isa. 66:24.

61 Mal. 3:18.

QUELQUES AGGADŌT CRITIQUÉES PAR YEFET BEN ʿĒLĪ

G. VAJDA ז"ל

L'attitude critique, voire hostile des Karaïtes vis-à-vis de l'*Aggada* est bien connue.[1] Elle est principalement motivée, on le sait également, par les anthropomorphismes et les bizarreries d'ordre eschatologique, angélologique ou mystique qui entrent pour une part notable dans l'exégèse midrashique. Mais les négateurs de la "tradition" rabbinique ne sont pas avares de réserves non plus lorsqu'ils rencontrent dans le Targum ou le Midrash des interprétations ou des amplifications du texte révélé appelées par un souci de précision appuyé sur l'imagination créatrice.

Dans la brève contribution que nous sommes heureux d'apporter à l'hommage offert à l'éminent maître des études karaïtes, nous voudrions signaler un petit nombre de critiques de cette dernière espèce, relevées chez l'un des plus féconds, sinon le plus fécond des exégètes karaïtes, Yefet ben ʿĒlī.

Nous empruntons les passages en question aux commentaires sur *Genèse* et *Exode*, pour lesquels nous avons disposé des manuscrits 278 et 280 du fonds hébreu de la Bibliothèque Nationale de Paris. Ils sont publiés à la suite dans une transcription en caractères latins.

I. Genèse 32:15–16 (Paris Hébreu 278, fol. 120 r-v).

Certaines personnes avancent pour le nombre total des têtes de bétail composant ces troupeaux — il est de cinq cent cinquante — une interprétation purement controuvée qui n'est suggérée comme probable et encore moins imposée par quelque preuve ou allusion que ce soit. Fidèles

1 Il suffit de renvoyer ici à Salmōn ben Yerūḥīm, *Sēfer Milḥamōt YHWH* (*The Book of the Wars of the Lord*), éd. I. Davidson, New York 1954, chap. XIV, pp. 108 *sq.*; J. Mann, *Texts and Studies in Jewish History and Literature,* II, Philadelphie 1935, pp. 38, 49 *sq.*; Z. Ankori, *Karaites in Byzantium,* New York — Jérusalem 1959, pp. 240, n. 77 et 264.

à leur méthode, ces gens offrent également des explications pour les détails contenus dans ces versets. Leur échec est, à n'en pas douter, complet. Celui qui possède de la connaissance (en la matière) n'occupe pas son imagination à produire de semblables balivernes et des inventions pures et simples. Ces gens n'entendent (même) pas le sens obvie du Livre (révélé) et ils s'amusent à des balivernes sans fondement dont Dieu couvre de honte les auteurs.

Le commentateur karaïte censure sans aménité les "balivernes" (*Khurāfāt*) excogitées par les adversaires qu'il pourfend sans toutefois préciser la teneur de leurs propos. Il est clair du moins que sa critique porte sur deux points: une motivation du nombre total des animaux envoyés par Jacob comme cadeau à son redoutable frère; une interprétation, non spécifiée, des détails (*tafṣīl*), donc sans doute de la composition des troupeaux.

Quant au second point, rien n'empêche de songer à l'exégèse qui rapprochait la répartition suivant les sexes du bétail offert par Jacob à Esaü avec la périodicité de l'accomplissement du devoir conjugal selon les professions de l'époux;[2] ce genre de traitement aggadique de l'Écriture avait en effet tout pour susciter l'indignation du docteur karaïte.

Pour ce qui est, en revanche, du décompte du nombre total des bêtes, l'affaire est moins claire, car outre une allusion dans le *Pirqey Rabbi Eliʿézer* qui n'est pas des plus limpides, le nombre en question n'est mis en relation avec le chiffre obtenu si l'on additionne les sacrifices prescrits dans la péricope *Pinḥas* (Nombres 28–29) ou bien (mais le calcul est obscur) avec la longueur de la période écoulée entre l'établissement de la royauté en Edom et en Israël respectivement que dans des textes postérieurs à notre Karaïte, le plus ancien étant une phrase de Rabbēnū Ḥanan'ēl (à la rigueur, contemporain plus jeune de Yefet), mais cité seulement par Baḥyé ben Asher, trois siècles plus tard. Yefet serait-il alors le premier en date des témoins d'une exégèse aggadique perdue par ailleurs, mais reprise, presque dans sa génération, par une grande autorité rabbanite? Je laisse à de plus savants et de plus habiles le soin d'en décider.[3]

2 *Cf. Genèse-Rabba*, éd. Theodor – Albeck, 76, 7, pp. 904 *sq.*, avec le commentaire de l'éditeur.

3 *Pirqēy Rabbī Eliʿezer*, chap. 37 et *cf.* la note 25 de David Luria dans son édition, Varsovie, 1852 (reproduction: Jérusalem 1963), 87a; Baḥyé ben Asher, *Bēʾūr ʿal ha-Tōrāh* à Gen. 32:15, éd. H. D. Chavel, Jérusalem 1966, p. 282; *cf.* aussi M. M. Kasher, *Tōrāh Šelēmāh*, VI,

II. Genèse 40:14-15 (ibid., fol. 201 r-v)

Certains pensent que Joseph est à blâmer à cause de ce qu'il a dit au grand échanson: *évoque mon cas devant Pharaon*; pour avoir mis sa confiance en un homme (l'issue favorable de son affaire) fut retardé(e) de deux ans. Mais c'est là une erreur manifeste, car s'il en était comme le pense (l'auteur de cette exégèse) il n'aurait pas été tiré de prison lorsque le grand échanson le mentionna.[4] Nous disons, quant à nous, que Joseph suivit les traces de son père Jacob qui mettait fondamentalement sa confiance en Dieu, mais n'en usa pas moins, ensuite, de divers stratagèmes (...). Lors donc que Joseph vit que le grand échanson reprendrait ses fonctions, il se dit:[5] cet homme est au courant de ma situation; il me doit de la reconnaissance pour l'avoir servi et il a la possibilité de me faire sortir d'ici; c'est sans doute le Maître de l'Univers qui avait disposé en vue de ma délivrance qu'il fût mis en prison et qu'il vît le songe que l'on sait; voilà pourquoi Joseph lui demanda de solliciter de Pharaon qu'il le remît en liberté.

Ici point de difficulté. Yefet fait allusion à une aggada bien connue et fort répandue.[6]

III. Genèse 42:27 (ibid., fol. 229v)

Un commentateur a pensé que par *l'un d'eux l'ouvrit* (l'Écriture désigne Lévi, car il est dit) (Gen. 49:5): *Siméon et Lévi sont frères*. C'est une déduction peu vraisemblable.

Le commentateur karaïte fait sans doute allusion à un *derash* identique ou similaire à celui cónservé dans le Targum palestinien au verset: "Lévi qui était

New York 1952, p. 1286, n. 87. – La motivation du nombre huit des rois ayant régné en Edom avant qu'il y eut un roi en Israël par les huit *mem*-s finaux dans le passage en question ou par l'appellation "mon Seigneur" huit fois appliquée par Jacob à Esaü (*cf. Gen.-R.*, 75, 11, p. 891, 2–4) n'entre pas en ligne de compte ici.

4 Pour le simple motif que...

5 J'ai tâché d'alléger la construction de l'original qui mêle lourdement le style direct au style indirect.

6 *Genèse-Rabba*, 89, 2–3, éd. citée, pp. 1088 *sq.*; *cf.* en dernier lieu les références rassemblées par E. B. Levine, "The Aggadah in Targum Jonathan ben 'Uzziel and Neofiti 1 to Genesis," excursus à Alejandro Diez Macho, *Neophyti 1*, t. II, Madrid – Barcelone 1970, pp. 567 *sq.*

resté seul (séparé) de son frère, ouvrit son sac..."[7]

IV. Genèse 42:37 (ibid., fol. 231).

L'intention de Ruben, lorsqu'il déclara: *tu tueras mes deux fils,* n'était pas de les exclure de l'héritage, contrairement à l'explication donnée par certains.

Dans la remarque plutôt fraîche, faite par le *Midrash* à propos de ces paroles inconsidérées de l'aîné des douze fils du Patriarche le motif d'exclusion de l'héritage n'apparaît pas.[8] Saadia avait quelque peu atténué l'expression en traduisant: "puisses-tu perdre (*'iṯkal*, impératif) mes deux fils" (puisque les petits-enfants sont en quelque sorte les enfants du grand-père), mais chez lui non plus il n'est pas question d'héritage.[9] Le motif apparaît par contre dans la compilation *Hadar Zeqēnīm*;[10] est-ce un cas de rencontre fortuite ou émergence d'une exégèse antérieure à la fin du Xe siècle reparaissant à deux endroits aussi distants l'un de l'autre dans le temps et dans l'espace que le commentateur karaïte d'Irak installé à Jérusalem et les rabbins de France ou du pays rhénan au XIIe-XIIIe siècle?

V. Genèse 46:27 (ibid., fol. 260v).

Le texte mentionne Joseph et ses deux fils, ce qui fait soixante-neuf. En comptant Jacob, le total général est de soixante-dix. C'est l'interprétation à laquelle j'incline. Un commentateur a pensé que c'est Jochebed (qu'il fallait compter) avec (les soixante-neuf). Un autre a soutenu que l'un des fils eut un enfant lorsque la famille de Jacob arriva à la frontière d'Égypte. (Il a avancé cette explication) parce qu'il lui a semblé invraisemblable que Jochebed ait donné le jour à Moïse à l'âge de 130 ans comme l'exigerait la chronologie.

7 *Cf.* Louis Ginzberg, *The Legends of the Jews*, V, 348 (n. 221); *Tōrāh Šelēmāh*, VII, chap. 42, n° 88, p. 1586; Levine, *loc. cit.*, p. 570.

8 *Cf. Genèse-Rabba*, 91, 9, éd. citée, p. 1132, 6; *Legends*, V, 349 (notes 224 et 225); *Tōrāh Šelēmāh, ibid.*, n° 103, p. 1590.

9 *Cf.* Y. Qāfiḥ, *Pērūsh Rabbēnū Sa'adyāh Gā'ōn 'al ha-Tōrāh*, Jérusalem 1963, p. 44. Rappelons en passant qu'il est difficile de se servir sans hésitation de ce travail très méritoire qui repose sur un original dont le texte a été établi mais non publié par le traducteur.

10 Cité dans *Tōrāh Šelēmāh*; je n'ai pas pu vérifier sur l'impression de Livourne.

Yefet a choisi parmi les solutions proposées[11] à la difficulté soulevée par le sens obvie du verset celle qu'avait adoptée Sa'adia en formulant sa traduction de manière à compter Jacob dans le total.[12] Que le nombre fût complète par Yochebed est une donnée aggadique répandue.[13] Quant à la troisième solution mentionnée par Yefet, elle est également connue.[14] En revanche, le motif de l'invraisemblance chronologique qui détourne d'identifier le soixante-dixième membre de la famille de Jacob avec la mère de Moïse n'apparaît pas, à ma connaissance, dans les textes antérieurs à notre commentateur karaïte: c'est plus tard qu'Abraham Ibn 'Ezra le fera valoir, s'attirant pour cette raison les foudres de R. Moïse ben Naḥman.[15] La référence que nous venons de relever chez Yefet montre qu'ici encore (*cf.* I) on pourrait avoir affaire à une source antérieure à la fin du Xe siècle qui reste à retrouver.[16]

VI. Exode 14:21 (Paris Hébreu 280, fol. 158).

L'emplacement qui se fendit fut égal à l'étendue du camp des Israélites, contrairement à l'opinion de ceux qui prétendent qu'il se fendit en douze (sentiers: un) pour chacune des douze tribus. En réalité, il se fendit morceau par morceau: l'eau s'ouvrait devant les Israélites et l'endroit (dégagé) séchait afin (de leur permettre) d'y passer.

L'aggada écartée est dans le Targum palestinien et ailleurs.[17]

VII. Exode 14:22 (Ibid., fol. 159 r–v).

Certains Docteurs ont pensé que le Seigneur des mondes fit apparaître dans la mer un ange chevauchant une cavale: lorsque les chevaux de

11 *Cf. Tōrāh Šelēmāh*, VIII, pp. 1690-1692, en particulier la fin de la note 152; voir aussi *Legends*, V, 359 (n. 321).

12 Qāfiḥ, *ibid.*, p. 46 (en rapprochant la traduction de 46:8 qui intercale "et ce sont" avant "Jacob et ses fils").

13 *Targūm Yerushalmi* et, avec plus de détails, *Genèse-Rabba*, 94, 9, édition citée, p. 1180.

14 Seraḥ fille d'Asher, *Genèse-Rabba*, *ibid.*, p. 1182, 4.

15 *Cf.* Abraham Ibn 'Ezra à Gen. 46:21 et Moïse ben Nahman à Gen. 46:15.

16 Autant que je puisse voir, cette difficulté ne figure pas dans les fragments repérés jusqu'ici du recueil de difficultés bibliques intitulé conventionnellement *Še'ēlōt 'Attīqōt* (indications bibliographiques: *HUCA*, 43 [1972], p. 136, n. 63).

17 *Cf. Legends*, III, 22 ; VI, 6 *sq.* (n. 36). Voir aussi David Luria à *Pirqēy Rabbī Eli'ezer*, XLII, notes 31 à 37 (99a); *Tōrāh Šelēmāh*, XIV, p. 66, n° 134.

Pharaon la virent, ils s'élancèrent à sa poursuite; pour cette raison, ils entrèrent (dans la mer) derrière les Israélites. (Les tenants de cette opinion) ont tiré argument de (Ex. 15:1) *Coursier et Cavalier, Il les a lancés dans la mer* et de (Cant. 1:9) *A une cavale attelée aux chars de Pharaon, je te compare, mon amie.*

Dans l'aggada visée, c'est Dieu lui-même qui apparaît ainsi.[18]

VIII. Exode 15:12 (Ibid., fol. 186r-v).

Les avis des Docteurs sont partagés au sujet de *la terre les engloutit.* Selon les uns, par cette parole (l'Écriture) désigne le rivage de la mer: lorsque la mer eut rejeté (les cadavres des Égyptiens), un certain endroit s'ouvrit et la terre les engloutit comme il advint (plus tard) à Dathan et à Abiram. Opinion peu vraisemblable, car à propos de ce qui arriva à ces derniers l'Écriture dit (Nom. 16:30): *Si le Seigneur crée une création et que le sol ouvre sa bouche et les engloutisse...*, tandis qu'ici, rien de tel ne s'est passé. D'après une autre opinion, le texte vise le fond de la mer qui les a engloutis après qu'ils eurent *sombré comme plomb* (Ex. 15:10).

Le Karaïte fait peut-être allusion au Targum de Palestine (I et II) et à la *Mekilta.*[19]

18 *Cf. Mekilta Bešallaḥ*, VII (6), Lauterbach, I, 247 = Horovitz – Rabin, p. 112; *Mekhilta de R. Shim'ōn bar Yoḥay*, éd. Epstein – Melamed, p. 68, 21 *sq.*; *Legends*, III, 26; VI, 9 (notes 44 et 47); *Tōrāh Šelēmāh*, XIV, 70, n° 149. Il est curieux que Yefet n'accompagne d'aucune censure cette *aggada* qui porte, contrairement au sept autres traitées ici, un caractère anthropomorphique et "naturiste" assez prononcé, surtout dans la version à laquelle il se réfère. Notons aussi qu'elle ne figure pas dans l'anthologie pourtant assez copieuse d'*aggadōt* "scandaleuses" que rapporte à sa façon son collègue plus jeune Juda Hadassi, dans *Eshkōl Ha-Kōfer*, alphabet 109.

19 Également dans *Neofiti; cf.* Levine, *ibid.*, p. 444; *Mekilta, Massekhta de Shir(t)a*, 9, Lauterbach, II, p. 67 *sq.* = Horovitz, p. 145; D. Luria, *loc. cit.*, notes 79–83 (100 a–b); *Legends*, III, 31; VI, 11 (n. 56); *Tōrāh Šelēmāh*, XIV, 138, n° 166.

APPENDICE

I

Waqad taʿāṭā qawm biʾithbāt maʿnā hādhā al-*ʿeder* alladhī jumlatuh khams miʾa wakhamsīn biqawl huwa daʿwā lā ġayr lā ʿalayh dalīl walā talwīḥ yujīzuh faḍla ʿan ʾan yūjibuh. waqad kāna sabīlhum ʾan yataʿāṭūna ʾayḍan ithbāt maʿnā litafāṣīlihā. wabilā maḥāla ʾinnahum ʿajazū ʿan dhālika. walladhi lahū maʿrifa lā yushghil wahmahū fī taḥṣīl al-khurāfāt wal-daʿāwī al-maḥḍ. fahum lā yaqifūna ʿalā basīṭ al-kitāb wayashtaghilū bil-khurāfāt alladhī laysa lahā ʾaṣl alladhī llāhu tabāraka wataʿālā yukhajjil qāʾilhā.

II

Waqad ẓanna baʿḍ al-nās ʾanna *Yōsēf* ghayr maḥmūd fī qawlih li-*sar hamashqīm kī ʾim zekhartānī ittekhā* waʾannahū ʾittakal ʿalā *ben ʾādām* falidhālik taʾakhkhar ʾamruh sanatayn. wahādhā ġhalaṭ bayyin wadhālika ʾannahū law kāna kamā ẓanna lamā kāna yakhruj min al-ḥabs bitadhakkurih *sar ha-mashqīm*. wanaḥnu naqūl ʾinna *Yōsēf* ʿa[layhi] l-s[alām] ʾakhadha fī ʿāthār *Yaʿaqōb* ʾabūh ʾalladhi kāna yattakil ʿalā rabbi l-ʿālamīn badiyyan thumma yaḥtāl biḍurūb min al-ḥiyal [...]. falammā *raʾā Yosēf* ʾanna *sar ha-mashqīm* sayaʿūd ʾilā martabatih waʾannahū qad ʿalima biḥāl *Yōsēf* waqad wajaba lahū ʿalayhi ḥaqq al-khidma waʾanahū qādir ʿalā ʾikhrājih qāla fī nafsih laʿalla rabb al-ʿālamīn sabbaba majīhi ʾilā l-ḥabs wanaẓarahū lihādhā l-manām likhalāṣī filidhālika saʾalahū masʾalat *Parʿōh* fī ʾikhrājih.

III

waqad zaʿama baʿḍ al-mufassirīn ʾanna *wayiftaḥ hāʾeḥād* huwa *Lēwī* liqawlih *Shimʿōn welēwī ʾaḥīm* wahuwa istikhrāj baʿīd.

IV

Walaysa kāna gharaḍ *Reʾūbēn* fī qawlih *ʾet shenēy bānay tāmīt* ʾisqāṭhum min al-*naḥalāh* kamā fassara qawm.

V

<u>dh</u>akara *Yōsēf* wawaladayḥ faṣārū tisʿa watisʿīn <u>th</u>umma jamala l-kull maʿa
Yaʿaqōb fahā<u>dh</u>ā lla<u>dh</u>ī ʿamīl ilayh. wabaʿḍ al-mufassirīn zaʿama ʾanna maʿahū
Yōkebed. waqāla baʿḍuhum ʾan jaʾa libaʿḍ al-awlād mawlūd ʿinda mā bala<u>gh</u>ū
ilā ḥadd Miṣr liʾannahū baʿuda ʿindahū ʾan takūn *Yōkebed* waladat li-*Mōsheh*
wahiya bnat miʾa wa<u>th</u>alā<u>th</u>īn sana kamā yūjibuh al-taʾrī<u>kh</u>.

VI

faʾammā l-mawḍiʿ alla<u>dh</u>ī n<u>sh</u>aqqa fakāna wāsiʿ bimiqdār saʿat ʿaskar *Yisrāʾēl*
laysa huwa kamā ẓanna qawm ʾannahū n<u>sh</u>aqqa fī *Y"B* mawḍiʿ liʾi<u>th</u>nay ʿa<u>sh</u>ar
sibṭ waʾinnamā kāna yan<u>sh</u>aqq qiṭʿa qiṭʿa faʾabdā (!) yan<u>sh</u>aqq al-māʿ
qudūmhum wayajiff <u>dh</u>ālika l-mawḍiʿ ḥattā yasīrū fīh.

VII

zaʿama baʿḍ al-ʿulamāʾ ʾanna rabb al-ʿālamīn ʾaẓhara fī l-baḥr malʾak rākib
ʿalā *sūsāh* fakamā naẓarūhā *sūsēy farʿōh* ṭalabūhā fali<u>dh</u>ālika da<u>kh</u>alū <u>kh</u>alfa
Yisrāʾēl waḥtajjū biqawlih *sūs werōkhbō rāmāh bayyām* waqawlih ʿay<u>dh</u>an
lesūsātī berikhbēy farʿōh dimmītīkh raʿyātī.

VIII

ʾi<u>kh</u>talafū l-ʿulamāʾ fī *tiblāʿēmō ʾāreṣ.* qāla baʿḍuhum ʾannahū yu<u>sh</u>īr bihi ʾilā
<u>sh</u>aṭṭ al-baḥr ʾalladī ʿinda mā qa<u>dh</u>afahum al-baḥr infataḥa mawḍiʿ wabtala-
ʿahum (!) al-ʾarḍ naẓīra mā laḥiqa *Dātān waʾAbīrām* wahuwa qawl baʿīd
liʾannahū lla<u>dh</u>ī laḥiqa fīh *Dātān waʾAbīrām* qāla fīh *weʾim berīʾāh yibrāʾ*
YWY ufāṣetāh ha-ʾadāmāh ʾet pīhā u-baleʿāh ʾōtām huwa lam yajri naẓīruh.
waqāla ʾā<u>kh</u>ar ʾannahū ʾyu<u>sh</u>īr bihī ilā qāʿ al-baḥr ʾannahū balaʿahum baʿda
ṣālalū ka-ʾōferet.

ON AN EARLY FRAGMENT OF THE QUR'ĀN

M. J. KISTER

Papyrus No. 28 of the *"Arabic papyri from Ḫirbet el-Mird,"* edited by Adolf Grohmann (Louvain-Leuven 1963, Bibliothèque du *Muséon*, vol. 52, pp. 30–32, Pl. XIV), is described by Grohmann as a "fragment of an official letter probably referring to the embola." His reading, translation and comments are reproduced here.

Mird A 31 a 1 (M.A.B.). 22 × 8,5 cm. IInd century A.H. (VIIIth century A.D.).

On the recto 16 lines are written in black ink in a cursive, inelegant hand at right-angles to the horizontal fibres. The verso (A 31b) bears fragments and vestiges of 13 lines written in black ink in a regular, skilled hand, parallel to the vertical fibres.

The fragment, coming from the middle of the letter, is very poorly preserved. Of the lines 12-16 only a small strip of papyrus, 1,7 cm wide, has survived. On the right side a piece, 3,5 cm high and 8,3 cm wide, has detached itself from the upper layer of the papyrus. The verso is so badly damaged that it is impossible to recover much more than some fragments of words, the translation of which is impossible.

Prototype : original.

١ [بســــــــــــــــ]م الله الرحمن [الرحيم]

٢ [من فلان بن فلان ا]لى سـ[ـليـ]ـمن بن حرث[ ]

٣ [امّـا بعد فإنى] احمد ا[ليـ]ـك الله [الذى]

٤ [لا اله ا]لّا هو [ ]

٥ [ ] و..؟ فانظ[ر]

٦]]نعمان الكيّال [ف]امنع [ ]
٧]]ن نفانه ولا يؤ̊ر ال[ ]
٨] [واعتصموا [ ]
٩] [. ولا نفر فو[ا]
١٠] [بنعمة الله [ ]
١١] [ ]ا[ ].....[ ]
١٢]]بوحـ[ ]
١٣]]...[ ]
١٤]]...[ ]
١٥]]...[ ]
١٦]]...[ ]

1. *[In the nam]e of God, the Compassionate, [the Merciful].*
2. *[From So and So, Son of So and So, t]o Su[lai]mān ibn Ḥāriṯ.*
3. *[Thereafter. Verily, I] praise un[t]o you God, [besides]*
4. *[whom there is] no god.*
5. [ ] *and . . . . So inspe[ct*]
6. [ ] *Nuʿmān, the corn-measurer. Therefore, prevent* [ ]
7. [ ] . . . . [ ]
8. [ ] *and they have had recourse [to*]
9. [ ] . . . *and no single person* . . . . [ ]
10. [ ] *with God's favour* [ ]
11. [ ] . . . . [ ]
12. [ ] . . . . [ ]
13. [ ] . . . . [ ]
14. [ ] . . . . [ ]
15. [ ] . . . . [ ]
16. [ ] . . . . [ ]

6. For the « corn-measurer » cf. APG nº 18, *3* and p. 66. He is presumably a successor of the μεσίτης of the Byzantine and early Arabic period, a trustee in the public barns in the province, who had to make the repartition of the impost in kind among the individual tax-payers. Cf. H. GERSTINGER, *Neue byzantinische Vertragsurkunden aus der Sammlung « Papyri Erzherzog Rainer » in Wien, The Journal of Juristic Papyrology,* XIII (1961), p. 57 (nº 3, VIth cent. A.D.).

However, Grohmann's reading does not correspond to what can be seen quite clearly in the papyrus. Consequently, his rendering and comments are not correct.

The correct reading of the papyrus is as follows:

٤. [لا اله ا] لا هو

٥. [......] قال في كتابه

٦. [......] يا [يها] الذي[ن] امنو[ا]

٧. [اتقوا الله حق] تقاته ولا تموت[ن]

٨. [الا وانتم مسلمون] واعتصموا

٩. [بحبل الله جميعا] ولا تفرقوا

١٠. [واذكروا] نعمة الله

The rendering of these lines is as follows:

4. [*there is no god*] *but He*
5. [. . . . .] *said in His Book*
6. [. . . . .] *O ye who believe*
7. [*Observe your duty to Allah*] *with right observance and do not die*
8. [*save as those who have surrendered unto Him*]. *And hold fast*
9. [*all of you together to the cable of Allah*] *and do not separate*
10. [*and remember*] *Allah's favor* . . . . . .

It is evident that the papyrus is not a "fragment of an official letter" but a fragment (lines 6–10) of the Qur'ān, containing Sūra III, verses 102–103.

There is no doubt whatsoever that this is the correct reading of the text; it seems to be of some importance that we have here one of the earliest specimens of the text of the Qur'ān, written in the second century of the Hijra.*

* I would like to express my sincere gratitude to Mr. A. Etan, Mrs. I. Pomeranz and Mrs. A. Sussmann of the Department of Antiquities and Museums, Ministry of Education and Culture, Jerusalem, Israel, who kindly prepared the photograph of the papyrus for me.

HERESY VERSUS THE STATE IN MEDIEVAL ISLAM

J. L. KRAEMER

States and societies tend to restrain nonconformity, and to suppress deviation from supreme values and principles which undermines societal and political foundations: law and order, and the legitimacy and authority of the sovereign.

In medieval Islam, deviation from fundamental religious principles in the form of apostasy and heresy was regarded juridically as treason against the state and revolt against the social order. The punishment inflicted upon deviants, apostates and heretics was the same as the retribution meted out to ordinary brigands, highwaymen and rebels. All were included in the category of those who make war upon Allah and His messenger, and they were penalized by execution, sometimes in the form of crucifixion.[1]

The major thesis of this paper is that the heretics (*mulḥidûn, zanâdiqa*) in the world of Islam who were truly heretics, not merely libertine poets, mystic visionaries or cultured secretaries, were objectively enemies of religion and

1 The heretic is liable to capital punishment by application of Sûrahs 5:33/36 and 26:49/49; see *Shorter Encyclopaedia of Islam*, s.v. "Zindīḳ" (L. Massignon), p. 659a. Sûrah 5:33/36 ("The only reward of those who make war upon Allah and His messenger and strive after corruption in the land will be that they will be killed or crucified, or have their hands and feet on alternate sides cut off, or will be expelled out of the land. Such will be their degradation in the world, and in the Hereafter theirs will be an awful doom" [trans. Pickthall]) is the authoritative verse for the punishment of brigandage (*qaṭ' al-ṭarîq*), the apostate from Islam (*murtadd*), and rebels (*bughāt*). What they all have in common is that they are outlaws who threaten the security of the state. In juridical works, brigandage, rebellion, apostasy and heresy are often classified under the same heading. In his observations on Roman law, in connection with its application in Judea, B. Jackson calls attention to the political implications of brigandage and the political overtones of Roman legislation regarding this offense, whereby *qui auctor seditionis fuerit* included brigandage. In this connection he mentions the political nature of the offense of the brigands crucified along with Jesus. See B. Jackson, *Theft in Early Jewish Law*, Oxford 1972, pp. 35, 37, 73, 251–253.

Islam and a real danger to the state and social order.[2] Hence, their persecution and suppression were the natural reaction of the state authorities.

In coordination with this major thesis, several minor theses are proposed. The arch-heretics of Islam (e.g., Ibn al-Muqaffaʿ, Abû ʿÎsâ b. al-Warrâq, Abu l-Ḥusayn b. al-Râwandî, or al-Rêwendî, and Abû Bakr Muḥammad b. Zakariyyâʾ al-Râzî) perpetuated an old and venerable tradition of polemic against the monotheistic revealed religions (Judaism and Christianity), which continued in a kind of underground movement against Islam. The polemical assaults of these arch-heretics against Islam are traceable, in the forms and themes of their argumentation, to the panoply of Gnostic and Manichean strictures against monotheism, and to the philosophical contentions of defenders of paganism such as Celsus, Porphyry, the Emperor Julian and Proclus. The weapons provided by these sources were no doubt reinforced by pre-Islamic Persian ideas, which lived on as antitheses to the creed of the Muslim conquerors. The heretical ideologies were associated, whether in the minds of the ruling élite or in actual fact, with programmes of heretical revolutionary movements which were aimed at the overthrow of the Islamic state. While it is possible to consider these *zanâdiqa* or *mulḥidûn* as rationalists or independent thinkers, it is imperative to realize that their rationalism was of a virulent strain: it attacked the revealed religions in general and Islam in particular. Rationalism *per se*, while it was a tender and vulnerable flower in the soil of medieval Islam, was not inevitably eradicated. Witness the relatively untrammelled lives of the Muʿtazilite theologians and the Aristotelian (or Neo-Aristotelian, Neo-Platonic) *falâsifa*. The *falâsifa* cherished elements of the same ancient heritage that was precious to the heretics, and like them upheld the supremacy of reason over revelation, but they expounded a system which retained the revealed Law of Islam intact and were consequently left in peace to pursue their philosophical lucubrations.

These themes would appear somewhat obvious on first reflection and in no need of defense or explication, were it not that they point in a direction which veers off from that marked by the great student of Islamic heresy, H. S. Nyberg, who studied the persecution of Ibn al-Râwandî in the context of a discussion of

2 The main terms for heretic are *zindîq* and *mulḥid* (pl. *zanâdiqa, mulḥidûn*; n. *zandaqa, ilḥâd*). For a recent discussion of these terms, see B. Lewis, "The Significance of Heresy in Islam," in *Islam in History,* London 1973, pp. 217–236, esp. 228–231. On the history of *zandaqa* in the ʿAbbâsid period, which mainly concerns us, see G. Vajda, "Les zindîqs en pays d'Islam au debut de la période abbaside," *Rivista degli Studi Orientali,* 17 (1938), 173–229; and Fr. Gabrieli, "La 'zandaqa' au 1er siècle abbasside," in *l'Élaboration de l'Islam*, Paris 1961, pp. 23–38.

classicism and cultural decline in Islamic history. Nyberg's assessment of Ibn al-Râwandî's experience and its repercussions may be summarized as follows:[3]

1. Ibn al-Râwandî was condemned and expelled by the Mu'tazilites *qua* Aristotelian philosopher. The conflict between him and his opponents was the first clash between Islamic *kalâm* and the new philosophy introduced in the third century A.H.

2. Actually, the violence of the Mu'tazilites' attack against Ibn al-Râwandî's writings was due to their own "mauvaise conscience," for he merely drew the logical, albeit extreme, consequences of their own premises.

3. Ten years after the death of Ibn al-Râwandî (i.e., in 922), the radical mystic al-Ḥallâj was executed in Baghdad. The persecution of Ibn al-Râwandî and the execution of al-Ḥallâj had far-reaching and enduring reverberations within Islam. From this time on, every "mouvement extraordinaire" had to conceal itself underground and was compelled, for self-preservation, to pose as orthodox Sunnite or as Shî'ite. Thus, dissimulation and hypocrisy (*taqiyya, kitmân*) became "de rigueur" for life.

4. Dissimulation and hypocrisy became inherent weaknesses of Islamic civilization. The practice of dissimulation paralyzed Islamic society, so that when the currents of modern secularization penetrated the Islamic world, there were no countervailing forces equipped to confront them.

The direction indicated by Nyberg was followed by M. Plessner in an article on heresy and rationalism in the early centuries of Islam. Echoing Nyberg's view, Plessner writes, concerning Ibn al-Râwandî, that "one receives the impression that he was merely more consistent than the Mu'tazilites in employing his reason for discussing theological subjects; in short, he was a rationalist, but not anti-religious." In the same spirit, Plessner, comparing Ibn al-Râwandî to al-Râzî, says that the latter was far from being a heretic, not to mention atheist. Plessner portrays al-Râzî as an individualist thinker who was merely anti-establishment or anti-orthodox.[4]

Portraying Ibn al-Râwandî and al-Râzî as merely rationalists and independent thinkers invests them with a cloak of innocence, while implying the guilt of the society in which they lived; i.e., it could not tolerate the independent exercise of reason. The assessments of Nyberg and Plessner raise a number of questions. If the persection and vehemence of the attack upon Ibn al-Râwandî

3 H. S. Nyberg, "'Amr ibn 'Ubaid et Ibn al-Rawendi, deux réprouvés," in *Classicisme et déclin culturel dans l'histoire de l'Islam,* Paris 1957, pp. 125–136, esp. 133–135.

4 M. Plessner, "Heresy and Rationalism in the First Centuries of Islam" (in Hebrew), in *The 'Ulamā' and Problems of Religion in the Muslim World: Studies in Memory of Professor Uriel Heyd,* ed. G. Baer, Jerusalem 1971, pp. 3–10, esp. 8–10.

are traced to the bad conscience of the Muʿtazilites, who were horrified by the conclusions of their own premises, then how can one account for the far-reaching historical reverberations? It would appear logical to assume that such an internal polemic and localized disagreement would not determine the future course of Islamic civilization's attitude to nonconformity. Moreover, if Ibn al-Râwandî was indeed simply a rationalist and not anti-religious, how does one explain the severe reaction to his views on the part of later writers? One is forced to conclude that the ruling Islamic establishment was hypersensitive to deviation from the norm; hence, even rationalism was considered anti-religious and subversive, though its adherents were innocent of harboring hostility to Islam.

Now, it is indeed true that anti-establishment thinking might be regarded by the authorities as heretical and even subversive. Many examples may be adduced of this kind of reaction to nonconformist ideas, particularly during the Umayyad period. The ideological opposition to the Umayyads centered upon issues such as the status of the grave sinner and the question of predestination, which carried implications bearing upon the legitimacy of Umayyad authority and the duty to acquiesce in its regulations and refrain from rebellion. The oppositionists often preached a purer form of Islam, ideals of justice and equality and adherence to the Qur'ân and the *Sunna*. But since they opposed the state and the dynasty of the Umayyads, their views were regarded as heretical, since the Umayyads believed that the Caliphate was divinely entrusted to their family; hence, disobedience to the Caliph and his surrogates was regarded as tantamount to infidelity to God. This is not to say that all the opponents of the Umayyads were of this type. In the last turbulent decade of Umayyad rule there were heresiarchs (e.g., al-Mughîra b. Saʿîd, Abû Manṣûr al-ʿIjlî, Ḥamza b. ʿAmmâra, Bayân b. Samʿân, ʿAbdallâh b. Ḥârith and others) who led what appear to have been heretical, subversive movements.

The theologian oppositionists to Umayyad ideology and rule espoused doctrines that threatened the dynasty, but they were not aimed against the Islamic state or Islam as such. Many were arrested and executed, not simply because of their nonconformist theology, but on account of their active participation in revolts against Umayyad rule. Several examples may be cited.

Maʿbad al-Juhanî, allegedly the first to discuss free-will (*qadar*), and said to have been a pupil of an Iraqi Christian convert to Islam who relapsed to his former faith, was tortured and executed by the governor al-Ḥajjâj, or by the Caliph ʿAbd al-Malik himself (ca. 704). Maʿbad is said to have denied that the wrongdoings of the Umayyads were divinely determined. But this was not his sole offense. He apparently participated in the revolt of Ibn al-Ashʿath (699–701 or 702), which had a religious character, at least in its advanced stage, and raised the standard of "the Book of God and the *Sunna* of His Prophet." It is significant that the famous pietist Ḥasan al-Baṣrî, a critic of the Umayyads who refused to accept the predestinarian rationale for their evil behavior, dissociated himself from Maʿbad's policy of insurrection and refrained from participating in this revolt, explaining (in a Calvinist vein) that the evil suffered under the hands of tyrants was to be accepted as divine chastisement. He escaped the fate of Maʿbad al-Juhanî.[5]

Ghaylân al-Dimashqî, a man of learning and piety and a follower of Maʿbad, also denied that evildoing was due to God's predetermination. He propounded his views on *qadar* in the days of ʿUmar II (b. ʿAbd al-ʿAzîz; 717–20), whose administration he criticized. The Caliph summoned him, demanding his recantation; but he apparently adhered to his views, since he was eventually forced to flee and, after his apprehension and interrogation in the presence of the Caliph Hishâm, he was executed (ca. 742). Quite typically, the form of execution was that reserved for criminal rebels against the state (amputation of hands and feet and crucifixion). His offense was not merely theological. He is said to have actively supported the rebellion of al-Ḥârith b. Surayj, the man with the black banner, who rebelled against the Umayyads in the name of the Book and the *Sunna* (734–46).[6]

Among the theologians who supported the rebellion of al-Ḥârith b. Surayj, Jahm b. Ṣafwân is also mentioned; indeed, he was the secretary of al-Ḥârith and an ideologue of the movement. According to reports, Jahm held a radical doctrine on the question of divine attributes (*taʿṭîl*: divesting God of His attributes), and claimed that God is not a being but above all existent beings, ideas that could easily be interpreted as outright atheism. He was captured and executed shortly before the leader of the movement (746).[7]

As distinct from the above-mentioned figures, Jaʿd b. Dirham, who was executed toward the end of the Umayyad period for his heretical ideas, appears

5 See, e.g., W. M. Watt, *The Formative Period of Islamic Thought*, Edinburgh 1973, pp. 85, 100 and 110. On the rebellion of Ibn al-Ashʿath, see *Encyclopaedia of Islam*, new edition (*EI*²), s.v. "Ibn al-Ashʿath," III, pp. 715–719 (L. Veccia Vaglieri).

6 See *EI*², s.v. "Ghaylān B. Muslim," III, p. 1026 (Ch. Pellat); and Watt, *Formative Period*, pp. 85–87. Watt (p. 335, n. 21) expresses doubt concerning Ghaylân's participation in the rebellion of al-Ḥârith b. Surayj. On the revolt, see *EI*², s.v. "al-Ḥārith B. Suraydj," III, pp. 223–224 (M. Kister). On Ghaylân's audience with ʿUmar II and the fateful interrogation before Hishâm, see M. S. Seale, *Muslim Theology*, London, 1964, pp. 17–21.

7 See *EI*², s.v. "Djahm B. Ṣafwān" and Djahmiyya, II, p. 388 (W. M. Watt). See also R. M. Frank, "The Neoplatonism of Ǧahm ibn Ṣafwân," *Le Muséon*, 78 (1965), 395–424; Seale, *Muslim Theology*, Index, p. 136; and Watt, *Formative Period*, pp. 143–148.

to have held truly deviant views. He was executed in Kûfa (or Wâsiṭ) by the governor, Khâlid b. ʿAbdallâh al-Qaṣrî, probably on the orders of the Caliph Hishâm, on the day of the Feast of Sacrifices (ʿÎd al-Aḍḥâ, in 742 or 743), allegedly because he claimed that "God did not take Abraham for a friend and did not speak to Moses," an unorthodox view which may have been related to his radical denial of divine attributes. He appears among the *zanâdiqa* (Manicheans) in Ibn al-Nadîm's *Fihrist*; according to al-Muṭahhar al-Maqdisî, his followers were beardless men (an expression associated with the Manichean elect), who accused the Prophet of lying and denied resurrection. To be sure, these are later reports, the historicity of which cannot be taken at face value.[8]

The upshot of the above sketch of persecution and suppression during the Umayyad period is that the victims were innocent in word (from the Islamic, if not the Umayyad, viewpoint), though not in deed. Their crime was disloyalty to the dynasty, not to the Islamic state as such or to the Islamic creed.

The *zanâdiqa* of the ʿAbbâsid period were not merely opponents of the regime but enemies of Islamic domination and the Islamic creed. Ibn al-Râwandî and men of his type, such as Ibn al-Muqaffaʿ, Abû ʿÎsâ al-Warrâq and Abû Bakr al-Râzî, were opposed to any form of Islamic belief and political expression.[9] They did not proclaim a purer form of Islam or summon people to obedience to the Book and the *Sunna*. In this respect, the dissident theologians executed by the Umayyads were more akin in their outlook to the heretics in

8 The prosecution of Jaʿd is the first recorded in connection with *zandaqa*; see Gabrieli, *op. cit.* (note 2 above), pp. 29–30; and Lewis, *op. cit.* (note 2 above), pp. 228–229. Gabrieli views Jaʿd as a theologian who remained entirely within the framework of Islam. On Jaʿd, see *EI²*, s.v. "Ibn Dirham," III, pp. 747–748 (G. Vajda); and Vajda, *op. cit.* (note 2 above), pp. 179–180, esp. p. 180, n. 1 (on pp. 180–181), citing al-Maqdisî, *Kitâb al-Badʾ wal-Taʾrîkh*, ed. C. Huart, vol. 6, pp. 54–55; and Ibn al-Nadîm, *Fihrist*, ed. Flügel, pp. 337–338, among other sources.

With respect to the name Jaʿd ("curly-haired") and the beardless men who were his followers, cf. the heretical *ḥadîths* mentioned by J. Fück, "Spuren des Zindīqtums in der islamischen Tradition," in *Studien zur Geschichte und Kultur des nahen und fehrnen Ostens* (Paul Kahle Festschrift), ed. W. Heffening and W. Kirfel, Leiden 1935, pp. 95–100, esp. p. 98: "I saw my Lord as a curly-haired (*jaʿd*) beardless youth in a green robe," and p. 99: "The dwellers of paradise are beardless youths, with the exception of Moses, whose beard reaches his navel." Cf. the comparison of the Lord to a youth with black curly locks in "The Hymn of Glory" by Rabbi Judah the Pious (d. 1217), included in the Sabbath morning service; *The Authorised Daily Prayer Book*, rev. ed. by J. H. Hertz, New York 5719/1959, p. 216.

9 On Ibn al-Râwandî, see below, note 11. On Ibn al-Muqaffaʿ, see P. Kraus, "Zu Ibn al-Muqaffaʿ," *Rivista degli Studi Orientali*, 14 (1933), 1–20, esp. 14–20; and D. Sourdel, "La biographie d'Ibn al-Muqaffaʿ d'après les sources anciennes," *Arabica*, 1 (1954), 307–23. Ibn al-Muqaffaʿ's heretical views are preserved in a refutation by the Zaydite *imâm*, al-Qâsim b.

Western Christendom who preached a return to a deeper spiritual life and to the true apostolic church, and to a life of poverty and simplicity in imitation of Christ, in a rebellion that was anti-establishment but not anti-Christian. In the Islamic milieu, the Ṣûfî martyrs al-Ḥallâj and al-Suhrawardî also resemble this model, since their intention was not to undermine Islam but to expose its deeper spiritual meaning. To be sure, the attempt by mystics to uncover the inner meaning of the faith often verged on a mode of pantheism and deification of man (through mystical love and union), i.e., notions that were not merely anti-establishment but veritably heretical.[10] The Western analogue to the phenomenon of *zandaqa* of the type under consideration can be found in the Manicheistic heretical movements, such as those of the Cathars and the Albigensians.

Paradoxically, the *zanâdiqa* of the ʿAbbâsid era, as distinct from the theologians accused of apostasy, heresy and rebellion during the Umayyad period, did not participate in revolts against the regime. However, their radical views were similar to the ideologies espoused by subversive heretical movements. It will be observed below that witch-hunts were launched against *zanâdiqa* and "fellow-travellers" during times of stress and upheaval, when

Ibrâhîm, *Kitâb al-Radd ʿalâ Ibn al-Muqaffaʿ al-Zindîq*, ed. and trans. M. Guidi, *La lotta tra l'Islam e il Manicheismo*, Rome 1927 (R. Accademia Nazionale dei Lincei); see the review by H. S. Nyberg, "Zum Kampf zwischen Islam und Manichäismus," *Orientalistische Literaturzeitung*, vol. 32,6, June 1929, pp. 425—441, and esp. p. 430, for a summary of the offending ideas. And see *EI*², s.v. "Ibn al-Muqaffaʿ," III, pp. 883—885 (F. Gabrieli). On Abû ʿÎsâ al-Warrâq, see C. Colpe, "Anpassung des Manichäismus an den Islam (Abū ʿĪsā al-Warrāq)," *Zeitschrift der Deutschen Morgenlandischen Gesellschaft*, 109 (N.F. 34), (1959), 82—91; *EI*², s.v. "Abū ʿĪsā al-Warrāq," I, p. 130 (S. M. Stern). Stern mentions a study by A. Abel, *Abū ʿĪsâ al-Warrâq*, Brussels, 1949 (unseen). The views of Abû ʿÎsâ are coupled with those of Ibn al-Râwandî by al-Khayyâṭ in *Kitâb al-Intiṣâr* (see note 11). On the heterodox views of Abû Bakr al-Râzî, see s.v. in *EI*¹, III, pp. 1225—1227 (P. Kraus and S. Pines); and P. Kraus, "Raziana II," *Orientalia*, 5 (1936), 35—56, 358—378, wherein fragments of al-Râzî's *Naqḍ al-Adyân* preserved by Abû Ḥâtim al-Râzî in his *Kitâb Aʿlâm al-Nubuwwa* are treated.

10 See, e.g., G. Leff, *Heresy in the Later Middle Ages,* Manchester — New York 1967, I, Prologue, pp. 1—47, esp. pp. 2—10, on the preaching of a return to the true apostolic church; and see R. E. Lerner, *The Heresy of the Free Spirit in the Later Middle Ages,* Berkeley — Los Angeles — London 1972, pp. 16—17, on the deification of man and dispensation with the intermediacy of the clergy; and N. Cohn, *The Pursuit of the Millennium* (2nd edition), New York 1961, pp. 150—152 and 185, on the heresy of the Free Spirit, where it is observed that the extreme individualism, self-deification and Neoplatonic pantheism of these Gnostics could easily be turned into social revolution, antinomianism and anarchy. See also G. C. Anawati and L. Gardet, *La mystique musulmane,* Paris 1961, p. 38, on the dangerous heretical excesses of mystical love.

revolutionary movements posed a military and political threat against the state.

The heretical views of Ibn al-Râwandî were not of the order of theological deviation on such questions as the status of the grave sinner and predestination; nor was his sin that of Aristotelianism or rationalism: it was a denunciation of the fundamental doctrines of Islam. The principal anti-Islamic theses of Ibn al-Râwandî were:

1. The eternity and primordiality of the universe.
2. The denial of the oneness of God.
3. Rejection of the mission of Muḥammad and depreciation of the prophets.
4. Denial that God is wise and compassionate.[11]

A comparison of the tenets of Ibn al-Râwandî with those of his predecessors Ibn al-Muqaffaʿ and Abû ʿÎsâ al-Warrâq and of his follower Abû Bakr al-Râzî reveals that the themes used as weapons by Celsus, Porphyry, the Emperor Julian and Proclus in their polemics against Judaism and Christianity were the very same as those wielded by Ibn al-Râwandî and his group against Islam and its parent religions. The heretics in the world of Islam inherited anti-religious *topoi* from pagan philosophers who waged last-ditch battles against the swelling tide of Christianity. The "pagan reaction," as well as Greek philosophy and culture, which had supposedly given up the ghost by the seventh century, were borne aloft in the ninth and tenth centuries by fresh defenders of "the old and true teaching" against the contemporary champion of the monotheistic camp in the guise of Islam.[12]

11 On these heretical views, see Ibn al-Khayyâṭ, *Kitâb al-Intiṣâr*, ed. H. S. Nyberg and trans. A. N. Nader, Beirut 1957, *passim*, esp. pp. 11–12. The text reproduced by Nader was first edited by Nyberg (Cairo 1925), along with a long Introduction in Arabic (pp. 10–62). Fragments of Ibn al-Râwandî's *Kitâb al-Zumurrudh*, preserved by the Ismâʿîlî *dâʿî*, al-Mu'ayyad fi l-Dîn al-Shîrâzî, have been edited and translated by P. Kraus, "Beiträge zur islamischen Ketzergeschichte," *Revista degli Studi Orientali*, 14 (1933–34), 93–129 and 335–379. On Ibn al-Râwandî's career and views, see H. Ritter, "Philologika VI: Ibn al-Ǵauzīs Bericht über Ibn ar-Rēwendī," *Der Islam*, 19 (1931), 1–17; J. van Ess' review of *Kitâb al-Intiṣâr*, published by A. N. Nader in *Archiv für Geschichte der Philosophie*, 45 (1963), 79–87; and *EI²*, s.v. "Ibn al-Rāwandī or al-Rēwendī," III, pp. 905–906 (P. Kraus–[G. Vajda]).

Ibn al-Râwandî's view on the eternity of the universe was expounded in his *Kitâb al-Tâj*. In *Kitâb al-Zumurrudh*, *Kitâb al-Farîd* (or *al-Firind/al-Farand*) and *Kitâb al-Dâmigh*, he attacked miracles, revelation and prophecy; and in *Kitâb al-Taʿdîl wal-Tajwîr* and *Kitâb Naʿt al-Ḥikma*, he inveighed against God's lack of wisdom and compassion.

12 P. de Labriolle, *La réaction paienne*, Paris 1934, p. 486, says that the long anti-Christian effort traced in his book remained paralyzed for a long time and that, from the point of view of Greek philosophy and culture, the fifth to the seventh centuries were a period of great silence.

The arguments employed by the challengers of the monotheistic faiths, from Celsus to al-Râzî, may be summarized in a list of ten predominant themes.[13]

1. Reason, or nature, which is universal, is a sufficient guide for mankind in order to apprehend reality and discriminate between good and evil.

2. Religion (i.e., monotheistic revealed religion) is anti-rational, demands blind acceptance of authority and prohibits reasoning. It contains absurdities, such as the belief in miracles and gross and superstitious conceptions of the deity. These absurdities cannot be explained away by allegorical interpretation, which is a feeble attempt to save childish fables.

3. The world is primordial and eternal; creation in time is negated.

4. Prophecy and revelation are rejected. The prophets are liars, imposters and sorcerers, who use magic tricks in order to deceive the ignorant and gullible multitude.

5. Those who follow the prophets and apostles are the uneducated, consisting mainly of women, slaves and children, who are easily deceived.

6. Religion is narrow and parochial rather than universalistic.

7. The various religions contradict one another and contradictions abound within the holy writ of each, thus undermining their credibility.

8. Religion is motivated by the pursuit of power and domination; it causes dissension and bloodshed.

9. God, as depicted by religion, is unwise, unjust and incompassionate.

10. What is true and noble in religion is plagiarized and forged from philosophy.

Along with these one finds Gnostic and Manichean ideas in the writings of the *zanâdiqa*, as well as pre-Islamic Persian motifs, which were also brought to bear in their anti-Islamic campaign.

The perpetuation and propagation of these radically anti-Islamic theses aroused the repressive apparatus of the state to action. But there was no automatic cause and effect mechanism operative here. There were some circumstances wherein radical views were propounded with impunity. For example, Abû Bakr al-Râzî, whose heretical views would have brought him under the executioner's sword under certain circumstances, died of infirmity and old age. While his reputation as a great physician may have contributed to his security, a more preponderant factor was no doubt the relatively tolerant *milieu* at Rayy under the aegis of Mardâwîj b. Ziyâr al-Jîlî.[14]

13 On another occasion I shall adduce detailed evidence for the claim that these themes, which appear in the writings of the pagan opponents of Christianity, reappear in the writings of the *zanâdiqa* under discussion.

14 Al-Râzî's *Naqḍ al-Adyân* (or *Makhârîq al-Anbiyâ'*), preserved in Abû Ḥâtim al-Râzî's *A'lâm al-Anbiyâ'*, was presented in a philosophical dispute between two citizens of Rayy in the

Active pursuit and suppression of *zanâdiqa* was often contemporaneous with heightened activity of heretical revolutionary movements. The direct military and political threat quickened the anti-subversive machinery that might have remained dormant in more tranquil times. It is reasonable to assume that the suppression of Abû ʿÎsâ al-Warrâq, Ibn al-Râwandî and al-Ḥallâj during the reign of the Caliph al-Muqtadir (908—32) was related to the successes of the Ismâʿîlî and general Shîʿite movements. During his reign, the Fâṭimids and Ḥamdânids achieved political independence and the Carmathians rebelled, controlling large tracts of territory, plundering Baṣra, harassing the pilgrim routes and even succeeding in carrying off the black stone of the Kaʿba. Al-Ḥallâj, a suspected *zindîq,* was accused of being a Carmathian agent and rebel and was crucified upon a gibbet.[15]

The correlation between waves of persecution and political and social turbulence caused by heretical revolutionary movements is discernible in the acts of the Caliph al-Mahdî (775—85), who unleashed the first systematic hunt of *zanâdiqa*. The beginning of his rule was marked by revolutionary, subversive activity in Khurâsân, whereupon, in 163/779—80, the Caliph initiated intensive police operations against *zanâdiqa*. It is related that in the course of a military expedition against the Byzantines, accompanied by his son Hârûn, while staying at Aleppo, the good news reached him concerning the end of the revolt of al-Muqannaʿ. The Caliph then ordered ʿAbd al-Jabbâr, the Muḥtasib, to round up and arrest the *zanâdiqa* in the region of Aleppo. They were brought before the Caliph, who was then at Dâbiq (north of Aleppo). He had a group of them executed and crucified, and their books cut into shreds. Four years later

court of Mardâwîj. Gabrieli expresses astonishment that Abû Bakr al-Râzî survived physically unharmed, and observes that this would not have been the case in Baghdad under al-Mahdî or al-Muqtadir; see *idem, op. cit.* (note 2 above), p. 35; and see pp. 36—37, on the tolerance in certain Islamic *milieux* of this period.

15 Ibn al-Jawzî cites Abû ʿAlî al-Jubbâʾî to the effect that the authorities pursued Abû ʿÎsâ al-Warrâq and Ibn al-Râwandî (Ritter, "Philologika VI," p. 5). According to this report, Ibn al-Warrâq was apprehended, arrested and died in prison; and Ibn al-Râwandî fled to the home of a Jew named Lâwî, where he died. Ibn al-Jawzî quotes Ibn ʿAqîl (p. 9) to the effect that Ibn al-Râwandî was crucified by one of the rulers, but doubt is expressed concerning the accuracy of this account. Ibn ʿAqîl is also quoted (pp. 3—4) as having expressed amazement that Ibn al-Râwandî remained alive after having composed books such as *al-Dâmigh* and *al-Zumurrudh* and accounts for this circumstance by impugning the purity of faith of Ibn al-Râwandî's contemporaries. On the accusations against al-Ḥallâj, and his execution, see *EI*[2] s.v. "al-Ḥallādj̲," III, esp. pp. 101—103 (L. Massignon [L. Gardet]).

(167/783–84), after further disturbances in Khurâsân, he intensified the pursuit of *zanâdiqa*, searching for them far and wide. In the first place, the hunt was directed against actual Manicheans, but the net was extended to enmesh those of dubious religious convictions, such as the poets Bashshâr b. Burd and Ṣâliḥ b. ʿAbd al-Quddûs. Thus the persecutions, which began in Syria, spread to Baghdad and other parts of the Empire.[16]

Al-Muqannaʿ, whose abortive revolt appears to have sparked al-Mahdî's anti-*zindîq* zeal, led a movement, the precise ideology of which is somewhat beclouded. He and his followers were accused of harboring antinomian ideas; al-Muqannaʿ was allegedly proclaimed the last divine incarnation of a series of prophets, including Abû Muslim. The Almuqannaʿiyya were also suspected of perpetuating Mazdakite tenets.[17]

The stringency of the state's reaction to various forms of nonconformism undoubtedly encouraged the adoption of the technique of dissimulation, which Nyberg views as a negative factor, contributing to the stagnation of Islamic civilization and restricting its receptivity to new ideas. However, it may be argued that the health and stability of Islamic state and society dictated expunging truly pernicious ideas. It is worth remembering the words of Steven Runciman: "Tolerance is a social rather than a religious virtue."[18]

The *zanâdiqa* were representatives of doctrines which the Islamic state could not possibly tolerate, for they undermined its foundations. The intolerable ideas were not simply in the guise of Aristotelianism or rationalism, which was adopted by the *falâsifa* (e.g., Alfarabi, Avicenna and Averroes). The latter did not suffer the fate of the *zanâdiqa*. They were conservative and prudent men, who refrained from assaulting the fundamental tenets of Islam. The *falâsifa*, in fact, defended religion by providing it with a philosophical rationale, for they believed that the system of religious symbols and practices embodied in the Islamic Law was necessary for the moral well-being of the society in which they lived. Reason may be universal, as some of the *zanâdiqa* claimed, but not all men are rational. The *falâsifa* adopted dissimulation not only to escape

16 Al-Ṭabarî, *Annales*, ed. M. J. de Goeje et al., III, p. 499 (anno 163), mentions the annunciation of the good news to the Caliph concerning al-Muqannaʿ's death during the Caliph's stay in Aleppo; and this is followed by the initiation of police action against local *zanâdiqa*. It is possible that the anti-Byzantine expedition of al-Mahdî also contributed to his anti-heresy zeal. The ardor of his son, Hârûn al-Rashîd, against *zanâdiqa* and *dhimmîs* was intensified during his Byzantine campaigns.

17 On al-Muqannaʿ and his movement, see B. Spuler, *Iran in früh-islamischer Zeit*, Wiesbaden 1952, pp. 198–200; and H. Laoust, *Les schismes dans l'Islam*, Paris 1965, pp. 74–75.

18 S. Runciman, *The Medieval Manichee*, New York 1961, p. 1.

persecution, a good reason in itself, but for the welfare of mankind (*ṣalâḥ al-khalq*).[19] Taking a cue from Socrates' fate, perhaps inevitable in the case of an outspoken nonconformist in a closed society, they assumed a prudent, discreet posture, thus escaping martyrdom. Just as Hârûn al-Rashîd, and even the pious al-Mutawakkil, drank wine in the privacy of their palace chambers, so the philosophers imbibed wisdom *in camera*. They were like the *dhimmîs* of the Islamic state, a tolerated minority, who remained relatively free from harm provided they maintained a low profile and did not openly attempt to convert others to their views. The *zanâdiqa* were quasi-*ḥarbîs*, internal members of the *dâr al-ḥarb*, who were treated as enemies whose blood could be spilled with impunity (*ḥalâl al-dam*).

The philosophers acceded to the magic spell of tradition and convention, whereas the heretics broke the spell. In this respect, the heretics were "spoil-sports" and the philosophers were "false players" and "cheats," in the sense of these expressions as applied by Huizinga in a passage which gives striking illumination to the phenomena under discussion:[20]

> The player who trespasses against the rules or ignores them is a "spoil-sport." The spoil-sport is not the same as the false player, the cheat; for the latter pretends to be playing the game and, on the face of it, still acknowledges the magic circle. It is curious to note how much more lenient society is to the cheat than to the spoil-sport. This is because the spoil-sport shatters the play-world itself. By withdrawing from the game he reveals the relativity and fragility of the play-world in which he had temporarily shut himself with others. He robs play of its illusion – a pregnant word which means literally "in-play" (from *inlusio, illudere* or *inludere*). Therefore he must be cast out, for he threatens the existence of the play-community... The spoil-sport breaks the magic world, he is a coward and must be ejected. In the world of high seriousness, too, the cheat and the hypocrite have always had an easier time of it than the spoil-sports, here called apostates, heretics, innovators, prophets, conscientious objectors, etc. It sometimes happens, however, that the spoil-sports in their turn make a new community with rules of its own. The outlaw, the revolutionary, the cabbalist or member of a secret society, indeed heretics of all kinds are of a highly associative if not sociable disposition, and a certain element of play is prominent in all their doings.

19 Algazali, in *Fayṣal al-Tafriqa bayn al-Islâm wal-Zandaqa*, ed. S. Dunyâ, Cairo 1381/1961, pp. 101–102, distinguishing between the *falâsifa* and the *zanâdiqa*, notes the principle of *ṣalâḥ al-khalq* adopted by the philosophers regarding the belief of the multitude in such matters as resurrection, God's knowledge of human events, and providence.

20 J. Huizinga, *Homo Ludens*, Boston 1950, pp. 11–12.

Sometimes the "spoil-sport" in the world of high seriousness of Islam sustained the illusion by playing the game. Al-Khayyâṭ relates that Ibn al-Râwandî wrote a treatise on the oneness of God (*Kitâb fî l-Tawḥîd*) in order to ingratiate himself with Muslims at a time when his life was in danger. In his *Kitâb al-Zumurrudh*, Ibn al-Râwandî ascribed his heretical views to fictitious Brahmans (*barâhima*). He is said to have held ultra-Shî'ite (Râfiḍite) views as a convenient cover for his true heretical beliefs. Râfiḍism was a position somewhere between that of the spoil-sport and the cheat or hypocrite; for it was possible, by the external profession of an ultra-Shî'ite doctrine, to play the game without really accepting its rules. By accusing Muḥammad's Companions, the first three Caliphs, the Traditionists and the community of believers of disobedience to the will of the Prophet, one could bludgeon Islam with its own weapons. Ibn al-Râwandî's Râfiḍite position was not a transitional step from his Mu'tazilism to absolute *zandaqa* but a stance he assumed after having left the pale of Islam.[21]

By their prudent and conventional conduct, the philosophers were able to preserve and transmit a cultural and philosophical tradition within the confines of Islam which survived, and occasionally flourished, during the late medieval period, particularly in Persia (e.g., the School of Iṣfahân). When modern currents drifted into the Islamic world from Europe, there were individuals, such as Jamâl al-Dîn al-Afghânî, who were equipped to assimilate them on their own terms by turning to the model of the *falâsifa*, who had successfully coped with analogous problems of cultural assimilation.

21 Al-Khayyâṭ describes Ibn al-Râwandî's *Kitâb al-Tawḥîd* as an attempt to find favor in *Kitâb al-Intiṣâr*, p. 19.4–5 (Nader).

Gabrieli sees in Ibn al-Râwandî's career a process from Mu'tazilism to Shî'ism, then to atheism, and his *Faḍîḥat al-Mu'tazila*, the book refuted by al-Khayyâṭ, as an internal quarrel among Muslims rather than a radical critique of revelation and prophecy; see Gabrieli, *op. cit.* (note 2 above), pp. 32–33. See also s.v. "Ibn al-Rāwandī" in *EI*², III, p. 905, where a temporary attachment to Shî'ism *prior* to his "free thought" (*zandaqa*) is mentioned. However, Ibn al-Khayyâṭ's account leads to the conclusion that Abû 'Îsâ al-Warrâq and Ibn al-Râwandî merely manifested Râfiḍism externally, while actually being *zanâdiqa*; see, e.g., Intiṣâr, p. 108. Gabrieli, *loc. cit.*, also views Ibn al-Râwandî's Shî'ism as the practical expedient of a man who put himself at the disposal of the best payer, but he does not regard it as a cloak with which he invested his *zandaqa*. That Shî'ism was often merely a respectable cover for *zandaqa* was suspected by medieval authors on heresy, such as 'Abd al-Qâhir al-Baghdâdî and Algazali; see, e.g., H. Laoust, "La classification des sectes dans le *Farq* d'Al-Baghdadi," *Revue des Études Islamiques*, 29 (1961), 45–47.

So far, the modern representatives of the *zanâdiqa*, those materialist atheists who have embraced the New Faith, have failed to provide the masses of believers with an ideology of sufficient charm and power to wean them from the Islamic heritage, and thereby to accomplish what their medieval predecessors failed to achieve.[22]

22 This article was completed in 1976 and does not reflect more recent views and literature.

ʿALI AL-MUNAYYAR

M. Perlmann

I

Tafhīm al-jāhilīn dīn al-yahūd al-maghḍūb ʿalayhim wa-l-naṣārā al-ḍāllīn is the long title of a short treatise of an Islamic refutation of the earlier monotheistic creeds. This *Enlightening the ignorant about the faith of the Jews with whom God is wrathful and of the Christians who are astray* is the work of ʿAlī al-Munayyar al-Shāfiʿī.

The tract was written for Egyptian readers. The time of writing is not indicated. However, the author introduces himself as a ṣufi disciple (*aḥadu-l-fuḳarā'*) of Sīdī ʿAlī al-Buḥayrī, who was the successor (*naḳīb*) of Sīdī ʿAlī al-Nabtītī, both deceased.

ʿAlī al-Buḥayrī is mentioned as a distinguished ṣūfī who died in 941/1534–5. A Turkish dignitary used to say about him that his name should rather be *al-Baḥrī*, alluding to his erudition (*tabaḥḥur*).[1]

Another man with the same name, a great Shāfiʿī erudite, is mentioned. He died in 953/1546–7. He was a teacher of Shaʿrānī for 20 years, active mostly in the countryside (*rīf*). He was absorbed in prayer, lacrimose, fearful of hell-fire (*wa-hal khuliḳati-nnāru illa li-miṯlī*), and was laid to rest in the zāwiya of Sīdī Muḥammad al-Munayyar outside the Siryaḳus *khanḳa*. Shaʿrānī considered him an illustrious master of both *shariʿa* and *ḥakiḳa*. Some considered him one of the forty righteous men of the age. He denied that such was his rank. But when he slept under the *mu'aḏḏin*'s bench at the Azhar mosque, he saw in his dream successive groups assuring him he was the leader of the forty.

Both notes may possibly refer to one and the same person.[2]

Around Sīdī Muḥammad al-Munayyar, of the circle of Ibrahīm al-Matbulī, a town developed. He died in the 930s (1520s) after having performed the hajj 67 times. For 30 years he used to read a *khatma* at night, another during the day.

1 Ibn ʿImād, *Shaḏarāt*, v. 8, p. 245.

2 *Ibid.*, p. 296; Shaʿrānī, *al-Ṭabaḳāt al-Kubrā*, Cairo 1965, v. II, p. 153; V. Vacca, *Vite e detti di santi musulmani*, Turin 1968, pp. 362 f. On Siryāḳūs, cf. ʿAli Mubarak's *Khiṭaṭ*, XVII, 2f.

Sha'rānī visited him frequently and accompanied him on a pilgrimage.[3] In the holy cities, Shaykh al-Munayyar would distribute food, sugar, soap, thread and needles. He was deeply troubled by the suggestion of another learned pilgrim that these gifts, coming from the hands of Cairo grandees and merchants, might be of tainted origin and perhaps unlawful. Grief over this suspicion was the cause of his death, says Sha'rānī. One wonders if the author of the tract under consideration was a descendant of this Muḥammad al-Munayyar.

About 'Alī b. al-Jamāl al-Nabtītī, an earlier revered master (died after 900/1494–5), we learn from Sha'rānī that he performed the pilgrimage annually and distributed grain, especially to the needy. Sha'rānī, who saw him only once, also knew 'Ali al-Nabtītī the blind (*al-ḍarīr*) who died in 917/1511.[4]

Brockelmann registered al-Munayyar as the author of responsa in problems of the canonic law, a writer whose time and place were unclear.[5] The Cairo ms. addenda list for 1936–1955 also mentions such responsa dated 1095/1683–4.[6] Thus we may conclude that the author of ***Tafhīm*** was a seventeenth-century Egyptian Shafi'ī scholar and ṣūfī. The ***Tafhīm*** is available in a copy preserved at the Cambridge University Library.[7]

II

The author explains that he was urged to write this refutation of Judaism and Christianity when he learned that those faiths were considered divine by certain Muslims, who consequently felt it was wrong to call Jews and Christians infidels. He considers this the probable result of ignorance, on the one hand, and of protracted contact with non-Muslims, on the other hand. Indeed, he locates this ignorance and these contacts: the people of the countryside (*aryāf*), presumably the peasants, removed as they are from centers of Muslim scholars and scholarship, are most susceptible to such aberrations and evil influences. The author was asked to write an instructive elucidation on this matter, to explain how the texts of the non-Muslim scriptures had been tampered with, and how the Jews came to assert that 'Uzayr was the son of God, and how the Christians came to worship Christ and his mother as deities. Seeing that nobody else in the countryside arose to refute the infidels, the author decided to

3 Sha'rānī, *op. cit.*, II, pp. 118 f.

4 *Ibid.*, p. 114; Ibn 'Imād, v. 8, pp. 163 f.

5 *Geschichte der Arabischen Literatur*, Supp. II, 975.

6 *Fihrist al-makhṭūṭāt*, etc.; I, Cairo 1380/1961, p. 48.

7 E.g., Browne, *Hand-list of Muhammadan mss.*, Cambridge 1900, p. 48. The library has put me under obligation by supplying a copy of the beautifully written ms. and consenting to my use of it in publication.

respond, lest the silence be taken by the ignorant as a sign of Muslim acquiescence in the Jewish and Christian tenets. If a non-Muslim says, "I testify that there is only one God" (without mentioning the name of His prophet, Muḥammad), is he a believer? Evidently not, from an Islamic point of view. Yet in the countryside the mistaken view is shared by many Muslims that the non-Muslim is a believer.

The author is aware of the existence of a substantial literature on the subject, and claims no originality. However, he has found that the best source is the Koran.

The questioner was evidently ignorant and influenced by contact with non-Muslims. He who doubts the unbelief of the Jews and the Christians abandons Islam and plunges himself into unbelief (p. 7; cf. Appendix).

But how do we know, e.g., that the non-Muslim scriptures are not of divine origin, at least in their present form?

If the reader expects the author to proceed into polemics, exegetic notes, to quote the criticized books and so on, he is in for utter disappointment. Our author may have read earlier polemical works but he has decided, apparently, that the argument from the Koran is the best. He is fully consistent in quoting only and exclusively the holy writ.

Throughout the ages Muslim polemicists ran into this difficulty of evaluating the Old Testament and the New Testament, of proving that their texts had been tampered with or misinterpreted, of looking for annunciations about Islam and Muḥammad in those books. Not so our shaykh: he ignores and avoids these reefs entirely. He quotes numerous Koran passages to demonstrate the Islamic teaching. *Hadīṯ* also serves the purpose (p. 28). Thus the author attains his proof. Moses and Jesus would have to follow Muḥammad (*hadīṯ* data; p. 10).

Jews may assert that they do not consider ʿUzayr to be God's son. But the Koran says they do (9:30; p. 13). Indeed, there may be a sect among the Jews that denies ʿUzayr's divine birth (p. 14). Here the author displays his learning about Jewish sects, such as the Samaritans, Sabians, ʿAnanians, etc. However, the majority are Rabbanites (p. 15). Some Sabians postulate a list of divine attributes, some recognize only negative attributes. This is quoted from Abū Manṣūr's (i.e., Baghdādī's) work.

Muḥammad's prophethood was all the more wondrous in that it appeared in a primitive milieu (p. 26; cf. Razi, also quoted by Ibn Kammūna, 85f/125). The Jews chose to reject the Prophet in their stubborn unbelief, motivated by envy. They have been reviled (p. 29) as enemies since the Prophet's time, through the ages. A long list of Jewish acts of unbelief (p. 31 f.) concludes this section. The author has boiled down to a resumé (33) what could have filled a stout volume.

He passes on to a discussion of Christianity. Christians, he says, also use the argument from the Koran: Islamic scripture mentions that Jesus is God's spirit and word. The Christians produced the theory of the trinity of the Godhead (34 f.) The philosophers do not believe in life beyond death (p. 39) but the Muslims and, for that matter, other religionists do. "Our proof is the divine word: 'Every soul tastes death' [(Koran, 2:182(185); 21:36(25); 29:57]. Now the one who tastes must necessarily remain [in existence] after tasting. But are the soul and the spirit one and the same thing or are they two different things? In truth, they are one and the same thing" (p. 40).

The *ṣūfī* master al-Buḥayrī quoted Ṣuyūṭī about the status of the Prophet's parents and other pre-Islamic figures: are they alive in Paradise or doomed on account of their unbelief (p. 45)? Ṣuyūṭī was positive about the salvation of the worthy.[8]

But how did the Christians develop the Trinity tenet and all their theology of the human and divine aspect in Christ? For 81 years the Christians lived in accordance with Christ's teachings. But then warfare broke out between them and the Jews. There was a Jew named Paul, a hater of Christians. He said to the Jews, "If Christ was right, we are guilty of unbelief, and doomed, and cheated too, for they go to Paradise, and we to Hell." He pretended to have repented, turned Christian, and displayed piety. He taught Nestor in Jerusalem the tenet of Trinity; proceeded to Rūm, where he taught about the hypostases, and preached that Christ was God's son. He further taught Mālik that Jesus was God (pp. 63–66). Paul then killed himself as a sacrifice to God and Christ. The various tenets that he taught caused fierce dispute among the Christians, and thus Paul the provocateur achieved his goal (p. 67). This is yet another version of the legend describing Paul as arch-misleader of the early community of Christians (65–67).[9]

The Christians, too, rejected Islam and its prophet, e.g., those of Najrān (82). Islam established in due course a system of treatment of the non-Muslims (89). A non-Muslim physician should not be consulted by the true believers, and no medicine should be accepted from him without previous test, for the unbelievers are treacherous (92).

8 He wrote half a dozen pamphlets on the subject.

9 Cf. the discussion of this lore by S. Stern, "ʿAbd al-Jabbar's Account on how Christ's Religion was Falsified by the Adoption of Roman Customs," *Journal of Theological Studies* (Oxford) (NS), 19 (1968), esp. 176–185.

III

At this point the author is through with theology and the last quarter of the pamphlet shows a different trend. It is an anti-Copt treatise, utilizing and repeating the standard motifs of such propaganda, directed especially against the employment of non-Muslims in the bureaucracy, which gives the Copts a semblance of power over Muslims.

Going into "sociology," ethnics, the author stresses that the infidels trick the Muslims by becoming accountants and physicians; in the former capacity they exploit Muslim wealth, in the latter they are apt to destroy Muslim lives.

The infidel accountants (*ḥussāb*) consider it lawful to rob the Treasury, because actually, they feel, Egypt is ***their*** country, which the Muslims took from them by force. The Jews, again, consider anyone who desecrates the Sabbath a miscreant, whose wealth and blood may be destroyed with impunity.

This is followed by the story of the monk-bureaucrat who, in the days of the Fatimid al-ʿĀmir (495—524/1101—1130), delivered a speech on the Copts' claims and quoted a poem which was taken to refer to the subject.[10]

It seems that al-Munayyar had nothing new to add to the anti-Copt lore. He merely re-introduced the subject and rewove it after three centuries in the guise of a theological opus. No indication is given of any more substantial pretext for the writing than the query (actual or a literary device?), or of any connection with public agitation against the infidels. With gusto, he reproduces accounts of the exposure and persecution of the infidels throughout the ages (up to 1400), with the righteous zeal of the true believer against the insolence and arrogance of those with whom God is wrathful and who are astray.

10 Belin, "Fetoua," etc., *Journal Asiatique* (1851), esp. p. 461; Ḳalḳashandī, *Ṣubh*, v. 13, pp. 369 f. Cf. R. Gottheil, "An Answer to the Dhimmis," *Journal of the American Oriental Society*, 41 (1921), esp. 393, 401/425, 429, 437; M. Perlmann, "Notes on Anti-Christian Propaganda in the Mamluk Empire," *Bulletin of the School of Oriental and African Studies*, 10 (1942), esp. 847 ff. *Idem* (Asnāwī), in *Ignace Goldziher Memorial Volume*, II, Jerusalem 1958, esp. p. 9 of the Arabic text; Cl. Cahen, "Histoire copte d'un cadi médiéval," *Bulletin de l'Institut Français d'Archéologie Orientale du Caire*, 59 (1960), esp. 141, 148.

تفهيم الجاهلين
دين اليهود المغضوب عليهم و النصارى
الضالين

تأليف

سيدنا و مولانا العبد الفقير المعترف بالذنب
الحبر الفهامة مفتى المسلمين و مرشد السالكين
الى رب العالمين
سيدى على المنير الشلفعى و يواليه دعاء له ولجميع
المسلمين ، آمين

(١)

(٣) بسم الله الرحمان الرحيم

الحمد لله الذى من علينا بالتوحيد وجعلنا مسلمين ولم يجعلنا من المغضوب عليهم وهم اليهود ولا من النصارى الضالين الذين يجعل(ون) مع الله الها آخر وشركاء وبنين . . . ولا ممن زاغ عن السنه وعقائد اهلها المعتمدين. سبحان ربك رب العزه عما يصفون والسلام على المرسلين والحمد لله رب العالمين حمدا يستغرق محامد الحامدين واشهد ان لا اله الا الله وحده ،لا شريك له ولا والد له ولا ولد له ،ولا اله معه الملك الحق المبين.

وبعد فيقول العبد الفقير ،المعترف بالذنب والعجز والتقصير ،على المنير الشافعى ،احد فقراء سيدى على البحيرى نقيب سيدى على النبتيتى ،غفر الله له ولهما وللمسلمين آمين.

اننى رأيت مع شخص سوءالا دائرا به فى البلاد بالارياف وهو :

ما قولكم ،رضى الله عنكم ،فى شخص من المسلمين يدعى العلم والمعرفه والفهم ،قال ان اليهود والنصارى كل منهما متمسك بدين صحيح ،لكون اليهود معهم التوراه ،وهى اصل

(٤) دينهم ،والانجيل مع النصارى ،وهو اصل

دينهم ،وانهما كلام الله تعالى . وكيف يكون من تمسك بكلام الله تعالى على باطل . وسألنى فى الجواب عن ذلك وعن بيان قول هذا ،وعن بيان اعتقاد اليهود والنصارى وما هما عليه ،ليحصل بذلك بيان كفرهما له ولكل جاهل به مثله

(٢)

خصوصا ممن عاشرهما و طالت صحبته بهما فى الارياق و غيرها ، حتى ظن من افعالهم فى صومهم و اعيادهم و عباداتهم الباطله و ذكرهم انهم على شيئ لجهله و لعدم معاشرته للعلماء ، وان ازيد على ذلك بيانا و اذكر سبب خروجهما عن ما فى التوراه و الانجيل ، و هل وقع فيهما تبديل و تحريف و تغيير ام لا ، و ما قالوه اليهود فى عزير انه ابن الله، تعالى و تقدس عن ذلك، و ما قالته النصارى فى عيسى عمَ انه ابن الله و ما خصوه به وجهلوه و امه الهين مع الله . . . فحطتنى الغيره . . . حين لم ار احدا تصدى اليه فى الارياق و لا تعرض عليه بالانكار ولا جواب . . .

و خشيت من السكوت عليه ان تعتقد العوام و من لا علم عنده من ذلك ان قوله صحيح ، خصوصا اهل الارياق الذين لا علم عندهم و لا علماء

(٥) بينهم و لا يعلمون شيئا من ذلك و لا يعرفون الفرق بين دين اليهود و النصارى و بين دين المسلمين و ربما اعتقدوا ان القول المذكور صحيح . و قد سمعت قبل ذلك بمدة من شخص سمع نصرانيا يقول : اشهد ان لا اله الا الله . فقال السامع المذكور : كيف يقولون هذا كافر و هو يشهد ان لا اله الا الله ؟ و لا يعلم ما هو عليه و لا ما هو كافر به الى غير ذلك من الجهل الذى زاد و اتسع بالارياف.

مع اننى لم اكن اهلا للجواب على ذلك و لا لبيانه على ما ذكره لانه يحتاج الى سعه علم . . . من الكتب المصنفة فى ذلك . . . فرأيت كتاب الله تعالى فيه الدليل و هو خير سبيل

(٣)

فرجعت اليه . . .

(٦) ولم اقل ذلك ليقال اننى ابتكر به . . فان الله تع بلغت حجته و دلت على وحدانيته و مخلوقاته و صنعته . . . و انما قلته ردا على الشخص المشار اليه كما تقدمت الاشارة اليه . . . خصوصا اهل الارياف التى خلت من العلم و العلماء وكثر فيها اهل الذمة اعداء الدين الغرماء . . .

(٧) و سميته تفهيم الجاهلين دين اليهود المغضوب عليهم و النصارى الضالين وعلى الله الكريم اعتمادى . . . فاقول . . . هذا الرجل القائل بتصويب اهل الضلاله من اليهود و النصارى لم يكن عالما و لا عارفا و لا فاهما و لا عاقلا نافعا ،بل هو عبد جاهل مغرور مفتون فى دينه استحوذ عليه الشيطان حتى اخرجه عن الاسلام . . . فان قال قائل :كيف خرج عن الاسلام و صار كافرا ؟ فالجواب :

من شك فى تكفير اليهود و النصارى فهو كافر ،كما نص عليه ائمة الدين وعلماء المسلمين ، فمع يقينه اولى بالكفر. و لعل سبب ذلك انه عاشر احدا من اليهود او النصارى و طالت عشرته بهم كما هو مشاهد فيمن اشقاه الله تع من المسلمين . . . او ان احدا من اليهود او النصارى حسن له كلاما من عقائدهم فمال قلبه اليه من جمله بالقاء الشيطان ذلك فيه لعماه . . .

(٨) و نزيد عليه من الادلة الشرعية من كتاب الله العزيز المحفوظ من التغيير و التبديل كما قال تعالى . . . فقوله ان التوراة و الانجيل كلام الله قلنا نعم اصلهما كلام الله تع من غير ريب و لا

(٤)

شك كما انزلا و ما وقع فيهما من التحريف و التغيير فليس ذلك كلام

(٩) الله . . . فان قال قائل منهم :كيف عرفتم المحرف و المغير و المكتوم و هما بلغه لا تعرفون معناها و هذا امر يستحيل عليكم؟ فجوابه :عرفنا ذلك من كتاب الله المبين و رسوله الصادق الامين فجميع ما اخبر الله به و رسوله صلعم انه فى التوراه و الانجيل و اليهود و النصارى ينكرونه ، فان كان الامر فى التوراه والانجيل ما يوافق انكارهم فهو مغير و مبدل او ان احبارهم الذين ادركوا النبى صلعم و انكروا نبوته و كفروا عنادا او حسدا و هم يعلمون نبوته من غير شك منهم و لا اشتباه كتموا ذلك كما وقع فى آيه الرجم من اليهود فى التوراة اوغيروه. فمن جاء بعدهم مشى على ما كانوا عليه فاستمر ذلك فيهم.و اما ماكان على اصله من التوراه و الانجيل ولم يغير ولم يبدل وكان ذلك يخالف شرعنا كان منسوخا بالقرآن العظيم . . .

(١٠) . . . و المعتمد ان شرع من قبلنا ليس بشرع لنا . . . لو فرض ان موسى عم ادرك نبينا صلعم ما وسعه الا تباعه و كذلك عيسى عم اذا نزل الارض انما يكون تابعا لشرع نبينا محمد صلعم و لا يعمل بشرعه الذى ارسل به.و لا خلاف ان اليهود و النصارى حرفوا التوراه و الانجيل ولهذا ان الاشتغال بكتابتهما ونظرها لا يجوز بالاجماع . و قد غضب النبى صلعم حين رأى مع عمر صحيفه فيها شيئى من التوراه فقال لوكان موسى حيا ماوسعه الا اتباعى . . .

(٥)

(١٢) ... ويكذبون نبينا ... وينكرون نبوته ورسالته ويكفـــرون بالقرآن ... ثم نرجع ونتكلم على شيئى من عقائدهم الباطلـه الفاسدة الضالة المضلة ...

... فان اهل الريف وغيرهم ممن عاشرهم وطالـــت عشرته بهم وذلك ان طائفة قالت عزير ابن الله . فان كان ذلك عندهم الآن فى التوراه فهو

(١٣) باطل ... قال احد منهم لم نقل عزير ابن الله . فقـــد قال الله تعالى :قالت اليهود عزير ابن الله و قالت النصـــارى المسيح ابن الله ... قال الزجاج ... قاله ابن العماد رآع فى شرح البردة

(١٤) ... وربما ان من انكر ذلك يكون من الطائفة التى لـــم تقل عزير ابن الله تعَ . ومن طوائفهم السامرة والصابئون وهم فرقان ،فرقه توافق النصارى فى اصل دينهم واخرى تخالفهـــم فتقول الفلك حى ناطق وتعبد الكواكب السبعة الاثار اليهـــا وتنفى الله تع ... وهم الذين افتى الاصطخرى بقتلهم فـــى زمن القاهره ... قال صاحب الانوار قال الاستاذ ابو منصـــور ان اليهود

اليوم فرق :عنانية ربانية سامرة وشاذانية والشاذانيـــه فيهم كأهل الاهواء فينا وجمهورهم الاعظم ربانية وبين الفرقتين خلاف فى اباحة الخمر وتوراة السامرة تخالف توراة الجمهـــور فى مواضع كثيرة وادعى الجمهور تسعة عشر نبيا بعد موسى . و اقرت السامرة ثلاثة منهم فقط.و قال الصابئون فرق احدهـــا

(٦)

قالت بحدوث العالم و ابنعاث الصانع و ان الصانع خلق الفلك حيا ناطقا سميعا بصيرا مدبر العالم و سموا الكواكب السبعة ملائكة. و الثانيه قالت بحدوث العالم و توحيد الصانع و لم يصرفوه باوصاف الكمال و وصفوه بنفى النقائص فقالوا لا نقول حتى عالم قادر ولكن نقول انه ليس بميت و لا جاهل و لا عاجزو قالوا ان هرمس المنجم كان نبيا و قالوا بثلاث صلوات مفروضات فى كل يوم . . .

(١٦) و حرموا الخنزير و الكلب و الحمار . . . و قالوا لا طلاق الا بحكم حاكم او بينة عن فاحشة و لا رجعة و لا جمع بين امرأتين .

الثالث قوم بناحية واسط دينهم خلاف دين صابية حران فى اكل الخنزير و فى صلواتهم الى القطب الشمالى و الحرانية تصلى و القطب وراءها . انتهى

(١٩) . . . و يكذبوا ما عدا طائفة العيسوية منهم يقولون برسالته الى العرب خاصة و يزعمون انه لم يرسل اليهم و لهذا ان احدهم اذا قال "اشهد ان محمدا رسول الله" لا يحكم باسلامه حتى يشهد له بالرسالة العامة و يتبراء من كل دين يخالف دين الاسلام و هذه الطائفه كافره ايضا . و اجمعت طوائفهم اجمعين على ان عيسى عم لم يكن نبيا و لا رسولا و ان الانجيل لم يكن كلام الله و لا انزله عليه و ان نبينا محمد صلعم لم يكن نبيا و لا رسولا ما عدا طائفة العيسوية . . .

(٢٠) . . . و لا يحتاج ذلك الى قولى هذا و انما ذكرته بيانا للعوام و القراء شهود الديوان فقد طالت عشرتهم باليهود و النصارى

(٧)

(٢١) الصيارف و هم يجهلون اعتقادهم و ما هم عليه . . .

(٢٦) . . . انه انزل فى زمن الفصاحة و البلاغة و هو صلعم امى لا يعلم الخط و لا الكتابة و لا الشعر و قومه جهال لا اعتناء لهم بعلوم الاديان و الزمان جاهليه بينهم و مع ذلك اتى بهذا القرآن — العظيم الذى لا تقدر الخلق اجمعين ان يأتوا بسورة منه واحكامه وغيره (وعبره ؟) و امثاله و مواعظه لا تحصى كامواج البحور ولهذا مدحه صاحب البردة و قال ابن الجوزى رضى الله عنه ان عده آيات القرآن العظيم ٦٦٦٠ آية . . .

(٢٧) . . . مع انهم كانوا قبل مبعثه يعترفون بظهوره و نبوته و يعرفون محله و هذا سبب رحيلهم من اقطار الارض و نزولهم بيثرب فى اوان مبعثه ينتظرون خروجه . . . فلما بعث جحدوا نبوته . . . بغيا و حسدا ولهذا كذبوا من عرفه منهم من احبار اليهود وآمن به كعبد الله بن سلام وغيره من اصحابه وغيروا و بدلوا صفته من التوراه و هذا جميعه و امثاله كفر عناد و حسد لا من شك و لا ريب . لا يخفى ذلك على من له ادنى عقل و فهم . و الحاصل ان اليهود امة شديدة الكفر مغضوب عليها كما ثبت عن النبى صلعم

(٢٩) انه قال فى تفسير قوله تعالى " غير المغضوب عليهم و لا الضالين" قال : المغضوب عليهم اليهود و الضالين النصارى و قد دل كتاب الله تعـ على ذلك و تكور القول فيهم و فى ذمهم و لعنهم و ان الذلة و المسكنة ضربت عليهم . . .

. . . فهم انجس الامم قلوبا و اخبثهم طوية و اردأهم سجية

(٨)

(٣٠) و اولا هم بالعذاب الاليم . فهم امة الخيانة لله و رسوله و دينه
و كتابه .
من زمن النبى صلعم و الى زماننا هذا و قبل ذلك بمأتين من
السنين . . .

(٣١) . . . و نجعل خاتمة هذا الكلام فى كفر طوائف اليهود لعنة
الله عليهم و اسبابه و تعداده و ان كان يعلم مما تقدم فجمعه
هنا بذكر الماضى و يعدده :فقولهم ان عزير ابن الله كفروانكارهم
نبوه عيسى عم كفر و رمى امه بالزنا كفر و انكارهم الا نجيل كفر و
قولهم انهم قتلوا

(٣٢) عيسى عم كفر ،و قولهم ان موسى عم خاتم النبيين و لا نبى بعده
كفر و كفرهم بنبينا محمد صلعم كفر و انكارهم القرآن العظيم انه
لم يكن كلام الله كفر و الطائفة التى منهم تعبد الكواكب السبعة
و تضييف الا ثار اليها كفر و الطائفة التى عبدت الشمس كفر
والطائفة التى عبدت العجل كفرو قولهم ان مستحل السبت كافر
و يحل دمه و ماله كفر و الطائفة التى عبدت النار كفر كفر متعدد
يطول الكلام عليه . و لهم غير ذلك اعتقادات كثيرة كقولهم ان
عيسى عم هو الدجال الذى يخرج فى آخر الزمان و جعلوا آخر
الزمان هو الزمن الذى بعث فيه عيسى صلعم و مع ذلك ان —
السحرة الذين يخرجون مع الدجال انما يكونون منهم فيمدونه
بالباطل و السحر فاقوالهم يناقض بعضها بعضا . فلو فرض ان
فيهم خصلة واحدة من هذه الخصال فى طوائفهم لعنة الله
عليهم اجمعين . فاعتمد ايها الرائى على ما قلناه. فاننى

(٩)

(٣٣) حققته من النقول المعتمدة لا سيما و الكتاب العزيز يوءيده و الله تعالى اصدق القائلين .

و هذا آخر ما تيسر الكلام عليه مع مراعاة الاختصار ولو اردنا الاطالة لجاء مجلدا اكبر اوفى هذا القدر كفاية لما نحن بصدده و قصدناه . . .

ثم نشرع بعد ذلك ان شاء الله تع فى امر النصارى الضالين لعنه الله عليهم اجمعين . . .

فانهم قالوا او بعضهم ــ ان عيسى عم ابن الله و هو غير مخلوق عند هم اجمعين بل جعلوه الٰها خالقا و اذا اردت تعرف حقيقه ذلك منهم فقل لهم : عيسى عم مخلوق ام غير مخلوق ؟ و يقولون انه روح الله و كلمته و كيف تكون روح الله و كلمته

(٣٤) مخلوقين ؟ و يسألون بعض من يقراء القرآن العظيم من المسلمين فيقولون له :فى القرآن كتابكم ان عيسى عم روح الله و كلمته و كيف يكون روح الله و كلمته مخلوقا ؟ فان ولا علم عنده من ذلك فيعجز عن الجواب لعدم علمه به . فمن هنا يجهلون المسلمون و ينسبونهم لعدم المعرفة بحقيقه عيسى عم مطلقا . . . قالوا ان الله ثالث ثلاثة . . . الاب و الابن و روح القدس الٰه واحد فيجعلون الثلاثة واحدا و الواحد ثلاثة . . .

فشرعت لك ايها الجاهل بذلك . . . ليظهر لك . . . و تفهم ما هم عليه من الباطل و التأويل و الاعتقاد الفاسد . . .

(٣٥) فاقول : الروح مخلوقة و كل شيئى مخلوق غير الله تع فهو القديم الخالق الذى لا اول لبدايته و لا آخر لنهايته فهو

(١٠)

الاول بلا بداية و الآخر بلا نهاية . فالروح من جملة مخلوقاته

(٣٩) ... و ذهبت اهل الملل من المسلمين و غيرهم (الى) ان الروح تبقى بعد الموت . و خالف فيه الفلاسفة . دليلنا قوله تعالى :

كل نفس ذائقة الموت . والذائق لا بد ان يبقى بعد الذوق .

(٤٠) و هل النفس و الروح شيئى واحد او شيئان . الصحيح ان — النفس و الروح شيئى واحد و قال بعض اهل السنّة ان الروح التى تقبض غير النفس .

... عيسى عمّ عبد الله و رسوله مخلوق و به روح الله مخلوقة كسائر المخاليق ... فلا خصوصية لعيسى .

(٤٤) ... و افادنى سيدنا و شيخنا و قدوتنا قطب زمانه و امامه الشيخ نور الدين على البحيرى نقيب سيدنا و مولانا الشيخ نور الدين قطب زمانه على النبتيتى رحمها الله تعالى و رضى عنهما انه سأل الشيخ جلال الدين السيوطى حافظ العصر عن ابوى النبى صلّعم هل احياهما الله تعَ و آمنا به و عن اهل

(٤٥) الفتره هل هم ناجون ام لا ؟ فاجابه فقال الذى اعتقده و القى الله تع به انهما احياهما الله تعَ اوصى امنا به و ان اهل الفتره من عيسى عمَ و الى محمد صلّعم ناجون و تلى قوله تع : و ما كنا معذبين حتى نبعث رسولا. و احتج بهذه الآية و قال البغوى رضى الله عنه فى تفسيره ...

(٥١) ... و فى هذه المقالات الكفر المبين الذى لا شك فيه و لا ريب و لا شبهة لمن له ادنى عقل و فهم ...

(١١)

(٦٥) . . . فان قال قائل : كيف وصل النصارى الى نسبة الولد لله تعالى وكيف جعلوه ثالث ثلاثة و ما ذكروه فى الاقانيم الثلاثة و اللاهوت و الناسوت و الجوهر وغير ذلك ؟ و الحال ان ذلك لم يكن فى الانجيل فيما انزل الله تعالى فيه . و لا يجسر احد على ذلك بل و لا يتصوره عقل و لا بعث به نبى و لا انزل فى كتاب و لا تكلم به احد قبلهم . والله تعالى منزه عن ذلك ولا عليه دليل و لا برهان و لا تقتضيه العقول و لا تصوره الافهام و لا الاوهام . فالجواب عن ذلك انهم ، بعد رفع عيسى عمّ كانوا على دينه احدى و ثمانين سنة ، ثم وقع بينهم و بين اليهود حروب كثيره وكان فى اليهود رجل يقال له بولس ، قتل جماعة من اصحاب عيسى

(٦٦) عمّ. ثم قال لليهود : ان كان الحق مع عيسى فكفرنا و النار مصيرنا فنحن مغبونون اذ دخلوا الجنة و دخلنا النار. فانا احتال و اضلهم حتى يدخلوا النار . وكان له فرس يقال له العقاب يقاتل عليه . فعرقب فرسه و اظهر الندامه و وضع على رأسه التراب. فقالوا له النصارى :من انت ؟ فقال بولس عدوكم ، نوديت من السماء : ليس لك توبة الا ان تتنصر و قد تبت فادخلوه الكنيسة و دخل بيتا سنة لا يخرج منه ليلا و لا نهارا حتى تعلم الانجيل.ثم خرج و قال :نوديت ان الله قبل توبتك فصدقوه و حبوه ثم مضى الى بيت المقدس و خلف عليهم نسطورا وعلمه ان عيسى عمّ و مريم رضى الله عنها و الاله كانوا ثلاثة . ثم توجه الى الروم وعلمهم اللاهوت و الناسوت و قال لهم :لم

(١٢)

يكن عيسى عم بانس ولا جسم ولكنه ابن الله . وعلم رجلا
منهم، يقال له يعقوب، ذلك . ثم دعا رجلا يقال مالكا ، فقال
له ان الاله لم يزل ولا يزال عيسى عم . فلما استمكن منهم دعا
هوءلاء لثلاثه واحدا واحدا بحيث لا يعلم الآخر، وقال لكل
واحد منهم : انت خالصتى ، وقد رأيت عيسى عم فى المنام ،
ورضى عنى . وقال
(٦٧) لكل واحد : انى غدا اذبح نفسى ، فادع الناس الى نحلتك
ثم دخل المذبح فذبح نفسه . وقال : انما افعل ذلك لمرضاة
المسيح عم. فلما كان يوم ثالث ، دعا كل واحد منهم طائفة
واختلفوا واقتتلوا . فهذا سبب ذلك وسبب فساد دينهم
ووصفهم المسيح عم بما تقدم . . .
فان قال قائل : كيف دخل عليهم ذبح نفسه وهو لا يحل ؟
فالجواب : ان من الامم الماضية ، قبل هذه الامة المحمدية ، من
كان مأمورا بقتل نفسه علامة لتوبته . فهو انما بالغ فى الحيلة
المذكورة بذلك بحيث انهم لم يبق عندهم شك ولا ريب فيما
قرره لهم . . . لصحة توبته وصدقه . . . وقد حفف الله تع
ذلك عن هذه الامة لشرف نبيها . . . وزادهم ضلالا وبغيا
مع ما وقع فى الانجيل ما معناه او لفظه : انى ولّدت عيسى
(٦٨) من العذراء، بتشديد اللام . كما يقول الشخص : انى ولّدت
البهيمة . وتقول الداية : انى ولدت المرأة . يراد بذلك
ان المولد اخرج المولود من بطن امه ، والله تع اخرج عيسى
من بطن امه بقدرته من غير واسطة . وهذا معناه . فلما تبدل

(١٣)

دينهم و مات قرأ الانجيل الذين لم يدركوا التبديل و ما وقع من بولس المذكور و حصل الاختلاف بينهم الذى قدمناه فى تقرير بولس لهم. قروؤا بتخفيف اللام من غير تشديد . فقالوا : انى ولدت عيسى من العذراء . فجعلوه ابن الله تعالى و تقدس و تنزه عن ذلك . كبرت كلمه تخرج من افواههم إن يقولون الا كذبا و حكمى انه كان فى الانجيل ما لفظه او معناه : و من يبتغ غير الاسلام دينا فلن يقبل منه . فتركوا لفظه (غير) و قالوا : و من يبتغ الاسلام دينا فلن يقبل منه

(٨٢) . . . و قد قدمنا ان اليهود انما كفروا بمحمد صلعم كفر عناد و حسد مع انهم عرفوه و عرفوا صفته و زمانه و مكانه و نبوته .
و كذلك وقع للنصارى حين قد وفد نصارى نجران حين حاجوه فى عيسى عم

(٨٩) ثم بعد ذلك تشرع فى اشياء مما يليق بالموءمن فعله و قوله مع اليهود و النصارى فالموءمن يجتنب معاشرتهم و مخالطتهم و يتخذهم اعداء كما انهم اعداء الله تع و رسوله صلعم الا ان تدعوه ضرورة شرعية الى ذلك . و ينكر عليهم بظاهره و باطنه . . .
شروط الامام عمر بن الخطاب . . . و لا يحسن لهم كلاما و لا يسلم عليهم و يتلطف بهم بالمودة . . .

(٩٢) . . . و لا يقبل قول طبيب منهم ، لا فى مرض و لا دواء ولا غير ذلك ما لم يصدق و لم يكن معلقا بالعبادة كالتيمم و فانهم اهل الخيانة و التدليس واعداء الدين . . . و من مكرهم بالمسلمين عملوا حسّابا و اطباء . فالحساب اكلوا اموال المسلمين

(١٤)

و الاطباء اتلفوا ارواح المسلمين و حسّاب النصارى يستحلـــو ن
اموال المسلمين . و ذلك انهم يعتقدون ان الارض كلها ملـــك
(٩٣) و حق لهم و ان اصحاب النبى صلعم اخذوها منهم بالسيف ظلما
فهى مستمرة على ملكهم و اذا اخذوا مال زارعها او ساكنها انمـــا
يأخذون حقهم . و اليهود يعتقدون ان كل من استحل السبت
كفر و حل ما له و دمه . فحسّابهم يستحلون اموال المسلميـــن و
كذلك غير حسابهم منهم و اطباؤهم و غيرهم يستحلون اخذ ارواح
المسلمين بالدواء و غيره و لهذا قال بعض الفضلاء شعرا و ينسب
للتامعى رضى الله عنه و هو هذا

لعن اليهود وكذا النصارى انهم من مكرهم صاروا لنا عملاء
صاروا اطباء و حسابا لنا
فتقاسموا الارواح و الاموال

اما اليهود فهذا مشهور فيهم لا خلاف فيه ،و هم اشد الاعادى
لنبينا محمد صلعم و اما النصارى . . . و هو انهم يقولون
ويعتقدون ان الارض ملكهم الى آخر ما تقدم . . .
. . . و حكى فى زمن الآمر بالله الخليفه استعمل من النصـــارى
كاتبا يعرف بالراهب و لقب بالاب القديس الروحانى النفيس .
فصار للعين عامه بالديار المصريه فخوفه بعض مشائخ الكتـــاب
و حذروه عواقب سوء افعاله و كان جماعة من كتاب مصر و قبطهـــا
فى مجلسه . فقام مخاطبا له مسمعا
(٩٤) للجماعة بحق ملاك هذه الديار حزبا و خراجا ملكها المسلمـــون
منا و تغلبوا عليها و استملكوها من ايدينا . فنحن مهما فعلنـــا

(١٥)

بالمسلمين فهو فى مقابل ما فعلوه بنا و لا يكون له نسبة الى
من قتل من روءسائنا و ملوكنا فى ايام الفتوح من اموال المسلمين
و اموال ملوكهم و خلفائهم حل لنا و بعض ما نستحقه عليهم فاذا
حملنا لهم ما كانت المنه لنا عليهم . و انشد اللعين يقول شعرا

بنت كرم غصبوها امها واهانوها قد ست بالقدم
ثم عادوا حكموها فيهم قلنا فيك بخصم احتكم

فاستحسن الحاضرون من النصارى و المنافقين ما سمعوه منه
و استفادوه وعضوه عليه بالنواجذ حتى قيل ان الذى احاط
عليه قلم هذا اللعين من املاك المسلمين قدره مئتا الف دينار
و اثنان و سبعون الف دينار و مئتا دينار و حوانيت و ارض باعمال
الدولة و استمر ذلك الى ان عارها الى اصحابها ابو على ابن
الافضل ثم ان الخليفه الآمر بالله انتبه من رقدته و افاق من
سكرته و ادركته حمية الاسلام و الغيره المحمديه فغضب لله تع (٩٥)
غضبه ناصر للدين و ثاثر للمسلمين فالبس اهل الذمه الغيار
و انزلهم بالمنزلة التى امرالله ان ينزلوا بها من الذل و الصغار
و امر ان لا يولوا شيئا من امر الاسلام و انشاء فى ذلك كتابا
يقف عليه الخاص و العلم و كتب عنه نسخه صورتها

الحمد لله المعبود فى ارضه و سمائه و المجيب دعاء من يدعوه
باسمائه المنفرد بالقدرة القاهرة المتوحد بالقوة الظاهرة و هو
الله الذى لا اله الا هو له الحمد فى الاولى و الآخرة هدى
العباد بالايمان الى سبيل الرشاد ،و وفقهم بالطاعات لما هو
انفع زاد المعاد ،و تفرد بعلم الغيوب يعلم من كل عبد

(١٦)

(٩٨) . . . و الامه الغضبيه هم اليهود بنص القرآن العظيم و امه

الضلاله هم النصارى المثلثه عباد الصلبان و قد اخبر الله تعالى

(٩٩) عن اليهود بانهم بالذله و المسكنه و الغضب موسومون .

(١٠٠) . . . فهم انجس الامم قلوبا و اخبثهم طويه و اردأهم سجيه

و اولاهم بالعذاب الاليم . . . امه الخيانه لله تعالى و رسوله

صلعم و دينه و كتابه و عباده الموءمنين . . .

(١٠٣) ذلك و انما استعناه فى هذا المحل حين كان الكلام فى

اعتقاد النصارى ان الارض ملكهم و حقهم و انهم اذا اخذوا —

خراجها . . . انما يأخذون حقهم . . .

(١٠٤) مما تقدم من حكايه الراهب الملقب بالاب

القديس و ماانشده فى قوله بنت كرم غصبوها امها

الى آخر الحكايه . . .

. . . . عمر بن الخطاب و ان شاء الله تع نختم هذا الكتاب

بما شرط على اهل الذمه

١١٨ . . . و قد تم كتاب

تفهيم الجاهلين زين اليهود المغضوب عليهم و النصارى الضالين

للشيخ الامام سيدى على المنير الشافعى رحمه الله تعالى .

CATALOGING AND CLASSIFICATION OF MATERIALS IN THE NEAR EASTERN LANGUAGES

S. R. BRUNSWICK

This paper had its origins in a lecture delivered in June 1966 at the first annual convention of the Association of Jewish Libraries. The years that have followed have proven the wisdom of the original thesis:

a. The best cataloging system available is that of the national library system, L.C.

b. Materials in the various Near Eastern languages are best represented in public catalogs in their own vernacular scripts.

In order to sell L.C., I must first appraise it vis-à-vis other university research libraries. First of all, L.C. is by far the largest library in the United States. The second largest library in the United States, Harvard's Widener Library, is approximately half the size volume-wise of L.C. Other major university research libraries are considerably smaller. L.C.'s holdings of printed books in the various Near Eastern languages are similarly quite extensive.

Because of the vastness of the size of the printed book collection at L.C., its officials were forced to develop classification schedules and subject headings on a much broader scale than that of any other research library. That is not to say that the classification tables and subject headings of individual libraries such as Cornell, Harvard, Princeton or Yale are not better on individual points; but I am considering library collection in toto.

It seems hardly desirable for large university libraries or specialized collections to think of undertaking reclassification to Dewey, no matter which edition. Professor M. F. Tauber gives many reasons for undertaking reclassification in his work on technical services (p. 265), but all the institutions studied were changing to L.C. from some other system. The majority of the libraries undertaking reclassification were using Dewey; others were using "local schemes."

Many of the older university research libraries in the United States found themselves heir to local schemes. The main entries were not necessarily those of L.C., and the subject headings were not those of any known list of subject headings.

In the case of some major Jewish theological seminary libraries that were saddled with the Freidus classification the decision was made to expand the Freidus scheme. This was a major error. They accepted and continued the use of a classification scheme which undoubtedly increased the work load of the cataloging staff of each institution involved. They would have been better advised to accept the L.C. classification schedules, wherein the work of classification is done at L.C. and printed on the L.C. unit cards. In addition, we must keep in mind the severe budgetary restrictions under which libraries operate nowadays, restrictions which seem to alternate with the shortages of well-trained professional librarians that we experienced a decade ago.

The same logic applies to the many other local schemes in use throughout the United States. Each classification scheme which requires real and extensive deviation from the L.C. system substantially increases the cost of professional help. This point was also made by Tauber in the above-mentioned book (p. 267), when he wrote: "There is strong reason to believe that the use of L.C. classification schedules is less expensive, since the classification numbers for individual titles are supplied on each L.C. printed card."

A veteran librarian once wrote me that "anyone who looks at the development of librarianship in recent years and who has foresight into the future will not question the fact that no single library can alone fulfill all its functions (meaning there is a need for cooperative effort). The volume of newly published books is increasing, as is the number of libraries. Is it not clear that we can build *only* through cooperative work? The Library of Congress and its professional work are not ideals but *they are the best available;* and we are living in a world of realities and not in a utopia."

There are a number of other benefits for the library that undertakes to use the L.C. unit card system:

a. No private library can match L.C. in the neatness of the unit cards that it produces and makes available through its Card Division.

b. When a professional cataloger has to do original cataloging, he first picks the proper subject heading. He can then refer to the master L.C. subject head lists and supplements, which will give him some suggestions as to where to class the book in hand. Then again, there is a series of L.C. sets of subject books, where the cards for titles already cataloged by L.C. or by libraries participating in cooperative cataloging are arranged by subject headings. If the cataloger searches these sets and compares the titles under the desired subject heading, he will have a very good idea of where to class the book.

c. Even if L.C. has not cataloged the specific edition of the title in hand, it has often cataloged other editions. In this case, the cataloger has the bulk of the work done for him.

d. The percentage of L.C. unit cards available for books in the various Near Eastern languages varies with the language. There are almost no L.C. unit cards for Ottoman Turkish books; by contrast, there are L.C. unit cards available for very many Yiddish books. About half the Arabic and Hebrew imprints extant are represented by L.C. unit cards. Persian imprints are represented by considerably fewer L.C. unit cards.

For all those titles for which L.C. unit cards are available, professional librarians are not needed except in a supervisory capacity. These titles can be searched and cataloged in preliminary fashion by trained sub-professionals under the supervision of professionals. This is the practice of many libraries.

e. For all Near Eastern languages written in a non-Latin script, the L.C. unit card establishes the form of spelling in Latin characters; once this is done it gives a full set of cross references to the established form of name, as well as a specific cuttering for each author.

f. Conformance to the L.C. system will further enable libraries to report their holdings to the local, regional and national catalogs.

One of the problems involved in cataloging Near Eastern materials is the question of how to represent non-Latin scripts to the reader. Is Arabic best represented in romanization or in the vernacular script? Libraries with strong holdings in Hebrew and Yiddish have traditionally maintained a separate catalog in the vernacular script for titles of these books.

The classical catalog, done over a hundred years ago by Joseph Zedner, has a special Hebrew title index by vernacular script to the British Museum form of entry in Latin script. The practice of many other libraries, such as Harvard, the Hebrew Union College and the Jewish National and University Library, has been similar. Most recently, the New York Public Library closed its card catalogs and went over to a new unified book catalog. They went to special efforts to represent Hebrew script materials to its readers in the vernacular script, as described in the Sept. 1977 issue of *Journal of Library Automation.*

Librarians dealing with materials in the Arabic and Persian scripts have sometimes reached a similar conclusion. In 1968, Harvard's Widener Library published its *Catalogue of Arabic, Persian, and Ottoman Turkish books*. The most outstanding feature of this catalog is its decision not to transliterate, but rather to catalog by use of the various vernacular alphabets. The late Labīb Zuwīyya-Yamak wrote, in part: "From the beginning the Library displayed great foresight in dealing with the problem of transliteration... Thus, instead of forcing the scholar to transliterate author and title in order to locate an Arabic book in the Roman-alphabet Public Catalogue, the Library has provided a separate file which is much easier to consult... The wisdom of [this] decision... has repeatedly been indicated."

A thorough evaluation of romanization is given by C. Sumner Spalding in the Winter 1977 issue of *L.R.T.S.* His first recommendation is very important. He recommends, in part: "Abandon romanization of headings in cataloging a work written in a non-roman writing system. File such a catalog record in a catalog consisting of author and title entries for publications in the given writing system, with headings in the same system."

As a final consideration I should like to discuss the question of recataloging and reclassification. This is really an expensive item; yet even large university libraries with thousands and thousands of volumes are willing to consider it, at costs that run into millions. Many schools have undertaken reclassification and recataloging or both. The question for many institutions is, is it really worth the expense involved?

Each library administrator must make this decision for himself. However, if he decides to do all new cataloging and classification by L.C., he may soon find himself with two separate catalog systems, one for the old cataloging system and another for the new one. Then the question becomes: do we send the readers forever to two separate catalogs with different forms of entry and different subject headings? Once one realizes the troubles this will bring upon the reader, recataloging and reclassification seem more essential, and in the interim years there will have to be two separate catalogs.

This problem bothered the people at Cornell University too. Felix Reichmann summed it all up when he wrote (*College and Research Libraries,* 23 [1962], 441): "The decision was made to start a new catalog in 1948. Many of us were unhappy about the idea of having two catalogs. We could foresee that the necessity of having to check two places would cause difficulties, annoyance, and mistakes for both the patrons and the staff. However, none of us could come up with a better proposal. Dr. Tauber, who participated in our discussions, spoke very strongly in favor of a new catalog, and today we acknowledge gratefully that he was right. We are happy that we followed his advice and were guided by his sage counsel."

The late Lucile M. Morsch once wrote me that "there is no parallel for L.C. cataloging." That is my conclusion, which I urge upon all librarians who have wrestled with the problems discussed here.

NATHAN MARCUS ADLER: A BIBLIOGRAPHY

RUTH P. GOLDSCHMIDT-LEHMANN

Nathan Marcus Adler, born at Hanover in 1803, served as Chief Rabbi of the United Congregations of the British Empire from 1844/5 until his death (Brighton, 1890).

1829
Antrittsrede
Dessau,
In Sulamith, vii, vol. 2, pp. 103—120
Delivered in the Synagogue of Oldenburg, 6 June 1829

1836
Des Israeliten Liebe zum Vaterlande. Eine Predigt zur Feier des Geburtstages Seiner Majestät des Königs Wilhelm IV. am Sabbathe כי תצא 5596 (27. August 1836), in der Synagoge zu Hannover gehalten
pp. 28. Hannover, 1836

1838
הסכמה
In פירוש על התורה מרבינו יעקב בן כבוד מרנא ורבנא רבינו הרא"ש זלה"ה
2nd ed., ed. by M. Rosenthal, Hannover, 1838

1843
Gutachten
In Rabbinische Gutachten über die Beschneidung... von Salomon Abraham Trier, Frankfurt am Main, 1844 pp. 4—14.
7 August

Due to the unavailability of complete files of the contemporary press and communal and other records, this bibliography of Adler's published works cannot claim to be entirely complete. Only items personally examined are included. Press reports of sermons, lectures, speeches, etc., are usually fairly full summaries; very brief notices are not included in the bibliography.

1845
(Letter)
pp. 1 Hannover, 1845
Reprinted in The Jewish Chronicle and Working Man's Friend, i, no. 11, p. 96
And in The Jewish Standard, 24.1.1890, pp. 3–4
And in The Voice of Jacob, iv, no. 96, p. 97
Letter in Hebrew and English addressed to "Estimable friends, synod of councillors, who love truth and delight in equity, men of worth, the guardians of the Congregation and leaders of the community, who are appointed by the United Congregations in London assembled" *accepting the office of Chief Rabbi. 11 Shevat 5605–19 January 1845*

Abschiedspredigt gehalten am Sabbath פ׳ שלח לך, תר״ה (den 28. Juni 1845) in der Synagoge zu Hannover... bei seinem Abgange von Hannover zum Antritte des Ober-Rabbinats in Grossbritannien
pp. 24. Hannover, 1845

Reply to address of welcome
London, 1845
In The Jewish Chronicle, i, no. 22, p. 197
9 July

שירי תהלה Form of service at the Great Synagogue, London, on Wednesday, the 9th July, 5605, at the installation of the Rev. Dr. Nathan Marcus Adler, Chief Rabbi of the United Congregations of Jews of Great Britain
pp. 11. London, J. Wertheimer, 1845
Reprinted in The Jewish Chronicle, i, no. 22, pp. 197–199 (*English summary only*)
Hebrew and English

Predigt beim Antritte seines Amtes als Ober-Rabbiner in Groszbritanien, gehalten in der Great Synagogue in London, am 4ten Tamus 5605 (8ten Juli 1845)
pp. 22. London, Longman, Brown, Green, & Longmans, 1845
With English translation by Barnard Van Oven
Reprinted in The Jewish Chronicle, i, no. 22, pp. 198–199
And in The Voice of Jacob, iv, no. 107, pp. 195–196
Based on Zechariah, iii, 7

Inaugural sermon in the Hambro' Synagogue
London, 1845
In The Jewish Chronicle, i, no. 23, pp. 208–209

And in The Voice of Jacob, iv, no. 108, pp. 211–212
Delivered in German, 19 July
Based on Micah, vi, 8

Sermon
London, 1845
In The Jewish Chronicle, i, no. 24, pp. 216–217
And in The Voice of Jacob, iv, no. 109, pp. 219–220
Delivered at the Great Synagogue, 2 August
Based on Jeremiah, ii, 13

(Letter)
London, 1845
In The Voice of Jacob, iv, no. 109, p. 221
Addressed to the Wardens of the Chatham Congregation, 4 August

Circular to the Presidents and Wardens of the Jewish Congregations in the British Empire
London, 1845
In The Jewish Chronicle, i, no. 25, p. 221
And in The Voice of Jacob, iv, no. 109, pp. 217–218
"...acquainting you with my primary intentions and wishes...", *13 August*

Visit to the New Synagogue, Great St. Helen's
London, 1845
In The Jewish Chronicle, i, no. 25, pp. 224–226
And in The Voice of Jacob, iv, no. 110, pp. 226–227
Sermon delivered in German on שבת נחמו*, 16 August*
Based on Isaiah, xl, 1

Visit to the Jews' Free School
London, 1845
In The Jewish Chronicle, i, no. 25, p. 226
Address to the children, 17 August

Western Synagogue
London, 1845
In The Jewish Chronicle, i, no. 26, pp. 232–233
And in The Voice of Jacob, iv, no. 110, pp. 227–228
Sermon delivered in German, 23 August
Based on Deuteronomy, x, 12

Sermon at the Great Synagogue

London, 1845
In The Jewish Chronicle, i, no. 26, pp. 235–237
And in The Voice of Jacob, iv, no. 111, pp. 235–236
Delivered on שבת פ׳ ראה
Based on Deuteronomy, xi, 26

Jews' Orphan Asylum
London, 1845
In The Jewish Chronicle, i, no. 27, p. 244
Address on the occasion of the examination of the children, 7 September

(Letter)
London, 1845
In The Jewish Chronicle, i, no. 28, p. 253
Addressed to the President and Members of the Edinburgh Hebrew Congregation, 12 September

Fenchurch Street Synagogue
London, 1845
In The Voice of Jacob, iv, no. 112, pp. 244–245
Sermon delivered, 20 September
Based on Deuteronomy, xxvii, 5

Sermon
London, 1845
In The Voice of Jacob, v, no. 113, pp. 6–7
Delivered at the Great Synagogue on שבת שובה
Based on Zechariah, i, 3

The Day of Atonement
London, 1845
In The Jewish Chronicle, ii, no. 1, pp. 5–6
Sermon delivered at the Great Synagogue, 10 October

Sermon
London, 1845
In The Voice of Jacob, v, no. 115, pp. 19–20
Delivered at the Crosby Square Synagogue on the first day of Tabernacles
Based on Leviticus, xxiii, 40

The Chief Rabbi's first visit to the Maiden Lane Synagogue
London, 1845
In The Voice of Jacob, v, no. 116, pp. 26–27

Sermon delivered on שבת פ׳ לך־לך

Duty to parents
London, 1845
In The Voice of Jacob, v, no. 117, p. 35 *and* v, no. 118, p. 43
Sermon delivered at the Great Synagogue

1846

The appeal of the Congregation of the West London Synagogue of British Jews to their brother Israelites throughout the United Kingdom
London, 1846
In The Jewish Chronicle, ii, no. 10, pp. 84–85
Correspondence with the Junior Warden of the West London Synagogue of British Jews, December 1845 – January 1846

Sermon
London, 1846
In The Voice of Jacob, v, no. 120, pp. 59–60
Delivered at the Crosby Square Synagogue on Sabbath ויגש*, 3 January*

Sermon
London, 1846
In The Voice of Jacob, v, no. 121, pp. 69–70
Delivered at the Fenchurch Street Synagogue, 17 January
Based on Exodus, iii, 1–6

The Russo-Polish Jews
London, 1846
In The Voice of Jacob, v, no. 123, pp. 85–86
Prayer in Hebrew and English, and sermon delivered, 21 February

תפלה A prayer offered by the United Congregations of the British Empire for the success of the philanthropic mission to Russia of Sir Moses Montefiore, F.R.S.,... Adar, 5606
pp. 3. London, 1846
Reprinted in The Jewish Chronicle, ii, no. 11, p. 93
And in The Voice of Jacob, v, no. 123, p. 86
And in Der Treue Zions-Wächter, 2, no. 11 (Hamburg 17.3.1846), pp. 95–96
Hebrew and English

Sermon
London, 1846
In The Voice of Jacob, v, no. 125, pp. 102–103

Delivered at the Great Synagogue, 21 March

Sermon
London, 1846
In The Voice of Jacob, v, no. 126, pp. 111–112
Delivered at the Great Synagogue on שבת הגדול*, 4 April*
Based on Genesis, xv, 9–17

תודה וקול זמרה Form of thanksgiving to Almighty G-d, as recited in all the German Synagogues throughout the British Empire, on the first day of Pesach, 5606, for the signal victories obtained by the British troops in India, over the army of the Sikhs
pp. 5. London, J. Wertheimer & Co., 1846
Reprinted in The Jewish Chronicle, ii, no. 14, p. 125
And in The Voice of Jacob, v, no. 127, pp. 119–120
Hebrew and English

Sermon
London, 1846
In The Voice of Jacob, v, no. 128, pp. 126–127
Delivered at the Great Synagogue on שבת *before* ר"ח אייר

Jews' Free School examination
London, 1846
In The Jewish Chronicle, ii, no. 17, p. 147
Address to the children, 24 May

סדר תפלה Order of service to be performed on the day of the anniversary, at the Synagogue of the Jews' Hospital, Mile End, for the support of the aged and for the education and employment of youth, Monday, 25th May, 1846–5606...
pp. 7. London, J. Wertheimer, 1846
Hebrew and English

Jews' Hospital and anniversary
London, 1846
In The Jewish Chronicle, ii, no. 17, p. 148
Prayer in Hebrew and English, and discourse delivered, 25 May

שיר תודה Form of thanksgiving on the occasion of the accouchement of Her Majesty the Queen, and the happy birth of a Princess, recited in the Synagogues throughout Great Britain on Sabbath the 5th day of Sivan, A.M. 5606
pp. 7. London, J. Wertheimer & Co., 1846

Reprinted in The Jewish Chronicle, ii, no. 17, pp. 151–152
Hebrew and English

Lecture
London, 1846
In The Voice of Jacob, v, no. 132, pp. 158–159
Delivered at the Great Synagogue, 20 June

(Letter)
London, 1846
In The Jewish Chronicle, ii, no. 20, p. 175
And in The Voice of Jacob, v, no. 134, p. 179
Addressed to the President, Wardens and Members of the Hebrew Congregation, Port Philip, Australasia, thanking for good-will message

(Reply)
London, 1846
In The Jewish Chronicle, ii, no. 22, p. 195
Addressed to the President, Treasurer and Committee of the Congregation "Beth Yisrael" in Sydney, thanking for congratulatory address, 28 July

Sermon
London, 1846
In The Jewish Chronicle, ii, no. 26, p. 222
Delivered at the Great Synagogue on New Year
Based on Psalms, lxxxix, 15

Opening of the Western Jewish Girls' Free School
London, 1846
In The Jewish Chronicle, iii, no. 2, pp. 13–14
15 October

תפלה Prayer to Almighty G-d, offered up in all the German Synagogues of the British Empire, on Sabbath, October 17th, 5607, and the two following Sabbaths, to avert the calamitous consequences of the famine which exists in parts of this country
pp. 2. London, J. Wertheimer & Co., 1846
Reprinted in The Jewish Chronicle, iii, no. 1, pp. 4–5
Hebrew and English

(Letter)
London, 1846
In The Jewish Chronicle, iii, no. 3, p. 27

Approving the conferment of the title חבר *upon Mr. Israel Levy of Manchester, 19 October*

1847

Laws and regulations for all the Synagogues ק"ק אשכנזים in the British Empire
pp. 23. London, John Wertheimer, 1847
Published anonymously

תפלה ביום עצרה Form of service to be used in all Synagogues throughout the United Kingdom, on Wednesday, 24th March, 5607 A.M., being the day appointed by command of Her Majesty to be observed as a general fast and day of humiliation
pp. 4. London, J. Wertheimer and Co.. 1847
Hebrew and English
Reprinted in The Jewish Chronicle, iii, no. 12, p. 100 *(English only)*

Sermon delivered in the Great Synagogue, Duke's Place, on the occasion of the Recent General Fast Day, Wednesday, the 24th March, A.M., 5607
pp. 15. London, Sherwood, Gilbert & Piper, 1847
"For the benefit of the Sufferers in Ireland and in the Highlands of Scotland"

Sermon
London, 1847
In The Jewish Chronicle, iii, no. 26, p. 232
Delivered in Hannover, July 1847
Based on Isaiah, xl, 7

Speech
London, 1847
In The Jewish Chronicle, iv, no. 2, pp. 268–270
Delivered in Birmingham, 10 October

(Letter)
London, 1847
In The Jewish Chronicle, iv, no. 3, p. 283
Copy of letter addressed to the President of the Hebrew Congregation of Birmingham, 12 October

תודה וקול זמרה Form of thanksgiving for the late abundant harvest, to be used in all the Synagogues of the British Empire in charge of the Chief Rabbi. October 17th, 5608
pp. 7. London, J. Wertheimer & Co., 1848
Reprinted in The Jewish Chronicle, iv, no. 2, p. 274

Hebrew and English

(Letter)
London, 1848
In The Jewish Chronicle, iv, no. 15, p. 394
Expressing thanks for the testimonial received from the Birmingham Cohanim, 31 December

1848
Relief granted to foreigners by the Metropolitan Synagogues
London, 1848
In The Jewish Chronicle, iv, 16, p. 400
Joint signatory to letter, 6 January

The Jewish faith. A sermon delivered in the Great Synagogue, Duke's Place. Sabbath, 24 Shevat, 5608 (29 January, 1848)
pp. 19. London, Effingham Wilson, 1848
Based on Ecclesiastes, xii, 13–14

תפלה על השלום Prayer offered up in all the Synagogues of the United Congregations, on Sabbath, the 29th of April, and the three following Sabbaths, for the continuance of peace and tranquillity
pp. 2. London, J. Wertheimer and Co., 1848 (*Hebrew and English*)
Reprinted in The Jewish Chronicle, iv, no. 30, p. 516 *(English only)*
And in ספר האסיף, edited by Z. Filipowski, Leipzig, K. F. Köhler, 1849, p. 134, *under the title* תפלה... אשר התפלל לעת השערוריות הנוראות בארצות אייראפא וגלילותיה בשנת ה׳ אלפים תר״ח לפ״ג *(Hebrew only)*

The Oral Law, etc.
London, 1848
In The Jewish Chronicle, iv, no. 30, p. 517
Sermon delivered at the Hambro' Synagogue on the second day of Passover Based on Leviticus, xxiii, 2

Address
London, 1848
In The Jewish Chronicle, iv, no. 32, p. 533
Delivered at the Jews' Free School, 7 May

Sermon
London, 1848
In The Jewish Chronicle, iv, no. 40, p. 593

Delivered, 1 July
Based on Numbers, xvi, 3–6

How can the blessings of the House of G-d be attained? A sermon delivered on the occasion of the consecration of the Synagogue at Canterbury, on the 21st day of Elul, 5608 – 19th September, 1848
pp. 16. London, Sherwood, Gilbert, and Piper, 1848

Western Jewish Girls' Free School: examination...
London, 1848
In The Jewish Chronicle, v, no. 4, p. 29
Speech delivered, 23 October

Jews' and General Literary and Scientific Institution, Sussex Hall
London, 1848
In The Jewish Chronicle, v, no. 5, pp. 40–41
Speech delivered at the opening of the Lecture Session, 26 October

1849

The Bonds of Brotherhood. A sermon delivered in the Synagogue שער השמים of the Spanish and Portuguese Congregation in London, on שבת בשלח the 11th Schwat, 5609
pp. 16. London, J. Wertheimer, 1849
Reprinted in The Jewish Chronicle, v, no. 18, p. 143

Jews' and General Literary and Scientific Institution
London, 1849
In The Jewish Chronicle, v, no. 45, p. 359
Copy of letter addressed to the Honorary Secretary thanking for being designated an Honorary Member, 6 August

Consecration of the new Synagogue at Norwich
London, 1849
In The Jewish Chronicle, v, no. 49, p. 392
Sermon delivered, 6 September

תפלה Form of prayer to used in all the Synagogues of the United Congregations in the British Empire on account of the great mortality caused by the cholera
pp. 2. London, J. Wertheimer and Co., 1849
Reprinted in The Jewish Chronicle, v, no. 50, p. 400
Hebrew and English
To be recited on צום גדליה

Sermon
London, 1848
In The Jewish Chronicle, vi, no. 7, p. 50
Delivered at the Great Synagogue on the Day of Thanksgiving for the cessation of the cholera, 15 November
Based on Psalms, cxvi, 12–19

1850

Visit to Portsmouth
London, 1850
In The Jewish Chronicle, vi, no. 14, pp. 105–106
Reply to address of welcome, speech at dinner, and sermon, 3–8 January

Visit to Portsmouth
London, 1850
In The Jewish Chronicle, vi, no. 15, p. 115
Correspondence regarding the recent visit

Marriage with deceased wife's sister
London, 1850
In The Jewish Chronicle, vi, no. 33, p. 258
Copy of letter addressed to the Secretary of the Marriage Commission, 13 March

Western Jewish Girls' Free School
London, 1850
In The Jewish Chronicle, vi, no. 28, p. 219
Address delivered at the third public examination, 15 April

Oration
London, 1850
In The Jewish Chronicle, vi, no. 49, pp. 386–387
Delivered at the funeral of the Late Baroness de Rothschild, 9 September

Sermon
London, 1850
In The Jewish Chronicle, vi, no. 50, pp. 393–395
Delivered at the Great Synagogue on שבת שובה
Based on Micah, vii, 18

Opening of the lecture session of the Jews' and General Literary and Scientific Institution
London, 1850

In The Jewish Chronicle, vii, no. 4, pp. 29—30
Speech delivered, 24 October

Laying of the corner-stone of the Manchester Hebrew School
London, 1850
In The Jewish Chronicle, vii, no. 10, p. 77
Prayer composed for the occasion, 9 December

1851

Jews' Free School
London, 1851
In The Jewish Chronicle, vii, no. 19, pp. 148—149
Speech delivered at the anniversary dinner, 11 February

Maiden Lane Synagogue
London, 1851
In The Jewish Chronicle, vii, no. 20, p. 154
Sermon delivered, 16 February

Western Synagogue, St. Alban's Place
London, 1851
In The Jewish Chronicle, vii, no. 28, pp. 220—221
Sermon delivered, 13 April

Inauguration of the new Jews' School, Cheetham Hill, Manchester
London, 1851
In The Jewish Chronicle, viii, no. 16, p. 123
Speech delivered, 22 May

Western Jewish Girls' Free School
London, 1851
In The Jewish Chronicle, vii, no. 37, p. 290
Address delivered at the fourth public examination of the children, 15 June

מזמור שיר חנכת הבית Order of service at the consecration of the Synagogue at Ramsgate, on Friday, 8th Elul (5th Sept.), 5611, after its having undergone a complete repair by the founders, Sir Moses Montefiore, Bart. and the Lady Judith, his wife, with a prayer composed for the occasion by the Chief Rabbi...
pp. 13. London, J. Wertheimer, 1851
Hebrew and English

New Synagogue, Great St. Helen's
London, 1851

In The Jewish Chronicle, viii, no. 2, p. 9
Sermon delivered on the first day of Tabernacles, 11 October
Based on Zechariah, xiv, 6–9

Hambro' Synagogue, Leadenhall St.
London, 1851
In The Jewish Chronicle, viii, no. 3, p. 19
Sermon delivered on שמיני עצרת*, 18 October*

1852
Address
London, 1852
In The Jewish Chronicle, viii, no. 14, pp. 108–109
Delivered at a public meeting to discuss the founding of a college, 4 January

Great Synagogue
London, 1852
In The Jewish Chronicle, viii, no. 16, p. 123
Lecture delivered, 17 January
On "The life of Moses"

Western Synagogue, St. Alban's Place
London, 1852
In The Jewish Chronicle, viii, no. 31, pp. 244–245
Discourse delivered, 1 May
On "Holiness, the principal characteristic of our religion"

Great Synagogue, Duke's Place
London, 1852
In The Jewish Chronicle, viii, no. 34, p. 268
Sermon delivered on the first day of Pentecost
On "Immutability"

Western Jewish Girls' Free School
London, 1852
In The Jewish Chronicle, viii, no. 37, pp. 292–293
Speech delivered at the fifth annual examination of the pupils, 14 June

(Letter)
In The Jewish Chronicle, ix, no. 45, pp. 357–358

And in Australian Jewish Historical Society Journal and Proceedings, i, part 9 (Sydney, 1943), pp. 300–301
Acknowledging the gift of a gold Kiddush Cup from the Jewish inhabitants of Victoria, July 1852

New Synagogue, Great St. Helen's
London, 1852
In The Jewish Chronicle, viii, no. 46, p. 363
Sermon delivered, 14 August
On "Immortality"

Sermon, preached... on Thursday, 19th Elul, 5612, on the occasion of the consecration of the Great Synagogue
London, 1852
In The Jewish Chronicle, viii, no. 49, pp. 385–386

Great Synagogue, Duke's Place
London, 1852
In The Jewish Chronicle, viii, no. 51, p. 402
Lecture delivered on שבת שובה*, 18 September*

Great Synagogue, Duke's Place
London, 1852
In The Jewish Chronicle, ix, no. 6, p. 47
Sermon delivered, 6 November
On "The lives of the Patriarchs"

Great Synagogue, Duke's Place
London, 1852
In The Jewish Chronicle, ix, no. 11, p. 83
Sermon delivered, 11 December
On "The Maccabees"

1853
הסכמה
In ספר בית אברהם, by Abraham Sussman, Königsberg, 1853, p. 1

Great Synagogue, Duke's Place
London, 1853
In The Jewish Chronicle, ix, no. 19, p. 147
Sermon delivered, 5 February
Based on Exodus, xxi, 15–17

Jews' Free Schools
London, 1853
In The Jewish Chronicle, ix, no. 21, p. 163
Speech delivered at the anniversary dinner in aid of the funds of the schools, 17 February

שיר תודה Form of prayer and thanksgiving to Almighty G-d, for the safe delivery of Her Majesty the Queen, of a Prince. Recited in the Synagogues of the United Congregations of the British Empire, on Sabbath, the 16th of April, 5613
pp. 3. London, J. Wertheimer & Co., 1853
Reprinted in The Jewish Chronicle, ix, no. 28, p. 219
Hebrew and English

Great Synagogue, Duke's Place
London, 1853
In The Jewish Chronicle, ix, no. 37, p. 291
Sermon delivered on the first day of Pentecost
On "Revelation on Mount Sinai"

Proposed mission to China
London, 1853
In The Jewish Chronicle, ix, no. 47, p. 370
Letter, 1 April

The return unto G-d
London, 1853
In The Jewish Chronicle, x, no. 2, pp. 9—10
Sermon delivered at the Great Synagogue on שבת שובה, *8 October*

New Synagogue, Great St. Helen's
London, 1853
In The Jewish Chronicle, x, no. 3, p. 17
Sermon delivered on the second day of Tabernacles
Based on Leviticus, xxiii, 2

1854

Die gegenwärtige Lage der Juden in Palästina... Rundschreiben an die Juden Grossbritannien
Leipzig, 1854
In Monatsschrift für Geschichte und Wissenschaft des Judenthums, iii, pp. 287—289

Solomon's judgment: a picture of Israel. A sermon delivered at the Great Synagogue, on שבת חנוכה (Sabbath of Dedication), 31st December, 5614
pp. 15. London, Wertheimer, 1854
Reprinted in The Jewish Chronicle, x, no. 14, p. 119

Pastoral letter to the Wardens, members and seat-holders of the United Congregations of Great Britain
London, 1854
In The Jewish Chronicle, x, no. 33, p. 284
Reprinted in History of Zionism 1600–1918, by Nahum Sokolow, ii, pp. 242–243, London, Longmans, Green, 1919
18 May

(Letter)
London, Office of the Chief Rabbi, 1854
Addressed to Sir Moses Montefiore in support of "our brethren in Palestine" *and enclosing the Pastoral Letter on the subject*
Reprinted in History of Zionism 1600–1918, by Nahum Sokolow, ii, p. 242, London, Longmans, Green, 1919
18 May

Re-opening of the Exeter Synagogue
London, 1854
In The Jewish Chronicle, x, no. 36, p. 306
English translation of the Hebrew prayer especially composed for the occasion, 1 June

Western Synagogue, St. Alban's Place
London, 1854
In The Jewish Chronicle, x, no. 39, p. 332
Sermon delivered, 24 June
Based on Leviticus, xv, 32–37

Maiden Lane Synagogue
London, 1854
In The Jewish Chronicle, x, no. 45, p. 582
Sermon delivered on שבת נחמו*, 5 August*
Based on Deuteronomy, iv, 40

Visit to the Exeter congregation
London, 1854
In The Jewish Chronicle, xi, no. 3, p. 20
Address delivered, 20 August

Based on Deuteronomy, xi, 26 and xxx, 19

Transition from fasting to feasting: digest of lecture
London, 1854
In The Jewish Chronicle, xi, no. 8, pp. 57–58
Delivered at the Great Synagogue on שבת שובה
Based on Jonah, iii, 8

Preparations for relieving the poor in the approaching winter
London, 1854
In The Jewish Chronicle, xi, no. 12, p. 89
Copy of letter addressed to the President and Treasurer of the Soup Kitchen Society, 26 October

Appeal on behalf of the poor
London, 1854
In The Jewish Chronicle, xi, no. 15, p. 116
Sermon delivered at the Great Synagogue, 18 November
Based on Genesis, xxiv, 17–22

Great Synagogue
London, 1854
In The Jewish Chronicle, and The Hebrew Observer, xii, no. 1, p. 5
Sermon delivered on שבת חנוכה*, 16 December*

1855

Anniversary dinner of the Portsmouth Hebrew Benevolent Institution
London, 1855
In Portsmouth Times and Naval Gazette, 29.1.1855
Reprinted in The Jewish Chronicle, and The Hebrew Observer, xii, no. 8, p. 59, and xii, no. 9, p. 66
Address delivered, 7 February

Consecration of the Branch Synagogue, Portland-Street
London, 1855
In The Jewish Chronicle, and The Hebrew Observer, xii, no. 16, p. 126
Discourse delivered, 29 March

Western Synagogue, St. Alban's Place
London, 1855
In The Jewish Chronicle, and The Hebrew Observer, xii, no. 25, p. 194
Sermon delivered on the second day of Pentecost
On "The Ten Commandments," *based on Proverbs, iii, 16–18*

Board of Deputies. – Report on the Dissenters' Marriage Bill
London, 1855
In The Jewish Chronicle, and The Hebrew Observer, xii, no. 29, p. 226
Letter

Re-opening of the New Synagogue
London, 1855
In The Jewish Chronicle, and The Hebrew Observer, xii, no. 39, p. 310
Sermon delivered, 6 September
Based on Haggai, ii, 9

Opening of the Jews' College
London, 1855
In The Jewish Chronicle, and The Hebrew Observer, xii, no. 49, p. 390
Reprinted in Jews' College Jubilee Volume, London, 1906, pp. xiv–xvi
Address delivered, 11 November

1856

(מ"מ ותקונים)
In ספר קובץ מעשי ידי גאונים קדמונים: פירוש רבינו רב האי גאון על סדר טהרות
edited by Judah ben Alexander Rosenberg, Berlin, 1856

Anniversary dinner of the Jews' Hospital
London, 1856
In The Jewish Chronicle, and The Hebrew Observer, xiii, no. 62, p. 492
Response made, 14 February

Jews' Hospital in New York
London, 1856
In The Jewish Chronicle, and The Hebrew Observer, xiii, no. 74, p. 586
Copy of letter addressed to the Committee of the Board of Directors on the subject of post-mortem examinations, 26 February

Metropolitan Free Hospital
London, 1856
In The Jewish Chronicle, and The Hebrew Observer, xiii, no. 69, p. 549
Letter in support of the hospital, 3 March

New Synagogue
London, 1856
In The Jewish Chronicle, and The Hebrew Observer, xiii, no. 71, p. 565

Sermon delivered on the second day of Passover

Sermon at the Great Synagogue
London, 1856
In The Jewish Chronicle, and The Hebrew Observer, xiii, no. 72, p. 575
Delivered on the last day of Passover
On "Antipathy to foreigners," *based on Leviticus, xix, 3, 34*

Manchester Reform Movement
London, 1856
In The Jewish Chronicle, and The Hebrew Observer, xiii, no. 74, p. 587
Letter addressed to the Wardens of the Hebrew Congregation in Manchester, 29 April

Thanksgiving Day
London, 1856
In The Jewish Chronicle, and The Hebrew Observer, xiii, no. 73, p. 581
Sermon delivered at the Great Synagogue, 4 May
Based on Psalms, lxxxv, 9–14

Notice
London, 1856
In The Jewish Chronicle, and The Hebrew Observer, xiii, no. 80, p. 640
Concerning the exercise of rabbinical functions by Dr. Schiller-Szinnessy in Manchester

Western Synagogue, St. Alban's Place
London, 1856
In Jewish Chronicle, and The Hebrew Observer, xiii, no. 81, p. 645
Discourse delivered, 28 June
Based on Numbers, xvi, 5

Consecration of the new Hebrew Synagogue, Birmingham
London, 1856
In The Jewish Chronicle, and The Hebrew Observer, xiii, no. 94, pp. 750–751
(*from the* "Birmingham Journal")
Sermon delivered, 24 September

1857

Laying of the foundation stone of a new synagogue
London, 1857
In The Jewish Chronicle, and The Hebrew Observer, xiv, no. 125, p. 994
Address delivered at the Manchester Hebrew Congregation, 20 April

Divorce Bill
London, 1857
In The Jewish Chronicle, and The Hebrew Observer, xiv, no. 132, p. 1053 *and* xiv, no. 133, p. 1063
Copies of letters addressed to the Secretary of the Board of Deputies, 16 June and 27 June

ערוגות הקדש, שירים וזמרים Order of service to be performed at the consecration of the Western Synagogue, St. Alban's Place, on Sunday, the 13th September, 5617, after its having undergone a complete repair
pp. 19. London, J. Wertheimer and Co., 1857
Hebrew and English

Address
London, 1857
In The Jewish Chronicle, and The Hebrew Observer, xiv, no. 153, pp. 1218–1219 (*from the* "Brighton Guardian," 11.11.1857)
Delivered in Brighton

1858

Consecration of a new synagogue at Manchester
London, 1858
In The Jewish Chronicle, and The Hebrew Observer, xv, no. 170, p. 107
Sermon delivered, 18 March
Based on Exodus, xxxix, 43

Consecration of the new cemetery, West Ham
London, 1858
In The Jewish Chronicle, and The Hebrew Observer, xv, no. 181, p. 197
Discourse and prayer delivered, 30 May

Inauguration of the new Westminster Jews' Free School, Greek Street, Soho... on Sunday, June 20th, 5618–1858
pp. 5. London, J. Wertheimer and Co., 1858
Hebrew and English

Western Synagogue, St. Alban's Place
London, 1858
In The Jewish Chronicle, and The Hebrew Observer, xv, no. 185, p. 229
Discourse delivered, 26 June
On "Israel's Vocation," *based on Leviticus, xxiii, 9*

Inauguration of the new building of the Infant School, Commercial Street, Spitalfields
London, 1858
In The Jewish Chronicle, and The Hebrew Observer, xv, no. 189, p. 261
Address delivered, 23 July
Based on Psalms, cxxvii

Discourse
London, 1858
In The Jewish Chronicle, and The Hebrew Observer, xv, no. 192, p. 285
Delivered "in commemoration of the admission of the Jews into Parliament" *on* שבת פרשת ראה *Based on Isaiah, lv*

ערוגות הקדש, שירים וזמרים Order of service to be performed at the consecration of the Maiden Lane Synagogue, Maiden Lane, Covent Garden, on Sunday, the 29th August, 5618, upon the completion of extensive alterations and repairs...
pp. 19. London, J. Wertheimer and Co., 1858
Hebrew and English
The sermon
In The Jewish Chronicle, and The Hebrew Observer, xv, no. 194, p. 301
Based on Isaiah, xxxiii, 26

Baron Rothschild's youngest son attaining his religious majority
London, 1858
In The Jewish Chronicle, and The Hebrew Observer, xv, no. 202, pp. 5–6
Sermon delivered on the occasion at the Great Synagogue, 23 October

1859
The "Royal Charter" disaster
New York, 1868
In The Works of Charles Dickens, vol. xvi, The Uncommercial Traveller, ii, p. 12
Reprinted in Anglo-Jewish Letters (1158–1917), edited by Cecil Roth, London, 1938, pp. 301–302
Copy of letter addressed to the Rev. Stephen Roose Hughes, Rector of Llanallgo, published in "The Shipwreck"

Sermon
London, 1859
In The Jewish Chronicle, and The Hebrew Observer, xvi, no. 212, p. 6
Delivered at the Great Synagogue on שבת וארא

Sermon
London, 1859
In The Jewish Chronicle, and The Hebrew Observer, xvi, no. 217, p. 6
Delivered at the Great Synagogue, 5 February

תפלה Prayer offered up in the London Synagogues of the United Congregations, for the success of Sir Moses Montefiore's Mission to Rome on behalf of Edgar Mortara of Bologna
pp. 3. London, J. Wertheimer and Co., 1859
Hebrew and English
Reprinted in The Jewish Chronicle, and The Hebrew Observer, xvi, no. 218, p. 5 (*English only*)

Annual meeting of the Jews' College
London, 1859
In The Jewish Chronicle, and The Hebrew Observer, xvi, no. 220, p. 5
Address delivered, 27 February

Sermon
London, 1859
In The Jewish Chronicle, and The Hebrew Observer, xvi, no. 222, p. 3
Delivered at the Great Synagogue on שבת שקלים

Jews' Free School anniversary dinner
London, 1859
In The Jewish Chronicle, and The Hebrew Observer, xvi, no. 235, p. 5
Reply to toast, 13 June

Western Synagogue, St. Alban's Place
London, 1859
In The Jewish Chronicle, and The Hebrew Observer, xvi, no. 237, p. 5
Sermon delivered, 25 June
Based on Numbers, xvi, 5

Sermon
London, 1859
In The Jewish Chronicle, and The Hebrew Observer, xvi, no. 238, p. 5
Delivered at the Great Synagogue, 2 July
Based on Numbers, xx, 10–13

Maiden Lane Synagogue
London, 1859

In The Jewish Chronicle, and The Hebrew Observer, xvi, no. 244, p. 5
Sermon delivered on שבת נחמו

To the Jewish public
p. 1. London, Office of the Ecclesiastical Administration, 1859
"...it is my duty earnestly to beseech the Jewish Public to abstain from eating... unporged hind-quarters..."

On the charities for dispensing food to the poor
London, 1859
In The Hebrew Review and Magazine for Jewish Literature, i, no. 11, pp. 175–176
And in The Jewish Chronicle, and The Hebrew Observer, xvi, no. 263, p. 7
Sermon delivered at the Great Synagogue on שבת חנוכה
Based on Genesis, xli, 16

תשובה
In שו"ת יד הלוי יו"ד, by Isaac Dov HaLevi Bamberger, סימן ל"ח, Jerusalem, 1965, pp. 107–108
On שחיטה

1860
Sermon delivered... at the Great Synagogue on **שבת שקלים**
London, 1860
In The Jewish Chronicle, and The Hebrew Observer, xvi, no. 272, pp. 7–8

The late S. L. De Symons
London, 1860
In The Jewish Chronicle, and The Hebrew Observer, xvi, no. 282, pp. 5–6
Funeral oration delivered, 7 May

Western Synagogue
London, 1860
In The Jewish Chronicle, and The Hebrew Observer, xvi, no. 283, p. 5
Sermon delivered, 12 May

Sermon
London, 1860
In The Hebrew Review and Magazine for Jewish Literature, i, no. 33, pp. 513–514
Delivered on the first day of Pentecost
Based on Joshua, i, 8

Maiden Lane Synagogue
London, 1860
In The Hebrew Review and Magazine for Jewish Literature, i, no. 36, pp. 563–566
And in The Jewish Chronicle, and The Hebrew Observer, xvi, no. 288, p. 6
Sermon preached on the occasion of the annual visit, 16 June

Sermon
London, 1860
In The Jewish Chronicle, and The Hebrew Observer, xvi, no. 296, p. 6
Delivered in support of the Syrian Relief Fund, 11 August

(Letter)
pp. 4. London, 1860
Reprinted in The Hebrew Review and Magazine for Jewish Literature, i, no. 48, pp. 767–777
Addressed to "The Jewish Community" *and referring to the plight of the Jews in Syria, 22 August*

Sermon
London, 1860
In The Jewish Chronicle, and The Hebrew Observer, xvi, no. 305, p. 5
Delivered at the Hambro' Synagogue on שמיני עצרת

1861

הסכמה
pp. 8, 118, 111, 7. Fürth, 1861–1862
In ספר שערי שמחה, by Isaac ben Judah ibn Ghayyat, edited by Isaac Dov Halevi Bamberger

Sermon
London, 1861
In The Jewish Chronicle, and The Hebrew Observer, xvi, no. 329, p. 6
Delivered at the Great Synagogue on the first day of Passover

Western Synagogue, St. Alban's Place
London, 1861
In The Jewish Chronicle, and The Hebrew Observer, xvi, no. 338, p. 6
Discourse delivered, 1 June

The Touro monument
London, 1861
In The Jewish Chronicle, and The Hebrew Observer, xvi, no. 336, p. 7
Copy of letter addressed to the Acting President of the Touro Monument, 1 August

מקיץ נרדמים
Lyck, 1861
In המגיד, v, no. 36, pp. 225–226
Joint signatory to letter supporting the foundation of a publication society, September

תפלה ותחנונים Form of service to be used in all Synagogues of the United Congregations of the British Empire, on Monday, the 23rd December, 5622, the day of burial of His Royal Highness the Prince Consort
pp. 11. London, J. Wertheimer and Co., 1861
Hebrew and English
The sermon
In The Jewish Chronicle, and The Hebrew Observer, no. 367, pp. 5–6

1862
תשובה
In שו"ת יד הלוי יו"ד, by Isaac Dov HaLevi Bamberger, סימן י"א, Jerusalem, 1965, pp. 89–90
On שחיטה

תפלה ל ל A prayer to Almighty G-d, offered up in the Synagogue at Ramsgate, on Sabbath, the 28th June, 5622–1862, after its having undergone repairs, the day being the fiftieth anniversary of the wedding of its founders, Sir Moses Montefiore, Bart., and Lady Judith Montefiore. Composed for the occasion
pp. 7. London, J. Wertheimer, 1862
Hebrew and English
Reprinted in The Jewish Chronicle, and The Hebrew Observer, no. 394, p. 5 (*English only*)

Bayswater Synagogue. Laying of the corner-stone
London, 1862
In The Jewish Chronicle, and The Hebrew Observer, no. 396, p. 5
Discourse delivered, 10 July

Western Synagogue, St. Alban's Place
London, 1862
In The Jewish Chronicle, and The Hebrew Observer, no. 396, p. 6
Discourse delivered, 12 July
On "Religious Zeal"

A pastoral
London, 1862
In The Jewish Chronicle, and The Hebrew Observer, no. 408, p. 5
Despatched "To the congregations scattered in the colonies", *25 July*

Sermon
London, 1862
In The Jewish Chronicle, and The Hebrew Observer, no. 402, p. 5
Delivered at the Great Synagogue, 23 August
On "The sanctity of an oath"

Funeral discourse delivered in Ramsgate, on the Fast of Gedaliah, 4th Tishri, 5623, at the burial of Lady Montefiore
pp. 4. London, J. Wertheimer, 1862
Reprinted in The Jewish Chronicle, and The Hebrew Observer, no. 407, pp. 5–6

Distress in the cotton manufacturing districts. – The forthcoming collection
London, 1862
In The Jewish Chronicle, and The Hebrew Observer, no. 415, p. 5
Pastoral concerning the collection to be made on 16 December

1863
(Letter)
London, 1863
In The Jewish Chronicle, and The Hebrew Observer, no. 423, p. 2
Copy of letter addressed to the President and Members of the London Committee of Deputies of British Jews, 14 January

Western Synagogue
London, 1863
In The Jewish Chronicle, and The Hebrew Observer, no. 444, p. 6
Sermon delivered, 13 June

Consecration of the Bayswater Synagogue
London, 1863
In The Jewish Chronicle, and The Hebrew Observer, no. 451, p. 5
Dedication sermon delivered, 30 July
Based on Psalms, xxvii

Maiden-Lane Synagogue. — A sermon
London, 1863
In The Jewish Chronicle, and The Hebrew Observer, no. 451, p. 6
Delivered, 1 August
Based on Deuteronomy, v, 7, 10

Funeral address
London, 1863
In The Jewish Chronicle, and The Hebrew Observer, no. 466, p. 6
Delivered at the funeral of the Rev. Barnett Abrahams, 16 November

1864

שיר תודה וקול זמרה Form of prayer and thanksgiving to Almighty G-d, for the Princess of Wales' safe delivery of a Prince, to be used in all the Synagogues of the United Congregations of the British Empire, on Sabbath, the 16th January, 5624
pp. 7. London, J. Wertheimer, 1864
Reprinted in The Jewish Chronicle, and The Hebrew Observer, no. 474, p. 5
Hebrew and English

Royal Society for the Prevention of Cruelty to Animals
London, 1864
In The Jewish Chronicle, and The Hebrew Observer, no. 479, p. 6
Sermon delivered at the Great Synagogue, 6 February

Spanish and Portuguese Synagogue special service
London, 1864
In The Jewish Chronicle, and The Hebrew Observer, no. 487, pp. 5–6
Sermon to mark the return of Sir Moses Montefiore from Morocco, 11 April

תודה ותפלה Form of prayer & thanksgiving for the success which attended the mission of Sir Moses Montefiore, Baronet, to Morocco, to be used in all the Synagogues of the United Congregations of the British Empire, on Sabbath, April 16, 5624
pp. 9. London, J. Wertheimer, 1864
Hebrew and English

Great Synagogue. – A special service
London, 1864
In The Jewish Chronicle, and The Hebrew Observer, no. 487, p. 26
Special prayer to be read at the Special Service in "celebration of the success which attended the mission of Sir Moses Montefiore to Morocco..." *at the Great Synagogue, 16 April*

הסכמה
In ספר קול אריה, by Aryeh Leb Harif, Jerusalem, 1866, pp. 80.

Sermon
London, 1864
In The Jewish Chronicle, and The Hebrew Observer, no. 499, p. 5
Delivered at the Western Synagogue, 2 July

Maiden Lane Synagogue. – A discourse
London, 1864
In The Jewish Chronicle, and The Hebrew Observer, no. 516, p. 5
Delivered on the occasion of the annual visit, 29 October

The late Barnett Abrahams. – Inauguration of the memorial tablet
London, 1864
In The Jewish Chronicle, and The Hebrew Observer, no. 522, p. 6
Discourse delivered, 3 December

(מכתב)
In הוספה למגיד, ix, no. 12, Lyck 1865
Addressed to Eliezer Lipman (L.) Silbermann, 4 Kislev 5625

1865

The Morning & the Evening Sacrifice: how to be represented in these days with special reference to the claims of deaf mutes in the Jewish community. A sermon delivered in the Great Synagogue, Duke's Place, on ש"ק פ' וארא ר"ח שבט תרכ"ה לפ"ק January 28th, 5625
pp. 16. London, Wertheimer, 1865

Jews' Orphan Asylum
London, 1865

In The Jewish Chronicle, and the Hebrew Observer, no. 534, p. 5
Speech delivered at the Triennial Festival, 8 March

The David Sassoon Memorial Fund
London, 1865
In The Jewish Chronicle, and The Hebrew Observer, no. 541, p. 5
Copy of letter addressed to Messrs. Albert and S. D. Sassoon, 19 April

Southampton. – Consecration of the Synagogue
London, 1865
In The Jewish Chronicle, and The Hebrew Observer, no. 546, p. 5
Words spoken on the occasion, 22 May

The Cattle Plague
London, 1865
In The Jewish Chronicle, and The Hebrew Observer, no. 566, p. 8
Form of prayer to be read at every Monday and Thursday morning service

Maiden Lane Synagogue
London, 1865
In The Jewish Chronicle, and The Hebrew Observer, no. 567, p. 2
Sermon delivered on the occasion of the annual visit, 21 October

1866

תפלה Prayer offered up in the Synagogues of the United Congregations, on the occasion of Sir Moses Montefiore's departure for the Holy Land. Adar, 5626
pp. 2. London, J. Wertheimer and Co., 1866
Hebrew and English
Reprinted in The Jewish Chronicle, and The Hebrew Observer, no. 584, p. 5 (*English only*)

Prayer for Sir Moses Montefiore
In The Jewish Chronicle, and The Hebrew Observer, no. 584, p. 5
Letter addressed to the Editor of The Jewish Chronicle, *enclosing* "copy of the Prayer which will be offered up in our Synagogues for Sir Moses Montefiore...", *16 February*

Reponse to Lord Chelmsford's circular
London, 1866

In Report of the Royal Commission on the Laws of Marriage, Command Paper 4059, pp. 45–46, London, 1868
And in The Jewish Chronicle, and The Hebrew Observer, no. 717, p. 3, London, 1868
And in The Jewish Record, i, no. 17, p. 6, London, 1868
Letter dated 30 April 1866

Jews' Free School. – Inauguration of the new buildings
London, 1866
In The Jewish Chronicle, and The Hebrew Observer, no. 596, p. 5
Address delivered, 13 May

Maiden Lane Synagogue
London, 1866
In The Jewish Chronicle, and The Hebrew Observer, no. 602, p. 6
Sermon delivered on the occasion of the annual visit, 23 June

Jews' Free School. – Award of the commemoration scholarship
London, 1866
In The Jewish Chronicle, and The Hebrew Observer, no. 607, p. 5
Address delivered, 26 July

מזמורים ותפלה Form of prayer to be used in all the Synagogues of the United Congregations of the British Empire for protection against cholera. Elul, 5626
pp. 4, London, J. Wertheimer, 1866
Hebrew and English
Reprinted in The Jewish Chronicle, and The Hebrew Observer, no. 610, p. 5
(English only)

תפלה לתודה A prayer and thanksgiving for relief from the plague amongst cattle, and for protection against the cholera, to be used in all the Synagogues of the United Congregations of the British Empire, on Sabbath, November 24th, 5627
pp. 4. London, John Wertheimer and Co., 1866
Hebrew and English
Reprinted in The Jewish Chronicle, and The Hebrew Observer, no. 623, p. 2
(English only)

1867
Proposed Society for Sabbath Keepers
London, 1867

In The Jewish Chronicle, and The Hebrew Observer, no. 638, p. 5
Sermon delivered at the Great Synagogue, 2 March
Based on Exodus, xxxv, 2-3

Consecration of the new Borough Synagogue
London, 1867
In The Jewish Chronicle, and The Hebrew Observer, no. 643, p. 5
Sermon delivered on the occasion

תפלה Prayer offered up in the Synagogues of the United Congregations of the British Empire, on Sabbath, 27th of July, 5627. For the success of Sir Moses Montefiore's mission to Jassy
pp. 5. London, Wertheimer, Lea and Co., 1867
Hebrew and English
Reprinted in The Jewish Chronicle, and The Hebrew Observer, no. 658, p. 6
(English only)

Maiden Lane Synagogue. – A discourse
London, 1867
In The Jewish Chronicle, and The Hebrew Observer, no. 673, p. 6
Delivered, 2 November
Based on Genesis, xi, 1

1868

Sermon
London, 1868
In The Jewish Chronicle, and The Hebrew Observer, no. 695, p. 6
Delivered at the consecration of the North London Synagogue, 29 March

Westminster Jews' Free School. – Anniversary dinner
London, 1868
In The Jewish Chronicle, and The Hebrew Observer, no. 701, p. 7
Response made, 20 May

The second days of the festivals. A sermon delivered at the New Synagogue, Great St. Helen's, on the second day of Passover, 5628
pp. 19. London, Trübner, 1868
(*Reviewed in* The Jewish Chronicle, and The Hebrew Observer, no. 704, p. 2)

[The second days of the festivals. A reply to a sermon delivered by the Rev. the Chief Rabbi. By two orthodox members of the Jewish community.
pp. 30. London, F. Pitman, 1868]

Western Synagogue, St. Alban's Place
London, 1868
In The Jewish Chronicle, and The Hebrew Observer, no. 704, p. 5
Sermon delivered, 6 June

Sermon
London, 1868
In The Jewish Record, i, no. 4, p. 7
Delivered at the Great Synagogue, 20 June

תפלה לתודה Form of prayer and thanksgiving for the preservation of the life of H.R.H. the Duke of Edinburgh, and for the success and safety of the Abyssinian Expedition, to be used in all the Synagogues of the United Congregations of the British Empire, on Sabbath, July 4th, 5628
pp. 2. London, Wertheimer, Lea and Co., 1868
Hebrew and English
Reprinted in The Jewish Chronicle, and The Hebrew Observer, no. 707, p. 6
(English only)

Sermon
London, 1868
In The Jewish Chronicle, and The Hebrew Observer, no. 714, p. 8
Delivered at Canterbury, 9 August
Based on Deuteronomy, xiv, 1–2

The Targum of Onkelos: a lecture delivered at the Jews' College on December the 9th...
London, 1868
In The Jewish Record, i, no. 29, p. 3
And in summarised form in The Jewish Chronicle, and The Hebrew Observer, no. 732, p. 2

1869

The Central Branch Synagogue
London, 1869
In The Jewish Chronicle, and The Hebrew Observer, no. 745, p. 5
Discourse delivered, 18 March
Based on I Samuel, vii, 12

Rabbi Akiba
London, 1869
In The Jewish Chronicle, new series, no. 7, p. 10
Sermon delivered at the German Synagogue on behalf of the Association for the Diffusion of Religious Knowledge

Sermon
London, 1869
In Supplement to the Jewish Record, lvi, p. 9
And summarised in The Jewish Chronicle, no. 13, p. 2, *as reported in the* Daily Post
Delivered at the Old Synagogue, Liverpool on Sabbath, 12 June
Based on Numbers, xvii–xxiii

Rabbinische Gutachten über die Statuten und Beschlüsse des ung.-isr. Kongresses
pp. 32. Pest, Schomre Hadath-Verein, 1869
In Rabbinische Gutachten über die Statuten und Beschlüsse des ung.-isr. Kongresses. Von den ehrwürdigen Herrn.... p. 5
25 June 5629/69

Sermon
London, 1869
In The Jewish Chronicle, no. 22, p. 10
Delivered at Birmingham, 21 August

Inauguration of the Lady Montefiore Jewish Convalescent Home
London, 1869
In The Jewish Chronicle, no. 28, p. 10
Address delivered at Norwood, 5 October

Maiden Lane Synagogue
London, 1869
In The Jewish Chronicle, no. 32, p. 6
Address delivered on the occasion of the annual visit, 30 October
Based on Genesis, xxv, 8–9

North London Synagogue
London, 1869
In The Jewish Chronicle, no. 37, p. 7
Sermon preached on שבת חנכה
On "Religious Safeguards," ***based on Zechariah, ii, 6–7***

1870

Famine in Jerusalem
London, 1870
In The Jewish Chronicle, no. 49, p. 3
Sermon delivered at the Great Synagogue, 26 February
Based on Exodus, xxxvi, 6

The Elementary Education Bill
London, 1870
In The Jewish Chronicle, no. 52, p. 8
And in The Jewish Record, no. 96, p. 9
Copy of letter addressed to the President (pro tem.) and Members of the London Committee of Deputies of the British Jews, 14 March

Consecration of the new Central Synagogue
London, 1870
In The Jewish Chronicle, no. 54, pp. 10–11
And in The Jewish Record, no. 97, p. 3
Sermon delivered, 7 April

Sabbath Hagadol
London, 1870
In The Jewish Chronicle, no. 55, p. 5
Sermon delivered at the Great Synagogue, 9 April
Based on Jeremiah, xxiii, 7–8

Passover
London, 1870
In The Jewish Chronicle, no. 56, p. 8
Sermon delivered at the Great Synagogue on the first day of Passover
Based on Song of Songs, ii, 11–12

Hambro' Synagogue
London, 1870
In The Jewish Chronicle, no. 57, p. 12
Sermon delivered on the seventh day of Passover
Based on Isaiah, xli, 14

The Central Synagogue
London, 1870
In The Jewish Chronicle, no. 61, p. 9
Sermon delivered, 21 May

Rabbi Jochanan ben Zaccai
London, 1870
In The Jewish Chronicle, no. 62, p. 15
And in The Jewish Record, no. 105, p. 3
Lecture delivered to the Jewish Association for the Diffusion of Religious Knowledge, 28 May

Pentecost
London, 1870
In The Jewish Chronicle, no. 63, p. 8
Sermon delivered at the Great Synagogue on the first day of Pentecost

Chatham Memorial Synagogue
London, 1870
In The Jewish Chronicle, no. 65, pp. 10–11
And in The Jewish Record, no. 108, p. 2
Consecration sermon delivered, 17 June

Distribution of prizes to the pupils of the Stepney Jewish schools
London, 1870
In The Jewish Chronicle, no. 67, p. 11
And in The Jewish Record, no. 110, pp. 5–6
Address delivered, 3 July

The War
London, 1870
In The Jewish Chronicle, no. 74, p. 8
Sermon delivered at the Great Synagogue, 20 August

Consecration of the Coventry Synagogue
London, 1870
In The Jewish Chronicle, no. 76, p. 10
And in The Jewish Record, no. 119, p. 5
Address delivered, 6 September

Western Synagogue
London, 1870
In The Jewish Chronicle, no. 78, p. 6
And in The Jewish Record, no. 121, p. 2
Sermon delivered at the service of re-consecration after repairs and alterations, 18 September

Sabbath תשובה
London, 1870
In The Jewish Chronicle, no. 80, p. 4
Sermon preached at the Great Synagogue, 10 October

Charity sermon
London, 1870
In The Jewish Chronicle, no. 87, p. 8
Delivered at the Great Synagogue on behalf of the Board of Guardians, 19 November
Based on Ezekiel, xviii, 21–22

1871
Rabbi Jehudah the Patriarch
London, 1871
In The Jewish Chronicle, no. 95, pp. 11–12, and no. 96, p. 12
And in The Jewish Record, no. 137, p. 3
Lecture delivered at Jews' College, 10 January

North London Synagogue
London, 1871
In The Jewish Chronicle, no. 96, p. 5
Sermon delivered on the occasion of the pastoral visit, 21 January
Based on Deuteronomy, vi,4

Election of First Reader to the Great Synagogue
London, 1871
In The Jewish Chronicle, no. 109, p. 10
And in The Jewish Record, no. 152, p. 2
Copy of letters to the Rev. H.D. Marks, 9 February and 19 March

The Swansea case
London, 1871
In The Jewish Chronicle, no. 102, p. 9
And in The Jewish Record, no. 145, p. 5
Copy of letter sent to the Western Mail "... in reference to the case of Mr. Moses of Swansea, who was prevented by the magistrates from prosecuting the case by reason of his refusal to violate the Sabbath," *3 March*

Great Synagogue
London, 1871

In The Jewish Chronicle, no. 106, p. 5
Sermon delivered, 1 April
On "The advent of a personal Messiah"

Pastoral visitation: Cheltenham
London, 1871
In The Jewish Chronicle, no. 120, p. 8
And in The Jewish Record, no. 163, pp. 4–5
Address delivered, 8 July
Based on Numbers, xxvii, 12

Pastoral tour: Dublin
London, 1871
In The Jewish Record, no. 164, p. 5
Sermon delivered at the Synagogue, Mary's Abbey, 15 July
Based on Numbers, xxxii, 6

Pastoral visitation: Swansea
London, 1871
In The Jewish Chronicle, no. 121, p. 9
Sermon delivered
Based on Numbers, xxv

Pastoral tour: Swansea
London, 1871
In The Jewish Record, no. 164, pp. 5–6
Address to the children of the Jewish school

Pastoral visitation: Glasgow
London, 1871
In The Jewish Chronicle, no. 122, p. 9
And in The Jewish Record, no. 165, p. 5
Sermon delivered, 22 July
Based on Nehemiah, ii

Great Synagogue
London, 1871
In The Jewish Chronicle, no. 126, p. 10
Sermon delivered, 19 August
Based on Deuteronomy, xxi, 1–9

(Letter)
London, 1871

In The Jewish Chronicle, no. 127, p. 2
Addressed to the President and Members of the Committee of the Manchester Hebrew Congregation, 24 August

Bristol
London, 1871
In The Jewish Chronicle, no. 129, p. 14
And in The Jewish Record, no. 172, p. 6
Sermon delivered at the dedication of the new Bristol Synagogue, 7 September Based on Isaiah, xxxiii

The Prince of Wales
London, 1871
In The Jewish Chronicle, no. 143, p. 14
English translation of the Prayer for the recovery of the Prince of Wales, used prior to the publication of the Special Prayer

תפלה Form of prayer for the recovery of His Royal Highness the Prince of Wales, and also on behalf of the Queen, the Princess of Wales and of all the Royal Family. To be read in all the Synagogues of the United Congregations of the British Empire
pp. 2. London, Wertheimer, Lea and Co., 1872
Hebrew and English
Reprinted in The Jewish Chronicle, no. 142, p. 9 *(English only)*
To be read 9 December 1871 etc.

1872

תפלת תודה A form of prayer and thanksgiving to Almighty G-d, for the recovery of His Royal Highness the Prince of Wales; to be used in all the Synagogues of the United Congregations of the British Empire, on Sabbath, 27th January, 5632
pp. 7. London, Wertheimer, Lea and Co., 1872
Hebrew and English
Reprinted in The Jewish Chronicle, no. 148, p. 12

Great Synagogue
London, 1872
In The Jewish Chronicle, no. 149, p. 11
Sermon delivered at the Special Thanksgiving Service on the recovery of the Prince of Wales, 27 January

Great Synagogue
London, 1872
In The Jewish Chronicle, no. 162, p. 65
Sermon delivered on שבת הגדול*, 20 April*

Burial Society
London, 1872
In The Jewish Chronicle, no 163, p. 77
Copy of letter addressed to the President and Council of the United Synagogue, 3 May

Science and religion: a sermon delivered... at the Central Synagogue on the Sabbath preceding Pentecost
London, 1872
In The Jewish Chronicle, no. 169, p. 167
Based on Exodus, xix, 24

Sermon
London, 1872
In The Jewish Chronicle, no. 171, p. 194
Delivered at the Western Synagogue, St. Alban's, 29 June
Based on Numbers, xiv, 31

Distribution of prizes at Stepney Jewish Schools
London, 1872
In The Jewish Chronicle, no. 171, pp. 200–201
Address delivered, 29 June

תפלה Prayer to be offered up in the London Synagogues of the United Congregations, on Sabbath, July 13th, 5632, for the safety of Sir Moses Montefiore's journey to Russia
pp. 2. London, Wertheimer, Lea and Co., 1872
Reprinted in The Jewish Chronicle, no. 173, p. 222
Hebrew and English

Consecration of the new Synagogue at Sheffield
London, 1872
In The Jewish Chronicle, no. 181, pp. 331–332
Sermon delivered, 10 September

Dedication of the Stepney Jewish Schools
London, 1872

In The Jewish Chronicle, no. 184, pp. 367–368
Address delivered, 29 September

Bayswater Synagogue
London, 1872
In The Jewish Chronicle, no. 191, p. 465
Sermon delivered, 16 November
Based on Genesis, xxi, 33

Maiden Lane Synagogue
London, 1872
In The Jewish Chronicle, no. 196, p. 544
Sermon delivered on the occasion of the annual visit, 20 December
Based on Genesis, xxxvii, 15–17

1873
תשובה
In **ס' תשובות מהרי"א: תשובות יהודה יעלה...** II (י"ד)
contained within **תשובה צ"ד**, Lemberg, 1873, p. 35b
On the kashrut of a new breed of chicken

Borough Jewish schools: distribution of prizes
London, 1873
In Supplement to The Jewish Chronicle, no. 217, pp. 121–122
And in The Jewish World, no. 14, p. 5
Address delivered, 11 May

Westminster Jews' Free School
London, 1873
In The Jewish Chronicle, no. 218, p. 145
And in The Jewish World, no. 16, p. 2
Response made at the anniversary festival, 22 May

Re-opening of the North London Synagogue
London, 1873
In The Jewish Chronicle, no. 233, p. 399
And in The Jewish World, no. 30, p. 5
Address delivered, 7 September

Consecration of a new Synagogue at Manchester
London, 1873

In Supplement to The Jewish Chronicle, no. 234, pp. 421–422
And in The Jewish World, no. 32, p. 2
Sermon delivered, 17 September

Maiden Lane Synagogue
London, 1873
In The Jewish Chronicle, no. 245, p. 592
And in The Jewish World, no. 43, p. 5
Sermon delivered on the occasion of the annual visit, 29 November

1874

ספר תורת ה׳... עם עשרה פירושים... (י) **נתינה לגר** באור על תרגום אונקלוס
5 vols. Vilna, 1874
Including his edited versions of ספר פתשגן, ״יאר״, מסרת התרגום
2nd ed. Vilna, 1876–1885
Another edition. Vilna, 1912
Photographic edition. Jerusalem, 1968, etc.

הקדמה כוללת לתרגום אונקלוס
Jerusalem, 1973
In אוצר מפרשי התורה V
Originally printed with his Pentateuch commentary נתינה לגר

Consecration of Aria College
London, 1874
In The Jewish Chronicle, no. 250, p. 681
And in The Jewish World, no. 48, pp. 5–6
Address delivered, 6 January

The famine in India
London, 1874
In The Jewish World, no. 66, p. 5
Copy of letter addressed to the Presidents of the Synagogues, supporting the Bengal Famine Relief Fund

Hospital Sunday
London, 1874
In The Jewish Chronicle, no. 273, p. 190
And in The Jewish World, no. 71, p. 5
Sermon delivered at the Great Synagogue, 13 June
Based on Job, xix, 21

Jews' Free School
London, 1874
In The Jewish Chronicle, no. 274, p. 207
And in The Jewish World, no. 72, p. 5
Address delivered at the distribution of prizes, 21 June

Consecration of a Synagogue at Middlesbrough
London, 1874
In The Jewish Chronicle, no. 274, pp. 201–202
And in The Jewish World, no. 72, p. 6
Consecration sermon delivered, 24 June

Consecration of the new Synagogue at Liverpool
London, 1874
In The Jewish Chronicle, no. 284, pp. 359–360
And in The Jewish World, no. 82, p. 2
Consecration sermon delivered at Princes Road Synagogue, 3 September
Based on Deuteronomy, xxxi

"Forbidden food"
London, 1874
In The Jewish Chronicle, no. 287, p. 421
Sermon delivered at the Great Synagogue, 19 September

Sermon
London, 1874
In The Jewish Chronicle, no. 295, p. 556
Delivered at Brighton, 14 November

Great Synagogue
London, 1874
In The Jewish Chronicle, no. 298, p. 598
And in The Jewish World, no. 96, p. 5
Sermon delivered, 5 December
Based on Genesis, xl, 7–8

1875
Sermon
London, 1875
In The Jewish Chronicle, no. 306, p. 725
Delivered at the Great Synagogue, 30 January
Based on Deuteronomy, iv, 9

Hospital Sunday
London, 1875
In The Jewish Chronicle, no. 325, p. 195
And in The Jewish World, no. 123, p. 3
Sermon delivered at the Great Synagogue, 12 June
Based on Leviticus, xix, 18

The Sabbath
London, 1875
In The Jewish Chronicle, no. 336, p. 365
And in The Jewish World, no. 134, p. 3
Sermon delivered at the Great Synagogue, 28 August
Based on Deuteronomy, xiii, 6, 8

Day of Atonement
London, 1875
In The Jewish Chronicle, no. 342, p. 466
And in The Jewish World, no. 140, p. 2
Sermon delivered at the Great Synagogue, 9 October
Based on Isaiah, lviii, 13–14

Jews' Deaf and Dumb Home
London, 1875
In The Jewish Chronicle, no. 346, p. 526
And in The Jewish World, no. 144, p. 5
Prayer offered up at the consecration of the new building in Notting Hill, 7 November

1876

The Michael Henry Memorial
London, 1876
In The Jewish Chronicle, no. 354, p. 654
Speech delivered at the unveiling of the memorial tablet at Stepney School, 2 January

The late Sir Anthony Rothschild, Bart.
London, 1876
In The Jewish Chronicle, no. 355, pp. 674–675
Funeral discourse delivered at the Willesden cemetery, 9 January

United Synagogue
London, 1876
In The Jewish Chronicle, no. 363, p. 797
Copy of letter addressed to the Vice-Presidents and Members of the Council of the United Synagogue concerning the appointment of a Dayan, 22 February

The East London Synagogue: laying the foundation stone
London, 1876
In The Jewish Chronicle, no. 369, p. 38
And in The Jewish World, no. 167, p. 3
Prayer composed for the occasion, 17 April

Hasty burials
London, 1876
In The Jewish Chronicle, no. 362, p. 783
Copy of letter addressed to the Secretary of the United Synagogue, 14 May

The Prince of Wales
London, 1876
In The Jewish Chronicle, no. 374, p. 117
And in The Jewish World, no. 172, p. 7
Prayer offered up at the Great Synagogue in thanksgiving for the safe return of the Prince of Wales from India, 20 May

The study of Hebrew literature
London, 1876
In The Jewish Chronicle, no. 390, p. 375
And in The Jewish World, no. 188, p. 2
Address delivered at the consecration of the new Beth Hamedrash, 7 September

The Borough Synagogue
London, 1876
In The Jewish Chronicle, no. 390, p. 375
And in The Jewish World, no. 188, p. 2
Sermon delivered at the ceremony of reconsecration, 10 September

Consecration of the St. John's Wood (Temporary) Synagogue
London, 1876
In The Jewish Chronicle, no. 391, p. 390
And in The Jewish World, no. 189, p. 2
Discourse delivered, 17 September

On Jewish morality
London, 1876
In The Jewish World, no. 191, p. 6
Sermon delivered at the Great Synagogue on שבת שובה
Based on Joshua, vii, 13

Western Synagogue
London, 1876
In The Jewish World, no. 201, p. 2
Sermon delivered on the eve of Chanucah, 10 December
Based on Proverbs, xx, 27

1877

Consecration of the East London Synagogue
London, 1877
In The Jewish Chronicle, no. 418, p. 7
And in The Jewish World, no. 216, p. 6
Dedicatory sermon delivered, 25 March
Based on Psalms, cxiii

Hambro Synagogue
London, 1877
In The Jewish Chronicle, no. 441, p. 13
And in The Jewish World, no. 239, p. 2
Sermon delivered on the occasion of the re-consecration, 2 September

Indian Famine Relief Fund
pp. 1. London, 1877
Reprinted in The Jewish World, no. 240, p. 6
Copy of letter addressed to ministers of Synagogues appealing to them to support the Fund, 5 September

Maiden Lane Synagogue
London, 1877
In The Jewish World, no. 252, p. 3
Sermon delivered, 2 December

1878

Great Synagogue
London, 1878

In The Jewish World, no. 271, p. 6
Sermon delivered on שבת הגדול*, 13 April*
Based on Leviticus, xiv, 48

Great Synagogue
London, 1878
In The Jewish World, no. 279, p. 3
Sermon delivered on the second day of Pentecost, 8 June
Based on Exodus, xix, 3

Hospital Sabbath
London, 1878
In The Jewish World, no. 282, p. 6
Sermon delivered at the Great Synagogue, 29 June
Based on Numbers, xiv, 18

Hand-in-hand asylum
London, 1878
In The Jewish Chronicle, no. 496, p. 7
And in The Jewish World, no. 294, p. 3
Address delivered at the consecration of the Synagogue in the new locale of the asylum, 22 September
Based on Isaiah, xlvi, 4

The death of Princess Alice
London, 1878
In The Jewish Chronicle, no. 509, p. 6
Sermon delivered at the Great Synagogue, 21 December
Based on Psalms, xxx, 7

1879
(Letter)
London, 1906
In Jews' College Jubilee Volume, p. liii
Asking the Council of the College to appoint a chairman of the council, 10 January 5639

The late Dr. Benjamin Artom
London, 1879
In The Jewish World, no. 809, p. 6

Copy of letter addressed to the Presidents of congregations asking for the Memorial Prayer to be read on Sabbath 11 January

(Letter)
pp. 1. London, Office of the Chief Rabbi, 1879
Addressed to the "President of the Hebrew Congregation" *concerning the constitution of a* בית דין *in the Australian colonies, 4 August*

(Letter)
London, 1879
In The Jewish Chronicle, no. 553, p. 10
And in The Jewish World, no. 351, p. 6
Copy of letter addressed to the Chairman and Members of the Executive Committee of the United Synagogue informing them of the need to reduce his Rabbinical activities due to ill-health, 13 October

(Letter)
pp. 1. London, Office of the Chief Rabbi, 1879
Reprinted in The Jewish Chronicle, no. 555, p. 4
And in The Jewish World, no. 353, p. 6
Copy of letter addressed to Presidents of Synagogues informing them of his correspondence with the Council of the United Synagogue, and of the appointment of Dr. Hermann Adler as Delegate, 10 November

1880

Gutachten
In Sod Haibur (סוד העבור): Grundlage und Festsetzung der Zeitberechnung, by David Friedländer, Budapest, 1880, p. 3

Reply... to the Conference of Delegates. Appendices
pp. 19. London, Wertheimer, Lea, 1880 (*Hebrew and English*)

The General Election
London, 1880
In The Jewish Chronicle, no. 574, p. 13
And in The Jewish World, no. 372, p. 8
Copy of letter addressed to the Times, *concerning the election scheduled to take place on the seventh day of Passover, 21 March*

Modifications of the Synagogue service
London, 1880

In The Jewish Chronicle, no. 586, pp. 12–13
Copy of letter addressed to the Honorary Secretary to the "Conference of Delegates to consider modifications in the Services of the Synagogues," *27 May*

(Letter)
London, 1880
In The Jewish Chronicle, no. 606, p. 7
Copy of letter addressed to the President of the United Synagogue, concerning his move to Brighton, 24 October

(Letter)
London, Office of the Chief Rabbi, 1880
In London Committee of Deputies of the British Jews. Session 5637–40 – 1877–80, the third annual report, pp. 21–23
Copy of letter addressed to the President of the London Committee of Deputies of British Jews, concerning the activities of the conversionists at Mission Hall

(Letter)
London, Office of the Chief Rabbi, 1880
In London Committee of Deputies of the British Jews. Session 5637–40 – 1877–80, the third annual report, pp. 25–26
Copy of letter addressed to the Secretary and Solicitor to the London Committee of Deputies of British Jews, concerning the scheduled Polling Day at Southwark coinciding with the seventh day of Passover

1881
Westminster Jews' Free Schools
London, 1881
In The Jewish Chronicle, no. 638, p. 7
Copy of letter addressed to the President of the schools, apologizing for not attending its meeting, 7 June

1882
The persecution of the Jews in Russia: public meeting at the Mansion House
London, 1882
In The Jewish Chronicle, no. 671, Supplement, p. 1
And in The Jewish World. Persecution of the Jews in Russia Special Supplement, no. 469, p. 1

Copy of letter addressed to the Lord Mayor, regretting his absence due to ill-health, from the Public Meeting at the Mansion House on 1 February, 31 January

תפלה על אחינו בני ישראל בארץ רוסיא Prayer for the Jews of Russia
pp. 3. London, Wertheimer, Lea, 1882
Hebrew and English

The persecution of the Jews in Russia
London, 1882
In The Jewish Chronicle, no. 672, p. 11
And in The Jewish World, no. 470, p. 3
Pastoral circular and Special Prayer, 5 and 7 February

The Oxford protest
London, 1882
In The Jewish Chronicle, no. 674, p. 14
And in The Jewish World, no. 472, p. 3
Copy of letter addressed to the Vice-Chancellor of the University of Oxford, thanking him for his "sympathy with my suffering coreligionists in Russia"

Anlage 14. Gutachten...
In Der Ohlsdorfer Begräbnissplatz in seinem Verhältniss zu den Israelitischen Gemeinden zu Hamburg, Hannover, 1889, pp. 36–37
Addressed to Oberrabbiner A. Stern in Hamburg, 11 May 5642

Thanksgiving service
London, 1882
In The Jewish Chronicle, no. 705, p. 7
Hebrew and English
Reprinted in The Jewish World, no. 503, p. 6 *(English only)*
"Order of Thanksgiving... for the signal success He has vouchsafed to our army in Egypt," *to be read on the first day of Tabernacles*

Mansion House Russian Jews' Relief Fund
London, 1882
In The Jewish Chronicle, no. 709, p. 6
And in The Jewish World, no. 507, p. 3
Joint signatory to an Address presented to the Lord Mayor, 25 October

1883
Jews' Free School

London, 1883
In The Jewish Chronicle, no. 727, p. 10
Copy of letter addressed to the President supporting the Building Fund appeal, 22 February

Eve of Passover: list of instructions
London, 1883
In The Jewish Chronicle, no. 733, p. 5
And in The Jewish World, no. 531, p. 3
Nisan 5643

"Tashlich"
London, 1883
In The Jewish Chronicle, no. 757, p. 5
Copy of the English version of a Yiddish notice circulated among the Chebroth appealing to Jews to avoid congregating at the Custom House Quay... "and all other public gatherings, for the purposes of Tashlich"

The Jews' Free School: consecration of the new building
London, 1883
In The Jewish Chronicle, no. 761, p. 7
Copy of letter addressed to Sir N. M. de Rothschild, regretting his inability to be present at the ceremony, 24 October

Ethical will
pp. 4. London, 1883
Marked "Confidential," *dated December 31 5644–1883*
Another printing. pp. 6. London, 1883

1884
(Letter)
In שלחן ערוך יורה דעה הלכות כבוד אב ואם, with commentaries by Naphtali Levy, Vienna, 1884, p. 15
Addressed to the author

שו"ת
In קדש נפתלי, by Naphtali Levy, printed with שלחן ערוך יורה דעה הלכות כבוד אב ואם, Vienna, 1884, p. 159

(Letters and תשובות)
In שו"ת בית אברהם, by Abraham Eber Hirschowitz, Jerusalem, 1923, pp. iv; 32; 33

On questions of Kashrut and shaatnez

The Jewish Board of Guardians
London, 1884
In The Jewish Chronicle, no. 783, p. 7
And in The Jewish World, no. 581, p. 3
Copy of letter addressed to L. L. Cohen tendering congratulations on the 25th anniversary of the Board of Guardians, 12 March

"Trefa" banquets
London, 1884
In The Jewish World, no. 585, p. 6
Copy of letter published in the Melbourne Jewish Herald

Jews' Free School dinner
London, 1884
In The Jewish Chronicle, no. 791, p. 4
Copy of letter addressed to the Right Hon. A. J. Mundella, M.P., regretting his absence from the anniversary dinner, 18 May

Provincial Jewish congregations
pp. 3. London, Office of the Chief Rabbi, 1884
Reprinted in The Jewish Chronicle, no. 792, p. 6
And in The Jewish World, no. 590, p. 6
Pastoral letter, May 5644

Postscript, July, 1884
London, Office of the Chief Rabbi, 1884
In כתר שם טוב, edited by Chaim Guedalla, pp. 70–71
Copy of letter addressed to Sir N. M. de Rothschild, President of the Council of the United Synagogue, recommending that a "Special Service of Prayer and Thanksgiving" *for Sir Moses Montefiore be held on 26 October, 26 May*

Sir Moses Montefiore
London, 1884
In The Jewish Chronicle, no. 795, p. 9
And in The Jewish World, no. 593, p. 5
Copy of letter addressed to the President of the Council of the United Synagogue recommending that a "Special Service of Prayer and Thanksgiving" *on the occasion of the 100th birthday of Sir Moses Montefiore be held on 26 October, 28 May*

The centenary of Sir Moses Montefiore
London, 1884
In The Jewish Chronicle, no. 799, p. 10
And in The Jewish World, no. 597, p. 6
Copy of letter addressed to the President of the Spanish and Portuguese Congregation recommending that a "Special Service of Prayer and Thanksgiving" *on the occasion of the 100th birthday of Sir Moses Montefiore be held on 26 October, 6 July*

The centenary of Sir Moses Montefiore
London, 1884
In The Jewish Chronicle, no. 800, p. 10.
Copy of letter addressed to the Presidents of the Colonial Jewish Congregations recommending that a "Special Service of Prayer and Thanksgiving" *on the occasion of the 100th birthday of Sir Moses Montefiore be held on 26 October*

תפלה למשה Service of prayer and thanksgiving to be used in all the Synagogues of the British Empire, on the occasion of Sir Moses Montefiore, Bart., completing his hundredth year. Sunday, 26th October, 5645-1884
pp. 11. London, Wertheimer, Lea and Co., 1884
Hebrew and English
Reprinted in The Jewish Chronicle, no. 813, p. 9
And in The Jewish World, no. 605, p. 2 *(English only)*

1885
(Letter)
pp. 4. Budapest, 1885
Promoting a forthcoming book on the Hebrew calendar by David Friedländer, p. 2

(Letter)
In שיבת ציון, by A. J. Slutzki, Warsaw, 1891, vol. 2, p. 5
Copy of letter in Hebrew addressed to Samuel Mohilever, dated 21 Tevet 1885 in Brighton

תפלה A prayer for Her Majesty's forces in the Soudan 5645—1885
pp. 3. London, Wertheimer, Lea & Co., 1885
Hebrew and English
Reprinted in The Jewish Chronicle, no. 831, p. 9

And in The Jewish World, no. 629, p. 6 *(English only)*
To be read on Sabbath 28 February

Death of Sir Moses Montefiore
London, 1885
In The Jewish World, no. 651, p. 6
Copy of letter addressed to the Wardens of all Congregations of the United Synagogue asking for the Memorial Prayer to be recited on Sabbath, 1 August

The will
pp. 3. London, 1885
Reproduced from hand-written document dated 27 December 1885

1887

תודה וקול זמרה Service of prayer and thanksgiving to be used in all the Synagogues of the British Empire, at the celebration of the jubilee of Her Gracious Majesty, Queen Victoria, on Tuesday, the 21st June, 5647–1887
pp. 15. London, Wertheimer, Lea & Co., 1887
Hebrew and English
Reprinted in The Jewish Chronicle, no. 951, pp. 8–9
And in The Jewish Record, no. 8, p. 7 *(English only)*
And in The Jewish World, no. 741, p. 6, *and* no. 749, p. 3 *(English only)*

The jubilee
London, 1887
In The Jewish Chronicle, no. 943, p. 16
Copy of circular addressed to the Ministers and Wardens of the Hebrew Congregations in the British Empire, and enclosing the Form of Prayer and Thanksgiving *to be used on 21st June*

United Synagogue
London, 1887
In The Jewish Chronicle, no. 976, p. 8
And in The Jewish World, no. 774, p. 7
Copy of letter addressed to Lord Rothschild stating that "our law is decidedly and emphatically opposed to the practice of cremation," *2 November*

(Letter)
pp. 1. London, Office of the Chief Rabbi, 1887
Copy of letter addressed to the Presidents of the Hebrew congregations, concerning the licensing of מוהלים *in provincial congregations, 10 November*

1888

Great Synagogue
London, 1888
In The Jewish World, no. 796, p. 3
Copy of letter addressed to L. Simmons concerning the use of a musical instrument at an afternoon service on a Sunday during Chanucah at the Great Synagogue, 6 January

Festival dinner of the Jews' Hospital and Orphan Asylum
London, 1888
In The Jewish World, no. 787, p. 5
Copy of letter addressed to the Chairman regretting his absence from the anniversary festival, 27 February

Mr. Angel and the Jews' Free School
London, 1889
In The Jewish Chronicle, no. 1031, p. 12
And in The Jewish World, no. 830, p. 7
Letter addressed to the Hon. Secretary of the Jews' Free School, 28 December 5649

1889

תשובה
In שו"ת יד הלוי II יו"ד, by Isaac Dov HaLevi Bamberger, סימן נז, Jerusalem, 1972, p. 37
Addressed to R. Seckel Bamberger of Schwersenz, 1889

(Letter)
Lyck, 1889
In המגיד, xxxiii, no. 2, pp. 13–14
And in המליץ, xxviii, no. 287, pp. 2932–2933, St. Petersburg, 1888–1889
Addressed to his Eastern European colleagues informing them of the plight of the Eastern European immigrants arriving to seek refuge in England

Jewish Provincial Ministers' Fund
London, 1889
In The Jewish Chronicle, no. 1040, p. 14
And in The Jewish Standard, ii, no. 51, p. 7
And in The Jewish World, no. 838, p. 5
Pastoral letter, 27 February

The proposed Hampstead Synagogue: reply on ritual
London, 1889
In The Jewish Chronicle, no. 1,075, p. 9
Copy of letter addressed to the Hon. Secretary to the Committee of the proposed Hampstead Synagogue, 24 October

1890
The Jewish Board of Guardians
London, 1890
In The Jewish Chronicle, no. 1,086, p. 12
Copy of letter addressed to the President of the Board of Guardians for the Relief of the Jewish Poor, 13 January

———

1897
הגדה של פסח containing a revision of the Hebrew text according to a MS. written in the year A.M. 5374, by... Rabbi Shabsi Sofer of Przemslow, also a valuable commentary copied from a MS. of the well known Rabbi Jonathan Eybeshuetz... together with explanations in Hebrew, and an English translation of some illustrative parables by the renowned Rabbi Jacob Magid of Dubno, and commentaries by the late Chief Rabbi Dr. N. Adler, the Chief Rabbi Dr. H. Adler, the late Rev. J. Reinowitz, the Rev. B. Spiers and the Rev. S. Cohen. Edited by the Rev. B. Spiers
pp. x, 96. London, J. Dickson, 1897
Reprinted 1909, 1922, 1954, 1956, 1960 *etc.*

Published without date

(Statement)
pp.1. Jerusalem, Deutsch. Israelit. Bicur-Cholim Hospital
In רחמים והצלה!, p. 1
Letter in German supporting the appeal for funds for the Hospital
Post-1890

JEWISH REFUGEES AT THE LIBRARY OF CONGRESS

T. WIENER

Among the sidelights of the tragic history of the Holocaust is the resurgence of those who were saved and made a new life for themselves in strange surroundings. America, indeed, proved to be a haven for a new group of refugees, as it had been in past generations. Of course, the years of affluence following World War II obscure the struggles that many had to undergo before they found their rightful place in this new land. Initially, it was particularly difficult for those with academic training to resume their interrupted careers, especially during the years of the great depression, when desirable jobs were naturally most difficult to obtain for people without American credentials and usually with an insufficient command of English. Yet, eventually the American success story was not to be withheld from a great many newcomers. True, they could not always find fields of work identical with those they had pursued in Europe; nevertheless, some have made significant contributions in their new endeavors.

Quite a few newcomers were attracted to library work, possible because the training was not too difficult to complete, requiring only one year after the undergraduate degree. At the Library of Congress, several former attorneys started new careers in which they distinguished themselves. Others brought different academic specialties to bear on their new tasks.

In the following pages we shall sketch the careers of a few of the more outstanding men and women from Hitlerian Europe who found a new vocation at the Library of Congress.

Among those who had made a name for themselves in Europe was David Baumgardt. Born in Erfurt, Germany, in 1890, he studied philosophy at the universities of Freiburg, Vienna, Munich, Heidelberg and Berlin, rising to the position of professor at the latter institution in 1932. Since he was a veteran of World War I, he was permitted to continue to lecture until 1935. At that time he served a brief term as visiting professor at the University of Madrid in Republican Spain, when the 800th anniversary of Maimonides' birth was celebrated. Eventually he came to the United States in 1939 and lectured at

Pendle Hill, a Quaker institution near Philadelphia, from 1939 to 1941. He was then appointed consultant in philosophy to the Library of Congress, as Archibald MacLeish, the newly appointed Librarian, embarked on a program of acquisitions to fill the gaps in the Library's collections. The annual reports of the Librarian of Congress between 1941 and 1954 record his contributions to this endeavor, among them *Philosophical Periodicals; an Annotated World List,* published by the Reference Department of the Library in 1952. Since his appointment had from the start been made possible only by special grants from foundations, fiscal retrenchments in 1954 brought about his retirement in that year. In 1955–1956 he served as visiting professor at Columbia University. He died in 1963, the same year that a *Festschrift* in his honor, *Horizons of a Philosopher,* published by Brill at Leiden, brought together many friends, professional and personal, to pay him tribute. Among them was a special greeting from Nobel laureate Hermann Hesse. The bibliography of his writings included in that volume testifies to his broad interests, not only in the field of philosophy but also in contemporary affairs. His main concern in the realm of ideas was ethics and mysticism. In America he wrote *Bentham and the Ethics of Today,* published by Princeton University Press in 1952 and reprinted in 1966. Characteristic of the loyalty of his students was the publication of a work based on his lecture notes from his Berlin University days, *Mystik und Wissenschaft; ihr Ort im abendländischen Denken* (1963), in part recovered from the notes of his pupil Helmut Minkowski, who had earned a doctorate under his supervision in 1932. An autobiographical sketch of Baumgardt was published posthumously in the Yearbook of the Leo Baeck Institute in 1965, which deals in particular with the Jews' place in German university life of Baumgardt's generation.

About the same time that Baumgardt's expertise in philosophy was being utilized at LC, Kurt Pinthus was employed for a shorter period as consultant on the Library's theater collections. He brought to this task a vast experience, gained over three decades. A fellow-townsman of Baumgardt, born likewise in Erfurt (in 1886), he studied literature, philosophy and history at the universities of Freiburg, Berlin, Geneva and Leipzig. After receiving his doctorate, he became reader at the prestigious Kurt Wolff Publishing House in Leipzig, while at the same time writing literary and theater reviews in leading German newspapers and magazines; he thus came into close contact with many German literary figures and formed lifelong friendships. Unique in his perception was an early recognition of the film as a new art form. In 1914 he edited *Das Kinobuch,* a collection of moving-picture plays by various German authors. This work was reprinted in 1963. During World War I he served in the German Army, at the same time editing two anthologies bearing on war in times past.

After the war he served briefly as a director in Max Reinhardt's theater in Berlin, but was mainly occupied with literary and theater reviews for the *8 Uhr Abendblatt,* a popular evening paper in Berlin, as well as with reviews for magazines and lectures at the Lessing-Hochschule, a school of adult education in Berlin, and over the radio, then the newest medium of expression. Possibly, however, his most lasting contribution during the inter-war period was an anthology of contemporary German poetry, *Menschheitsdämmerung* (1920; latest edition 1974, with 95,000 copies printed). This work is recognized as a milestone in German expressionism and has evoked serious studies both in Germany and elsewhere.

All this came to an end in 1933 when Pinthus, along with all other German Jews, was excluded from the German literary scene and had to confine his activities to the Jewish community, writing and lecturing with unreduced enthusiasm in this narrowed sphere. In 1938 he came to America, lecturing at the New School for Social Research in New York until 1940 and then serving at LC for a number of years. From 1947 to 1960 Pinthus lectured on theater history at Columbia University. From 1953 onward, he began to make visits to Germany, lecturing at the Free University of Berlin and renewing old friendships. In recognition of his literary activity he was granted the title of professor and the Grand Cross of Merit of the German Federal Republic in 1966. During the following year he settled permanently at Marbach, Germany, the location of the Schiller-National-Museum, a center for the study of German literature, to whose library and archive of German literature he presented his own extensive library and memorabilia of contemporary German writers. On the occasion of his 85th birthday in 1971, the Museum published a selection of his writings, under the title *Der Zeitgenosse, literarische Portraits und Kritiken.*

Another European scholar who had built a respectable position for himself and was suddenly uprooted by the advent of Hitlerism was Francis Joseph (Franz Josef) Weiss (1898–1975). A native of Vienna, he studied at the University there, receiving doctorates in chemistry and economics. He lectured at his *alma mater* and served as scientific consultant to the Austrian agricultural cooperatives and secretary-general of the International Hail Insurance Committee. While in Vienna he wrote a work on economic history, *Grundlagen der Volkswirtschaftspolitik in ihrer geschichtlichen Entwicklung* (1929), in which he applied his knowledge of food chemistry and economics to the practical problems besetting the modern world.

On coming to the United States in 1939, Weiss became associated with the National Planning Association. For this organization he wrote such studies as *The Alaskan Reindeer Industry* (1941), *Chemical Utilization of Fish Products in Alaska* (1941) and *Industrial Utilization of Agricultural Products (Cellulose,*

Lignin, and Allied Raw Materials) (1943). He also served as consultant to the Board of Economic Warfare and the Office of Technical Services of the Commerce Department during World War II. From 1946 to 1958 he was consultant to the Senate Subcommittee on Labor and Labor-Management Relations. During that time he wrote *Tobacco and Sugar* (1950) for the Sugar Research Foundation and prepared a report, *Manpower, Chemistry, and Agriculture* (1952), for the Senate Subcommittee. In 1954 the Senate issued another of his reports, *New Outlets for Wheat; a Report on "Parboiled Wheat," a Practical Solution to a Grave and Urgent World Problem, Food Shortage in the Rice Areas.* From 1958 to 1969 he served as Bibliographer and Science Specialist in the Science and Technology Division at LC. While there he worked on several projects sponsored by the U.S. Atomic Energy Commision, dealing with agricultural applications of atomic energy. Weiss's labors did not cease with his retirement in 1969. He participated in the Third International Congress of Food Science and Technology in Washington, D.C., presenting a paper, *The Food in the Bible* (1970). During his stay in Washington, he served at different times as consultant to the U.S. Fish and Wild Life Service, the International Cooperation Administration and the governments of Puerto Rico and Nicaragua.

Two refugee legal scholars who made important contributions in reference work were William Siegfried Strauss (1910–1967) and Fred Karpf (1903–1969). Strauss, a native of Nuremberg, J.D. recipient of the University of Würzburg, reached the United States in 1935. After studying U.S. law at the George Washington Law School, he joined the staff of the Copyright Office at LC in 1947, serving as Assistant General Counsel of the Library from 1962 until his death. In 1955, as part of his concern with copyright law, he wrote *The Moral Right of the Author,* first published in the *American Journal of Comparative Law.* In 1959 he helped to prepare a supplement to *Bibliography on Design Protection,* under the auspices of the Copyright Office. One prodigious task that he accomplished was the preparation in 1961 of an annotated compilation, *Air Laws and Treaties of the World,* under the auspices of the Committee on Science and Astronautics of the U.S. House of Representatives. An enlarged edition of this work appeared in 1965 at the request of the U.S. Senate Commerce Committee. In 1968, his *Guide to Laws and Regulations on Federal Libraries: a Compilation and Analysis* was published posthumously under the aegis of the Federal Library Committee. He thus left a permanent imprint on the legal literature of his time.

Fred Karpf joined the staff of LC in 1947, the same year as Strauss. Born in Vienna, where he received his doctorate of law in 1928, he worked in the legal department of a large insurance company there. Coming to the United States in

1938 he settled in Chattanooga, Tennessee, where he again attended law school and was eventually admitted to the Tennessee bar before coming to LC. He worked for several years as specialist in European law in the European Law Division of the Library, receiving several incentive awards for the solution of many difficult reference problems and finally being promoted to assistant chief of that division in 1962, a post he held until his death. While in Washington, he served on the Board of Governors of the Washington Foreign Law Society, and as board member and also president of the LC credit union. Thus another career interrupted by the tragic fate of European Jewry acquired a new, fruitful direction in a new environment.

While the bibliographic and reference function of a great library, as exemplified in the work of Baumgardt, Karpf, Pinthus, Strauss and Weiss, is extremely important, the processing of the materials that flow into the library in a never-ceasing stream is no less significant, especially since the unit cards prepared at the Library of Congress – with bibliographic description, classification and subject headings – are being used without modification by an increasing number of U.S. libraries. In the following pages we shall sketch the contributions in this area of several refugee librarians at LC.

Several of these, trained in law in Europe, made important contributions to American librarianship in various ways. Charles Conrad Bead (Karl Cohn-Biedermann, 1905–) was one of the Jewish law students at German universities when Hitler came to power in 1933. Under the regulations, he was permitted to receive his doctorate from the University of Erlangen, on the basis of a dissertation on German property law, but was not admitted to the bar examination. Upon coming to the United States, he received a Master of Library Science degree from the University of Illinois and came to LC after serving in the U.S. Army during World War II. For most of the time from 1945 until his retirement in 1972 he worked in the cataloging divisions. In 1962 he became Senior Subject Cataloger for the Social Sciences in the Subject Cataloging Division, in 1967 Assistant Chief and in 1969 Chief of that division, which is in charge of classifying and assigning subjects to all books processed by LC. As LC classification schedules and subject headings are being adopted by an increasing number of libraries throughout the country, the importance of this responsibility cannot be overestimated.

A colleague of Bead in the Subject Cataloging Division was Werner Bruno Ellinger (1908–1972). He earned his doctorate from the University of Heidelberg with a thesis on German and Austrian copyright law. Arriving in the U.S. in 1937, he studied library science at Columbia University Library School. From 1941 to 1971 he was on the staff of the Library of Congress, first in the Descriptive Cataloging Division and then in the Subject Cataloging Division.

From 1951 to 1969 he was Senior Subject Cataloger in Law and thereafter, until his retirement, Specialist in Law Classification.

The one area in which there was at the time no classification schedule was law, and it was here that Ellinger did pioneering work. In 1949 he published a scheme of his own, *Subject Classification of Law,* first as an article in *Library Quarterly*. This was followed in 1953 by an official publication of the Subject Cataloging Division, *Class K: Law; Working Papers,* an experimental publication intended to elicit comments from law librarians. In 1963 there appeared *Subject Headings for the Literature of Law and International Law,* the law subjects included in the 6th edition of LC subject headings. The second edition of this work was published in 1969, based on the 7th edition of LC subject headings. Both of these works appeared under the auspices of the American Association of Law Libraries, in whose councils Ellinger was active throughout his library tenure. In 1970 the Subject Cataloging Division issued his *Classification. Class K: Law; Draft Outline.* Thereafter the first working schedule of American law took its place among the official classification schedules of LC, facilitating the cataloging of these materials in law libraries throughout the U.S.A.

An earlier work of Ellinger was a bibliography, *Sea Power in the Pacific, 1936–1941,* co-authored with Herbert Rosinski in 1942. In addition, he served on the general committee of the American Library Association, which co-sponsored the *Anglo-American Cataloging Rules* (1967) for descriptive cataloging, another attempt to standardize cataloging practice even on an international level. In 1961 he attended the International Conference on Cataloging Principles in Paris, as a delegate of the International Association of Law Librarians. Closer to home, he served as president of the District of Columbia Library Association.

Ellinger's successor and former close associate, John Fischer, was born in Hungary in 1910. After receiving a doctorate of law degree from the University of Szeged, he practised law until 1943, resuming his law practice in Budapest after the War in 1946. By 1949 he had reached the United States and was studying at the George Washington Law School in Washington, D.C., from which he received the degree of Master of Comparative Law in 1951. At the same time (1949) he joined the staff of LC, becoming Subject Cataloger in law in 1962 and Law Classification Specialist ten years later. As a result of his work, the Subject Cataloging Division was able to augment its tools with yet another classification schedule in law (*Classification. Class K, Subclass KD: Law of the United Kingdom and Ireland, 1973).* In the early phase of his service at LC, Fischer participated in the activities of the Mid-European Law Project and helped to compile *Hungary, Churches and Religion* (1951) and

Forced Labor and Confinement without Trial in Hungary (1952), putting his intimate knowledge of the contemporary Hungarian legal system to good use.

A former European lawyer who did not utilize his legal expertise in his library work is Johannes Leopold Dewton (formerly Deutsch). Born in Vienna in 1905, he received his doctor of laws degree from the local university and practised law there until 1938. After graduating as a librarian from the University of Illinois in 1944, he served in 1945 as technical adviser to the U.S. Army Air Force when the latter was setting up its Air Research Documentation Center in London. At LC since 1945, he became Assistant Chief of the Union Catalog Division in 1957. (This branch of the Library receives cataloging data from hundreds of American libraries, maintaining a union catalog of all these data and the locations of the books they represent; it also answers enquiries from outsiders regarding the location of individual books.)

Since 1956 the *National Union Catalog* has been appearing in published form, with a record of the current acquisitions of participating American libraries. In 1961 Dewton was responsible for editing *The National Union Catalog, 1952–1955 Imprints; an Author List Representing Library of Congress Printed Cards and Titles Reported by other American Libraries*. This thirty-volume title was forerunner for the monumental *National Union Catalog, pre-1956 Imprints,* begun in 1968, a project which will comprise more than 600 volumes when completed. This is the largest bibliographic project ever undertaken, and a special unit in the Library, the National Union Catalog Publication Project, was set up in 1967 with Dewton at its head. He retired in 1975, continuing as a consultant. Between these two massive tasks, he pioneered another innovation at LC, serving as Acting Chief of the new Shared Cataloging Division from 1966 to 1967. To speed up the processing of books from outside the U.S.A., bibliographic information furnished by the national bibliographies of various countries was utilized in cataloging the books originating there. This called for a cataloging procedure other than beginning with the book *de novo*. The Shared Cataloging Division was set up for this purpose, and Dewton thus put his imprint on another important LC project.

Dewton's successor at the Shared Cataloging Division was Nathalie Delougaz. Born in Russia in 1910, she settled with her family in France, receiving a degree of Licencié en Droit in Paris in 1935. After coming to the United States during World War II, she worked as a cataloger at the University of Chicago Library while studying there for a degree in librarianship and an M.A. degree. She received her degree on the basis of a thesis on *A Survey of Book Publishing in Soviet Russia* (1948) In 1950 she transferred to the Library of Congress, to become Head of the Slavic Section in the Descriptive Cataloging Division, as greater interest in Russian publications led to expanding acquisitions of books from the Soviet Union. Later in the 1950s she was part of a UNESCO unit assisting at the Jewish National and University Library in Jerusalem, remaining there for a number of years as senior librarian and instructor in the new Graduate Library School. On returning to the United States in 1965, she soon became involved in the new acquisition program from abroad, for which the Shared Cataloging Division was to serve as the processing arm. She established overseas offices for LC in London and Paris for the purpose of acquiring works in those countries and preparing preliminary cataloging data on the basis of the respective national bibliographies. This gave her a different view of the program that she was eventually to administer in Washington as Chief of the Shared Cataloging Division, from 1967 on.

Another senior librarian in the cataloging field was Marion Schild. Born in Fiume of Hungarian parents in 1907, she received a Ph.D. degree from the University of Munich in 1933, with a thesis entitled *Die Musikdramen Ottavio Rinuncinis*. After her arrival in the United States, she graduated from Columbia University Library School and in 1941 joined the staff of Columbia University Library as cataloger of Hungarian books. From 1946 onward she worked at the Library of Congress, concerned throughout her service there with descriptive cataloging. In 1950 she received a superior accomplishment award for drafting preliminary rules for the cataloging of Incunabula, at the time the gifts of Lessing Rosenwald were being processed at LC. She was the cataloger of the 1954 edition of *The Rosenwald Collection; a Catalogue of Illustrated Books and Manuscripts, of Books from Celebrated Presses, and of Bindings and Maps, 1150–1950. The Gift of Lessing J. Rosenwald to the Library of Congress*. In 1962 she became head of the English Language Section of the Descriptive Cataloging Division, which of course handles a significant portion of LC's acquisitions. In 1964 she was appointed Deputy Principal Cataloger and a few years later Principal Cataloger of the division, where all the problems connected with the introduction of the new *Anglo-American Cataloging Rules* had to be dealt with. From 1968 to 1974 she served as Field Director for Acquisitions of Italian Books in Florence, Italy. From 1974 until her retirement in 1977 she was again Deputy Principal Cataloger. At various times she served on the Subcommittee on the National Union Catalog of ALA.

This article has presented the contributions of only a few of the more prominent staff members of the Library of Congress whom Fate brought to these shores during the turbulent years of the Hitler period. There were a considerable number of others, who served in less visible positions, but nevertheless found a new place for themselves in the New World. These examples of lives interrupted by the Holocaust and taken up again in a new and strange environment are a tribute to the resilience of the human spirit.

BIBLIOGRAPHICAL NOTE

Biographical sketches of Bead, Delougaz, Dewton, Ellinger, Fischer and Schild are included in the *Biographical Directory of Librarians in the United States and Canada, 1970*. The *LC Information Bulletin* described the careers of Fred Karpf (July 3, 1969) and Francis Joseph Weiss (May 8, 1969 and February 7, 1975). For David Baumgardt there is an entry in the *Encyclopaedia Judaica* (1971). He was furthermore listed in *Wer ist's?* (1935) during the Nazi period (where he insisted on proclaiming his descent from Wolf Heidenheim, the Hebrew printer) and also in *Kürschner's Deutscher Gelehrten-Kalender* (1961). There is an article on Pinthus in the *Universal Jewish Encyclopedia,* with additional listings in *Kürschner's Deutscher Literatur-Kalender* (1967) and *Wer ist wer* (1971). His anthology *Menschheitsdämmerung* is referred to in *Lexikon der Weltliteratur des 20. Jahrhunderts* as one of the most important collections of contemporary German poetry. William Strauss was eulogized in the *New York Times* of June 1, 1967.

A PROBE INTO HEBREW PRINTING IN HANAU IN THE SEVENTEENTH CENTURY OR HOW QUANTIFIABLE IS HEBREW TYPOGRAPHY?[1]

H. C. ZAFREN

What kinds of information can the book, examined as an artifact, reveal? Since my use of the word typography is not limited to the type used for printing or to the design of the book, but rather extends to all aspects of the book as artifact, it may logically cover the type, metal ornaments, woodcuts, engravings, paper, ink, binding and other material used; it may also cover the text (and especially the text of the title page, preliminary matter and colophon); and it may involve measurement, counting, statistical analysis, chemical analysis and any other kind of examination or comparison. It is quite another question to determine just how far to go, that is, to face the realities of quantifiability and the equally difficult question of whether the yield is commensurate with the labor.

I have on occasion thought of devoting several lifetimes, were they only granted to me, to doing typographic profiles of Hebrew printers and places of printing in the belief that if we had all the data about who used what type, where and when; about how ornaments and illustrative cuts traveled and were copied; and about other related things dealing with paper, presswork, design, the tradesmen, etc., we could probably write a good history of Hebrew printing that would not be a chronicle but an intellectual, social and economic history of the Jews in microcosm and indeed a model of the non-Jewish world as well. This, I believe, might be possible, even if there were no documentation other than the books. In the presence of non-book documentation — the usual sources of history — the artifacts may act as controls or fill in details.

Let us probe into Hanau Hebrew printing in the seventeenth century to see

1 This paper was presented at the Seventh World Congress of Jewish Studies in Jerusalem in August, 1977, under the title "How Quantifiable is Hebrew Typography?" Documentation has been added and minor revisions have been made for publication. The research was supported in part by a grant from the Penrose Fund of the American Philosophical Society.

what the artifacts yield for this place and time. Except for a maverick book or two with only occasional Hebrew type, dating back to 1604,[2] books in Hebrew began to emerge in 1610 from the shop of Hans Jakob Henne.[3] Some ten to thirteen books from 1610 to 1612 bear the name of the printer Henne[4] and the place of printing (Appendix, Section A). From 1614 to 1622, probably fourteen books appeared that did not bear a printer's name but did bear the imprint Hanau (Appendix, Section B). Here I might interject the very considerable problem that no investigator can reasonably get all of the books together in one place or find standardized descriptions. Thus, even counting the number of books is not easy, because books bound with others may or may not be counted separately. And statements made by very reliable scholars often prove to be wrong, as, for example, Steinschneider's assertion that the imprint Hanau is not to be found on Hanau books after 1617,[5] though I have seen three with place printed and dated 1620 and 1621[6] and I believe that Steinschneider's own description of the tractate *Chulin* of 1622[7] strongly implies that the place is printed in that book.

It is now apparent that only twenty-four to twenty-seven Hebrew books can be attributed to Hanau on the basis of internal direct evidence, and this evidence represents a major difference from those that do not have Hanau printed in them. Fifteen more books, dated from 1623 to 1630 (Appendix, Section C), and six more without date (Appendix, Section D) have been attributed by Steinschneider and others to Hanau of this period, and an additional six to ten (there are "bound-withs" involved) are attributed to Hanau though they say internally that they were printed elsewhere (Appendix, Section E).

Attributions of the post-1622 books to Hanau have been made on the basis of the type, the typesetters or other tradespeople and one woodcut that were

2 An edition of Johann Buxtorf's *Synagoga Judaica* (Hanoviae, G. Antonius, 1604) has a few scattered Hebrew words in it.

3 B. Friedberg, ...תולדות הדפוס העברי בערים האלה... הענא (Antwerp 1935) provides details on Henne and on printing in Hanau but relies on Gustav Könnecke, *Hessisches Buchdruckerbuch* (Marburg in Hessen 1894), especially pp. 136–138 and 148–149. See also J. Benzing, *Die Buchdrucker des 16. und 17. Jahrhunderts in deutschen Sprachgebiet* (Wiesbaden 1963), pp. 177–178.

4 Henne's burial is recorded on 17 March, 1613. See Könnecke, p. 137 and Benzing, p. 178.

5 M. Steinschneider, *Catalogus librorum hebraeorum in Bibliotheca Bodleiana...*, 3 vols. (Berlin 1852–1860), 3099.

6 The titles are עולם הבא, ישועות ונחמות and משניות מסדר טהרות.

7 Steinschneider, *Catalogus*, 250/1631.

connected with one or more books definitely printed in Hanau before 1623. Let us examine these a little more closely.

Eight people, serving variously as typesetters, editors and proofreaders, are named in one or more of the almost fifty books. Four of them served in the period from 1610 to 1617,[8] two served in the period from 1625 to 1630,[9] and two served in both periods.[10] I must point out that some scholars have at times been confused by a similarity of names.[11] But Steinschneider's summary yields the above breakdown; and, except for the fact that I could not check on one person[12] who seems to have appeared in one or two early books, my examination of the books corroborates Steinschneider. Since typesetters and others frequently left one city for another, presumably to find work, it must be said that an attribution of a book to a place because one or more typesetters are known to have worked there is not sufficient reason. Our two workers who are mentioned in both periods may have left Hanau together if Hebrew books were no longer printed there after 1622.

From 1610 to 1622, the date of the last book to have Hanau printed in it, Henne and those who followed him used at least nine fleurons,[13] or metal ornaments cast like type. From 1623 to 1630 there were also nine fleurons used. Three of the fleurons *appear* to have been used in both periods. Four head pieces, twelve tail pieces, several small frames, a few title pages — all woodcuts — and a number of woodblock letters were used from 1610 to 1622. Three head pieces, five tail pieces, and one title page — all woodcuts — were used from 1623 to 1630. One of these ornaments only appears to have been used in both periods. (There were additional woodcuts in dated and undated books, but they do not present or solve any problems because they appear in only one book each, as far as I know.)

In the early period, the printers used square Hebrew type in the following approximate sizes: 1.3 mm, 2.1 mm, 3.3 mm, 4.3 mm and 5.8 mm. In the later period the sizes were 1.4 mm, 2.0 mm, 2.5 mm, 3.75 mm and 5.5 mm. The

8 Seligman Ulma ben Moshe Shim'on, Eliyahu ben Seligman Ulma, Eliezer ben Chayim Eliyahu Ulma ben Yehuda and Avraham ben Eliezer.

9 David Tevel ben Yechezkel from Troppau and Eliyahu ben Yehuda Ulma.

10 Avraham ben Yekutiel from Burga and Mordechai ben Yaakov from Prossnitz.

11 Friedberg, p. 58, has "merged" the two Eliyahus, as has the *Jewish Encyclopedia,* 12 (New York 1906), 311.

12 Avraham ben Eliezer.

13 For facsimiles of most of the fleurons, woodcuts and type fonts, the reader must wait for the publication of a typographic profile. The original books are, of course, available in scattered libraries.

smallest size used might well be the same type; the others are sufficiently different in size or face to rule out sameness.[14] The rabbinic, or Rashi, type sizes are 1.2 mm, 1.7 mm and 2.5 mm for the early period and 1.2 mm and 2.3 mm for the later period. Only the 1.2 mm type may be the same in both periods. A 2.25 mm type for Yiddish *was* the same in both periods. A second, smaller Yiddish type is found only in one book,[15] printed in Basel if the title page is to be believed. Thus three types *may* be the same in both periods, while six are exclusive to the first period and five to the second.

The words *Cum Licentia Superiorum* appear on the title pages of books from the early period only. In fact, the latest book that I have seen with these words is dated 1620. While I am studiously limiting myself here to the artifacts and excluding documents, I take the liberty of suggesting that we may have here some artifactual support for the printing privilege that was apparently granted for ten years only.[16] May we speculate that the lapse of the privilege is the reason for omitting the formula and perhaps the reason that Hanau was abandoned as a center of Hebrew printing two years later.

There is certainly reason to wonder why the name of the city Hanau was not printed after 1622, why almost all the ornaments are used on either one side of this date or the other, and why most of the type splits at this time. On the other hand, a couple of possibly shared ornaments and a couple of typesetters, plus three possibly shared typefaces, *may* be bridge enough over the otherwise huge chasm. Were the 1623 to 1630 books printed in Hanau, as bibliographers long ago assumed, or were they printed elsewhere?

Let us see how strong the bridge is.

Throughout Hebrew and general printing history we have many examples of the use of the same types, ornaments (wood and metal) and typesetters by different printers. There are also countless instances of imitation, sometimes so close that it is virtually impossible to be certain whether the impressions were made from the same metal or wood or from imitations. The amount and the content of the ink used, the degree of pressure at the press, the skill of the pressman, the cleanliness of the type or ornament, the absorptive quality of the paper — these and other variables render a quantitative analysis meaningless when the measurements are fine. While measurements as close as possible are

14 Close scrutiny will sometimes be necessary to detect the differences, especially in the approximately 2.0 mm size.

15 חמשה חומשי תורה... צאינה וראינה and also חמש מגלות והפטרות, which is really part 2 of the *Chumash*. The first part only is dated — 1622.

16 Könnecke, p. 137.

desirable to separate similar designs, when the designs are very similar in appearance and size, refined measurements are often inappropriate for the unrefined nature of that which is being measured.

I believe that two of the fleurons and two of the typefaces fall into the category of being too close and unrefined to be differentiated by measurements. They are small – the typefaces are between 1.2 mm and 1.4 mm in "x" height, and I know no way of being certain whether the two squares (Figs. 1 and 3) and the two rabbinics (Figs. 2 and 3) are respectively the same as, or different from each other.[17] Similarly with two of the fleurons. One of them is really a collection of six basic arabesques – which are endemic to printing in Europe – that fit together in many configurations to make many designs (Figs. 1 and 4). They were probably standard material at many type foundries; but even when they were made at home, so to speak, they look like all the rest. To add to the

קפח 188

נביאים אחרונים

חזון

Fig. 1. Bible, Hanau 1610. Basic arabesques, "loops" fleuron, smallest square type.

17 I believe they are different. The *fe* seems more slanted (broader base than top) and the *bet* seems to have a more slanted top in the early period square type. In the rabbinic type, the later period seems to favor rounder qualities in the *alef, mem, tsadi* and *resh,* among others.

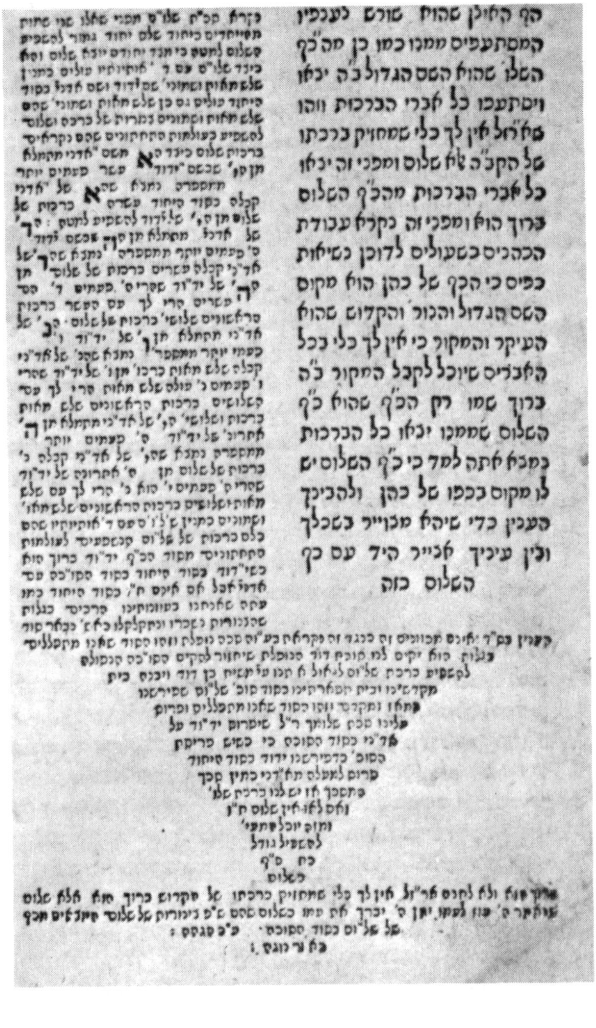
הף האין שהוא שורש נענפין
המסתעפים ממנו כמו כן מה כ"ף
השלו' שהוא השם הגדול ב"ה יבאו
ויסתעפו כל אברי הברכות וזהו
מאח"זל אין לך כלי שמחזיק ברכתו
של הקב"ה אלא שלום ומפני זה יבאו
כל אברי הברכות מהכ"ף השלום
ברוך הוא ומפני זה נקרא עבודת
הכהנים כשעולים לדוכן נשיאות
כפים כי הכף של כהן הוא מקום
השם הגדול והגבור והקדוש שהוא
העיקר והמקור כי אין לך כלי בכל
האברים שיוכל לקבל המקור ב"ה
ברוך שמו רק הכ"ף שהוא כ"ף
השלום שממנו יבאו כל הברכות
נמצא אתה למד כי כ"ף השלום יש
לו מקום בכפו של כהן ולהבינך
הענין כדי שיהא מצוייר בשכלך
ובין עיניך אצייר היד עם כף
השלום כזה

Fig. 2. שפע טל, Hanau 1612. Rabbinic types 1.2 mm (smallest) and 1.7 mm.

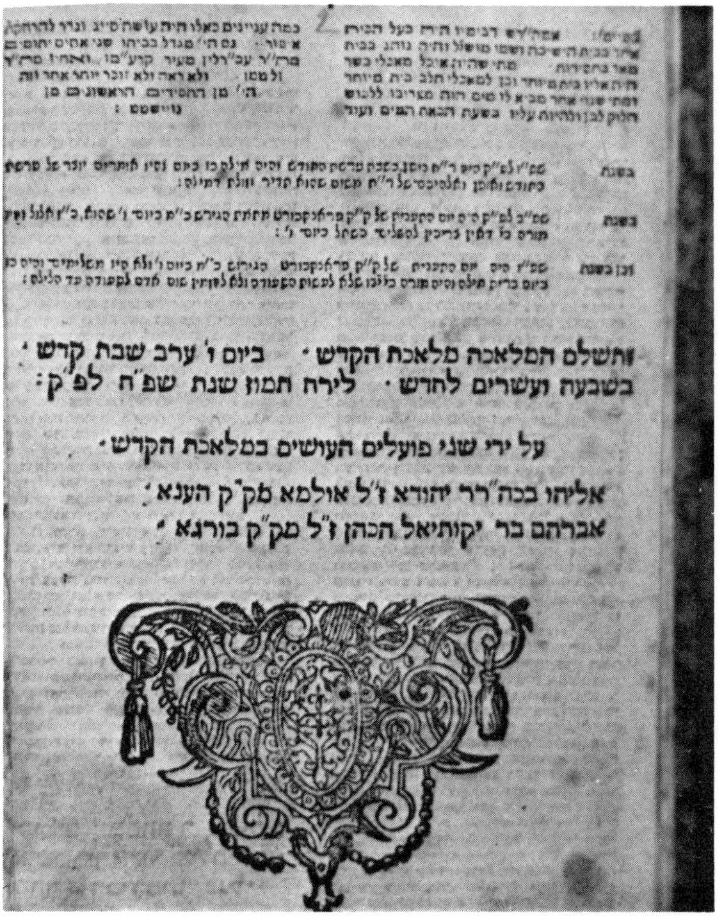
ותשלם המלאכה מלאכת הקדש · ביום ו' ערב שבת קדש :
בשבעה ועשרים לחדש · לירח תמוז שנת שפ"ח לפ"ק :
על ידי שני פועלים העושים במלאכת הקדש ·
אליהו בכה"רר יהודא ז"ל אולמא מק"ק הענא :
אברהם בר יקותיאל הכהן ז"ל מק"ק בורגא :

Fig. 3. ספר מהריל, 1. 64b, 1628. Smallest square and rabbinic types, "tassel" woodcut ornament, names of two typesetters.

עם הנהורת והחרושים שליקט ואסף
ההר צבי ין בר יצחק יעקב זל : ממרה
שבא לידו וברק ונסה זרה כמה שנים :
והוגה אות באות על פי הגאון מוהרר משה
איסרליס זל וגם מה שהוסיף הגאון תמצא
בהנהורת גם כן והלכורת ניקר
בקצרה :
לא אגרעתי מהם ולא אחזרתי
מהראשונים דבר :
אכן הם מדויקים יותר
מהראשונים :

Fig. 4. בדיקות [1623–30]. Basic arabesques, "loops" fleuron (near bottom on both sides), square types 2.0 mm., 3.75 mm. and 5.5 mm.

problem, each piece is small, perhaps 6 mm square. The second fleuron is also small (less than 3 mm square) and very common; it looks like two small elongated loops (Figs. 1, 4 and 6). Incidentally, this fleuron appears in the Hanau book of 1604 previously mentioned (see note 2 above), in which the several Hebrew words are in a characteristic Basel type.

One fleuron, a rectangular double whirl about 11 × 5.5 mm, is not common and does seem to be a bridge between the two periods, though I have seen it used in only one book in each period (Fig. 5). And the one larger woodcut ornament with a "tassel" motif (Fig. 3) was used several times in each period. Similarly, the Yiddish type, which spans both periods, is certainly an important link. The *demonstrable* "links" are thus one fleuron, one woodcut and one type font.

Let us turn to the typesetters. That two of them are active in both periods

Fig. 5. **Fleuron (rectangular double whirl) used** in both periods.

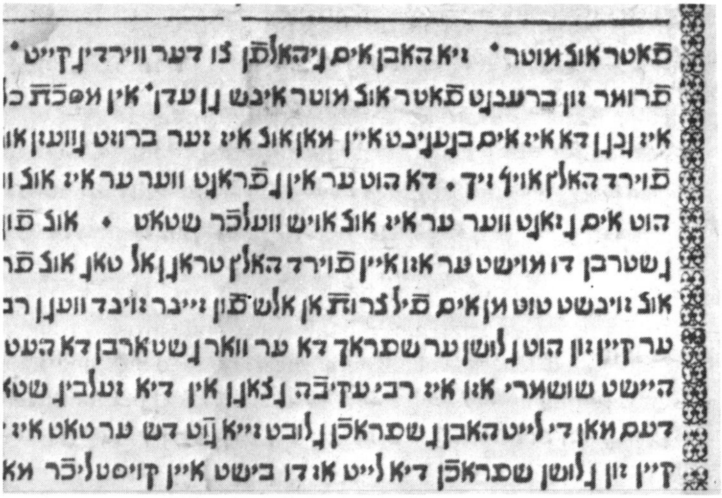

פֿאטר אונ מוטר • זיא האבן אים ניהאלפֿן צו דער ווירדיגקייט •
פֿרומר זון ברענגט פֿאטר אונ מוטר אינש גן עדן • אין מסכת כ
איז גנגן דא איז אים בגעגנט איין מאן אונ איז זער ברוזט גוועזן א
פֿירד האלץ אויף זיך • דא הוט ער אין גפֿראגט ווער ער איז אונ ו
הוט אים גזאגט ווער ער איז אונ אויש וועלכר שטאט • אונ פֿו
גשטרבן דו מוישט ער אזו איין פֿירד האלץ טראגן אל טאג אונ פֿר
אונ זיבשט טוט מן אים פֿיל צרות אן אלש פֿון זייבר זיבד ווענן רב
ער קיין זון הוט גלושן ער שפראך דא ער וואר גשטארבן דא העט
היישט שושמרי אזו איז רבי עקיבה גצאגן אין דיא זעלבין שט
דעם מאן די לייט האבן גשפראכן גלובט זייא גוט דש ער טאט איז
קיין זון גלושן שפראכן דיא לייט אזו בישט איין קויסטליכר מא

Fig. 6. ברנט שפיגל, 1626. "Yiddish" type used in both periods. Also "loops" fleuron.

proves nothing, as indicated earlier. The key to the puzzle may lie in the name of one who is known to have served from 1625 to 1630. This typesetter is named, in every book where I have seen his name, Eliyahu [ben] Yehuda Ulma "Mikak" Hanau (Fig. 3). This seems to match the other typesetters whose places of origin are also mentioned. But in the early period, while those typesetters who came from Prossnitz or Burga are so designated, those whose homes were in Hanau have no place of origin connected to their names. The very fact that Eliyahu ben Yehuda Ulma is described as being from Hanau suggests that he was then (1625–1630) working elsewhere.

Now add in the other ingredients that oppose Hanau as the place of printing of the post-1622 books. Very important is the undisputed fact that not a single book says that it *was* printed in Hanau. More important still is the fact that there is a break at 1622, after which at least six Hanau typefaces were not used in the later books, six fleurons were no longer used, and two dozen or more woodcuts of various kinds were no longer used. And, while the printers of the books attributed to Hanau in the later period used up to, but not more than, three typefaces, three fleurons and one woodcut from the early period, these were not sufficient; and they quickly added more to their repertoire. It would have been natural, if the press had been continuous in Hanau, to *add* to the repertoire as time passed but not to drop the major part of the repertoire precipitously. That only a small part of the old was used with the new suggests the possibility that someone, perhaps the two typesetters who figure in both periods, managed to acquire a bit of the printing repertoire in Hanau, moved elsewhere, and added more when setting up in the new place.

It seems to me, therefore, that the so-called Hanau books of 1623 to 1630 were *not* printed in Hanau. Where they were printed I do not yet know. If there were printing profiles for other cities in Europe for this period, we might be able to match up the 1623–1630 profile, which should really be separated from the 1610 to 1622 Hanau profile, with some place that fits it better. Perhaps we shall never know. My own attention will go first to Frankfurt am Main and Basel because there were many connections between them and Hanau.

Other quantifiable characteristics could certainly be brought into consideration: elongated letters, vocalization, ligatures, Roman and italic type and arabic numerals, signatures, size of the printed part of the page, space between lines, number of lines, dimensions of the paper used, watermarks, and other measurements borrowed from archeology and codicology, perhaps. It is my judgment that, in this case, nothing conclusive would emerge from such quantification, but I would be delighted to be proved wrong.

It may be proper to suggest a few "predictions," based on the summary of the Hanau and the 1623–1630 books that has emerged. I have not seen the following books but feel confident in saying that:

1. The *Tefilot* and the *Zemirot shel shabat* of 1623 (a kind of borderline year), because they do not contain a place of printing, probably match the post-1622 books rather than the earlier ones.
2. The quarto *Tefilot* of 1625 has Eliyahu ben Yehuda Ulma as a typesetter. His name will have his place of origin attached, because in 1625 he was probably not living in Hanau.

Less amenable to proof at the present is my confidence that the undated books attributed to Hanau can now be better dated than they have been. The *Sefer Hagan* has been attributed to 1620;[18] I would say (from the microfiche I

18 *Yiddish Books on Microfiche*, p. 7. This is the catalog prepared by Inter Documentation Company for its Jewish Studies Microfiche Project, 4.3 Yiddish Languages and Literature, Project Publication No. 6/1976.

have seen) that it has to be dated after 1622. A *Machzor* has been attributed to 1610–1630; we ought certainly to be able to say which side of 1622 it really is. The *Tsukht Spigl* was attributed by Steinschneider to 1610–1613.[19] The characteristic Yiddish type is not used in the *Yudisher Teryak* of 1615 or in the *Sidur* of 1616 but is used in the *Chumash* of 1617; it may have been introduced to the Hanau repertoire in late 1616 or 1617. Its presence in, or absence from, the *Tsukht Spigl* might be a factor in dating the book.

Is there more conventional historical evidence to support the artifactual evidence that I have adduced? Are there conflicts? Can the artifactual evidence be a control for the conventional and *vice versa?* It would be foolhardy to think otherwise.

APPENDIX

Here, in tabular, short-title form are the books printed in Hanau and attributed to Hanau. Elsewhere, I plan to publish a fuller bibliography and typographic profiles. The following notation is used: * = not seen; fac = facsimile of parts of the book only seen; mic = microfiche only seen.

Section A: 1610–1612 – With name of printer, Hans Jakob Henne, and place of publication

תנ"ך 8° Plant and animal title page 1610
* תנ"ך 8° Moses and Aaron motif title page 1610
fac תנ"ך 32° 1610
ארבעה טורים 1610
שאלות ותשובות שלמה בן אדרת 1610
שאלות ותשובות יעקב ווייל 1610
שאלות ותשובות יעקב סגל 1610
* תפלות 1611
* תהלים Undated; relates to תפלות of 1611
נשמת אדם 1611
שפע טל 1612
1612 Schindler, Lexicon
fac חומש Started in 1611

19 Steinschneider, *Catalogus*, 2581/7172:1.

Section B: 1614–1622 – Hanau printed as place of printing; no printer's name

גנת אגוז 1614
גדולת מרדכי 1615
יודישר טירייאק 1615
סדור תפלות 1616
* סליחות 1616
בן דעת על תהלים 1616
* דרוש על עשרת הדברות 1616
mic חומש 1617
* נדה 1618
mic ישועות ונחמות 1620
mic עולם הבא 1620
משניות מסדר טהרות 1621
* חולין 1622
* מראות אלהים 1622

Section C: 1623–1630 – No place, no printer's name

* תפלות 1623
* זמירות של שבת 1623
* תפלות 1625 8°
* תפלות 1625 4°
מחזור 1625
* סליחות 1625
ברנט שפיגל 1626
עדות יעקב 1627
mic שוין פרויאן בויכליין (מצות הנשים) 1627
תפלות 1628
* מנהגים 1628 (Benjacob 336/1406; spurious?)
ספר מהריל 1628
שלחן ערוך 28 – 1626
תורת החטאת 1628
ספר הרוקח 1630

Section D: No date, no place, no printer's name[20]

בדיקות

mic ספר הגן

mic טייטש עשרים וארבע

* מחזור

* מראה המוסר [דר צוכט שפיגל]

שיר היחוד לבני משה (A fragment of a *Sidur* at the Schocken Library, Jerusalem)

Section E: Title pages show a place of printing other than Hanau and questionable dates[21]

fac חמשה חומשי תורה... צאינה וראינה Basel, 1622

mic חמש מגלות והפטרות Part 2 of above; Basel, no date

* תפלות Placed and dated from the attached Psalms, which actually says Prag, 1625

כונות Venice, 1620

סאה סלת Venice, 1579

שיח יצחק Basel, no date

תעלמות חכמה

Including בחינת הדת (Basel, 1629), תעלמות חכמה (Basel, 1629), and נובלות חכמה (Basel, 1631)

20 There are good reasons for assigning the first three titles in Section D to the same printing establishment as the books that I have seen in Section C, but this requires further study.

21 The books in Section E are quite mixed. סאה סלת is different from Hanau and from other books ascribed to Hanau. The *Chumash* (both parts) and תעלמות חכמה are ascribed to Hanau by J. Prijs, *Die Basler hebräischen Drucke* (Olten und Freiburg i. Br. 1964), pp. 475–479. These, כונות and שיח יצחק certainly have some features in common with some books in Sections C and D. It should be noted that books in Sections D and E *may* be further identified when Section C is pinned down; they cannot help at all with the problem of identifying the place of printing of the books in Section C.

ג) ק. מאטשולסקי: וולאדימיר סאלאוויאָוו, לעבן און לערע[50]

די פריינדשאפט פון סאלאוויאוון מיט געצן דויערט ביזן סאמע טויט פון פילאסאף. שוין אין ערשטן בריוו צו אים זאגט ער ארויס זיין טיפע סימפאטיע צום יידיש פאלק. ״די לעצטע צייט האב איך געהאט א געלעגנהייט זיך צו איבערצייגן — שרייבט ער — אז אין דער אקטיווער רוסישער אינטעליגענץ איז דער סאמע ערלעכסטער עלעמענט דאך דער יידישער״. (148)

דער ארטיקל וועגן יידנטום איז איינער פון די געלונגנסטע פון סאלאוויאוון. ער איז געווען דער ערשטער רוסישער דענקער, וועלכער האט דרייסט געלאזט וויסן, אז ״די יידישע פראגע איז א קריסטן־פראגע. נאכן אויפטראט פון סאלאוויאוון איז דער ״אידעאלאגישער אנטיסעמיטיזם״ מער נישט געווען מעגלעך. ער האט פון אים ארונטערגעריסן אלע מאסקעס און אויפגעוויזן זיין אנטיקריסטלעכן, חיהשן כאראקטער. אויף וואס עס זאל זיך נישט ווען עס איז שטיצן די ״קריסטלעכע פאליטיק״, וועט זי זיך נישט קאנען נישט רעכענען מיט סאלאוויאווס אידעען: זיין דרייסטע און ערלעכע האנדלונג האט עפעס־וואס געענדערט אין תוך פון דער קריסטלעכער וועלט. (150)

דער מחבר דערציילט איבער פאקטן פון סאלאוויאווס באציאונג צו געצן: ער האט אים געגעבן רעקאמענדאציע־בריוו צו די צענזארן בעת געץ האט געהאט בדעה ארויסצוגעבן א זשורנאל. ער שיקט אים אויך א פאררעדע צו זיין בוך ״דער באשולדיקטער האט דאסווארט״ אין פארעם פון א בריוו, אין וועלכן ער רייסט ארונטער דעם שלייער פון אנטיסעמיטיזם. אגב איז דאס בוך באלד קאנפיסקירט געווארן און סאלאוויאווס שתדלנות איז געווען אן אומזיסטע.

כדי אפצושאצן די טעטיקייט פון סאלאוויאוון אין שוץ פון די יידן האלט דער מחבר פאר פאסיק צו ציטירן די ווערטער פון געצן, וואס ער האט ארויסגענומען פון געצס ארטיקל (זע אונדזער ביבליאגראפישע נאטע (31). מיר וועלן נאכטאן זיין ביישפיל:

מען קאן אנפעלערדיק פעסטיקן — שרייבט ער — אז זייטן טויט פון לעסינגן איז נישט געווען קיין קריסטלעכער געלערנטער און ליטעראַרישער טוער, וועלכער זאל געניסן פון אזא בכבודיקער באוואונדערונג, פון אזא ברייטער פאפולערקייט און אזא אויפריכטיקער ליבע ביי די יידן ווי וול. ס. סאלאוויאוו און מען קאן פארויסזאגן, אז אויך להבא, צווישן די איידלמוטיקע קריסטלעכע פארטיידיקער פון יידנטום אין איין ריי מיט די נעמען פון אבאט גרעגואר, מיראבא און מאקאליי וועט מיט יראת־הכבוד, מיט ליבע און אנערקענונג אויך דערמאנט ווערן דורכן דאנקבארן יידישן פאלק דער נאמען פון וול. ס. סאלאוויאוו. (151)

50 К. Мочульский, Вл. Соловьев, жизнь и учение, Париж 1951.

די קבלה איז אויפגענומען ווי א דענקמאל, וואס טראגט דעם חותם פון אן אלטער העברעאישער טראדיציע אין באזיץ פון באשטימטע תנכישע אמתן. דאס וואס ציט צו ספעציעל דעם אויפמערק פון פילאסאף איז די דאקטרין פון מאניזם צווישן פארעם און אינהאלט. (41)

די רעעלע און מיסטישע צווישנשייכות, וואס איז פאראן ווי א פארקערפערונג פון אן איינציקן און אבסאלוטן תוכן בילדעט דעם אויסגאנגספונקט און דעם גרונטפרינציפ פון דער קבלה; א באוווסטזיניקער און סיסטעמאטישער אנטראפאמארפיזם איז איר פארענדיקונג. (1896) (42)

ער (סאלאוויאוו — נ.ג.) דערקלערט אין א בריוו פון 1890, אז זיין רוסישע קולטור שטערט אים נישט צו זיין א ייד, וואס דארף ווארשיינלעך מיינען, באזיצן א יידישע מענטאליטעט, וואס איז געווענדעט צו רעאליזירן די רוחניות אין גשמיות. (44)

"און אלע פעלקער פון דער ערד זאלן זיין געבענטשט אין דיר", אזא איז די חתימה פון גאט אויף דעם דאזיקן ערשטן אפמאך פון תנך, אן אפמאך אויסגעדריקט דורך דעם זעלבן ווארט, וועט זיך אנטפלעקן אין דער ברית חדשה, ווו עס רעדט זיך וועגן אוניווערסאליזם. סאלאוויאוו האלט, אז די דאזיקע נבואה גלייך ווי יענע, וואס גאט האט געזאגט צו הגרן, קאן נישט ווערן אויסגעטייטשט דורך קיין שום קריטיק. (147)

לויטן מחבר האלט נישט סאלאוויאוו, אז די סלאוון בילדן א פארזיכיקן טיפ פון ציוויליזאציע. נישט עקאנאמיש, נישט פילאסאפיש, נישט וויסנשאפטלעך און נישט ליטעראריש האבן די רוסן

געשאפן עפעס אריגינעלס, פון וואס עס לאזט זיך ריידן ווי וועגן א טיפ פון ציוויליזאציע, וואס איז אומאפהענגיק פון מערב־אייראפע...

באשטייענדיק אויף א נאציאנאלן עגאאיזם, איזאלירנדיק זיך פון דער קריסטלעכער וועלט, איז רוסלאנד תמיד געוועזן אוממאכטיק ארויסצוגעבן פון זיך עפעס פון גרויסן באטייט. ערשט אין אינטימען הסכם, דרויסנדיק ווי אינעווייניק, מיט אייראפע האט דאס רוסישע לעבן ארויסגעגעבן געשעענישן ווירקלעך גרויסע: "די רעפארם פון פיאטר דעם גרויסן, די פאעזיע פון פושקין" (ציטירט לויט סאלאוויאווס ווערק, באנד 5, ז. 95/96). (201)

סאלאוויאוו קלערט אויף, אז ער האט קיין מאל נישט געהאלטן פאר נישט מאראליש דעם נאציאנאלן פרינציפ, נייערט דווקא דעם נאציאנאליזם, וואס איז נישט עפעס אנדערש, ווי א נאציאנאלער עגאאיזם. (202)

דער קאמף קעגן רעאקציאנערע עלעמענטן, די ארגאניזאציע פון הילף פאר אויסגעהונגערטע באפעלקערונגען, האבן אים דערפירט צו א נייער פארבינדונג, מער אינטימער ווי אמאל, מיט די ליבעראלע מערבניקעס (זאפאדניקי — נ.ג.). (218)

אלגעמיין אנגענומענער אייראפעאישער אוממאראלישער פאליטיק; די יידן ווידער... זיי האבן אלטע חשבונות, און ס'איז גריילעך, אז זיי נוצן אויס די געלעגנהייט, זיי אויסצוגלייכן. אויף אזעלכע דערשיינונגען דארף מען נישט קוקן נאר פון זעפונקט פון די פארגייעוודיקע פאליטישע אינטערעסן פון אותו רגע.

— זייט מוחל, דאס דאזיקע אלגעמיינע...

— איז וואס? דארפן מיר זיך, הייסט עס, לאזן אויפעסן פון פאראייניקטן יידנטום?

— אויב ס'איז פאראן א סכנה פון "ווערן אויפגעגעסן", אין וואס כ'בין נישט זיכער, דארף מען זיך קעגנשטעלן, ווער עס זאל נישט ארויסווייזן אן אפעטיט — יידן צי אנדערע.

— זעט איר דאך! דאס מיינט, אז מען דארף קעמפן?

— יא, נישט מיט אלע מיטלען. צווערשט דארף מען זיין יושרדיק און מענטשלעך אין באצוג צו אלעמען, צו פריינד און שונאים.

— זייט מוחל, דאס דאזיקע אלגעמיינע...

— עס דארף זיין אן אלגעמיינע דערשיינונג; בפרט בנוגע יידן מוז מען אפטער לאזן פילן, אז אומיושר דראט זיי נישט. דעמאלט וועט דערגרייכט ווערן דער שלום-בית, וואס די געשיכטע האט פארהאמעוועט.

— איר נעמט שוין ברייטע ליניעס...

— יא, אין די שמאלע איז מיר ענג — האט גוטמוטיק פארענדיקט דער באשיידענער פילאסאף, האלטנדיק אז דער ענין איז אויסגעשעפט.

דער מחבר גיט צו פון זיך אזא מין אפשאצונג:

עס קאנען זיין כלערליי מיינונגען וועגן דער יידן-פראגע און דעם אופן פון איר לייזונג, עס לאזט זיך אבער אויף קיין פאל נישט לייקענען, אז וואס פאר א ווילטועטדיקע ווירקונג עס אנטהאלט אזא פענאמען ווי וולאדימיר סערגייעוויטש סאלאוויאוו: א פלאמיקער קריסט, א הייסער פארטיידיקער פון קריסטלעכן אמת אין צווישן-מענטשלעכע באציאונגען, וואס וועקט ביי די יידן אומענדלעכן צוטרוי און ליבשאפט צו אים...

ב) ד. סטרעמאאוכאף: וולאדימיר סאלאוויאוו און זיין משיחיש ווערק

סטרעמאאוכאף איז געווען פראפעסאר פון שטראסבורגער אוניווערסיטעט. אים האט אינטערעסירט איין געביט פון סאלאוויאווס שאפונג: זיין משיחיזם, זיין מיסטיק. אין שייכות מיט דעם אספעקט פון זיין טעטיקייט האט דער מחבר נישט געקאנט אויסמיידן יידישע מאמענטן. אייניקע פון זיי דרוקן מיר איבער און שטעלן אין קלאמערן די זייט פון בוך.

הגם סאלאוויאוו רופט נישט אן זיין סיסטעם מיט נאמען משיחיזם, אידענטיפיצירט ער די קריסטלעכע אידעע מיט דער משיחישער, וואס גיט אונדז דאס רעכט צו קוואליפיצירן זיין קאנצעפציע פון קריסטנטום ווי א משיחישע.(9)

סאלאוויאוו... טראכט אז די רעליגיע פון פרייעם גייסט האט זיך אין אלטערטום ווידער באוויזן נאר ביים יידישן פאלק... דער יידישער מאנאטעאיזם, באטראכט ווי גאר א ספעציעלער פענאמען... (30)

גערייצטקייט אויסהערן אויף א ביטערן אמת פון א מענטשן, אין וועמענס גוטפריינדשפט זיי זיינען איבערצייגט.

. . . .

מיר איז אויך אויסגעקומען בייצוזיין ביים ווייטערדיקן כאַראַקטעריסטישן סכסוך וולאַדימיר סאָלאָוויאָווס אין שייכות מיט דער דרייפוס־אַפערע. אַן אָנהענגער פון פראַנצייזיש־רוסישן בונד און פאַרערער פון דער רומפולער פראַנצייזישער אַרמיי האָט געפרעגט דירעקט:

— צי האַלט איר אַז דרייפוס איז שולדיק?

— איך ווייס נישט — האָט סאָלאָוויאָוו געענטפערט — היות פון סאַמע אָנהייב איז דער ענין געווען בכיוון פאַרפּלאָנטערט און מ׳האָט ביי דרייפוסן צוגערויבט די יורידישע גאַראַנטיעס, וואָס יעדער באַשולדיקטער האָט נייטיק, נאָר דערפאַר, ווייל ער איז אַ ייד און ס׳איז געשטאַנען אין קאָן דער כבוד פון אַ מיליטערישער אינסטיטוציע. דערנאָך זיינען די יידן און מענטשן, וואָס פילן זיי מיט אויך אַריינגעפאַלן אין אַן אָנקעריקן פּאַרטייאישן עקסטרעם; סוחרישע אונטערנעמונגען די א.ג. צייטונגען, האָבן אָנגעהויבט אַזאַ באַרג מיט אויסטראַכטענישן און ליגנס, אַז איצט איז שוין שווער זיך צו דערגרונטעווען צום אמת. פון דער ערשטער ביז דער לעצטער מינוט איז דאָס נישט קיין משפט נאָר אַ פּאַרטייקאַמף...

— נאָר דערלויבט! די דאָזיקע אַפערע האָט אויפגעטרייסלט אַ גאַנצע גרויסע מלוכה, האָט אויפגעבראַכט גאַנץ אייראָפּע! גיט אַ טראַכט, צי וואָלט נישט געווען איינפאַכער עס זאָל אומקומען איין מענטש. אַפילו ווען זיין שולד איז נישט אין גאַנצן באַוויזן, איידער אַ גאַנץ לאַנד מיט אַ פילמיליאָניקער באַפעלקערונג זאָל ליידן צוליב אים?..

— דאָס האָב איך דערוואַרט און כ׳שטרייך עס באַלד אונטער! ס׳איז אַ פאַטאַלע איראָניע פון גורל, וואָס אין ענין דרייפוס זיינען די קריסטן געניגט צו טראַכטן, ווי די יידישע היפּאָקריטן און פּרושים בנוגע קריסטוסן: בעסער זאָל אומקומען איין מענטש איידער עס זאָל ליידן און זיין אומרואיק אַ גאַנץ פאָלק. דאָס איז אַ מאַטעמאַטישע, אָבער נישט אַ קריסטלעכע אויסרעכענונג. אַ מענטשלעכע פּערזענלעכקייט איז דאָך אַן אומבאַדינגטע ווערדע — און מקריב זיין זי אַפילו צוליב אַ רואיקייט פון אַ גאַנץ פאָלק איז בשום אופן נישט דערלאָזלעך.

— אָבער איר זייט מודה, אַז דער צד פון דרייפוסן האָט אונטערגענומען אַ גאַנצע אַגיטאַציע?

— אוודאי, דאָס איז אין אָרדענונג. היות מ׳האָט דערצו דערפירט איז די אַגיטאַציע אַ באַרעכטיקטע.

— דאָס איז אַ טיפּישע דייטש־יידישע אינטריגע!

— ס׳איז נישט באַוויזן, נאָר כ׳נעם אָן...

— און וואָס?

— און גאָרנישט.

— וואָס הייסט?

— גאַנץ איינפאַך. אויב עס איז אַזוי, פירט זיך דייטשלאַנד אין הסכם מיט דער

ביז גאר אינטערעסאנט און רירנדיק איז וולאדימיר סערגייעוויטשס באציאונג צו יידן. ער געפינט, אז א פאלק, וואס איז אין לויף פון פיל יארהונדערטער געווען דער פאקל־טרעגער פון מאנאטעאיזם און געגעבן דער וועלט נביאים, האט צוגעגרייט דעם באדן פארן קריסטנטום און איז אויסדערוויילט געווארן דורך דער השגחה עליונה צו פארקערפן דעם גאט־מענטשן — אזא פאלק קאן נישט ווערן באטראכט ווי אבסאלוט שלעכט אדער שעדלעך און אומצוטריטלעך פארן קול פון אמת. און נאך דעם, ווי דאס דאזיקע פאלק, וואס האט געהאט אויסצושטיין דעם פארדינטן כעס פון גאט, איז געווארן צעזייט איבער דער גאנצער וועלט און האט אנגעהויבן צו ליידן פון דעמאראליזירנדיקע רדיפות, האט עס דאך נישט אויפגעהערט ארויסצוגעבן נאבלע דענקערס און בולטע פארשטייערס פון קונסט.

....

מיר איז אמאל אויסגעקומען צו זיין אן עדות פון זיין (סאלאוויאווס — נ.ג.) פאלעמיק מיט אן אנטיסעמיט דערביי, אויף וויפל מיר דוכט, האט דער פארשטארבענער וולאדימיר סערגייעוויטש דעמאלט פארמולירט זיינע אנשויאונגען גלונגענער אפילו איידער אין די ארטיקלען, וואס באהאנדלען די דאזיקע טעמע. איך דערמאן מיך ווי ער האט געזאגט בערך אזוי:

— איך פארשווייג נישט די יידישע חסרונות נישט די נייטיקייט זיי צו בזייטיקן. היות אבער די פרווון צו היילן די דאזיקע דעפעקטן דורך שנאה, חוזק אדער דיסקרימינאציע האבן דערגרייכט א קאפויערדיקן רעזולטאט — באקומט זיך אז מען דארף האנדלען אנדערש. אין אונדזער געזעלשאפט לאזט זיך מערקן א צווייאיקע באציאונג צו יידן: איינע געפינען, אז אלץ יידישע איז עקלדיק, אלע יידן — אומדערטרעגלעך און דעריבער... מאלע וואס צו וועלכע אויספירן קאן מען זיך דערקייקלען ארויסגייענדיק פון אזא זעפונקט. די אנדערע, וועלכע קערעווען זיך מיט קאסמאפאליטישן און מאראלישן גלייכגילט, פסקנען אז אלץ איז וווּיל און אז די חסרונות וואס מען שרייבט צו די יידן ווי אויך זייער שעדלעכע השפעה אויפן לעבן פון ארומיקע אז דאס אלץ זיינען פוסטע מעשיות און דעריבער איז דאס בעסטע, וואס מען קאן טאן פארן לייזן די יידן־פראגע איז צוגעבן, אז זי עקסיסטירט נישט. דיביידע מיינונגען — האט סאלאוויאוו געזאגט — האלט איך פאר נישט ריכטיקע. מען דארף נישט פארהוילן וועמענס ס'זאל נישט זיין פעלערן, נישט מגזם זיין, פאראלגעמיינערן אדער צושפיצן זיי, נייערט איז נייטיק משפיע צו זיין אויף זיי מיט דערציערישע מיטלען. יעדע קריסטלעכע מדינה... איז א דערציערישע אינסטיטוציע. די באזע ווידער פון יעדער דערציאונג קאן זיין נאר ליבע און קעגנזייטיקער צוטרוי. און וועגן דעם דארף מען קודם כל געבן א טראכט. די פיל־דורותדיקע יידישע געשיכטע האט אין זיי אויסגעבילדעט יענע נערוועזע שטימונג, וואס מערסטן טייל שליסט זי אויס צוטרוי צו ווערטער פון אנדערש גלייביקן, אפילו ווען ער איז גוטסגינעריש. דער פועל יוצא איז, אז צו ערשט דארף מען צורעכטשטעלן די "מאראלישע פארבינדונג", כדי שפעטער גענעזעריש משפיע צו זיין אויף דער יידישער סביבה. די יידן וועלן דעמאלט אן

האבן פאר דער אנטיסעמיטישער אגיטאציע. פון דער צווייטער זייט ווערט זיך דאס רוסישע פאלק דער דאזיקער אגיטאציע נישט אונטערגעבן.

ווען סאלאוויאָוו איז אין זומער 1900 געשטארבן האט אים באווײנט די גאנצע יידישע באפעלקערונג. אין די לעצטע טעג פון זיין לעבן זאל סאלאוויאָוו האבן געבעטן זיינע ארומיקע: "שטערט מיר צו שלאפן, צווינגט מיך צו טאן תפילה פארן יידישן פאלק, איך מוז בעטן פאר אים" און ער האט אויף לשון קודש געזאגט תהלים.[49]

די יידישע פרעסע אין אלע שפראכן האט וועגן אים געשריבן, אין די שולן האט מען אפגעריכט תפילות, די געזעלשאפטלעכע אינסטיטוציעס האבן ארגאניזירט פארלעזונגען איבער דער פערסאנאליטעט פון פארשטארבענעם. די געזעלשאפט "מפיצי השכלה" האט איר ערן־מיטגליד באערט מיט א הספד, אין וועלכן עס האבן גענומען א חלק דער רב ד"ר דראבקין, נ. אי. באקסט, מ. אי. קולישער אונטערן פארזיץ פון באראן האראצי א. גינזבורג. אויף סאלאוויאָווס נאמען זיינען באשטימט געווארן 4 סטיפענדיעס און אין לאקאל פון דער ביבליאטעק האט מען אויפגעהאנגען א פארטרעט פון וולאדימיר סערגייעוויטש סאלאוויאָוו.

4. רוסישע שרייבערס וועגן סאלאוויאָווס נייגונג צו יידישקייט

אין די ביזאיצטיקע אויספירן האבן מיר געהערט די שטימע פון סאלאוויאָוון אליין און פון יידישע מחברים וועגן אים. אין דאזיקן כאר פעלן נאך אפשאצונגען פון דער רוסישער ליטעראטור וועגן סאלאוויאָווס פאראינטערעסירונגען מיט דער יידישער פראגע אין דער קעגנווארט, ווי אויך מיט פראבלעמען פון יידישקייט און יידישן פאלק בכלל. א פאר אלגעמיינע ארויסזאגן זיינען ציטירט געווארן אין אריינפיר. דא ווילן מיר זיך אפשטעלן אויף א פאר שרייבערס,ועמענס צושטייער דערגאנצט אונדזערע ידיעות איבערן יידישן אספעקט פון סאלאוויאָווס טעטיקייט, כדי צו ווארפן אן אלזייטיק ליכט אויף דער פערסאנאליטעט פון סאלאוויאָוון אין די ראמען פון אונדזער טעמע. צו דעם צוועק וועלן מיר זיך באנוגענען מיט ציטאטן און קורצע אנאליזן פון עטלעכע מחברים בלויז, כדי נישט צו באלאסטן דעם דאזיקן עסיי מיט איבערחזרונגען, וואס לאזן זיך אין אזא פאל נישט אויסמיידן. דער סדר פון די מחברים איז א כראנאלגישער.

א) וו. ל. וועליטשקא: וולאדימיר סערגייעוויטש סאלאוויאָוו. לעבן און שאפונג

דער מחבר איז געווען א פערזענלעכער פריינד פון סאלאוויאָוון. אין זיין בוך, וואס איז דערשינען אין יאר 1902 אין פעטערבורג, געפינען מיר פאראלעל מיט אפשאצונגען אויך באריכטן וועגן סאלאוויאָווס ארויסזאגן איבער יידישע פראבלעמען, וואס ער האט אליין געהערט. די דאזיקע גבית עדותן בילדן פאקטיש דאקומענטן פון דער ערשטער האנט.

אין איצטיקן פאראגראף ציטירן מיר גאנצע אפזאצן פון בוך צווישן די זייטן 89—94.

49 זע 38.

גייסטיקע פעאיקייטן און דעריבער בילדן זיי א קאנקורענץ פאר דער איינגעווארצלטער באפעלקערונג. דעם איינציקן מיטל פון קעגנווירקן זעען זיי אין א לעגאלער באגרענעצונג פון יידישער קאנקורענץ־פעאיקייט, כדי צו פארהאלטן זייער באוועגונג פארויס. דער דאזיקער מיטל רופט זיך באיקאט. סאלאוויאוו גיט צו אז

די דאזיקע כלומרשטע פאטריאטן פארגעסן אין גאנצן נישט בלויז די לערעס פון הומאניזם און מענטשן־ליבע, נאר זיי היטן אפילו נישט אפ די סאמע עלעמענטארסטע פרינציפן פון רעכט און יושר. זיי ווילן נישט וויסן, אז הגם די עווענטועלע קולטורעלע העכערקייט פון די יידן איז נאך בכלל נישט קיין באוויזענער פאקט, קאן זי אבער נישט דינען ווי א מין בארעכטיקונג (קארפוס דעליקטי) פארן צוריבן די אינטעגראלע מענטשלעכע און בירגערלעכע רעכט ביי א פילמיליאניק פאלק, וואס טראגט אויף זיך אלע מלוכהשע פליכטן באגלייך מיט דער איבעריקער באפעלקערונג פון לאנד און וואס איז נישט באגאנגען קיין שום פארברעך...[46]

די "פאטריאטן" רעכענען זיך אויך נישט מיטן וויל פון לאנד און זיין גוטן נאמען. אזא קינסטלעך אטראפירן פון א גאנצער נאציע, וואס איז א טייל פון דער מלוכה שאפט א פאראזיטישן גליד אין מלוכהשן ארגאניזם און דאס וועט זיך מוזן נוקם זיין אין דער מלוכה גופא. מיט אלע זיינע כחות באקעמפט סאלאוויאוו אזא דיסקרימינאציע. דאס איז אן אנטי־קריסטלעכע טענדענץ פון נאציאנאליזם, וואס וועט זיך אויסווירקן נישט בלויז אויף די יידן נייערט אויך אויף אנדערע נאציאנאליטעטן און ראן דערפירן צו אינטערנאציאנאלע קאמפליקאציעס:

א געזונטע פאליטיק איז קודם־כל א קונסט צו פארווירקלעכן אויפן בעסטן אופן מאראלישע צילן אין נאציאנאלע און אינטערנאציאנאלע ענינים. דעריבער דארף דער לייטנדיקער מאטיוו פון דער פאליטיק זיין נישט נאציאנאלער אייגננוץ און זיכיקייט נייערט פליכט און פאראנטווארטלעכקייט.[47]

א פאלק איז נאר א טייל פון דער מענטשהייט, מיט וועלכער עס איז מחויב צו זיין סאלידאריש. דער היפוך פון דעם איז דער פאלשער פאטריאטיזם, וועלכער אונטער דער מאסקע פון ליבע צום פאלק באפעסטיקט דעם נאציאנאלן עגאאיזם, ד.ה. אז ער ווינטשט דעם פאלק שלעכטס און איילט צו זיין אונטערגאנג. און

כל זמן מיליאנען רוסישע איינוווינער וועלן צוליב פאלשע פאליטישע מאטיוון... זיין מיט געוואלד איזאלירט פון דער איבעריקער באפעלקערונג און אונטערגעווארפן א נייעם מין פון פארקנעכטונג, כל זמן דער סיסטעם פון פארברעכערישע שטראפן וועט באדראען רעליגיעזע איבערצייגונגען... אזוי לאנג וועט רוסלאנד אין אלע זיינע ענינים פארבלייבן מאראליש געפענטעט און גייסטיק פאראליזירט.[48]

סאלאוויאוו האט געטרייסט זיין פריינד געץ פארזיכערנדיק אים, אז דאס יידישע פאלק, וואס האט אזוי פיל דורכגעמאכט אין זיין געשיכטע, האט נישט וואס מורא צו

46 דארט, ז. 193.

47 דארט, ז. 194.

48 דארט, ז. 196.

אויף דער עסטרייכישער גרענעץ האב איך געהאט א געלעגנהייט זיך צו איבערצייגן אויף אייגענער דערפארונג וועגן דער ווירקונג פון חילול השם־פרינציפ ביי יידן. היינו: אן עלטערער ייד טוישט מיר רוסיש געלט אויף עסטרייכיש דורכן פענצטער פון וואגאן. מיט א מאל רירט זיך דער צוג פון ארט און דער ייד דערצאלט מיר נישט עטלעכע גילדן. דער ייד קומט צו לויפן צו דער נאענטסטער סטאנציע און ברענגט מיר דאס איבעריקע געלט טענהדיק, אז ער וויל נישט איך זאל האבן א גרונד פירצוווארפן א יידן אפנארעריי.[43]

נישט געקוקט אויף זיין שטעקן אין די פילאסאפיש־טעאלאגישע פראבלעמען איז סאלאוויאוו נישט אפגעריסן פון דער רעאלער ווירקלעכקייט. ער שרייבט צו דעם זעלבן אדרעס אט וועגן די באשולדיקונגען קעגן די יידן אין עקספלואטאציע און וואכער. פאררופנדיק זיך אויף קאטקאווס ארטיקלען וועגן יידן שרייבט ער, וואס מיר וויסן אויך פון אנדערע מקורים:

> שכרות איז אין מערבדיקן לאנד נישט בלויז נישט גרעסער, נייערט פיל ווייניקער אנטוויקלט איידער אין איבעריקן טייל פון רוסלאנד און די פויערים דארט לעבן אין פארגלייך פיל בעסער, נישט ערגער; אין מערבדיקן לאנד הערשט באמת א שרעקלעכע ארעמקייט, אבער דאס איז נישט קיין פויערישע ארעמקייט נאר א יידישע...

ער גיט צו: "צו די דאזיקע ווערטער פון קאטקאוון קאנען זיך נישט אונדזערע אנטיסעמיטן באציען ווי זיי וואלטן זיך באצויגן, למשל, צו מיינע מיינונגען".

סאלאוויאוו זאגט ווייטער, אז מען וואלט אפשר באדארפט שטעלן די פראגע, צי קאטקאוו זאגט דעם אמת. מען פארנעמט זיך איצט זייער פיל מיט יידן־סטאטיסטיק, מען האט אבער בלויז פארגעסן אנצוווענדן א פארגלייכנדיקע סטאטיסטיק צווישן די מערבדיקע אוןווארצלדיקע גובערניעס. די אנטיסעמיטן מיידן אויס די דאזיקע פארגלייכן, אבער די פארשונגען פון באקאנטן סטאטיסטיקער בליאך, גיען אליין און טשיטשערין באשטעטיקן קאטקאווס אפשאצונגען. טשיטשערין צ.ב. איז געווען פארוואלטער פון צוויי גיטער, איין אין טאמבאווער און דאס צווייטע אין פאלטאווער גובערניע און ער באשטעטיקט, "אז אין צווייטן (ד.ה. דארט ווו די יידן האבן וווינרעכט — נ.ג.) זיינען די פויערים רייכער און פארמעגלעכער און די באדינגונגען זיינען בעסערע".[44]

די יידן עקספלואטירן די פויערים, נישט ווייל זיי זיינען יידן, נאר ווייל "געלט הערשט אומעטום". אבער נישט די יידן האבן אויסגעטראכט די הערשנדיקע סיסטעמען.

מען באשולדיקט די יידן אין נאציאנאליזם און קאסמאפאליטיזם — צוויי באצייכענונגען, וואס זיינען זיך סותר. "וווהין האט זיך אפגעווייטערט דער כח פון קריסטלעכן אוניווערסאליזם, ווען מען שטעלט אנטקעגן דעם שמאלן נאציאנאליזם, עגאאיזם פון יידן?"[45]

פאטריאטן־נאציאנאליסטן זאגן, אז די יידן האבן א העכערע קולטור און גרעסערע

43 זע 31, ז. 184.
44 דארט, ז. 187.
45 דארט, ז. 190.

א יאר שפּעטער שרייבט סאָלאָוויאָוו אין אַ בריוו:

עס זיינען שוין פאַרביי צען יאָר זינט "דער פאָטער פון שקר" האָט אויפגעוועקט אין אונדזער געזעלשאַפט די אַנטיסעמיטישע באַוועגונג. פאַר דער צייט איז מיר אויסגעקומען אַ פאַר מאָל אָנצוּווייזן (פריער פון דער קאַטעדרע און שפּעטער אין דער רעליגיעזער און וועלטלעכער פּרעסע) אויף יענעם אומספּקדיקן אמת, אַז די יידן־פראַגע איז קודם כל אַ קריסטן־פראַגע. די פראַגע באַשטייט דווקא אין דעם אויף וויפל די קריסטלעכע געזעלשאַפטן זיינען פעאיק זיך צו פירן אין דער פּראַקטיק לויט די פּרינציפּן פון דער עוואַנגעלישער לערע, וואָס זיי נעמען אויף מיט ווערטער... ווער עס פּרעדיקט אַ כוללדיקע שנאה צו אַ גאַנץ פאָלק, ווייזט ער במילא אַז דער קריסטלעכער קוקווינקל איז אים מער נישט מחייב.[42]

אויף אַ פאַרשלאַג פון דער צייטונג "מאָסקאָווסקיע וועדאָמאָסטי" מיטצואַרבעטן, ענטפערט סאָלאָוויאָוו מיט אַ באַדינג, די רעדאַקציע זאָל אים נישט שטערן צו שרייבן אין שוץ פון יידן. היות די רעדאַקציע איז אויף דעם נישט איינגעגאַנגען האָט ער זיך אָפּגעזאָגט פון מיטאַרבעט אַרויסזאָגנדיק דערביי אַ מיינונג, אַז די פרישע רעדאַקציע וויל נאָכטאָן דעם שלעכטן ביישפּיל פון קאַטקאָוון (אַ באַרימטער זשורנאַליסט־אַנטיסעמיט — נ.ג.) און ביי אַ געלעגנהייט אַריינשפּאַנען אין לאַגער פון די יודאָפאָבן. ער האַלט, אַז צו די עבֿרות פון רוסלאַנד געהערט די באַציאונג צו יידן, וועמען "מיין פעדער איז שטענדיק גרייט צו פאַרטיידיקן".

די יידישע געזעלשאַפטלעכקייט האָט פּאָזיטיוו אָפּגעשאַצט סאָלאָוויאָווס באַציאונג צום יידישן פאָלק. די "חברה מפיצי השכלה" האָט אים אויסגעוויילט פאַר אַן ערן־מיטגליד (1894) און ווען זי גייט אַרויס אַ זאַמלונג לטובת איר שול גיט סאָלאָוויאָוו זיין צושטייער. ער איזאויך באַטייליקט אין דער יידישער היסטאָריש־עטנאָגראַפישער געזעלשאַפט. פאַר גענצן איז סאָלאָוויאָוו אין זיין באַציאונג צו יידן אַ יחיד במינו אין רוסלאַנד און ער שטעלט זיך די פראַגע, וואָס האָט אים געבראַכט צו זיין תמיד גרייט צו קעמפן לטובת די יידן. דעם ענטפער געפינט ער אין אַ בריוו פון 8טן מערץ 1891, וווּ סאָלאָוויאָוו ציטירט אַ זאָץ פון נביא יחזקאל וועגן אַ פליכט צו וואָרענען אַ בעל־עבֿירה.

סאָלאָוויאָוו זוכט באַקאַנטשאַפט מיט יידן, ער לייענט יידישע פּרעסע. אין די יידן זעט ער די פאַרקעמפער פאַר גייסטע און אידעאַלע ווערטן. אין אַ שמועס מיט גענצן האָט ער זיך אַמאָל אַרויסגעזאָגט וועגן יידישער "פּחדנות", וועלכע ער האַלט פאַר אַן אויסגעטראַכטע." די ערשטע קריסטלעכע מאַרטירערס און דאָס יידישע פאָלק — דאָס זיינען קלאַסישע מוסטערן פון קעמפער פאַר פרייהייט פון געוויסן, ביי זיי דאַרפן מיר זיך לערנען ווי אַזוי צו פאַרטיידיקן אייגענע איבערצייגונגען". ער באַדויערט נאָר, וואָס צווישן די יידן זיינען פאַראַן גלייכגילטיקע צו די דאָזיקע ווערטן און זיי זיינען נישט ראוי צו זיין נאָכפאָלגערס פון די אבֿות. אויסער דער אַזוי צו זאָגן היסטאָרישער סיבה זיך אָנצונעמען די יידישע קריוודעס זיינען געווען אויך אַנדערע, סוביעקטיווע: ער האָט געהאַט אַ חוש פאַר יושר, אַ נאָבל געוויסן און אַ גוט האַרץ. אין אַ בריוו פון זאַגרעב צו גענצן (6 יולי 1888) שרייבט ער מיט פרייד וועגן אַ פאַל, ווו יידן זאָרגן ס'זאָל נישט קומען צו חילול השם:

42 Восход, 13 августа 1900.

סאלאוויאווס אני מאמין בנוגע יידן ווערט פארשטענדלעך ווען ער זאגט:

איינע באטראכטן מיך ווי א אוהב ישראל, אנדערע טאדלען מיך פאר מיין בלינדער סימפאטיע צו יידישקייט... כ׳בין אבער א בעלן צו וויסן, אין וואס באשטייט מיין יידן־פריינדשאפט אדער מיין יידישקייט־סימפאטיע? צי פארשווייג איך דען זייערע חסרונות אדער בארעכטיק זיי? איך פארבארג נישט, אז דער גורל פון יידישן פאלק גייט מיך שטארק אן, אבער דאס איז דערפאר, ווייל ער איז פאר זיך אליין אין א העכסטער מדרגה אינטערעסאנט און באלערעוודיק אין פיל שייכותן. און וואס כ׳נעם מיך א מאל אן פאר יידן? יא, נאר כ׳באדויער וואס נישט אזוי אפט ווי איך וואלט וועלן און ווי כ׳בין מחויב צו טאן ווי א קריסט און א סלאוו: ווי א קריסט, בין איך מודה, אז איך בין די יידן שולדיק א גרויסן דאנק, ווייל מיין אויסלייזער איז געווען א ייד, יידן זיינען אויך געווען די נביאים און אפאסטאלן און דער ווינקלשטיין פון דער אלגעמיינער קירכע איז גענומען געווארן אין דעם בית־ישראל; ווי א סלאוו טראג איך א גרויסע שולד לגבי די יידן און כ׳וויל זי אויסקויפן מיט וואס איך קאן.[39]

ער באדויערט וואס די רוסישע אינטעליגענץ טוט ווייניק לטובת די יידן. זיך אליין האלט סאלאוויאוו פאר א נישט גענוגנדיקן אויטאריטעט אויף צו נעמען די איניציאטיוו אין דעם זין, אבער ער איז גרייט אונטערצושרייבן יעדן פראטעסט קעגן יידן־רדיפות. אים האט מען נישט געדארפט בעטן, ווייל ער האט דאס געהאלטן פאר זיין מאראלישן חוב. ערשט אין 1890 האט ער רעאגירט אויף דער צארישער אנטי־יידישער פאליטיק און צוזאמען מיטן ענגלישן פראפעסאר דילאן, אנגעשריבן א פראטעסט, וואס איז געווען פארעפנטלעכט אין די לאנדאנער "טיימס" פון 10טן דעצעמבער 1890.[40] לעוו טאלסטאי, צו וועמען סאלאוויאוו האט זיך געוואנדן וועגן א חתימה, האט געענטפערט מיט א בריוו, אין וועלכן מיר לייענען:

איך ווייס פון פאראויס, אז אויב איר, וולאדימיר סערגייעוויטש, וועט אויסדריקן דאס, וואס איר טראכט וועגן דאזיקן ענין, וועט איר פאר איין וועגס אויסדריקן אויך מיינע געדאנקען און געפילן, ווייל דער גרונד פון אונדזער עקל צו די מעטאדן, מיט וועלכע מען אונטערדריקט די יידישע נאציע, איז איינער און דער זעלבער: דער באוווסטזיין פון ברידערלעכער פארבינדונג מיט אלע פעלקער און אוודאי און אוודאי מיט די יידן, פון וועמענס מיט עס קומט ארויס קריסטוס און וועלכע האבן אזוי פיל געליטן און ליידן נאך פון פאגאנישער איגנאראנץ מצד די אזוי גערופענע קריסטן.

פארשטייט זיך אז דער דאזיקער ענטפער האט סאלאוויאוון שטארק דערפרייט. אים האט אויך הנאה געטאן א בריוו פון קאראלענקא, טשיטשערין א״א, וועלכע ער האט גערן געוויזן אלעמען. טאלסטאי איז געווען דער ערשטער, וואס האט געחתמעט און צוזאמען מיט אים איבער הונדערט שרייבערס און פראפעסארן.[41]

39 זע 30.

40 אסיע לאמונאווא, הונדערט יאר "אנא קארענינא", מאסקווע, סאוועטיש היימלאנד, נומער 2, 1974.

41 זע 31.

פארטיפן זיך אין דער תלמודישער ליטעראטור אדער אין פירושים אויפן תנך האבן אים נישט אפגעוווענדט פון אקטועלן מצב פון יידישן פאלק, וועמענס סיטואציע האט אים פארשאפט זארגן און אויף וועלכער ער פלעגט רעאגירן.

וועגן דער זייט פון סאלאוויאווס באציאונג צו דער יידישער פראגע לייענען מיר ביי גרוזענבערגן: "אויב דער רואיקער טעארעטיקער־אידעאלאג קאן בלייבן א גלייכגילטיקער עדות פון די ליידן פון א גאנץ פאלק, קאן נישט דער פובליציסט־בירגער און האט קיין רעכט נישט זיך נישט אנצונעמען פאר די געטרעטענע רעכט פון אן אונטערדריקטער נאציע", און ער ציטירט סאלאוויאווס ארויסזאג:

> ווען עס גייט נישט אין טעארעטישע אידעען, נאר אין א פראגע, וועמענס אזא אדער אנדערע לייזונג האט דירעקטע פראקטישע קאנסעקווענצן פאר א גרויסער צאל פון לעבעדיקע מענטשן, ווען דער טריאומף אדער דורכפאל פון א באשטימטער מיינונג איז פארבונדן מיט א וווילטאג אדער אומגליק פון אנדערע נאענטע, — אין אזא פאל איז דער פילאסאפישער אביעקטיוויזם און גלייכוואג אין גאנצן נישט אויפן ארט; דא פאדערן שוין זייערע רעכט הן דער מאראלישער אויפברויז און הן די רעליגיעזע דבקות; דאס איז שוין נישט גענוג אויפצוקלערן דעם אמת נאר מען מוז אן רחמנות דעמאסקירן דעם שקר.[35]

אין הסכם מיט דער שטעלונג פארעפנטלעכט ער א ריי ארטיקלען און ארבעטן, וועגן וועלכע מיר ריידן אויף אן אנדער ארט.

דערוויסנדיק זיך פון די צייטונגען וועגן די פאגראמען אין רוסלאנד, שרייבט ער פון זאגרעב צו געצן: "די ידיעה וועגן נייע פאגראמען האט מיר פארשאפט עגמת־נפש... ווי זשע גיט מען זיך אן עצה מיט אט דער צרה".[36] אויף דער ידיעה וועגן איינפירן די פראצענט־נארמע רעאגירט ער אין א בריוו מיט די דאזיקע ווערטער:

> איך גרייט צו צום דרוק אויף פראנצייזיש אן אפהאנדלונג וועגן די עיקרדיקע פארפליכטונגען פון רוסלאנד... איינע פון די דאזיקע פארפליכטונגען איז דאס אנערקענען פון פולע בירגערלעכע רעכט פאר די רוסישע יידן... אויב איר וועט געפינען אז איך קאן טאן נאך עפעס, וואס זאל דינען דעם דאזיקן ענין, מעגט איר, קאנענדיק מיינע געפילן צו אייער פאלק, זיין זיכער, אז פאר יעדן אנוויז וועל איך אייך זיין דאנקבאר.[37]

אין די 80ער יארן "ווען די פראפאגאנדע פון מענטשן־שנאה, גאווה און עם־הארצות האבן לכתחילה טריאומפירט פראקלאמירנדיק זיך פאר די איינציקע געזעצלעכע אויסדרוקן פון רוסישע פרינציפן", האט אפגעהילכט די שטימע פון סאלאוויאוון אין זיין ארטיקל "רוסלאנד און אייראפע", ווו ער זאגט, אז טאלעראנץ און רעליגיעזע פרייהייט שטעלן מיט זיך פאר אזא וואגיקע און דרינגענדיקע נויטוועדיקייט פארן איצטיקן רוסישן לעבן, ווי מיט זיך 40 יאר צוריק איז געוועזן די נויטוועדיקייט צו באפרייען די פויערים.[38]

35 דארט.

36 זע 31, ז. 160.

37 דארט.

38 Восход No 69, 3 сентября 1900.

אַפּט ציטירט און וואָס מיר ווילן נישט איבערחזרן. מיר וועלן אין איצטיקן קאַפּיטל רעזומירן דער עיקר די אָפּהאַנדלונגען פון פ. געץ, מיט וועמען סאָלאָוויאָוו איז געווען יאָרנלאַנג פאַרבונדן, בפרט נאָך אַז מיר טרעפן דאָרט אויטענטישע אַרויסזאָגן פון אים ווי אויך אויסצוגן פון זיינע בריוו צום מחבר איבער דער טעמע, וואָס אינטערעסירט אונדז. מיר וועלן פון דעסט וועגן נישט פאַרנאַכלעסיקן אויך אַנדערע מקורים. כדי צו דערגרונטעווען און פריי ריידן וועגן געטלעכער אַנטפּלעקונג ווי וועגן אַ היסטאָרישן פאַקט, צו דיסקוטירן וועגן רעליגיעזע סודות און קירכלעכע קאָנפליקטן, און דערצו נאָך ריידן מיט טאַלאַנט פון פילאָסאָפישן זעפּונקט — צו דעם פאָדערט זיך ערודיציע, דיאַלעקטישע פעאיקייטן, אָבער אויך טיפער גלויבן און מאָראַלישע געוואַגטקייט צו פאַרטיידיקן אייגענע מיינונגען.

די ערשטע אַרבעטן פון סאָלאָוויאָוו איבער טעאָלאָגישער ליטעראַטור, געשיכטע פון פילאָסאָפיע און נאַציאָנאַלער פראַגע האָבן אים געפירט צו פאָרשונגען איבערן גורל פון יידנטום און יידישער ליטעראַטור. באַציענדיק זיך געוויסנהאַפטיק און ערנסט צו זיינע פאָרשונגען, זוכט סאָלאָוויאָוו אַ קאָנטאַקט מיט אַ מענטשן, וועלכער זאָל אים עפענען די טויערן פון תלמוד. דער ערשטער ייד, מיט וועמען ער באַקענט זיך אין יאָר 1879, איז פ. ב. געץ, אונטער וועמענס לייטונג ער לערנט תנך, העברעאיש אא״וו. סאָלאָוויאָוו באַגנוגנט זיך נישט מיט עטימאָלאָגישן און גראַמאַטישן אַנאַליז פון טעקסט, נאָר הויפּטזאַכלעך אינטערעסירן אים די קאָמענטאַרן פון די תלמודישע און רבנישע מפרשים. סאָלאָוויאָוו פלעגט טייל מאָל קומען צו גיין אַרום 10 אוונט און זיך פאַרזיצן ביז 2 פאַר טאָג, כדי צו שטודירן דעם תנך און די מפרשים. זיינע תנך קענטענישן האָבן אים צוגעהאָלפן ביים שרייבן געוויסע אַרבעטן. סאָלאָוויאָוו האָט דורכשטודירט די מסכתא ״אבות״, ״עבודה זרה״, ״יומא״, ״סוכה״ און זייער פיל געלייענט וועגן דער תלמודישער ליטעראַטור, אין וועלכער ער דרינגט אַריין, כדי בעסער צו פאַרשטיין די גייסטיקע קרובהשאַפט צווישן די איסיים און די גרונדלייגערס פון קריסטנטום און במילא שוין די ברית החדשה. לויט אים איז קיין ספק נישטאָ, אַז די איבערוויגנדע פאָרעם פון עוואַנגעלישע דרשות פאַרמאָגט נישט קיין קריסטלעכע ספּעציפישקייט; דאָס איז אַ פּשוטע פאָרעם פון תלמודישע אגדות.[33]

דאָס קריסטנטום האָט געשעפּט זיין רעליגיעזע מאַכט און לעבנס־חכמה פון די צדוקים, די תורה אין איר פּראַקטישער אָנווענדונג — פון די פרושים און דעם אויסקוק אויף מלכות אל — פון די איסיים.

אין איינעם פון זיינע בריוו צו געצן שרייבט סאָלאָוויאָוו:

> אַ חוץ דער תורה און היסטאָרישע ספרים האָב איך איבערגעלייענט אַלע נביאים און גענומען לייענען תהלים. איצט, געלויבט איז גאָט, קאָן איך כאָטש טיילווייז מקיים זיין מיין חוב פון רעליגיעזער ערלעכקייט, צוגעבנדיק צו מיינע טעגלעכע תפילות אויף העברעאישע פסוקים.[34]

זיינע פאַראינטערעסירונגען מיט יידישע ענינים האָבן זיך נישט באַגרענעצט בלויז צו דער א.ג. ״וויסנשאַפט דעס יודענטומס״, ווי דאָס האָט זיך געראָפן אין דייטשלאַנד. דאָס

33 זע 31, ז. 167.
34 זע 30.

עמנו־אל

מיט אונדז איז גאט! ניט אינעם הימלבלא דעם קלארן,
ניט הינטער גרענעצן פון וועלטאלן אן א צאל,
ניט אין יארהונדערטער, וואס שלאפן אין זכרון,
ניט אין דעם בײַזן פלאם און ניט אין שטורעמס קול.

ער איז אט דא, אט איצט — און אויב דו ווייסט עס גלייביק
אין לעבנס מוטנעם שטראס פון צופאל און באראט,
באגליקט דיך דאס געהיימעניש: מיר זיינען אייביק!
קיין שליטה האט ניט מער דאס שלעכטס. מיט אונדז איז גאט!

דער סנה

. . . .
מיין זינד איז גרויס. נאר א גייסט א נייער
אין מיר זינט נעכטן פלאמט און יערט:
דער דערנערקוסט. וואס ברענט אין פייער,
וואס ברענט און ווערט ניט פארט פארצערט.
איך האב דערהערט: "מיין פאלק, א דארן
ביסט דו אין שונא'ס אויג אצינד.
נאר כ'האב ביי אייביקייט געשווארן —
דיין הייליקייט ניט מער פארשווינדט.
א, ציטערט, געטער פון מצרים,
ווי רויק איז אייער רום — נאר זע,
עס בליט ישראל איצט פון נייעם,
ווי ס'גליט דער ברענענדיקער סנה!"

3. יידישע מקורים וועגן סאלאוויאווס באציאונג צו דער יידן־פראגע

פון יידישע מקורים וועגן סאלאוויאוון פארדינט אונדזער אויפמערק דער ווייטערדיקער צעטל פון ארטיקלען, וועמענס מחברים עס זיינען געווען גרוזענבערג,[30] געץ[31] און א פאר אנאנימען אין "וואסכאד" אין שייכות מיטן טויט פון פילאסאף.[32] פארשטייט זיך אז אלע מחברים זיינען אייניק אויף איינס, אז סאלאוויאוו האט אויסגעדריקט מער ווי פיל אנדערע שרייבערס זיין באציאונג צו יידן און צום יידנטום אין זיינע שריפטן, וואס ווערן

30 Семен Грузенберг, Соловьев В.С., Евр. Энциклопедия.
31 Ф. Гец, "Об отношении В.С. Соловьева к еврейскому вопросу," Вопросы философии и психологии, год 12, книга 1 (56), янв. 1901, Москва, 159—198.
32 Восход, 3 и 13 августа 1900.

איבער ווידער א מאל אין א נעקראלאג נאכן טויט פון זיינס א פריינד יוסף בן דוד ראבינאוויטש. ראבינאוויטש איז געווען א ייד, וועלכער האט זיך געשמדט אויס איבערצייגונג און אויפגעשטעלט אין קישינעוו א בית־תפילה אין נאמען פון ישו און עס אנגערופן "בית־לחם".

די יידן, פארשטייט זיך, האבן אים פארשאלטן, אבער סאלאוויאָוו האט געגלייבט, אז ער האט געהאנדלט אין הסכם מיט זיין איבערצייגונג און געזען אין אים אן אנזאגער פון א נייער תקופה, ווען עס וועלן זיך פארווישן די אונטערשיידן צווישן רעליגיעס און דער הויכער עטישער ניווא וועט אלעמען אויסגלייכן.

אין דערמאנטן נעקראלאג שרייבט סאלאוויאָוו, אז ראבינאוויטש איז, נישט געקוקט אויפן שמד, געבליבן א ייד. ביי דער געלעגנהייט רעכנט זיך סאלאוויאָוו ווידער א מאל אפ מיט דער קריסטלעכער וועלט, שרייבנדיק:

> מיט וואס פאר א רעכט (נישט געבנדיק אליין קיין ביישפיל) וועלן מיר דאס (דעם שמד — נ.ג.) פארלאנגען פון אלע יידן אדער אפילו פון א מערהייט פון זיי אדער נאר פון א קליינער מינדערהייט? עס איז באשיימפערלעך, אז דאס יידנטום זעט אין דער קריסטלעכער וועלט נאר דאס, וואס די וועלכע באטראכטן זיך פאר קריסטן ווייזן זיי אין דערווירקלעכקייט. עס וואלט געווען א צו מאדנע פאנטאזיע צו דערווארטן, אז די יידן זאלן, מאסנווייז און אויס אויפריכטיקער איבערצייגונג אריבערגיין צום קריסטנטום, ווי צו א רעליגיע פון ליבשאפט בעת עס קומען פאר פאגראמען און ביים אקאמפאניאמענט פון קריסטלעכע אויסרופן: "א טויט די יידן! שלאגט די יידן!"[28]

ו. לידער

אין זיינע ארטיקלען און רעצענזיעס איז סאלאוויאָוו באריידעוודיק. ער שטעלט זיך נישט אפ ביז ער שעפט נישט אויס אלע ארגומענטן, וואס דארפן בארעכטיקן זיין קאנצעפציע.

אנדערש זיינען זיינע לידער.[29] זיי זיינען געפאסט און דריקן אויס זיינע מיינונגען, האפענונגען, אידעאלן.

די זאמלונג נעמט ארום אריגינעלע לידער ווי אויך איבערזעצונגען פון דער וועלט־ליטעראַטור. צווישן די איבערגעזעצטע מחברים געפינען זיך דאנטע, פלאטאן, מיצקעוויטש, פעטראַרקא א"וו.

מיר האבן נישט בדעה צו געבן אן אפשאצונג פון זיין פאעטישער שאפונג. צום איצטיקן קאפיטל, ווו מיר באהאנדלען סאלאוויאָווס "יידישע" שריפטן פאסן זיך אריין די ווייטערדיקע לידער, וואס מיר ברענגען אין דער איבערזעצונג פון מ. ליטווין, וועלכער האט זי צוגעגרייט ספעציעל פאר דער דאזיקער אפהאנדלונג. מיר דריקן אים אויס אונדזער אויפריכטיקן דאנק.

28 סאל., באנד VIII, ז. 442—444.

29 Стихотворения Владимира Соловьева, С.Петербург 1900.

דאס יידישע יאגן זיך נאך געלט איז א פועל יוצא פון אייער ציוויליזאציע. ווען מיר זיינען געווען אומאפהעגניק האבן מיר געשמט מיט אונדזער רעליגיע, נישט מיט געלט, מיטן בית המקדש און נישט מיט דער בירזשע.

אלץ וואס מיר פארמאגן גוטס נעמט זיך פון אברהמען און משהן, אלץ שלעכטע אין אונדזער נאטור און לעבן איז א רעזולטאט פון אונדזער צופאסן זיך צו דער געזעלשאפט אין וועלכער מיר לעבן. און דאך זיינען מיר געבליבן געטריי צו אונדזער תורה און אויפגעהיט סאלידארישקייט פון איינעם צום צווייטן ווי אויך גוטע משפחה — מידות. צוניפשמעלצן זיך מיטן קריסטנטום וואלט פאר אונדז באטייט, פארלירן אונדזערע מאראלישע יסודות און נישט באקומען פאר זיי קיין קאמפענסאציע. ביי אונדז האט דער סנהדרין באשטימט דריי כללים, וואס דארפן אויספילן דאס מענטשלעכע לעבן: תורה, עבודה ומעשים טובים. מיר טיילן זיי נישט אפ, טעאריע גייט מיט פראקטיק האנט ביי האנט. ביי אייך איז די טעאריע אפשר א גוטע, זי שטימט אבער נישט מיט דער ווירקלעכקייט. איר אלע, קריסטן, מיינט אז אזוי דארף זיין. לויט אייך קאן דאס אידעאלע נישט זיין פראקטיצירט און די פראקטיק קאן נישט זיין אידעאל. מיר זיינען פרינציפיעל קעגן אזא אויפפאסונג. איינס פון די ביידע: לאזט זיך אייער רעליגיע רעאליזירן — טא זייט איר די ערשטע צו געבן א גוטן ביישפיל; לאזט זי זיך נישט רעאליזירן — איז זי א פוסטע, אומבאגרינדעטע פאנטאזיע.

נאך דעם לאנגן, אויסגעטראכטן מאנאלאג גיט סאלאוויאוו צו אין נאמען פון די קריסטן, אז זיי האבן נישט קיין רעכט צו פאדערן די יידן זאלן זיך אפזאגן פון צוקונפטיקן מלכות־משיח, אויב זיי קאנען זיי נישט פארזיכערן א איצטיקע. דער עיקר חסרון פון דער אידעע צו פאראייניקן ביידע גלויבנס איז נישט אזוי "די צו שטארקע ווירקעוודיקייט פון תלמוד ווי די נישט גענוגנדיקע ווירקעוודיקייט פון דער עוואנגעליע".[26]

דער ארטיקל פארענדיקט זיך מיט אזא מין סך הכל:

> פון אונדז אליין, און נישט פון די יידן, איז אפהענגיק די געוואונטשענע לייזונג פון דער יידן־פראגע. צווינגען די יידן זיך אפצוזאגן פון תלמודישע געזעצן זיינען מיר נישט בכוח, אבער אנווענדן לגבי זיי עוואנגעלישע געבאטן איז שטענדיק אין אונדזער מאכט. עס זיינען פאראן צוויי מעגלעכקייטן צו פארענטפערן די יידן־פראגע: זיינען די יידן נישט אונדזערע שונאים — איז דאך במילא קיין יידישע פראגע נישט בנמצא; זיינען זיי יא אונדזערע שונאים — אין אזא פאל איז דאס באציען זיך צו זיי אין גייסט פון ליבע און שלום איז די איינציקע קריסטלעכע לייזונג פון דער יידן־פראגע.[27]

ה. י. ד. ראבינאוויטש

פון די ציטירטע שריפטן, בפרט פון דער לעצטער, איז בולט קלאר סאלאוויאווס קאנצעפציע וועגן דער פאראייניקונג פון פארשיידענע גלויבנס. זיין מיינונג חזרט ער

26 סאל., באנד VI, ז. 29.
27 דארט.

שמועסן מיט לייבן.[25] די באשולדיקונג פון די אנטיסעמיטן איז ווייט פון זיין אמתדיק. נישטא אין תלמוד קיין געזעצן וועגן נישט־יידן.

נאך דעם דאזיקן אריינפיר רעדט סאלאוויאוו וועגן צוויי אנטיסעמיטישע ביכער: איינס פון פראפ. ראלינג, "דער תלמוד־יודע", און דאס צווייטע פון ד"ר יוסטוס (א פסעוודאנים), "דער יודענשפיגעל". בכלל איז אויסגעוואקסן אין די לעצטע יארן פון 19טן י.ה. א ברייטע פאלעמישע ליטעראטור וועגן יידן. סאלאוויאוו פאררופט זיך אין זיין ארטיקל אויף אכט ביכער פון וועלכע די מחברים זיינען יידן (2), קריסטן (3) און אנטיסעמיטן (3). די דאזיקע פארטיילונג שטאמט פון סאלאוויאוון, וועלכער באטראכט נישט, ווארשיינלעך, די אנטיסעמיטן פאר קריסטן. ער אנאליזירט די ציטירטע, דורך די מחברים, טעקסטן און געפינט אויס, אז זיי זיינען פאלסיפיצירט און די מחברים — אומקאמפעטענטע. עס וואלט אים געוווּנדערט, ווען דער שולחן ערוך, וואס איז אויפגעקומען אין 16טן י.ה., זאל טראקטירן די יידן און נישט־יידן אויף דעם זעלבן אופן, בעת אין די קריסטלעכע לענדער, אין די סאמע פארגעשריטענע, צייגט די עמאנציפאציע פון אלע בירגער נישט מער ווי א פאר צענדליגנ יארן.

דער מחבר הייבט ארויס דריי פרינציפן פון יידנטום: 1. קדוש השם — אן אידעאל פאדערונג, 2. חילול השם — אן איסור, אויב די טואונג פון מענטשן קאן דערפירן צו חילול השם און 3. דרכי שלום.

סאלאוויאוו שטעלט זיך אריין אין דער לאגע פון די יידן און פירט אן אויסגעטראכטן מאנאלאג, וועמען ער אדרעסירט צו דער קריסטלעכער וועלט:

אויב איר קריסטן ווילט, אז די יידן זאלן נישט זיין איינגעעקשנט אין זייער נאציאנאלער אייגנקייט, שטעלט זיי אנטקעגן אייערע, אן אלגעמיין רעליגיעזע, אבער נישט אין ווערטער בלויז, נאר אין מעשים. אויף סתם רעליגיעזע דרשות קאנען אייך די יידן ענטפערן, אז דאס קריסטנטום ווי א רעליגיע דארף זיין א לעבנס־סיסטעם און נישט א סיסטעם פון טעאלאגישע געדאנקען. מיר יידן משפטן וועגן א בוים נישט לויט דער גרייס פון זיין האלצלייב אדער דער שיינקייט פון זיינע בלעטער, נייערט לויטן טעם און נארהאפטיקייט פון זיינע פרות. אזוי האט אויך געטראכט קריסטוס.

וואס האט דאס קריסטנטום אויפגעטאן אויפן סאציאלן געביט? די קירכע באריימט זיך, אז זי האט באקעמפט די שקלאפעריי. אבער דאס האט שוין מיט 1500 יאר פאר איר געטאן משה איינפירנדיק שמיטה־ און יובל־יארן.

די קריסטלעכע אידעע רייסט ארונטער די קנעכטשאפט, אבער פראקטיש איז זי אפגעשאפן געווארן אין 18טן און 19טן י.ה. גראד ווען דער כוח פון דער קירכע איז אפגעשוואכט געווארן. דאס זעלבע איז נוגע דעם סיסטעם פון פייניקונגען אין דער יוסטיץ.

מיר יידן געדענקען ווי דאס האט אויסגעזען אין די צייטן פון געצנדינעריי און זעען א קנאפן אונטערשייד מיט דער איצטיקייט.

איר בעט צו גאט פון אמת און ליבע, אבער איר דינט דעם גאלדענעם קאלב, וואס אירווארפט אונדז פיר. דער טיפישער דינער פון גאלדענעם קאלב אין דער ליטעראטור איז נישט שיילאק (ביי שעקספירן) נאר דער "קאַרגער ריטער" (פושקין).

25 שאול מ. גינסבורג, היסטארישע ווערק, באנד 3, ניו יארק 1937, צווי רעליגיעזע מארטירער.

סכאלאסטישן באלאסט און דער א.ג. לערע פון די קירכע־פּאַטערס און מען ראט זיי זיך אומצוקערן צו דער ריינער עוואַנגעליע ווי למשל די מאלאקאנער־סעקטע.

לויט אים איז דער תלמוד "דער ליטעראַרישער אויסדרוק פון יענער ארגאנישער פארמע, וואס האט זיך אויסגעבילדעט אין לויף פון פיל יארהונדערטער דורכן לעבן פון יידישן פאלק נאכן פארלירן די פאליטישע אומאפהענגיקייט".[22]

ווייטער דערציילט ער די געשיכטע פון תלמוד, זיין באגרינדונג און מאכט דעם אויספיר אז "די רעליגיעז־נאציאנאלע באזונדערקייט פון יידנטום איז א דאנק דעם תלמוד פארזיכערט געווארן אויף פיל יארהונדערטער".[23]

דער מחבר ברענגט אויסצוגן פון תלמוד, וואס מאכן בולט דעם מאראלישן גייסט פון דאזיקן דענקמאל. די תורה, שרייבט סאלאוויאוו, איז געגעבן געווארן פאר מענטשן, נישט פאר מלאכים. דער תלמוד זאגט זיך נישט אפ פון פולקומקייט ווי א ציל, ווי א מאראלישער אידעאל, אבער כדי אים צו דערגרייכן דארף מען זארגן פארן וועג, וואס פירט צו אים. דער וועג אבער ציט זיך דורך נישט פולקומע מענטשלעכע נאטורן.

ווונדערלעך קלינגט אין אונדזערע אויערן די אפשאצונג פון דעם פלאץ, וואס די יידישע געשיכטע פארנעמט אין גערעם פון אלגעמיינער געשיכטע. סאלוויאוו זאגט ווארט־ווערטלעך: "דורכגייענדיק די גאנצע געשיכטע פון דער מענטשהייט פון סאמע אנהייב ביז צו אונדזערע טעג (וואס מען קאן נישט זאגן וועגן אנדערע פעלקער) שטעלט דאס יידנטום מיט זיך פאר א מין אקס פון דער אלוועלטלעכער געשיכטע".[24] האבנדיק דאס אין זין, ווונדערט זיך סאלאוויאוו ווי אזוי קאן מען פירווארפן די יידן דאס פעלן פון פאטריאטיזם פאר א לאנד, בעת זיי זיינען פאטריאטן פון יידישן פאלק.

קאמיש קלינגען אויך אין זיינע אויערן די פירווארפן אין קאסמאפאליטיזם לגבי דעם איינציקן פאלק, וואס האט זייט די עלטסטע צייטן, נישט געקוקט אויף רדיפות, אפגעהיטן זיין נאציאנאלע אייגנקייט און אין דער זעלבער צייט באשולדיקט מען דאס דאזיקע פאלק אין נאציאנאלער איזאלירטקייט.

ביידע באשולדיקונגען זיינען פאלש. יידן האבן זיך אונטערגעווארפן פרעמדע השפעות און אפילו געביטן ס׳לשון: זיי האבן גערעדט אין בבל — ארמיש (תרגומיש ווי עס שלאגט פאר מאקס וויינרייך), אין אלעקסאנדריע — גריכיש, אין קארדאבע — אראביש, אין מזרח־אייראפע — יידיש און האבן אומעטום זיך גערופן מיט פרעמדע נעמען. מען זאגט, אז זיי זיינען פיאנערן פון ליבעראליזם. א שאד, וואס ביי אונדז האבן זיי נישט געהאט קיין השפעה!

די יידן שעפן זייערע אידעען פון דער תורה, דעריבער האלט מען זיי פאר אפגעשטאנענע. די אנטיסעמיטן באשולדיקן דעם תלמוד, וואס הייסט פיינט האבן גוים. עס וואלט נישט געווען קיין ווונדער ס׳זאל זיין אזוי. ווייניק האבן די יידן זיך אנגעליטן? אין 1738 האט מען אין פעטערבורג פארברענט אויף א שייטער א יידן לייב בארוכאוו און א רוסישן אפיציר וואזניצין, ווייל דער לעצטער האט זיך מגייר געווען א דאנק די

22 דארט, ז. 2.
23 דארט, ז. 8.
24 דארט, ז. 15.

אינטערעסאנט לאז איך זי אדורך, ווייל זי ווייכט אפ פון אונדזער טעמע. איך וויל בלויז אנווייזן געוויסע שטעלעס זיינע, וואס כאראקטעריזירן זיין אפשאץ פון יידנטום.

עס איז אן אנספקדיקער פאקט, אז א קליינע און דערצו א צעדרויבלטע נאציע האט איבערגעלעבט אין די אמאליקע צייטן — און דאס מיט א געווין פאר זיך, מיט אינעוויייניקסטן וווקס און דערהייבונג — אזעלכע היסטארישע קאטאסטראפעס, פון וועלכע עס זיינען אין רעזולטאט פארשוונדן אומפארגלייכלעך שטארקערע, באהאפטענע און קולטורעלע נאציאנאלע גופים. הייסט עס, דאס יידישע פאלק האט דאס דורכגעלעבט נישט א דאנק א מאטעריעלן נייערט א גייסטיקן כח. אט דער גייסטיקער כח איז גאנץ באשטימט פארבונדן מיט דער נאציאנאלער רעליגיע, היות קיין אנדערער באטייטיקער אויסדרוק פון נאציאנאלן גייסט איז ביי די יידן נישט געווען...

אין דער רעליגיע פון די יידן איז געווען עפעס גרעסערס ווי די אויבנאויפיקע נאציאנאלע פארמע, ס'איז געווען א מין אינעוויייניקסטע העכערקייט, א דאנק וועלכער עס האט זיך פארפעסטיקט דער גייסט פון פאלק, וואס איז געווארן פעאיק איבערצולעבן דעם חורבן פון זיין פאליטישן גוף. אט דאס גרעסערע, וואס טיילט אויס די נאציאנאלע רעליגיע פון די יידן אין פארגלייך מיט אלע איבעריקע און וואס קומט דער עיקר צום אויסדרוק ביי די נביאים, איז געווען נישט אן אבסטראקטע אידעע פון מאנאטעאיזם, נייערט א לעבעדיק באוווסטזיין און געפיל, אז דער באזונדערער גאט, וועלכער איז די השגחה עליונה פון גאנצן פאלק און פון יעדן באזונדער איז אויף ראשית־כל אן אלוועלטלעכער גאט, וועלכער האט אלץ אין זיין מאכט, ושנית, אז ער איז נישט בלויז דער גאט פון כח נאר אויך דער גאט פון אמת, נישט דעם אבסטראקט־געדאנקלעכן, נייערט דעם רעאל ווירקנדיקן און ממשותדיקן.[21]

מאכנדיק אן אויספיר פון זיינע ארגומענטן שרייבט סאלאוויאוו, אז די נביאים האבן געלעבט א טייל פאר גלות בבל, א טייל בעתן גלות בבל, אין הסכם מיט דער טראדיציע און פארשונגען. דער תנך, בפרט די נביאים, זיינען א נביאישער אויסדרוק פון העכסטן און ריינסטן גייסטיקן כח, וואס ווירקט אין דער מענטשהייט.

ד. דער תלמוד און די נייסטע פאלעמישע ליטעראטור וועגן אים אין עסטרייך און דייטשלאנד

אין אריינפיר צום ארטיקל רוקט סאלאוויאוו ארויס דעם יידן־פראבלעם, וועגן וועלכן מען זאגט, אז ער וואלט געקאנט לייכט געלייזט ווערן ווען די יידן זאגן זיך אפ פון תלמוד, וואס נערט זייער פאנאטיזם און שטארקט זייער איזאלירטקייט; זיי וואלטן געדארפן זיך באגנוגענען בלויז מיט דער תורת משה ווי די קראימער.

אויף דעם ענטפערט סאלאוויאוו מיט א קעגן ארגומענט און פרעגט וואס וואלטן די רוסן געענטפערט, ווען מען הייסט זיי זאלן זיך אפזאגן פון זייערע קירכלעכע כללים, פון

21 דארט, ז. 540.

דער טייל יידן, וואס לעבט אויף דער טעריטאָריע פון דער רוסישער אימפּעריע איז דער שטאַרקסטער יידישער שבט און וועט קאָנען אויף דעם אופן דערפילן א וויכטיקע שליחות.

ב. די יידן, זייער תורה און מאראל

דער דאזיקער ארטיקל איז א קורצע, אבער אומרחמנותדיקע קריטיק פון א שטודיע, וואס עס האט אנגעשריבן א געוויסער ס. יא. דימינסקי אויף דער דערמאנטער טעמע. די ארויסגעבער האלטן דעם מחבר פון בוך פאר א גאר גרויסן בקי. סאלאוויאָוו מאכט א גענויעם אנאליז פון בוך, באווייזט אז דער מחבר האט דעם תלמוד קיין מאל פאר די אויגן נישט געהאט און אז די ציטאטן, וואס ער ברענגט זיינען פאלשע. דעם אויספיר פון סאלאוויאָוון גיבן מיר איבער אין גענויער איבערזעצונג, כדי דער לייענער אליין זאל זען זיין באציאונג צו די קרייזן, ווו אזא ליטעראטור גילט פאר א גוטער סחורה.

פון דעם אויבן געזאגטן, מיין איך, איז גענוג קלאר, אז די ארויסגעגעבענע דורך אומבאקאנטע פארשוינען שריפט פון דימינסקין פארמאגט נישט ווי איין יידישן טעקסט, אפילו נישט אין אן איבערזעצונג, און עס ווערט בולט די פולע עם־הארצות פון מחבר אין יידישע כתבים בכלל און אין תלמוד בפרט. זי פארדינט אפשר בלויז אן אויפמערק ווי אן עדות פון קולטור־ניוואָ פון דער חברה, ביי וועלכער דער דאזיקער אומגעלומפערטער און גראָביאַנישערפאמפלעט גייט אן פאר א באטייטיקער און למדנישער פארשונג.[20]

ג. ווען האבן געלעבט די יידישע נביאים?

אין פראנצייזישן זשורנאל "רעווי דע דע מאָנד" (Revue des Deux Mondes) און דערנאך אין א סעפאראטן אפדרוק איז דערשינען א בראשור וועגן די נביאים: ערנסט האווע, "דער מאדערניזם פון די נביאים", פאריז, 1891. סאלאוויאָוו דערציילט גענוי איבער דעם אינהאלט פון דער דאזיקער ארבעט און פאלעמיזירט מיטן מחבר, וועלכער גיט אן די כראנאלאגיע פון די נביאים א פיל שפעטערע, ווי דאס איז אנגענומען.

האווע אליין איז זיך מודה, אז קיין העברעאיש קען ער נישט און אז ער האט "א גאַנץ יאָר" שטודירט די דאזיקע טעמע און געגעבן אפילו א קורס. שוין פון דעם אליין איז צו זען, מיינט סאלאוויאָוו, אז די ארבעט איז נישט קיין ערנסטע.

סאלאוויאָוו ווארפט אפ די טעזע, אז דאס **גאַנצע פאָלק** אין פאלעסטינע האט גערעדט גריכיש און אז העברעאיש איז שוין געווען א טויטע שפראך. ער פרעגט באלד פון וואנען האבן זיך גענומען די נביאישע ווערק, וואס זיינען געשריבן אין העברעאיש. א משל, **עלעהיי עמעץ זאל היינט צו טאג אין רוסלאנד זיך נעמען שרייבן אין אלט־**סלאוויש לשון. סאלאוויאָוס קריטיק איז א צעשמעטערנדיקע. ער פאררופט זיך אויף די נביאים, ציטירט זיי אין אריגינאל און קאמענטירט זיי. הגם די גאנצע פאלעמיק איז

20 סאל., באנד VI, ז. 345—346.

צו דער פֿראַגע נומער 2: די ייִדן האָבן אָפּגעוואָרפֿן די לערעס פֿון קריסטוסן, ווײַל אין אַלעמען זוכן זיי אַ רעזולטאַט און טראַכטן וועגן אַ קאָלעקטיווער פֿאַראייניקונג מיט גאָט. זיי האָבן נישט געקאָנט פֿאַרשטיין די נויטווענדיקייט פֿון אַן אינדיווידועלן וועג צום דאָזיקן ציל.

די קריסטלעכע לערע וועגן אַלמענטשלעכער ברודערשאַפֿט איז אין ייִדישע אויגן צו ברייט און נישט רעאַל, אַבסטראַקט. פֿון דער צווייטער זײַט, דאָס פֿאַרבינדן די אַלוועלטלעכע אויסלייזונג מיט איין פּערסאָן — יעזוסן — זעט בײַ זיי אויס צו שמאָל, אומבאַגרינדעט און נישט גענוגנדיק. דעריבער זעען די פּראַקטישע און רעאַליסטישע ייִדן אין קריסטנטום אַ נישט רעאַלע און במילא אַ פֿאַלשע אידעע. איבערצייגן זיי קאָן מען בלויז מיט פֿאַקטן, ד.ה. דורך רעאַליזירן די קריסטלעכע אידעען. אַזוי־אַרום איז די ייִדן פֿראַגע אַ קריסטן פֿראַגע.[18]

צו דער פֿראַגע נומער 3: בײַ ייִדן האָט די נבואה געהאַט אַ גרעסערן באַטײַט ווי מלכות און כהונה. דאַ גייט סאָלאָוויאָוו אַריבער צו ריידן וועגן רוסלאַנד און פּוילן, זייערע רעליגיעס ווי אויך וועגן דער נאַציאָנאַלער פֿראַגע. לויט אים קאָן פּוילן דינען פֿאַר אַ בריק צווישן מזרחדיקן און מערבדיקן קריסטנטום.

נאָך די דאָזיקע באַטראַכטונגען שטעלט ער די פֿראַגע צי זײַנען ייִדן אַ שעדלעכער און פּאַראַזיטישער עלעמענט אין רוסיש־פּוילישן לאַנד. ער ענטפֿערט זיך אַליין, אַז אויב ייִדן האָבן בײַ אומגינציקע אומשטענדן געקאָנט באַהערשן די שטעט אין מערב־רוסלאַנד, איז דאָס אַ סימן אַז זיי זײַנען פֿעאיקער איידער דאָס רוסישע פֿאָלק אָדער די פּוילישע שליאַכטע צו בילדן אַ שטאָטיש־אינדוסטריעלן קלאַס.

אומעטום אויף דער וועלט עקספּלואַטירט דער אינדוסטריעלער קלאַס דעם פּויער אַנשטאָט אים צו העלפֿן; טוען עס די ייִדן אויך. צו לאַנג זײַנען זיי געווען אויף דער לערע בײַ דער פּוילישער שליאַכטע, בײַ די פּוילישע פּאַנעס, וועלכע האָבן אונטערדריקט סײַ דעם ייִדן און סײַ דעם פּויער. אויב די פּויערים נייטיקן זיך אין די ייִדן און טאָלערירן זיי איז דאָס מחמת זייער סאָציאַל־עקאָנאָמישער אומבאַהאָלפֿנקייט. דאָס איז אָבער נישט די שולד פֿון די ייִדן. דער פּויער גייט בעטן בײַם ייִדן הילף, ווײַל די אייגענע העלפֿן אים נישט. אויב דער ייִד העלפֿנדיק דעם פּויער עקספּלואַטירט אים אין איין וועגס, טוט ער עס נישט מחמת דעם וואָס ער איז אַ ייִד, נאָר ווײַל ער איז אַ געלטמענטש, און געלט־ענינים באַשטייען אין אויסנוצן איינע דורך די אַנדערע. נישט די ייִדן האָבן זיך געשטעלט פֿאַר אַ ציל פֿון זייער עקאָנאָמישער טעטיקייט דאָס באַרײַכערן זיך און נישט די ייִדן האָבן אַ מחיצה צווישן עקאָנאָמיק און רעליגיעז־מאָראַלישע פּרינציפּן. דאָס האָט די אויפֿגעקלערטע אייראָפּע אײַנגעפֿירט אין דער סאָציאַלער עקאָנאָמיק אַנגעטלעכע און אוממענטשלעכע פּרינציפּן, און טענות צוליב דעם האָט מען צו די ייִדן, וועלכע פּראַקטיצירן זיי. אדרבה, זאָל די קריסטלעכע וועלט ווײַזן אַ בײַשפּיל, פֿאַראייניקן די קירכעס, שאַפֿן אַ קריסטלעכע מלוכה און אויפֿשטעלן אַ געזעלשאַפֿט אויף קריסטלעכע יסודות, וועלן די ייִדן זען אַז די זאַך איז ערנסט און בײַטראָגן אויך זייער צושטייער.[19]

18 דאָרט, ז. 143
19 דאָרט, ז. 165.

"מיר זיינען מחויב" — שרייבט ער — "צו זיין איינס מיט די יידן נישט אפזאגנדיק זיך פון קריסטנטום, נישט קעגן קריסטנטום, נאר אין נאמען און צוליב דעם קריסטנטום; און די יידן זיינען מחויב צו זיין איינס מיט אונדז נישט קעגן יידישקייט נאר אין נאמען און צוליב דער אמתדיקער יידישקייט. מיר זיינען דערפאר אפגעזונדערט פון די יידן מחמת מיר זיינען נאך נישט קיין פולקומע קריסטן און זיי זונדערן זיך אפ פון אונדז מחמת זיי זיינען נאך נישט קיין פולקומע יידן".[16] קריסטוס אליין איז געווען א ייד פון בלוט און פלייש. שוין צוליב דעם אליין שניידט אין די אויגן דאס פאראורטיילן דאס גאנצע יידנטום דווקא אין נאמען פון קריסטוסן. גרינגשאצן דאס יידנטום איז נאריש; זידלען זיך מיט זיי איז אומנוציק; בעסער וועט זיין זיי צו פארשטיין, הגם דאס איז שווערער.

אין המשך פון זיין ארבעט שטעלט סאלאוויאוו דריי פראגעס:

1. פאר וואס איז קריסטוס געווען א ייד און ביי יידן איז אויפגעקומען די וועלטקירכע?

2. פאר וואס האבן די יידן נישט אנערקענט דעם משיחן און מיידן אויס א קריסטלעכן טעמפל?

3. פאר וואס געפינט זיך דער שטארקסטער טייל (אין רעליגיעזן זין) פון יידנטום גראד אין רוסלאנד און פוילן?

אט זיינען די ענטפערס:

צו דער פראגע נומער 1: די יידן בילדן א רעליגיעז פאלק. זיי פארמאגן א נאציאנאלן באוווסטזיין און זיי זיינען מאטעריאליסטן. זייער מאטעריאליזם דריקט זיך אויס אפילו אין זייער שריפט: זיי נוצן בלויז קאנסאנאנטן, ווייל אויס שפארזאמקייט אין אותיות האבן זיי נישט אויסגעבילדעט קיין וואקאלן.

ווי אזוי קאנען הויזן אין איין ייד די דערמאנטע דריי שטריכן: א רעליגיעזע אידעע, א נאציאנאלער באוווסטזיין מיט א נארמאלער מענטשלעכער טעטיקייט און דער יידישער מאטעריאליזם? דאס איז מעגלעך ווייל

> די רעליגיע דארף זיין נישט א פארניכטונג פון מענטשן אין דער אוניווערסאלער גאטהייט, נייערט א פערזענלעכע קעגנזייטיקייט צווישן געטלעכן און מענטשלעכן איך. גראד דערפאר וואס דאס יידישע פאלק איז פעאיק געווען צו פארשטיין אויף אזא אופן גאט און רעליגיע האט עס געקאנט ווערן א פון גאט אויסדערוויילטע פאלק.[17]

עס קומט נאך א גאנצע מסכתא וועגן יידישער געשיכטע, רעליגיע, תפילות, וואס האבן משפיע געווען די יידן זאלן זיין אזוי. אפילו דער יידישער מאטעריאליזם איז אנדערש פון פראקטישן מאטעריאליזם און פון וויסנשאפטלעך־פילאסאפישן פון גריכיש־רוימישן מקור: ער איז א רעליגיעזער. יידן אנערקענען נישט קיין אידעאל, וואס איז נישט בכוח גובר צו זיין די ווירקלעכקייט און זי איבערגעשטאלטיקן. צוליב די אויסגערעכנטע מעלות איז ישראל געווארן דאס אויסדערוויילטע פאלק און ישו איז דא געקומען אויף דער וועלט.

16 Сол., т. 4, Еврейство и христианский вопрос, с. 123.

17 דארט, ז. 128.

ג. ווען האָבן געלעבט די ייִדישע נביאים (1896);
ד. דער תּלמוד און די נײַסטע פּאַלעמישע ליטעראַטור וועגן אים אין עסטרײַך און דײַטשלאַנד.

2. סאָלאָוויאָווס "ייִדישע" שריפֿטן

איידער מיר וועלן איבערדערציילן, וואָס אַנדערע האָבן געשריבן אין מאָנאָגראַפֿיעס, אָפּהאַנדלונגען און זכרונות וועלן מיר מאַכן אַ קורצן סך־הכּל פֿון עטלעכע זײַנע שריפֿטן, וואָס האָבן אַ דירעקטע שײַכות צום ייִדנטום.

א. דאָס ייִדנטום און די קריסטלעכע פֿראַגע

די ייִדן האָבן זינט תּמיד און אומעטום געקוקט אויפֿן קריסטנטום און זיך באַנומען לגבי אים אין הסכּם מיט די פֿאַרשריפֿטן פֿון זייער רעליגיע, לויט זייער גלויבן און לויט זייער תּורה. די ייִדן האָבן זיך צו אונדז באַצויגן תּמיד ווי ייִדן.

דאַקעגן מיר, די קריסטן, פֿאַרקערט; ביז איצט האָבן מיר זיך נישט אויסגעלערנט צו באַציִען צום ייִדנטום ווי עס פּאַסט פֿאַר קריסטן.

זיי האָבן, וואָס שייך אונדז, קיין מאָל נישט עובֿר געווען אויף זייערע רעליגיעזע געזעצן, מיר אָבער האָבן תּמיד עובֿר געווען, און טוען דאָס נאָך ווײַטער, לגבי זיי אויף די אָנווײַזן פֿון דער קריסטלעכער רעליגיע.

אויב עס איז נישט גוט צו זײַן געטרײַ אַ שלעכט געזעץ, איז נאָך ערגער צו זײַן אומגעטרײַ צו אַ גוט געזעץ. אַנשטאָט זיך צו מודה זײַן אין דעם, זוכן מיר אויף וועמען אַרויפֿצוּוואַרפֿן די שולד פֿאַר אונדזער האַנדלונג. פֿריִער זײַנען געווען שולדיק דער מיטלעלטערלעכער פֿאַנאַטיזם, די קאַטוילישע קירכע. אָבער איצט רודפֿט מען די ייִדן בײַ אונדז און מיר וואַרפֿן אַרויף די שולד אויף די קרבנות גופֿא: זיי פֿירן זיך ייִדישמעסיק — דאַרפֿן מיר, כּלומרשט, האַנדלען ווי געגן־דינערס; זיי ווילן אונדז נישט ליב האָבן — דאַרפֿן מיר זיי האַסן; זיי איזאָלירן זיך — דאַרפֿן מיר זיי אויסוואָרצלען.

נישט אומעטום רודפֿט מען די ייִדן. אין ענגלאַנד פֿאַרנעמען זיי אַ גאָר אָנגעזען אָרט. די שׂנאה צו ייִדן נעמט זיך דערפֿון, וואָס די קריסטלעכע וועלט לעבט נישט קריסטלעכמעסיק. דער הויפּט־אינטערעס אין אייראָפּע איז געלט. היות ייִדן זײַנען געניט אין די דאָזיקע ענינים — האָבן זיי אַ השפּעה אין אייראָפּע. אין דעם פּרט איז נישטאָ קיין חילוק צווישן דער ייִדישער און נישט ייִדישער וועלט. אָבער בעת אַ ייִד ווערט רײַך, ווערט רײַכער דאָס ייִדנטום, ווײַל די ייִדן זײַנען סאָלידאַריש, בעת די קריסטן האָבן ליב געלט — איז דאָס נישט צוליב אַ העכערן ציל.

סאָלאָוויאָוו גלייבט אַז בהדרגהדיק וועט קומען צו אַ רעליגיעזער ליַיזונג פֿון דער ייִדן־פֿראַגע: עס וועט זיך פֿאַראייניקן דאָס הויז פֿון ישׂראל מיטן אָרטאָדאָקסישן און קאַטוילישן קריסטנטום אויף איין טעאָקראַטישן באָדן — ווי עס האָט געלערנט דער אַפּאָסטל פּאָול אין זײַן בריוו צו די רוימער.

שלמה המלך סודות פון רעליגיעז־מיסטישע לערנונגען, קבלה און מאסאנישע טראדיציעס. פון דעם אלעמען האט ער גארנישט דערגרייכט. דער שבט האט ביי אים צוגעגנבעט זיין זייגערל און צעקוועטשט זיין צילינדער. פון די אינטערעסאנטע באקאנטשאפטן, וואס ער האט דא געמאכט איז כדאי אויסצורעכענען בלויז לעסעפסן, דעם בויער פון סועץ־קאנאל.

אין אריינפיר האבן מיר ציטירט אפרופן וועגן דער ראלע, וואס סאלאוויאוו האט געשפילט אין דער פילאסאפיע און ליטעראטור. דאס זיינען געוועזן מיינונגען פון מענטשן צו מיינסטן פון ענלעכע איבערצייגונגען. עס וועט אפשר זיין אויפן ארט איבערצוגעבן אן אפשאצונג פון דער סאוויעטישער ענציקלאפעדיע, כדי דאס בילד זאל זיין פול:

> סאלאוויאוו... ער האט אויף א דעמאגאגישן אופן זיך ארויסגעזאגט פאר באזייטיקן די סאציאלע און נאציאנאלע ווידעראנאנדן, אבער במקום אויף א רעוואלוציאנערן האט ער גערופן אויף א פאלשן, רעליגיעזן וועג. צום ביישפיל, ארויסטרעטנדיק קעגן די יידישע פאגראמען, האט ער געפאדערט נישט א קאמף פאר דעמאקראטיזאציע פון געזעלשאפטלעכן לעבן פון צארישן רוסלאנד. נאר א רעליגיעזע לייזונג פון דער יידן־פראגע ד.ה. א פאראייניקונג פון יידנטום מיטן קריסטנטום.[14]

ווי אזוי עס האט געזאלט אויסזען דער צונויפשמעלץ פון קריסטנטום מיטן יידנטום — דאס איז גאר אן אנדער פראבלעם, וואס וועט געפינען זיין אויפקלערונג אין המשך פון דאזיקן ארטיקל.

סאלאוויאוו איז געשטארבן אין יאר 1900 איבערלאזנדיק א רייכע ליטעראריש־פילאסאפישע ירושה, צו וועלכער עס געהערן זיינע פראנצייזישע שריפטן ״די רוסישע אידעע״ (1888), ״רוסלאנד און די אוניווערסאלע קירכע״ (1889), ביידע געדרוקט אין פאריז, און צ.אנד. ליטעראַרישע ווערק ״דריי רעדעס צום אנדענק פון דאסטאיעווסקין״ (1884). די רעדעס וועגן דאסטאיעווסקין ווערן באטראכט ווי דאס בעסטע און טיפסטע, וואס איז וועגן אים געווארן געשריבן. זייט 1873 זיינען זיי געווען באפריינדעט. דאסטאיעווסקי קומט זיך צוהערן צו די לעקציעס פון סאלאוויאוון. דערנענטערט האט זיי די נייגונג צו מיסטיציזם. דער הויכפונקט פון זייער נאענטקייט פאלט אויס אין 1878, ווען זיי ביידע פארן קיין אפטינא פוסטין, כדי צו באזוכן דעם סטארעץ אמברואז אדער מיט זיין וועלטלעכן נאמען א. מ. גרענקאוו. אן אפקלאנג פון שמועס צווישן סטארעץ און סאלאוויאוון געפינען מיר אין ״די ברידער קאראמאזאוו״ (באנד 2, קאפ. 5). עס איז קיין ספק נישט, אז ״דאסטאיעווסקי און סאלאוויאוו האבן געביטעריש געוועגדט דעם רוסישן געדאנק צו גלויבנס־ענינים״.[15]

כדי זיך צו דערנענטערן צו אונדזער טעמע וועלן מיר דא אויסרעכענען אייניקע ארבעטן סאלאוויאווס, וואס האבן א שייכות צו יידן:

א. דאס יידנטום און די קריסטלעכע פראגע (1884);

ב. די יידן, זייער תורה און מאראל (1891);

14 Большая Сов. Энциклопедия, Т. 40.

15 Вячеслав Иванов, Борозды и межи, Москва 1916, с. 98.

סאלאוויאווס דאצענטור האט נישט לאנג געדויערט. נאכן אטענטאט אויפן צאר אלעקסאנדער דעם 2טן (1 מערץ 1881) האט זיך געשטארקט אין רוסלאנד די רעאקציע. ארעסטן און טויטאורטיילן זיינען געווארן אן אפטע דערשיינונג. די אטמאספערע פון אדמיניסטראטיוון טערארר האט באהערשט דאס לאנד.

אין אט דעם מאמענט האט סאלאוויאוו געוואגט זיך עפנטלעך ארויסצוזאגן אין נאמען פון זיין קריסטלעכקייט קעגן טויטשטראף, וויסנדיק אז דורך דעם שטעלט ער אין סכנה זיין פאסטן און אפשר אויך זיין צוקונפט. צו טיף אבער איז געווען זיין גלויבן אין הומאניטארע פרינציפן ער זאל זיך אפשרעקן פארן ארויסזאגן זיי. אין יענער צייט האט סאלאוויאוו געלייענט לעקציעס אין פעטערבורגער אוניווערסיטעט און אויף העכערע ווייבלעכע קורסן א.ד.ט. "אלוועלטלעך היסטארישער באטייט פון יידנטום". היות מען פארווערט אים אויפצוטרעטן עפנטלעך מיט פארלעזונגען איז ער געצוווּנגען צו פארלאזן דעם אוניווערסיטעט. אויף אזא אופן ווערט פאר אים פארשלאסן דער וועג צו א פראפעסור און צו א וויסנשאפטלעכער קאריערע. ער האט אבער געהאנדלט אין הסכם מיט זיין קריסטלעכער איינשטעלונג און זיין מיינונג קאן מען נישט אפזאגן קיין לאגיק און קאנסעקווענץ. זיין ארגומענטאציע איז געווען אזא: דער צאר פערסאניפיצירט זיין פאלק. דאס פאלק איז טיף קריסטלעך, דעריבער דארף דער צאר האנדלען לויטן אידעאל פון קריסטוסן. ער דארף באגנעדיקן די מערדער און אזוי ארום באשטעטיקן דעם כוח פון די קריסטלעכע פרינציפן. אויב ער וועט דאס נישט טאן האט די געזעלשאפט די פליכט אפצולייקענען די מאכט פון דער רעגירונג.

די דאזיקע רעדע האט געמאכט א שטארקן רושם אין דער געזעלשאפט און גורם געווען צו א שפּאלטונג: די רעאקציאנערן זיינען קעגן אים, די רעוואלוציאנערן אפלאדירן אים אויס שנאה צום אריסטאקראטישן רעזשים, הגם די מאטיוון זייערע גייען זיך פונאנדער. סאלאוויאוו האט זיך איבערצייגט, אז דער הערשנדיקער רעזשים טויג נישט און דעריבער פארנעמט ער זיך אויפן וועג פון אקטיווער טעטיקייט, נישט ווי אין די פריערדיקע יארן, ווען ער האט זיך באגרענעצט בלויז צו פילאסאפיע. סאלאוויאוו וויל געפינען א סינטעז צווישן סאציאלער גערעכטיקייט און קריסטלעכן גלויבן. ער אינטערעסירט זיך מיט טעאקראטיע, וואס דערפירט אים צו שטודירן דעם תנך, כדי צו זען איר גענעזע. סאלאוויאוו איז גרינטלעך און געוויסנדיק אין זיין ארבעט און האט ליב צו דערגראבן זיך ביז צום קוואל. דער קוואל פון תנך איז לשון קודש און דעריבער נעמט סאלאוויאוו לערנען די שפראך פון די נביאים. אין דער תקופה פון זיין לעבן גיט ער זיך אפ מיטן שטודירן די נאציאנאלע פראגע.

דאס באזייטיקן אים פון דער קאטעדרע האט סאלאוויאוון נישט צעבראכן. ער רעזיגנירט נישט פון זיינע איבערצייגונגען, נייערט ער איז ממשיך זיינע פארשונגען און ברענגט זיי צו דער עפנטלעכקייט אין זיינע ביכער, ארטיקלען, רעפעראטן און לידער. א טייל פון זיינע שריפטן זיינען געשריבן אין פראנצייזיש. ער קניפט אויך אן פארבינדונגען מיט אידעאלאגיש נאענטע פּערזענלעכקייטן אין אויסלאנד, וווהין ער פארט פון צייט צו צייט. די ערשטע רייזע האט אים געפירט קיין לאנדאן, כדי צו שטודירן אין בריטיש מוזעאום די ליטעראטור, וואס האט געהאט א שייכות צו זיינע פאראינטערעסירונגען. ער איז אויך געווען אין פאריז, אין זאגרעב און האט זיך אויך געלאזט קיין עגיפטן, ווו ער האט געגלייבט צו געפינען א בעדואינער שבט, וועלכער האט געירשנט דירעקט פון

קאנצעפציע וועגן "דאס אייביק ווייבלעכע", איבער וועלכער מיר געפינען געוויסע אויפקלערונגען און קאמענטארן צ. אנד. אין דער קארעספאנדענץ פון אלעקסאנדער בלאק און אנדריי ביעלי.[10]

אט ווי פאליוואנאווא באשרייבט די ערשטע לעקציע, אייגנטלעך דעם פראפעסאר אליין:

א הויכע, זייער מאגערע געשטאלט און געדיכטע, טונקלע האר. די שטימע א קלינגענדיקע, א הארמאנישע, א דורכדרינגענדיקע... מיך האט שטארק פארכאפט דאס באצויבערנדיקע קול... עס האט זיך ביי סאלאוויאוון נישט געמערקט די מינדסטע שעמעוודיקייט. ער האט גערעדט רואיק, ווי א גענייטער פרעלעגענט, הגם ער איז געווען ערשט א פריש געבאקענער... מיט רואיקייט אָן יעדער קליינלעכער פארריסנקייט און דעריבער פשוט און רואיק. הערלעכע אויסשפראך און וואנדערשיינע שטימע. אויף זיין מאט־בלייכן פנים איז געווען אויסגעגאסן א גייסטיקער אויסדרוק פון ·אויסערגעוויינטלעכער גוטסקייט. זיין מאגערקייט האט גורם געווען מען זאל אים באטראכטן ווי א מענטשן אָן אומהאפטיקן.[11]

נאכן אפזיין צוויי יאר אין מאסקווער אוניווערסיטעט פארט ער קיין פעטערבורג אויף דער פארבעטונג פון בילדונגס־מיניסטעריום, כדי דא צו לייענען לעקציעס אויף רעליגיעזע און פילאסאפישע טעמעס, ווי א דאצענט פון פעטערבורגער אוניווערסיטעט. דא גרייט ער זיין דאקטאר־טעזע א.ד.ט. "די קריטיק פון אבסטראקטע פרינציפן", וואס ער פארטיידיקט מיט דערפאלג אין יאר 1880.

זיינע שאפערישע היסטאריאסאפישע מעדיטאציעס האבן אים דערפירט צו א קאנקלוזיע, "אז די געשיכטע האט פאר אונדז ארויסגערוקט דריי גרויסע פראגעס, וואס דארפן קריגן א בכבודיקע, מענטשלעכע לייזונג: די פוילישע, די מזרחדיקע אדער סלאווישע און די יידישע".[12] דאס פוילישע פאלק איז אים געווען נאענט ווי א קאטויליש פאלק, וואס איז אונטערדריקט. וואס שייך דער צווייטער פראגע האט עד געהאט א מיינונג, אז רוסלאנד איז בארופן צו פאראייניקן פעלקער און נישט זיך ארויסהייבן איבער זיי, ווי דאס טוען די דייטשן, פאר וועלכע די העכערע קולטור לייגט כלומרשט אויף זיי ארויף א מיסיע און דערמיט בארעכטיקן זיי זייער אגרעסיווקייט און אוממענטשלעכקייט. דאס איז א שעדלעכער און פאלשער פרינציפ. קולטורעלע העכערקייט איז צו באגריסן, ווען זי דינט צו מענטשלעכער פארשטענדיקונג, אבער ווען מען דערהייבט זי צו א פרינציפ לטובת דעם אייגענעס פאלק אליין איז דאס גלייך צו א לעגאליזירונג און פאראייביקונג פון נאציאנאלע סכסוכים. איבער נאציאנאלע סכסוכים דארף מען שטעלן דאס קריסטנטום. וואס שטארקער דער נאציאנאלער כוח איז, אלץ העכער דארף ער זיך דערהייבן איבערן נאציאנאלן עגאאיזם... אויב עס קומט צו א קאנפליקט צווישן פאטריאטיזם און געוויסן, זאל זיך אונטערוווארפן דער פאטריאטיזם.[13]

וועגן דער דריטער פראגע וועלן מיר ריידן ברייטער אין א וויטערדיקן קאפיטל.

10 Александр Блок и Андрей Белый, Переписка, Москва, Гос. литер. музей. Вступительная статья В.Н. Орлова.

11 Лукьянов с. 44.

12 В.Л. Величко, Владимир Соловьев, жизнь и творения, С.Петербург 1902, с. 205.

13 דארט, 83–84.

1. ביאָגראַפֿישע פּרטים

נאָך דעם ווי מיר האָבן סיטואירט סאָלאָוויאָווס אָרט אין דער וועלט פֿון גייסט, וועלן מיר נאָכפֿאָלגן זיין אַנטוויקלונג פֿון סאַמע אָנהייב.

וולאַדימיר איז געבוירן אין מאָסקווע אין יאַנואַר 1853. זיין פֿאָטער סערגיי סאָלאָוויאָוו איז געווען אַ באַרימטער היסטאָריקער, פּראָפֿעסאָר פֿון מאָסקווער אוניווערסיטעט און מחבר פֿון אַ פֿילבענדיקער געשיכטע פֿון רוסלאַנד.

שוין אין די קינדעריאָרן האָט וולאַדימיר אַרויסגעוויזן גרויסע פֿעאיקייטן. זייענדיק אַ שילער אין גימנאַזיע האָט ער שוין דורכגעמאַכט פּאַזעס פֿון ניהיליזם, מאַטעריאַליזם, אָבער באַזונדער האָט אים פֿאַרכאַפּט ספּינאָזאַ, וועמען ער האָט געהאַלטן פֿאַרן גרעסטן פֿילאָסאָף. דער אַרויסגעבער פֿון זיינע געזאַמלטע ווערק און ביאָגראַף ע. ראַדלאָוו:

ספּינאָזאַ איז געווען די ערשטע ליבע פֿון סאָלאָוויאָוון אויפֿן געביט פֿון פֿילאָסאָפֿיע און די דאָזיקע ליבע האָט ער אָפּגעהיט זיין גאַנץ לעבן און זיך געהאַלטן פֿאַר אַ בעל־חוב ספּינאָזאָס נישט בלויז אין באַצוג צו פֿילאָסאָפֿיע נייערט אויך צו רעליגיע.[8]

אין דער יוגנט האָט אים אינטערעסירט אויך פֿיל אַנדערע פּראָבלעמען פֿון גייסטיקן לעבן, ביז עס האָט זיך אויסקריסטאַליזירט זיין וועלטבאַנעם: ער שטודירט געשיכטע פֿון רעליגיעס, דעם בודדיזם, די פֿילאָסאָפֿיע פֿון שאָפּענהאַוערן, האַרטמאַנען או״וו. ער פֿאַרטיפֿט זיך אויך אין דער אידעאָלאָגיע פֿון די סלאַוואָפֿילן.

נאָכן פֿאַרענדיקן די גימנאַזיע, ווערט ער אַ סטודענט פֿון מאַטעמאַטיק און פֿיזיק אויפֿן מאָסקווער אוניווערסיטעט. נאָך צוויי יאָר גייט ער אַריבער אויפֿן היסטאָריש־פֿילאָסאָפֿישן פֿאַקולטעט. גלייכצייטיק באַזוכט ער אויך לעקציעס אין דער גייסטלעכער אַקאַדעמיע. צו 21 יאָר פֿאַרטיידיקט ער זיין מאַגיסטער־דיסערטאַציע אויף דער טעמע: "דער קריזיס פֿון דער מערבדיקער פֿילאָסאָפֿיע" (1874), וווּ ער טרעט אַרויס קעגן דער דאָמינירנדיקער דעמאָלט פּאָזיטיוויסטישער פֿילאָסאָפֿיע.

די דיסערטאַציע האָט געמאַכט אַ שטאַרקן איינדרוק און אַרויסגערופֿן אַ שאַרפֿע פּאָלעמיק מיטן אָפֿיציעלן אָפּאָנענט פּראָפֿ. לעסעוויטש, וועלכע ווערט קאָנטינואירט אין דער פּרעסע.[9] פֿאַרענדיקט די אוניווערסיטעט־שטודיעס פֿאַרבלייבט סאָלאָוויאָוו ביים מאָסקווער אוניווערסיטעט: ער לייענט לעקציעס וועגן פֿילאָסאָפֿיע.

עס איז אינטערעסאַנט זיך צו באַקענען מיטן רושם, וואָס זיין ערשטע לעקציע וועגן דער פֿילאָסאָפֿיע פֿון פּלאַטאָ (דעם 14טן יאַנואַר 1875) האָט געמאַכט אויף דער צוהערערין אין אינסטיטוט פֿון וול. אי. געריע, יע. מ. פּאָליוואַנאָוואַ. דאָ וויל איך צוגעבן, אַז סאָלאָוויאָוו איז געווען פֿאַרליבט אין דער דאָזיקער צוהערערין זיינער און געהאָפֿט צו פֿאַרבינדן זיין לעבן מיט איר, אָבער מער ווי אַ גוטע פֿריינדשאַפֿט איז פֿון דער באַקאַנטשאַפֿט נישט געוואָרן, וואָס סאָלאָוויאָוו האָט זיין גאַנץ לעבן באַדויערט. אַן אָפּקלאַנג פֿון דער אומגליקלעכער ליבע איז צו געפֿינען אין זיין דיכטונג און אין זיין

8 Э. Радлов, Вл. С. Соловьев, אין סאָל., באַנד 9, זייט 4.

9 С.Л. Лукьянов, О Вл.С. Соловьеве в его молодые годы, Материалы к биографии, Книга 3, выпуск 1, Петроград 1921.

וואס האבן אויפגעשפראצט אין רוסלאנד אין אנהייב פון 20סטן יארהונדערט.[3]

ענדלעך געפינען מיר אין דער הקדמה צו דער דייטשער אויסגאבע פון סאלאוויאווס געזאמלטע ווערק, פאלגנדיקע מיינונג:

וולאדימיר סאלאוויאוו, דער גרעסטער פילאסאפישער גאון מיט וועמען די סלאווישע וועלט קאן זיך באריםען, שטייט אן גוזמא אין איין ריי מיט די קאריפייען פון דער מערבדיקער מחשבה. צווישן די גרויסע קאטוילישע דענקערס פון די לעצטע צוויי הונדערט יאר שטייט ער אין יעדן פאל אויפן ערשטן ארט.[4]

עס איז נישט אָן אינטערעס צו ציטירן א דאקומענט פון א מיטצייטלער, וועלכער רופט זיך אפ אין א פריוואטן בריוו אויף סאלאוויאווס אפהאנדלונג א.ד.ט. "קריטיק פון אבסטראקטע פרינציפן". דער מיטצייטלער איז דער רוסישער קאמפאזיטאר פיאטר טשייקאווסקי וועלכער שרייבט דעם 12טן אקטאבער 1879 צו זיין פריינדין פאן מעק:

צי האט איר שוין געלייענט די פילאסאפישע ארטיקלען פון וולאדימיר סאלאוויאוו (דער זון פון פארשטארבענעם רעקטאר און היסטאריקער) אין 'רוסקי וועסטניק'? זיי זיינען פרעכטיק געשריבן אין דעם זין, וואס זיי זיינען פולקום צוטריטלעך פאר א נישט־ספעציאליסטן און אויפגעקלערט מיט א גרויסן טאלאנט און שארפזין. איך ווייס נישט צו וועלכע ענדגילטיקע אויספירן דער מחבר וועט דערגיין, אבער אין לעצטן (אויגוסט־) נומער באווייזט ער מיט א פרעכטיקער איבערצייגעוודיקייט און פקחות די אומהאפטיקייט פון פאזיטיוויזם וועלכער פארלייקנט די התבוננות, האלט די מעטאפיזיק פאר אן אויסטראכטעניש, קאן זיך אבער נישט באגיין אן דער פילאסאפיע...[5]

איך באגרענעץ מיך בלויז צו די פאר זאצן, כדי קלאר צו מאכן, וואס פאר אן איינדרוק סאלאוויאוו האט געמאכט מיט זיינע שריפטן. מיר פארגעסן נישט אז בעת טשייקאווסקי האט געלייענט די דערמאנטע פילאסאפישע אפהאנדלונג אין "רוסקי וועסטניק", ווו זי איז געווען פארעפנטלעכט אין המשכים אין די יארן 1877—1879, איז סאלאוויאוו אלט געווען בסך הכל 26 יאר.

פון די אויבן ציטירטע אפקלאנגען איז קלאר אז די ביבליאגראפיע, וואס איז נוגע די פילזייטיקייט פון סאלאוויאווס שאפן, איז זייער רייך. היות אבער אונדזער טעמע באציט זיך בלויז צו א באשטימטן אספעקט פון זיין אקטיווקייט, וועלן מיר נעמען אין אכט אויסשליסלעך יענע ווערק, וואס האבן א שייכות צו אונדזער טעמע. מיר שיקן אפ דעם פאראינטערעסירטן לייענער צו דער ביבליאגראפיע פון וולאדיסלאוולעוו.[6] וואס שייך די ווערק פון סאלאוויאוון האבן מיר זיך באנוצט מיט דער אויסגאבע פון יאר 1902.[7]

3 D. Strémooukhoff, *Vladimir Soloviev et son oeuvre messianique, Publication de la faculté de Lettres de l'Université de Strasbourg,* Fascicule 69, 1935, 9—13.

4 Wladimir Szylkarski, *Das philosophische Werk von Wladimir Solowjew...,* Krailling vor München 1950. Sonderdruck der Einleitung zur deutschen Gesamtausgabe der Werke von W. Solowjew.

5 Модест Чайковский, Жизнь Петра Ильича Чайковского, Москва—Лейпциг 1901, Т. 2, стр. 325 (Письмо к Н.Ф. фон Мекк).

6 И.В. Владиславлев, Русские писатели, Москва 1924, стр. 290—294.

7 Собрание сочинений Владимира С. Соловьева, Том. 1-9, Ст. Петербург 1902... (וייטער: סאל., באנד..., אָדער Сол., Том...)

דאס יידישע פאלק און זיין געשיכטע אין דער אויפפאסונג פון וולאדימיר סאלאוויאוו

נ. גריס

צו די פערזענלעכקייטן, וואס האבן געלייגט זייער שטעמפל אויפן גייסטיקן לעבן פון רוסלאנד אין די לעצטע צוויי צענדליק יארן פון פארדעמדיקן יארהונדערט, געהערט אן ספק וולאדימיר סערגייעוויטש סאלאוויאָוו. כדי דער לייענער זאל זיין אריענטירט וועגן פלאץ וואס ער האט פארנומען, איז געגנוג צו ציטירן עטלעכע ארויסזאגן פון מחברים פון פארשיידענע צייטן, לענדער און וועלטבאנעמען.

באלד נאכן טויט פון סאלאוויאוון לייענען מיר אין נעקראלאג פון דער רוסיש־יידישער צייטונג "וואסכאד", אז דער פארשטארבענער "איז געווען א נביאישער אנזאגער פון אמת און גוטסקייט, א פארטיידיקער פון גערודפטע און באליידיקטע..."[1]

א רוסישער ליטעראטור־היסטאריקער, וועלכער איז געווען קריטיש געשטימט לגבי זיין קוק אויף דער נאציאנאלער פראגע, שרייבט אין יאר 1903:

> ער האט פארמאגט יענעם טעמפעראמענט פון א רוסישן אידעאלאג, וואס קומט צום אויסדרוק אין פולער אומאייגננוציקייט און זיך פארגעסנקייט, אין געטריישאפט צום אידעאל און צו גייסטיקער פרייהייט. וולאדימיר סאלאוויאווס נאמען איז דער לעצטער אין דער מגילה פון הייליקע נעמען פון 19טן יארהונדערט.[2]

א פראפעסאר פון שטראסבורגער אוניווערסיטעט מיינט, אז סאלאוויאוו

> האט געשאפן אין רוסלאנד א גרויסע באוועגונג פון אידעען... די מאראלישע פילאסאפיע און היסטאריאסאפיע פון סאלאוויאוון האבן שטארק באווירקט דענקערס אזוי פארשיידענע ווי דער פירשט יע. טרובעצקוי און נ. א. בערדיאיעוו... ער איז געווען דער דירעקטער פארגייער פון די רוסישע סימבאליסטן אנדריי ביעלי (פסעוודאנים פון באריס בוגראוו — נ.ג.), אלעקסאנדער בלאק... סאלאוויאוו האט נישט געשאפן קיין שול, ער האט א דאנק זיין שטארקער פערסאנאליטעט משפיע געווען אויף א גאנצער תקופה און געגעבן א מעכטיקן אימפולס פאר פילאסאפישע, רעליגיעזע און ליטערארישע אידעען,

1 .Восход, 3 августа 1900, год 19, нум. 60

2 Николай Энгелгардт, История русской литературы 19-го столетия, Том 2, 1850—1900, .Ст. Петербург 1903, стр. 415

גאולה מאת ר׳ יעקב בר יצחק

יַשְּׁרִי יוֹנָה סְלוּל אָורְחֵךְ
וּפִצְחִי רִינָּה בְּגָרוֹן וָחֵיךְ,

עַנְּדִי עַצְמֵךְ בְּמֶרְקָחֵךְ
וְזִיכְרֵךְ הַטּוֹב וְגַם רֵיחֵךְ.

קַשְּׁרִי בְזֶמֶר עֲדִי חֵחֵךְ
זֵר זָהָב שְׁתִי מִזְחֵךְ,

בְּבוֹאִי לְמִקְדַּשׁ בֵּית מְנוּחֵךְ
וְיַעֲבוֹר לְפָנַיִךְ מְשִׁיחֵךְ.

כִּי נִשְׁבַּעְתִּי נְאֻם גּוֹחֵךְ,
אֲנִי לָעַד לֹא אַזְנִיחֵךְ.

רְדִיָּיה תִרְדִּי בְּמַדִּיחֵךְ
בְּצֵאתֵךְ לִרְוָיָה מֵרֶשֶׁת פַּחֵךְ,

יוֹפִי אֶשְׁלַח לְהַנִּיחֵךְ
וּבְיַד צָר לֹא אֲנִיחֵךְ.

צְבָאֵךְ יִבְנֶה מִזְבְּחֵךְ
וְאָז אָרִיחַ בְּנִיחוֹחֵךְ.

חֶדְוַת תָּמִיד יְהִי נִיכְחֵךְ
בְּשַׁבַּתֵּךְ חַגֵּךְ וּפִסְחֵךְ.

קַרְנֵךְ אָרִימָה וּמִצְחֵךְ
וְנֶצַח לֹא יֹאבֵד נִצְחֵךְ.

חִדְלִי מִכַּעַס מְרִי שִׂיחֵךְ
וְהַרְחִיבִי קוֹצֶר רוּחֵךְ.

זַמְּרִי לִשְׁמִי כְּפִי כּוֹחֵךְ
כִּי לֹא יֵאָסֵף יְרֵיחֵךְ.

קַבֵּץ אֲקַבֵּץ נִדָּחֵךְ
וּמִמַּעֲרָבֵךְ וּמִזְרָחֵךְ.

הערות

1. יונה, כינוי לכנסת ישראל. 3. ענדי, תקשטי עצמך. בכתב־היד: עבדי. 5. עדי חחך, קישוטיך.
6. מזחך, חגורתך. 9. גוחך, הקב״ה, ע״פי תהלים כב, י. 10. רדייה, בשלטון תמשלי על האויב.
20. ונצח, בניגוד למה שנאמר באיכה ג, יח. 24. כי לא יאסף, ע״פ ישעיה ס,כ.

א

תוכחה ל"זכרונות מאת ר' יהודה הלוי

יָהּ אִם עֲוֹנִי כְשִׁכּוֹר / הִתְעַנִּי וַיִּעְכּוֹר / בְּרוֹגֶז רַחֵם תִּזְכּוֹר (חבקוק ג, ב).
אַל תְּחַפֵּשׂ מַצְפּוּנַי / בְּיוֹם תִּפְקוֹד עֲוֹנַי / זְכוֹר רַחֲמֶיךָ אֲדֹנָי (תהלים כה, ו)
נַפְשִׁי לְרֹעַ פָּעֳלַי / תִּבְכֶּה וְעוֹד מַעֲלָלַי / תִּזְכּוֹר וְתָשׁוֹחַ עָלַי (איכה ג, יט)
יְגוֹנַי הִרְבּוּ פְשָׁעַי / אָכֵן מִתּוֹךְ פְּצָעַי / זְכַרְתִּיךָ עַל יְצוּעָי (תהלים סג, ו)
יָהּ חוֹב אִם תְּדִינֵנִי /עֲשׂוֹת רְצוֹנְךָ לַמְּדֵנִי /זָכְרֵנִי וּפָקְדֵנִי (ירמיה טו, טו)
הֵן זְדוֹנוֹתַי אָיוֹם / אַזְכִּיר וּבְעַד פִּדְיוֹם / אֶת חֲטָאַי אֲנִי מַזְכִּיר הַיּוֹם (בראשית מא, ט)
וְאָמְנָם הֵן זָחַלְתִּי / לְמַעַן אֲשֶׁר מָעַלְתִּי / זָכַרְתִּי וְנִבְהָלְתִּי (איוב כא, ו)
דָּאַגְתִּי לְרֹב עֲוֹנוֹת / בְּהִפָּתַח לְחִשְׁבוֹנוֹת / אֶת סֵפֶר הַזִּכְרוֹנוֹת (אסתר ו, א)
הַדּוּפִים חֵן תִּלְבְּשׁוּ / וְקוֹשׁוּ וְהִתְקוֹשֲׁשׁוּ / זִכְרוּ זֹאת וְהִתְאוֹשָׁשׁוּ (ישעיה מו, ח)
הֲיוֹאִיל בְּיוֹם דִּין כֹּפֶר / וּמָוֶת גְּאוֹנְכֶם יָפֵר / זִכְרוֹנֵיכֶם מִשְׁלֵי אֵפֶר (איוב יג, יב)
קָרוֹב אֵל לַחֲסִידָיו / לַשָּׁבִים בֶּאֱמֶת עָדָיו / וּלְזוֹכְרֵי פִּקֻּדָיו (תהלים קג, יח)
טַהֲרוּ לֵבָב קָשֶׁה / וְאֵל מֵעֲוֹנְכֶם יַשֶּׁה / זִכְרוּ תּוֹרַת מֹשֶׁה (מלאכי ג, כב)
נַשְּׁקוּ בַר נֶאֱמָנַי / וְשׁוּבוּ לִשְׁמֹר אֱמוּנַי / וְנִזְכַּרְתֶּם לִפְנֵי אֲדֹנָי (במדבר י, ט).

הערות

1. ויעכור, את רוחי. 4. יגוני, פשעי הרבו יגוני. 5. חוב, אם לחוב תדינני. 9. הדופים, על ידי האויבים. וקושו, ע"פ צפניה ב,א. 12. ישה, ישכח. 13. נשקו בר, תהלים ב, יב.

שני פיוטים עתיקים

א. מ. הברמן ז״ל

על ספרים נאמר ״הכל תלוי במזל, ואפילו ספר תורה שבהיכל״, ודברים אלה כוחם יפה גם לגבי פיוטים. יש פיוטים שהם יפים וגם מחבריהם חשובים, ואף־על־פי־כן לא ראו אור הדפוס ולא הגיעו לידי קוראים.

כאן מתפרסמים שנים מפיוטים אלה. הראשון הוא מתחום הפיוט הספרדי, והשני מתחום הפיוט האשכנזי־צרפתי.

הפיוט הראשון הוא ״תוכחה לזכרונות״ של ראש השנה, וחתום בו: אני יהודה הקטן. לדעתי נתחברה ״תוכחה״ זו על־ידי המשורר והפייטן הנודע רבי יהודה הלוי. הוא לא נהג להוסיף תמיד לשמו ״הלוי״, וכן חתם לפרקים בפיוטיו ״הקטן״ כדרך שאר הפייטנים בימים ההם. מבנה הפיוט וצורתו מסייעים לדעה זו. משקלו הוא בדרך כלל שש תנועות בכל צלעית מבלי להתחשב בשוואים, ותוכנו הוא בקשה למחילת עוונות. כל בית בו מסתיים בפסוק שעניינו זכרון. לא מצאתי זכרו ברשימות, והוא מתפרסם כאן על פי כתב־יד המוזיאון הבריטי סי׳ 7963 דף כו, ב.

הפיוט השני הוא ״גאולה״. מחברה חתום בה: יעקב בר יצחק חזק, ואין מועדה קבוע. פיוט זה הוא שווה־חרוז, ועניינו דברי נחמה וגאולה בפי הקב״ה לכנסת ישראל. מבחינת הצורה והסגנון הוא קרוב לפיוט הספרדי, אבל הפייטן היה אשכנזי או צרפתי בן המאה השתים־עשרה בערך. ״גאולה״ זו ידועה כפיוטו היחידי של הפייטן, השווה דברי צונץ ב״ליטראטורגשיכטה״ שלו עמ׳ 489. מקורות כתב־יד ברלין סי׳ 179 דף צא, א.

ספרנות וביבליוגרפיה

מאמרים בעברית וביידיש

תוכן העניינים

מסת"ב 0—032—226—965

נדפס בישראל תשמ"ג
בדפוס ידע־סלע בע"מ, ת"א

מחקרים
ביהדות, בקראות ובאיסלאם

מוגשים ליהודה אריה נמוי ביום הולדתו השמונים

עורך:
שאול ר. ברונסוויק

מערכת:
זאב ג. בראודה, חיים יונה גרינפלד, דניאל שפרבר

הוצאת אוניברסיטת בר אילן